D0914482

Political Exile in the Global Twentieth Century

POLITICAL EXILE IN THE GLOBAL TWENTIETH CENTURY

Catholic Christian Democrats in Europe and the Americas

Edited by
Wolfram
KAISER
& Piotr H.
KOSICKI

LEUVEN UNIVERSITY PRESS

© 2021 Leuven University Press/Presses universitaires de Louvain/Universitaire Pers Leuven, Minderbroedersstraat 4, B-3000 Leuven (Belgium)

ISBN 978 94 6270 307 0
eISBN 978 94 6166 422 8
D/2021/1869/51
https://doi.org/10.11116/9789461664228
NUR: 686

TABLE OF CONTENTS

ACKNOWLEDGEMENTS

From the beginning we have conceived of this book as a collaborative endeavour to bring together and integrate emerging fresh research on Catholic Christian Democrats in political exile during the global twentieth century. At an intermediate stage of the project, we organised a conference to discuss draft manuscripts. Our exchanges at the workshop and beyond and the subsequent editing process have also allowed us to bring out connections across the different groups of exiles, regions and timespans covered in this book.

We would especially like to thank the Konrad Adenauer Foundation and the Civitas organisation for their generous funding of the conference. We would similarly like to thank all discussants and participants at the conference as well as three anonymous reviewers of the book manuscript for their valuable comments which helped us very significantly to revise and hopefully improve our chapters. Finally, we are grateful to Victoria Boscaro for her excellent support with the formal side of editing the book.

Portsmouth/Montreal, February 2021

CATHOLIC CHRISTIAN DEMOCRATS IN POLITICAL EXILE IN THE GLOBAL TWENTIETH CENTURY

Wolfram Kaiser and Piotr H. Kosicki

Exile can be a challenging experience: insufficient language skills; no abili-ty to work, or at least to work in one's established profession; limited funds for living expenses and few social contacts. When Luigi Sturzo, the founder of the Italian Popular Party after the First World War, arrived in England in October 1924, he could speak French well, but had no knowledge of En-glish. Moreover, much of the Catholic Church and leading Catholic thinkers supported the fascist regime in Italy and were neutral or even hostile to-wards him personally. Sturzo might have been truly miserable had he not met Barbara Barclay Carter at a dinner in December 1924 organised by the St. Joan's Social and Political Alliance, which advocated women's rights and political participation. When Sturzo could no longer live in Church-owned accommodation, she and her friend Cicely Marshall invited him to move in with them in 1926. They created a "survival system" that carried Sturzo through the years leading up to his move to the United States in 1940: they managed the household, translated his texts, helped him get published, and put him in touch with Catholic dissenters opposed to fascism and ap-peasement, as well as Catholic exiles from other European countries.[1]

Politicians like Sturzo faced additional obstacles in exile compared to academics, artists, novelists and others. Several depended on the sup-port of their governments-in-exile. If exiled politicians were lucky, they disposed of private or political contacts which allowed them to move to their host country and receive some local support, even if they never really "integrated" with their new place of residence.[2] Alongside private

---

1   Giovanna Farrell-Vinay, "The London Exile of Don Luigi Sturzo (1924-1940)," *Heythrop Journal* 45, no. 2 (2004): 158-177, at 163.
2   On the choice of "integration" vs. "representation" faced by political exiles, see Michel Dumou-lin and Idesbald Goddeeris, "Introduction," in Michel Dumoulin and Idesbald Goddeeris, eds, *Intégration ou représentation? Les exilés polonais en Belgique et la construction européenne* (Louvain-la-Neuve: Bruylant, 2005), 5-12.

networks, host country institutions, including secret services or political foundations, for example, provided such support. This was the case for some younger Christian Democrats who fled Chile after the 1973 military coup d'état, for example, and who were able to study at Western European universities with the help of grants from organisations such as the Konrad Adenauer Foundation with affiliated sister parties, in this case the West German Christian Democratic Union.

Usually, however, politicians in exile could neither participate in the politics of their host country nor have a real impact on their home country during periods of authoritarian and dictatorial rule there. They were often restricted to small circles of exiles from the same country, or the same political persuasion, and in danger of stewing in their own juices. Some were deprived of citizenship altogether, all while refusing (or being refused the opportunity) to adopt the nationality of their host country, thereby joining the swelling ranks of the "stateless".[3] More often than not, it was not the exiles abroad who ultimately shaped transitions to democracy, but rather other groups: those who had gone into internal exile, dissidents and members of resistance movements, or simply the next generation(s), who may have neither understood nor particularly cared about the priorities voiced by exiles in distant bistros and club rooms over years or even decades. These exiles then returned to a country that they no longer knew well enough to exercise any influence in an era of democratic politics.

This book focuses specifically on the political exile of Catholic Christian Democrats. More research has been done on socialists, communists and even liberals in political exile, who constituted larger groups, at least in the case of refugees from right-wing regimes.[4] Research on Catholic Christian Democrats in exile in turn has largely focused on celebrated individuals like Sturzo.[5] These were normally influenced in some way by socio-economic reformism in the spirit of Catholic social teaching and strongly opposed to either clerical, military, fascist and national-socialist dictatorships from the Right or, after 1945, communist regimes from the Left.[6] To be clear, this was often not the same as support for pluralist

---

3   Mira L. Siegelberg, *Statelessness: A Modern History* (Cambridge, Mass.: Harvard University Press, 2020).

4   See, e.g., Anthony Glees, *Exile Politics during the Second World War: The German Social Democrats in Britain* (Oxford: Clarendon Press, 1982).

5   See, e.g., Or Rosenboim, *The Emergence of Globalism: Visions of World Order in Britain and the United States, 1939-1950* (Princeton, NJ: Princeton University Press, 2017), 241-271.

6   On the impact of the totalitarian regimes on the engagement of the Catholic Church and Catholics with modernity, see also James Chappel, *Catholic Modern: The Challenge of Totalitarianism and the Remaking of the Church* (Cambridge, Mass.: Harvard University Press, 2018).

Wolfram Kaiser and Piotr H. Kosicki

democracy – let alone market economy – which were at odds with fashionable neo-corporatist concepts of state and society (not "state corporatism") that were influential during the inter-war period and to some extent spilled over into post-war debates and political practices.[7]

Only some of these political exiles would, like Sturzo, have used the term "Christian Democrat" to describe their political identity, at least initially. After all, the term has its origins in the inter-war period but only became widespread as the hallmark of a particular political orientation and form of party organisation in Europe and Latin America after 1945.[8] In fact, Jacques Maritain, who exercised intellectual leadership not least with his work in exile in the United States, refused the label "Christian Democrat" for himself.[9] Nonetheless, he profoundly influenced the Christian Democratic movement – especially in Latin America after the Second World War – and he maintained close links with self-identified Christian Democrats like Sturzo in a manner that clearly warrants his inclusion in a book about Christian Democrats in political exile.

In the light of this lack of clarity as to who was, or considered himself to be, a "Christian Democrat", and at what point in time, we try to take a middle path and include individuals and groups of exiles who saw themselves as Christian Democrats or were connected in some way, however loosely, with this worldview or associated networks through their thinking or social contacts. Not all of these exiles were emphatically democratic or obviously Christian-inspired in their political beliefs – something that the individual chapters in this book will seek to clarify for their respective protagonists.

Moreover, we focus on the political exile of Christian Democrats during the (short) global twentieth century from the end of the First World War to the end of the Cold War. We do so for two main reasons. Although the origins of Christian Democracy as inspired to a large degree by Catholic social teaching lie in the late nineteenth century, as a political ideology it only came of age in interwar Europe and as a political movement of organ-

---

7   On this question of continuity see also Martin Conway, "The Rise and Fall of Western Europe's Democratic Age, 1945-1973," *Contemporary European History* 13, no. 1 (2004): 67-88.

8   Wolfram Kaiser, *Christian Democracy and the Origins of European Union* (Cambridge: Cambridge University Press, 2007); Michael Gehler and Wolfram Kaiser, eds, *Christian Democracy in Europe since 1945* (London: Routledge, 2004); Tom Buchanan and Martin Conway, eds, *Political Catholicism in Europe 1918-1965* (Oxford: Oxford University Press, 1996).

9   See, e.g., Paul E. Sigmund, "Maritain on Politics," in Deal W. Hudson and Matthew J. Mancini, eds, *Understanding Maritain: Philosopher and Friend* (Macon, GA: Mercer University Press, 1987), 153-170.

ised political parties, after the Second World War, both in Europe and in Latin America.

We sometimes think of political exile as a phenomenon of the long nineteenth century from Royalist exiles from Revolutionary France to Lenin's exile from Tsarist Russia. While the nineteenth century saw mass migration from Europe to the Americas, which was often induced by socio-economic plight, not political concerns, the twentieth century was overshadowed by the unprecedented phenomenon of forced population movements effected by the totalitarian regimes.[10] At the same time, these regimes were characterised by a new quality of equally systematic and brutal repression of domestic dissent, which induced more politicians – including Catholic Christian Democrats – to go into exile to avoid imprisonment or death.

Where studies on Catholic Christian Democrats in exile during the global twentieth century go beyond the biographical approach, they normally still adopt a national lens.[11] We seek to take the first step toward overcoming this national introspection by bringing national and transnational perspectives together in a global and longitudinal approach to the phenomenon of Christian Democrats in political exile, to lay foundations for future research in this direction. Thus, the book includes chapters on continental European exile in the United Kingdom and North America through 1945; on Spanish exile during the period of the Franco dictatorship after the Civil War of 1936-39; on East-Central European exile after the defeat of Nazi Germany and the establishment of communist rule from 1944-48 through the end of the Cold War and Latin American exile in Europe and North America through the lens of Chile after the 1973 coup d'état.

All chapters are based on fresh (archival) research. We do not claim to treat the exile of Catholic Christian Democrats in a comprehensive manner. However, the combined chapters set out many issues of political exile which invite further research on transnational and comparative aspects, for example to explore the different experiences of Latin American Christian Democrats in exile during the 1970s and 1980s.[12]

---

10 See Pertti Ahonen et al., eds, *People on the Move: Forced Population Movements in Europe in the Second World War and its Aftermath* (Oxford: Berg, 2008).
11 See, e.g., Janusz Zabłocki, *Chrześcijańska Demokracja w kraju i na emigracji, 1947-1970* (Lublin: Ośrodek PZKS w Lublinie, 1999).
12 Without a specific focus on Catholic Christian Democrats see Mario Sznajder and Luis Roniger, eds, *The Politics of Exile in Latin America* (Cambridge: Cambridge University Press, 2009); Pablo Yankelevich and Silvina Jensen, eds, *Exilios, destinos y experiencias bajo la dictadura militar* (Buenos Aires: Editorial del Zorzal, 2007).

In the case of the Christian Democrats, "global" essentially means Europe and the Americas if we want to avoid the Orientalist pretence that there must be Christian Democracy to be found in Africa and Asia as well.[13] This broad spatial scope also allows us to start exploring inter-regional exchanges and transfers that go beyond a continental perspective limited to Europe or North America, for example. In this volume, the two chapters on Chile demonstrate, for example, how experiences of centrist cooperation in Europe facilitated the rapprochement between Christian Democrats and democratic socialists before and during the Chilean transition back to democracy in the late 1980s. We hope that our book will incentivise more research in this direction in the future. Such research could explore the structures of, and the relations within, trans-regional networks, including those of political exiles, and their contributions to the transfer of institutions and practices during political transitions or in the context of incipient regional integration.

The chapters in this book explore four key themes. The first concerns the social and political composition of the Christian Democrats in political exile in a broad sense. Who were they, where did they locate themselves in their respective national party traditions, and how should we understand their decision to emigrate? Sometimes these departures took place under duress, as the result of persecution or violence. In other cases, they were voluntary, constituting a positive choice not to withdraw into private life but instead take on the new regime from abroad. How did these political exiles interact with pre-existing domestic traditions: alongside Christian Democracy, other flavours of political Catholicism, such as Christian socialism or Catholic conservatism? How did the exiles decide where to go? How did they manage to get to the host country, for example: did they draw on the help of pre-existing party contacts, or charities and relief organisations?

The second theme concerns the host countries themselves, their political and social cultures and how they received the political exiles. After all, exiles could put great strain on internally divided countries with weak economies, as in the case of France in the 1930s. Did the political

---

13 Arguably analogous political forms in Africa and Asia nonetheless follow their own distinctive (sometimes, post-colonial) trajectories: see, e.g., David Halloran Lumsdaine, ed, *Evangelical Christianity and Democracy in Asia* (Oxford: Oxford University Press, 2009); Paolo Borruso, "The Impossibility of a Christian Democracy in Africa? The Uganda Experience," in Jean-Dominique Durand, ed, *Christian Democrat Internationalism: Its Action in Europe and Worldwide from post-World War II until the 1990s*, vol. 3 (Brussels: P.I.E. Peter Lang, 2014), 97-106; Carlo Invernizzi Accetti, *What is Christian Democracy? Politics, Religion and Ideology* (Cambridge: Cambridge University Press, 2019), 317-344.

exiles gain access to the host country's government or relevant leaders of political parties? Did they try to influence those countries' relations with their home country, where this was even an option? What shaped their social integration with fellow exiles from the same home countries, or other Christian Democrats from different countries, or with the local host population? This may have been especially difficult in predominantly Protestant countries like the United Kingdom and the United States, with a Catholic Church and Catholic minority cultures that were strongly ultramontane in the nineteenth century and quite supportive of right-wing European dictatorships that the Vatican tacitly endorsed or tolerated.

The political organisation of exiles constitutes the book's third main theme. Once abroad, how did Sturzo, for example, interact with other Italian exiles like the liberal diplomat and key member of the Mazzini Society, Count Carlo Sforza, following the latter's move to the United States in 1940? National and transnational solidarities receive equal consideration here: Christian Democrats in exile sought to bring together political exiles from a wider Catholic Christian Democratic spectrum in order to develop social contacts and have meaningful discussions about reconstruction after a possible future transition out of war and/or into democracy. The resulting organisational structures included the Secrétariat International des Partis Démocratiques d'Inspiration Chrétienne, which Sturzo initiated from his exile together with the French Parti Démocrate Populaire in 1925;[14] the International Christian Democratic Union (ICDU) formed in London with the help of the People & Freedom Group in 1940 and discussed by Wolfram Kaiser in his chapter in this book; and the Christian Democratic Union of Central Europe (CDUCE) which operated from New York beginning from 1950 onwards.[15] How did Spanish, East-Central European and Latin American Christian Democrats in exile interact with those in Western Europe who, beginning in 1945, rebuilt parliamentary democracies

---

14 Guido Müller, "Anticipated Exile of Catholic Democrats: The Secrétariat International des Partis Démocratiques d'Inspiration Chrétienne," in Wolfram Kaiser and Helmut Wohnout, eds, *Political Catholicism in Europe 1918-45* (London: Routledge, 2004), 252-264.

15 Piotr H. Kosicki, "Christian Democracy's Global Cold War," in Piotr H. Kosicki and Sławomir Łukasiewicz, eds, *Christian Democracy across the Iron Curtain: Europe Redefined* (London: Palgrave Macmillan, 2018), 221-256; Stanisław Gebhardt, "The Christian Democratic Union of Central Europe," in Piotr H. Kosicki and Sławomir Łukasiewicz, eds, *Christian Democracy across the Iron Curtain* (London: Palgrave Macmillan, 2018), 411-424; Peter Van Kemseke, *Towards an Era of Development: The Globalization of Socialism and Christian Democracy, 1945-1965* (Leuven: Leuven University Press, 2006), 172-181.

and took new paths towards international collaboration through regional integration in what is now the European Union? Did these exiles adopt distinctly Christian Democratic structures and practices also for their work under the auspices of non-Christian Democratic organisations like the Free Europe Committee or the United Nations?[16]

The fourth theme, lastly, concerns the political exiles' intellectual and programmatic work. What ideas did they develop for a new post-war or post-Cold War order in Europe and beyond? Did these ideas matter during the reconstruction and transition periods after both hot and cold wars? Or were these ideas and plans marginalised as a result of dynamic social, economic and political developments on the ground during processes of reconstruction and transition that these exiles could not effectively influence, either from abroad or following their return to the home country? Even if it perhaps did not have much impact on reconstruction and transition processes, what (if any) distinctively Christian Democratic ideology and agenda emerged under the conditions of exile?

In Europe, Catholics had experience with exile throughout the long nineteenth century. At the time of the Prussian-German (and European) culture wars over the relationships between politics and religion and the state and church, priest-politicians as well as many other clergy went into exile.[17] Political exile of self-declared Catholic Christian Democrats only began with the priest-politician Sturzo in 1924, however. He resolutely refused to accept Benito Mussolini's fascist usurpation of power and abolition of democracy or to support the Vatican's search for accommodation and compromise with the new regime.

The illiberal turn in European politics in the 1920s and 1930s posed hard questions for Catholics actively involved in politics, which at that time still included priest-politicians like Sturzo, whose situation and personal decision-making was further complicated by their dependency on the Church hierarchy. In several countries the Church hierarchy as well as most Catholic believers supported newly established dictatorships that were inspired in different ways by traditional conservative notions of Catholicism and social order. This was the case in Portugal, for example,

16 See, e.g., Idesbald Goddeeris, "Exiles' Strategies for Lobbying in International Organisations: Eastern European Participation in the *Nouvelles Équipes Internationales*," *European Review of History/Revue européenne d'histoire* 11, no. 3 (2004): 383-400; Józef Łaptos, "L'apport des exilés d'au-delà du rideau de fer à la construction européenne," in Michel Dumoulin and Idesbald Goddeeris, eds, *Intégration ou représentation? Les exilés polonais en Belgique et la construction européenne* (Louvain-la-Neuve: Bruylant, 2005), 187-212.

17 See Christopher Clark and Wolfram Kaiser, eds, *Culture Wars: Catholic-Secular Conflicts in Nineteenth-Century Europe* (Cambridge: Cambridge University Press, 2003).

where António de Oliveira Salazar created the Estado Novo in the early 1930s, thus transforming the military dictatorship established in 1926 into a Catholic-inspired corporatist authoritarian dictatorship. It was also true of Spain during and after the Civil War of 1936-39, where the majority of Catholics supported Francisco Franco's Nationalists against the Republican Government in Madrid; or of the First Slovak Republic when it was created in 1939 as a Nazi German puppet state building on the mobilisation of Catholic Slovak nationalism under the leadership of priest-politician Jozef Tiso. Even in Germany, the Vatican pressured the Centre parliamentary party in the Reichstag to support Adolf Hitler's so-called Enabling Act in 1933 – this, in the hope of negotiating a concordat that would fully protect the interests of the Catholic Church and Catholics in the newly established totalitarian regime.

In these circumstances, only relatively few Catholics went into exile compared to socialists and communists, who were viciously persecuted by the new right-wing regimes. They opposed the new regimes on different grounds: some saw them as a fundamental threat to civil (not necessarily religious) liberties; or they had developed a strong stake in and were keen to defend parliamentary democracy; or they were critical of capitalist economic structures but did not regard what they called "state corporatism" propagated by some of these regimes as a legitimate alternative. Many of those who went into political exile were persecuted for their prior opposition to the new political parties and elites that established the new right-wing regimes and went into political exile as a result. Several among those in the Centre Party who had opposed support for the 1933 Enabling Law in internal discussions prior to the vote in Parliament, like Carl Spiecker, for example, fled quickly to avoid internment in the new concentration camps.

In the first chapter in this first section about the political exile of continental European Catholic Christian Democrats, Wolfram Kaiser takes a transnational perspective on the relatively small group of Catholic Christian Democrats in London, from the time of Sturzo's arrival there in 1924 through to the end of the war. Based on archival documents and media reports as well as autobiographical accounts, he explores the great importance of solidarity networks of mostly female progressive Catholics like Barbara Barclay Carter and Virginia Crawford for the well-being and at least partial integration of Christian Democratic political exiles in the United Kingdom. These middle-class Catholics became engaged in charity work to support exiles from Italy and Spain in the first instance, and they also helped Sturzo to create the People & Freedom Group to establish British and transnational contacts. However, Kaiser also shows that leading Catholics in governments-in-exile (notably, the Benelux countries) focused on their countries' military contribution and concrete post-war planning. With the partial exception of Basques and East-Central Europeans, the ICDU meetings were mostly attended by individuals on the margins of mainstream Catholic and Christian Democratic politics. Moreover, their proposals for the dismemberment of Germany and the creation of a democratic world organisation, not European integration, were quickly overtaken by post-war developments in Western Europe as the Cold War began.

In the second chapter in this section, based on archival as well as published sources, Paolo Acanfora explores Sturzo's exile in the United States in depth, focusing on how his contacts with American Catholics and other Italian political exiles shaped Sturzo's views of the United States and of the future post-war faces of Italy and the international system alike. Acanfora demonstrates how Sturzo became convinced that only the United States, if supported by the moral influence of the Catholic Church, could act as the engine of a new international order based on the principles articulated in the 1941 Atlantic Charter. To Sturzo, the fight for such a new international order was essential to protect the interests of Italy in what he considered to be a just peace treaty that would distinguish sharply between those responsible for fascism and the Italian people as a whole. In the end, however, Sturzo was unable to influence American decision-makers in a significant manner. As Acanfora also shows, the Holy See asked him to remain in the United States for more than one year after the end of the war, not least because of his Republican inclinations which would have made it more difficult for Alcide De Gasperi, the leader of the newly created Democrazia Cristiana, to unite his party and dominate Italian politics. As a Catholic Italian priest, Sturzo even at this point remained under the political yoke of the Vatican.

In the third chapter, Carlo Invernizzi Accetti uses the lens of political theory to study how the experience of exile in the United States shaped the ideas of Luigi Sturzo and Jacques Maritain. Based on the analysis of their publications during exile, he argues that both became fascinated with the United States as an alternative political system and culture that articulates politics and religion in a different key. Whereas European Catholics had long been sharply critical of what they saw as materialistic, individualistic and Protestant-dominated American politics and culture with its separation of church and state, the experience of exile led Sturzo and Maritain to reconsider and revise these views, for example by appreciating the peculiarly American notion of liberty. This, Invernizzi Accetti argues, profoundly shaped the more positive attitudes of Christian Democrats towards the United States and the Atlantic Alliance in Cold War Western Europe. However, these attitudes remained somewhat ambivalent, as is also reflected in Sturzo's renewed criticisms of the United States towards the end of the Second World War and in the war's immediate aftermath, when he accused the US of having surrendered the principle of global organisation and presided over what he considered the unfair treatment of Italy.

The second section starts with a chapter by Christopher Stroot about exile and Catholic politics in Spain from the 1930s through the death of Franco in 1975, drawing on extensive archival research as well as autobiography. In Spain, Catholic politics came of age with the creation of the Confederación Española de Derechas Autónomas founded to oppose anticlerical politics and policies. Many of its founders were at best semi-loyal to the Republic, however. As Stroot explores for the two cases of José María Gil Robles and Manuel Giménez Fernández, several of these exiles subsequently endorsed democratisation and Europeanisation in opposition to Franco, however. Their experience of exile – two decades in France and Portugal in the case of Gil Robles and internal exile in the case of Giménez Fernández – facilitated the shift from semi-loyalty to support for parliamentary democracy and regional integration based on the post-war Western European model. Both men helped to mobilise international and domestic support for the anti-Franco democratic opposition. This in turn facilitated the transition in the 1970s, though Christian Democracy as a distinctive political movement largely failed in the first free elections in 1977.

Based on research in Basque and international archives, Leyre Arrieta in the second chapter in this section explores the peculiar case of the Basque Nationalist Party. Imbued with in-vogue Christian Democratic ideas in the first half of the 1930s, Basque nationalist leaders, despite their strong Catholicism, opted for the Republic and against Franco in 1936. Many of them fled Spain as Franco's troops occupied the Basque Country. These Basque leaders worked hard in exile in Western Europe and the United States to build networks and to play a role in international organisations like the ICDU and then the Nouvelles Équipes Internationales (NEI) after 1945. For them, as Arrieta shows, this cooperation served to justify their opposition to Franco in the eyes of Catholics and, more particularly, the

Vatican. They also believed that the newly emerging integrated post-war (Western) Europe could constitute an ideal home for stateless nations like the Basques.

The third chapter in this section is devoted to the Catalan politician Josep Maria Trias Peitx from the Unió Democràtica de Catalunya, who was one of approximately 440,000 people who fled Spain during the winter of 1938-39. Based on archival research in Catalonia, France and the United States as well as oral history interviews, Gemma Caballer analyses his attempted mediation between the Republican government and the Holy See to re-establish relations and guarantee religious freedom. She goes on to explore Trias Peitx's exile in France until his death in 1979, painting a vivid picture of his humanitarian work in the south of France. In the end, he became increasingly marginal to his party's politics during the transition to democracy – a fate that many Christian Democratic political exiles shared.

The third section is devoted to Christian Democratic political exiles from East-Central Europe who settled in Western Europe and the United States as a consequence of the establishment of communist rule over their home countries in the years 1944-48.[18] Exile and migration form one of the defining thematic axes of the historiography of modern East-Central Europe.[19] Multiple waves of outward migration reshaped the region in the mid-twentieth century, first in the wake of the German and Soviet invasions of Poland in 1939, and subsequently, following the war's conclusion, when the short-lived post-war strategy of "popular fronts" gave way to rule throughout the region by full-blown Stalinist regimes steered from the Kremlin. Some of the exiled wartime intellectual and political leadership remained in the United Kingdom, the United States or France after the Second World War; others remained in or returned to Budapest, Prague or Warsaw, only then to escape or be pressured into exile yet again.[20]

In this era of "double exile" for East-Central European activists and politicians, Christian Democracy played a role whose visibility and significance far outweighed its electoral power – even in countries where Chris-

18 Norman M. Naimark and Leonid Gibianskii, eds, *The Establishment of Communist Regimes in Eastern Europe, 1944-1949* (Boulder, CO: Westview Press, 1998); Anne Applebaum, *Iron Curtain: The Crushing of Eastern Europe, 1944-1956* (New York: Random House, 2012).

19 See, e.g., Tara Zahra, *The Great Departure: Mass Migration from Eastern Europe and the Making of the Free World* (New York: W.W. Norton & Co., 2016); Anna Mazurkiewicz, ed, *East Central Europe in Exile* (Cambridge: Cambridge Scholars, 2013), 2 vols; Anna Mazurkiewicz, ed, *East Central European Migrations during the Cold War: A Handbook* (Berlin: de Gruyter, 2019).

20 See, e.g., Jarosław Rabiński, "The Elimination of Christian Democracy in Poland after World War II," in Piotr H. Kosicki and Sławomir Łukasiewicz, eds, *Christian Democracy across the Iron Curtain: Europe Redefined* (London: Palgrave Macmillan, 2018), 153-176.

tian Democrats had done quite well at the ballot box, such as Lithuania. In inter-war Czechoslovakia as in Hungary, in inter-war Lithuania as in Poland, politicians professing some form of inspiration or identification with Catholic social teaching either ran governments or ranked among the most prominent members of the opposition.[21] The Second World War cemented the strategic significance of Catholic statesmen in and from the region, as their declared commitments to social justice made it difficult for Soviet agents to discredit them out of hand as capitalists. With the exception of the Baltic states, where Christian Democrats' wartime anti-Sovietism had in many cases led to cooperation with the Nazi German invaders, Christian Democrats in the region entered "national unity" and "popular front" governments in the immediate post-war with an "anti-fascist" imprimatur from Moscow.[22]

By 1948-49 at the very latest, however, Christian Democrats were having teeth and eyes knocked out in interrogation rooms, while those fortunate enough to have fled the region before the solidification of an Iron Curtain sought American support to keep their political movements alive. The American Cold War strategy of "political warfare" against the Soviet Union included substantial funds for political exiles, with Christian Democrats in the front of the ranks, and the result was the formation of the CDUCE, a transnational lobby group funded by Americans, recognised and admired by Western Europeans and active even across the Global South, most notably in Latin America. The United States also provided support through (among others) the Ford Foundation, the Central Intelligence Agency and Radio Free Europe, which employed many political exiles.

Even though they were part of the CDUCE, the Baltic contingents of East-Central European Christian Democracy remained a world apart in virtue of their homelands having been fully annexed by the Soviet Union under the terms of the 1939 Molotov-Ribbentrop Pact. Arguably, Lithuania's Christian Democrats had been the most prominent in all of inter-war East-Central Europe.[23] And yet, as Justinas Dementavičius shows in the first chapter of this section, the real story in Lithuanian Catholic political exile belonged not to former Christian Democratic statesmen, but to its theorists and ideologues. Dementavičius explores the writings of Antanas

---

21 See, e.g., Arnold Suppan, "Catholic People's Parties in East Central Europe: The Bohemian Lands and Slovakia," in Wolfram Kaiser and Helmut Wohnout, eds, *Political Catholicism in Europe 1918-45* (London: Routledge, 2004), 217-234.

22 Piotr H. Kosicki, *Catholics on the Barricades: Poland, France and "Revolution," 1891-1956* (New Haven, CT: Yale University Press, 2018), 93-113.

23 V. Stanley Vardys, *Lithuania: The Rebel Nation* (Boulder, CO: Westview Press, 1997), 34-37.

Maceina and of Mykolas Krupavičius. The divergence between these two men and their approaches to the preservation of Catholic politics in exile reflected important conclusions reached already in the 1930s by French philosopher Jacques Maritain on the difference between confessional partisanship and political inspiration derived from religious ethics (in Maritain's parlance, *agir en tant que chrétien* vs. *en chrétien*).[24] Maceina, in particular, drew on Maritain already in the 1930s, well before leaving Lithuania behind in 1945. Dementavičius successfully establishes that, whatever the electoral fate of Christian Democratic parties in post-Soviet Lithuania, exile served as an incubator for a transnationally informed ideology that outlasted the Cold War itself.

The second chapter in this section, by Sławomir Łukasiewicz, takes up the thread of the CDUCE while posing a crucial question, previously unexplored in the historiography: how successful were exiled East-Central European Christian Democrats at imparting their agenda to newer and younger generations? Łukasiewicz offers a sobering account of the fleeting livelihood of East-Central European Christian Democratic youth movements in exile, with Poles as his case study. A small handful of the generation of activists born in the 1920s and 1930s and come of age during the war committed seriously to the cause; among these, only one man, Stanisław Gebhardt, made a successful career of Christian Democratic activism. Problems of legitimacy and continuity plagued the CDUCE and its member parties, with the result that few serious, politically minded Christian Democrats were left by the end of the Cold War to keep Christian Democracy alive. Poland was the clearest and most striking failure on this score, but the problems of generational continuity spanned the region.

Finally, Katalin Kádár Lynn explores the trajectory of perhaps the only Christian Democratic party in the region to have successfully returned from exile following the Cold War. Hungary's Christian Democratic People's Party was but one of several political groupings in inter-war Hungary claiming a political agenda drawn from Catholic social teaching, but the post-war popular front years oversaw an important dialogue between the more traditional Christian nationalism of the People's Party and the more "progressive", Catholic-socialist approach of a new faction under the leadership of István Barankovics. Pushed into exile by 1949, these groups found a modus vivendi that enabled them to fall in line with the Cold War agenda of the Free Europe Committee, working together also within the CDUCE. Hungarian Catholic leaders in exile were called upon again and

---

24 Jacques Maritain, "Structure de l'action," *Sept*, 12 April 1935.

again in the face of Cold War flare-ups centred on Hungary, whether this involved denouncing the arrest and show trial of József Cardinal Mindszenty or broadening their ideological umbrella to pronounce solidarity with the young Budapest revolutionaries crushed by Soviet tanks in the autumn of 1956. By the end of the Cold War, the US-supported Hungarian National Council was defunct, but some of its leaders returned to active politics in post-communist Hungary. The Hungarian case offers an important, if singular, testament to the ability of exiled Christian Democracy to survive the Cold War, all while confirming the lessons of Dementavičius's and Łukasiewicz's chapters.

Finally, the fourth section deals with political exile of Catholic Christian Democrats from Latin America in Europe and the United States during the periods of military dictatorship. Political parties inspired by Catholic social teaching flourished in Latin America from the 1950s and 1960s onwards.[25] Thus, representing the Comité de Organización Política Electoral Independiente (COPEI), the second largest political party there, Rafael Caldera became President of Venezuela for the first time during 1969-74 and again during 1994-99. In other examples, in El Salvador and Guatemala Christian Democratic parties became strong from the 1960s onwards.

A particular form of Christian Democracy with a strong socio-economic reform agenda also took hold in Chile from the 1930s onwards. There as elsewhere in Latin America, a new generation of young Catholics broke with the more staunchly conservative party-political traditions. Like in the case of the Nouvelles Équipes Françaises, which were formed in late 1930s France by several later leaders of the post-war Mouvement Républicain Populaire, these young Catholics were concerned about socio-economic underdevelopment and inequality in their countries and keen to develop a "progressive" Christian Democratic alternative to communism to address low levels of education, poverty and so on. They were inspired by leading thinkers like Maritain, in particular.[26]

In Chile these young politicians in 1957 created the Partido Demócrata Cristiano, which originated in the Falange Nacional, and were able to mobilise the grassroots support of many Catholic clergy who were equally keen on non-communist reforms to address the social question.[27] In 1964,

---

25 Scott Mainwaring and Timothy R. Scully, eds, *Christian Democracy in Latin America: Electoral Competition and Regime Conflicts* (Stanford: Stanford University Press, 2003).

26 Olivier Compagnon, *Jacques Maritain et l'Amérique du Sud: Le modèle malgré lui* (Villeneuve d'Ascq: Septentrion, 2003).

27 For the intellectual roots and politics of the PDC see Andrea Botto, *Catolicismo chileno: controversias y divisiones (1930-1962)* (Santiago: Ediciones Universidad Finis Terrae, 2018).

the PDC's candidate, Eduardo Frei Montalva, won the presidential elections, and the party won a majority of seats in parliament in 1965. Facing multiple domestic difficulties, however, the PDC government lacked the financial means to implement its far-reaching socio-economic reform agenda. In 1973 the Chilean military then ousted the socialist President Salvador Allende in a violent coup d'état.

Although the Chilean military dictatorship mainly persecuted, imprisoned and assassinated its socialist and communist opponents, many Christian Democrats on the left of the party also went into political exile, although some then returned during the 1980s. Elsewhere in Latin America, Christian Democrats supportive of democracy, rule of law and Christian-inspired socio-economic reform agendas were not organised as effectively as a political movement or party, but nevertheless experienced persecution at the hands of juntas in Uruguay during 1973-85 and in Argentina during 1976-83.

In the first chapter in this section, Joaquín Fermandois takes an inside-out perspective on relations between leaders of the Chilean Christian Democrats grouped around Eduardo Frei, who remained in Chile after the coup d'état by the army against the government of Salvador Allende, and other members of the PDC who went into exile between 1973 and the start of the 1980s. Based on the private papers of Frei, Patricio Aylwin and Gabriel Valdés, as well as memoirs and published sources, Fermandois shows that the main dividing line was the question of future cooperation with the Socialists and what form of (Christian) socialism, if any, was desirable – with the exiles landing mostly on the Left in this debate. The chapter also shows that the political exiles had no significant direct impact on the transition towards the end of the Pinochet regime. However, their contacts, and those of the Chilean socialists in exile in Europe, with reformed social democracy facilitated a transformation during the 1980s that saw a resurgent Left shed its Marxism. The result was the Concertación between the Christian Democrats and the Socialists between 1990 and 2010.

In the final chapter of the book, Élodie Giraudier offers an outside-in perspective to reconstruct the experience of Christian Democratic political exiles from Chile in Europe and North America and their contacts with the party in their home country. Drawing on fresh archival sources from the Jean Jaurès, Frei and Konrad Adenauer Foundations, in addition to interviews and press reports, this chapter explores why many exiles from the left of the PDC went to Italy, the Netherlands and France, where they already had contacts because the Christian Democratic parties there had compatible "left-Catholic" sections. The German Konrad Adenauer Foundation also provided support, but the right wing of the Christian Democratic Union and its sister party in Bavaria, the Christian Social Union, tacitly supported the Pinochet regime, at least at the start. The chapter goes on to argue (complementing Fermandois) that despite heated controversies within the PDC and among Christian Democrats in exile, the Chilean exile experience clearly helped to bring together Christian Democrats and socialists to cooperate in achieving a democratic transition in Chile. In other words, the experience of Western European politics provided a meaningful template for Chile's political future after the dictatorship.

The spatial and temporal diversity of the chapters in this book, which are all based on fresh (mostly archival) research, provide pointers for desirable future research, but also limit the potential for generalisations. Much of the research on the history of Catholic and Christian Democratic politics (as on other political ideologies and histories of political movements and parties) has become professionalised, shedding its older, more strongly normative orientation geared towards supporting contemporary parties, their policies and narratives. Nevertheless, Christian Democracy in exile could still appear as a morally "pure" form of intellectual thought and political engagement. This meant transnational activism on behalf of democracy and international organisations divorced both from the widespread Catholic support for fascist and clerical military dictatorships and from their continued ambivalence about pluralist democracy and the post-transition need to make moral and political compromises in government.

As several chapters in this book demonstrate, however, many Christian Democrats in exile were quite isolated socially. Those who had fled right-wing regimes suffered from tense relations with the Catholic Church and faithful who largely supported those regimes, whether in Mussolini's Italy, Franco's Spain or Pinochet's Chile. Even East-Central Europeans allied with the Cold War agenda of the United States were hardly immune to this isolation: many ultimately chose integration with host countries over continued (and increasingly tenuous) claims to representation of their homelands – increasingly so as they lost proper access to host country political networks (let alone governments).

Christian Democrats in political exile often espoused political ideas that they upheld for their own sake, but also used instrumentally for advancing more traditional, national(istic) agendas. Thus, as Kaiser demonstrates, the Polish participants in the ICDU strongly advocated the dismemberment of Germany, Poland's western expansion irrespective of any territorial loss to the Soviet Union in the East and mass expulsion of Germans from these territories. As Acanfora argues, Sturzo supported the 1941 Atlantic Charter and a more lenient treatment of Germany without larger territorial changes not least because he hoped that the Allies would award Italy a post-war status similar to Austria, effectively as a victim of Nazi Germany. Sturzo's approach may well have contributed to the post-war Italian amnesia about the national experience of fascism and its crimes. Lastly, the Basque nationalists – as Arrieta demonstrates in her chapter – invested so much time and energy in cooperating in organisations like the ICDU and the NEI precisely to secure the support of their Christian Democratic allies for Basque statehood in a somehow united Europe, or at the very least the restoration and expansion of its autonomous status within Spain.

The history of Christian Democrats in exile in the global twentieth century also cannot, and should not, serve the sanctification of Christian Democracy, for another reason: these exiles sometimes did not live to return to their home country, and when they did, they were frequently cut out of the new political life after the war or transition to democracy. In extreme cases, their exile, despite its own forms of hardship, even became a social and political stigma, as not only actively participating in opposition to the authoritarian and dictatorial regime was glorified, but also enduring repression, internal exile and war. As Sławomir Łukasiewicz shows, the younger generations of Christian Democrats increasingly lacked these identifications, seeing themselves instead as cosmopolitans and transnationalists for whom patriotism was but one priority within a larger constellation of global aims.

Thinkers like Maritain exercised intellectual influence on Christian Democracy from exile in the longer term. In contrast, with the limited exception of Hungary, no Christian Democrat in exile in any of the cases covered in this book succeeded in returning to his home country to co-shape post-war or post-transition politics in any truly significant manner.[28] In extreme cases like Trias Peitx from Catalonia, they did not even return when they could have, as they had become so isolated even within their own ideological family or organised political party. Clearly, contemporary Christian Democracy or Christian Democratic politics were not made in political exile.

---

28   See, e.g., Piotr H. Kosicki, "Beyond 1989: The Disappointed Hopes of Christian Democracy in Post-Communist Central and Eastern Europe," in Michael Gehler, Piotr H. Kosicki and Helmut Wohnout, eds, *Christian Democracy and the Fall of Communism* (Leuven: Leuven University Press, 2019), 305-326.

I.B. 113

No. _____ S.39434 _____

Date _____ 15th August, 1940 _____

Authority issuing certificate :—HOME OFFICE.
Indication de l'autorité qui délivre le certificat

Place of issue of certificate :—LONDON.
Lieu ou l'on délivre le certificat

CERTIFICATE OF IDENTITY.
CERTIFICAT D'IDENTITE.

Valid until _14th August, 1941_
Valable jusqu'

The present certificate is issued for the sole purpose of providing the holder with identity papers in lieu of a national passport. It is without prejudice to and in no way affects the national status of the holder. If the holder obtains a national passport it ceases to be valid and must be surrendered to the issuing authority.

Le présent certificat est délivré à seule fin de fournir au titulaire une pièce d'identité pouvant tenir lieu de passeport national. Il ne préjuge pas la nationalité du titulaire et est sans effet sur celle-ci. Au cas où le titulaire obtiendrait un passeport national, ce certificat cessera d'être valable et devra être renvoyé à l'autorité qui l'a délivré.

Signature of Holder,
Signature du titulaire,

Surname. _____ STURZO _____
Nom de famille.

Forenames _____ Luigi Sturzo _____
Prénoms.

Date of birth _____ 26th November, 1871 _____
Date de naissance.

Place of birth _____ Caltagirone _____
Lieu de naissance.

Nationality of origin _____ Italian _____
Nationalité d'origine.

Surname and forenames of Father. STURZO Felice
Nom de famille et prénoms du père.

Surname and forenames of Mother. BOSCARELLI Caterina
Nom de famille et prénoms de la mère.

Name of wife (husband). _____ ----- _____
Nom de la femme (mari).

Names of children. _____ ----- _____
Noms des enfants.

Occupation. _____ Catholic priest and author _____
Profession.

Former residence abroad _____ Rome _____
Ancien domicile à l'étranger.

Present residence in the United Kingdom _ 32, Chepstow _
Résidence actuelle dans le Royaume Uni.

_____ Villas, London.W.11. _____

Police Registration Certificate _____ 236817 _____
Certificat d'enregistrement délivré par la Police.

The undersigned certifies that the photograph and signature hereon are those of the bearer of the present document.

Le soussigné certifie que la photographie et la signature apposées ci-contre sont bien celles du porteur du présent document.

DESCRIPTION.
SIGNALEMENT.

Age _____ 68 years _____
Age

Height _____ 5 ft 5 ins _____
Taille

Hair _____ grey _____
Cheveux

Eyes _____ hazel _____
Yeux

Face _____ oval _____
Visage

Nose _____ normal _____
Nez

Special peculiarities _____
Signes particuliers

Remarks
Observations

Signature of the issuing authority,
Signature de l'autorité,

[signature]

H.M. CHIEF INSPECTOR,
IMMIGRATION BRANCH,
HOME OFFICE,
LONDON, S.W.1.

This Certificate is available during its validity for the holder's return to the United Kingdom without visa.

Durant la période de sa validité le présent certificat sera valable pour la rentrée du titulaire dans le Royaume Uni sans formalité de Visa.

This Certificate must be endorsed with an Exit Permit for Embarkation and Vised by a British Consular Authority abroad for return to the United Kingdom. [S.O. 6625]. Wt. 46550/660. 5 000. 5/39. C.T. Gp. 680

CERTIFICATE OF IDENTITY FEE. 7 6 2270

Luigi Sturzo's United Kingdom-issued Certificate of Identity dated 15 August 1940.
[Document in possession of the Istituto Luigi Sturzo, Fondo Luigi Sturzo, Terza parte (1940-1946), fasc. 617, doc. 10, and reproduced with its permission]

SECTION I

EXILE IN THE UNITED KINGDOM AND THE UNITED STATES 1924-1945

1

EUROPEAN CHRISTIAN DEMOCRATS IN EXILE IN THE UNITED KINGDOM

Socially Isolated and Politically Marginal

Wolfram Kaiser

Spending time in political exile could be a lonely and frustrating experience, not least for continental European anti-fascist Christian Democrats in London during the 1930s and the Second World War. Few of them had a privileged role as politicians or officials in one of the nine governments-in-exile. The others swapped their actual or anticipated persecution by Nazi, fascist or collaborationist regimes, internment or possibly death, for a temporarily unclear legal status, difficult professional situation, relative social isolation, food rationing and generally poor living standards combined with the experience of the Blitz, or German Luftwaffe bombardments.

Additionally, Christian Democrats in political exile in London had limited and often uneasy relations with other exiles of different ideological persuasion and party affiliation from their own country. Communists, socialists and even liberals from countries like Italy, Spain, and France were strongly influenced by the widespread support among continental European Catholics for clerical dictatorships and fascist and collaborationist regimes from which they had fled. With few exceptions, moreover, for most Christian Democrats their exile in London ended any aspirations to resuming or starting a political career after the war. When they returned after 1944-45, they often found themselves replaced by politicians who had suffered milder persecution, if any, in different varieties of domestic exile or clandestine life; by those who had been active in the Resistance; or by a younger generation of up-and-coming politicians – or after temporarily having had a major influence on Catholic thought and politics, as in the case of Poland during 1945-47, they were forced back into exile once more as a result of the creeping communist usurpation of power in East-Central Europe.

The anti-fascist, pro-democratic Christian Democrats in exile faced a Catholic community in Britain, moreover, which was overwhelmingly not very welcoming to the newcomers. Many British Catholics were initially quite philo-fascist, supported Franco during the Spanish Civil War and endorsed the policy of Appeasement until 1939.[1] Although British government policy towards political refugees has been researched comprehensively,[2] much less is known about British societal networks for refugees – such as the Scottish associations formed to support the Polish refugees and Air Force soldiers based there, for example.[3] Only a small number of British Catholic and Protestant anti-fascist individuals specifically supported Christian Democrats in political exile. Many of them were middle-class women who helped political exiles to connect with each other and with British citizens and politicians. As this chapter argues, these women's combined charitable and political activism was frequently crucial to enabling political exiles to create social contacts and contribute something meaningful to political life in exile – as in the well-known case of Luigi Sturzo, who largely depended on the American writer and women's rights advocate Barbara Barclay Carter for managing his personal life, creating contacts with sympathetic British citizens, networking with Catholic journals and translating his writings into English. These women also played a key role in facilitating transnational communication and joint thinking among continental Christian Democrats in London about a post-war order for Europe.

Historical literature on exile in the United Kingdom is quite extensive.[4] Research on *political* exile is more limited, however. Moreover, the analysis of political exile is often confined to a particular national group;[5] it

---

1   See Tom Villis, *British Catholics & Fascism: Religious Identity and Political Extremism Between the Wars* (Basingstoke: Palgrave, 2013).

2   Jeremy Seabrook, *The Refuge and the Fortress: Britain and the Persecuted 1933-2013* (Basingstoke: Palgrave Macmillan, 2013); David Cesarini and Tony Kushner, eds, *The Internment of Aliens in Twentieth Century Britain* (London: Frank Cass, 1993). For broader context see, e.g., Colin Holmes, *John Bull's Island: Immigration and British Society 1871-1971* (Basingstoke: Macmillan, 1988).

3   Peter D. Stachura, "The Poles in Scotland, 1940-50," in Peter D. Stachura, ed, *The Poles in Britain 1940-2000: From Betrayal to Assimilation* (London: Frank Cass, 2004), 48-58; Keith Sword, Norman Davies, and Jan Ciechanowski, *The Formation of the Polish Community in Great Britain, 1939-1950* (London: School of Slavonic and East European Studies, 1989).

4   See, e.g., J.M. Ritchie, *German Exiles: British Perspectives* (New York: Peter Lang, 1997).

5   With a strong focus on Belgium despite the broader title, Martin Conway and José Gotovitch, eds, *Europe in Exile: European Exile Communities in Britain 1940-45* (New York: Berghahn, 2001).

Wolfram Kaiser

focuses on the numerically larger communists and socialists;[6] or it is pre-occupied with the activities of the nine governments-in-exile during the Second World War.[7] In contrast, this chapter will focus on their transnational cooperation in London, and their deliberations about post-war Europe. When they met in forums like the meetings organised by the People & Freedom Group created in November 1936 and the International Christian Democratic Union (ICDU) formed in February 1941, they often held views on the future of their country, and of Europe, that were fundamentally at odds with each other, however. The chapter concludes that transnational networking in exile in the United Kingdom during 1924-45 had little to no impact on post-war reconstruction or the particular shape that European integration in the present-day European Union was to take with the creation of the European Coal and Steel Community in 1951-52 and beyond.[8] Exploring the discussions among exiles nevertheless sheds light on their views and mentalities as part of the wider study of exile and war.

To make these points, the chapter will first map the political exile of Christian Democrats in London between Sturzo's arrival in October 1924 and the end of the Second World War. It will go on to set out the basic characteristics of Catholicism in the host country during the 1930s, which these exiles found quite disturbing. The chapter's second section will sketch the British support networks for these political refugees, focusing especially on the biographies and activities of Barbara Barclay Carter, Virginia Crawford and Katherine Murray-Stewart, the Duchess of Atholl. Finally, based on their speeches and discussions in the People & Freedom Group and the ICDU and wartime publications, the third section will analyse the dominant ideas among continental European Christian Democrats in political exile for European reconstruction after 1945.

---

6   See, e.g., Anthony Grenville and Andrea Reiter, eds, *Political Exile and Exile Politics in Britain after 1933* (Amsterdam: Radopi, 2011).
7   See, e.g., with a heavy focus on Czechoslovakia, Vít Smetana and Kathleen Geaney, eds, *Exile in London: The Experience of Czechoslovakia and the other Occupied Nations, 1939-1945* (Prague: Charles University Karolinum Press, 2017); see also Julia Eichenberg, "Macht auf der Flucht: Europäische Regierungen in London (1940-1944)," *Zeithistorische Forschungen* 15, no. 3 (2018): 452-473.
8   Wolfram Kaiser, *Christian Democracy and the Origins of European Union* (Cambridge: Cambridge University Press, 2007), chapters 4-6.

Anti-fascist Christian Democrats in exile in the United Kingdom

Compared to communists and socialists, only relatively few anti-fascist Catholic politicians went into exile between 1922 and 1925, as Mussolini consolidated power in Italy, and in the years 1938-40. In turn, only very few of these Catholic exiles would initially have described themselves as Christian Democrats imbued with ideas of Christian-inspired socio-economic reform. Some only came in touch with Christian Democracy as a political ideology for the first time through contact with Sturzo in London.

Initially, many conservative Catholics worked with the fascist and Nazi regimes or with the German occupation forces, especially in Vichy France. Others, like the German and Italian post-war leaders Konrad Adenauer and Alcide De Gasperi went into internal exile, with De Gasperi working in the Vatican Library. Many younger, politically and socially more re-form-minded Christian Democrats joined the national resistance, where they cooperated with socialists. Georges Bidault succeeded Jean Moulin as leader of the French Resistance, working closely with Pierre-Henri Teitgen, Paul and Alfred Coste-Floret and François de Menthon, all of whom became leading figures in the Mouvement Républicain Populaire (MRP) after 1944.[9] Other Catholic politicians in the Resistance included Josef Müller, the first leader of the Bavarian Christian Social Union, and Felix Hurdes, the first secretary general of the Austrian People's Party after the war. Moreover, while most communists fled to the Soviet Union and many social democrats to Britain due to their links with the Labour Party, the less numerous Catholic politicians in exile were more dispersed, as several chapters in this book demonstrate.

Among the small group of Italian members of the Partito Popolare Italiano (PPI), its founder Luigi Sturzo went to London in October 1924, apparently since he, as a Catholic priest, expected to be less subject to Vatican control in majority-Protestant Britain than, for example, in France.[10] After Italy's entry into the war, Sturzo left Britain for the United States in September 1940, partly to avoid the internment that most German and

---

9   On the French Christian Democrat Resistance and the formation of the MRP see Pierre Letamendia, *Le Mouvement Républicain Populaire: Histoire d'un grand parti français* (Paris: Beauchesne, 1995).

10 Francesco Piva and Francesco Malgeri, *Vita di Luigi Sturzo* (Rome: Edizioni Cinque lune, 1972), 295.

Wolfram Kaiser

Austrian political refugees had suffered in the preceding spring.[11] Other PPI politicians initially settled in Paris or Brussels.[12]

The German Centre Party exile was particularly dispersed. Thus, Heinrich Brüning, Reich chancellor from 1930 to 1932, left Germany in 1934. He first lived mainly in the Netherlands and Britain and then settled permanently in the United States when he became law professor at Harvard University in 1937. However, Brüning opposed "refugee politics"[13] and never played a prominent public role in the German political exile community. Carl Spiecker, who had been a member of the Reichsbanner leadership and special Reich representative for the fight against National Socialism during 1930-31, was first in France, then in Britain and finally, in Canada. Joseph Wirth, also a former Reich chancellor, settled in Switzerland.[14] Still other Centre Party politicians fled to Brazil and elsewhere in Latin America.

The Austrian Christian Social refugee group was even smaller. Kurt Schuschnigg was arrested after the German annexation of Austria. The Association of Austrian Christian Socials in Great Britain numbered only 15, with no prominent politicians among them.[15] The former Austrian ministers Hans Rott and Guido Zernatto fled to Canada and the United States respectively.[16] However, they were very isolated within the Austrian refugee community due to their participation in the establishment of the authoritarian *Ständestaat* and the outlawing of the Social Democratic Party in 1933-34. Moreover, they were marginalised by the politically hyperactive conservative legitimists around Otto and Robert von Habsburg who had quite close links with the American and British governments.[17]

---

11 Francesco Malgeri, *Luigi Sturzo* (San Paolo: Cinisello Balsamo, 1993), 239; on the British internment policy see Peter and Leni Gillman, *'Collar the lot!' How Britain interned and expelled its Wartime Refugees* (London: Quartet Books, 1980); Michael Seyfert, "'His Majesty's Most Loyal Internees': Die Internierung und Deportation deutscher und österreichischer Flüchtlinge als 'enemy aliens': Historische, kulturelle und literarische Aspekte," in Gerhard Hirschfeld, ed, *Exil in Großbritannien: Zur Emigration aus dem nationalsozialistischen Deutschland* (Stuttgart: Klett Cotta, 1983), 155-182.

12 Charles F. Delzell, *Mussolini's Enemies: The Italian Anti-Fascist Resistance* (Princeton, NJ: Princeton University Press, 1961), 55.

13 Joachim Radkau, *Die deutsche Emigration in den USA: Ihr Einfluß auf die amerikanische Europapolitik 1933-1945* (Düsseldorf: Bertelsmann, 1971), 184.

14 Ulrike Hörster-Philipps, *Joseph Wirth 1879-1956: Eine politische Biographie* (Paderborn: Schöningh, 1998).

15 Helene Maimann, *Politik im Wartesaal: Österreichische Exilpolitik in Grossbritannien 1938-1945* (Vienna, Cologne and Graz: Böhlau, 1975), 101.

16 Franz Goldner, *Die österreichische Emigration 1938 bis 1945* (Vienna and Munich: Herold, 1972).

17 Maimann, *Politik im Wartesaal*, 94.

The Catholic political refugees from Italy, Germany and Austria were initially very isolated politically. Their main challenge was whether, how and on what terms to form links with the non-Catholic democratic political refugees, and especially with the socialists. When the Italian Socialists and Republicans founded the Anti-Fascist Concentration in 1927, they excluded the PPI refugees because of the Vatican's support for Mussolini.[18] After a brief period of Popular Front collaboration between the Socialists and Communists after 1935, Sturzo established a close personal relationship with Count Sforza and other liberal and socialist refugees in the United States.[19] At the same time, many Austrian Christian Social exiles clung to the *Ständestaat* model for much longer than Catholics within Austria and in the Austrian Resistance, precluding closer contacts with the Social Democrats.

Catholic refugees from the Netherlands, Belgium, Luxemburg, France and East-Central European countries, especially from Poland and Czechoslovakia, were primarily oriented towards their national governments-in-exile in London and official planning for postwar reconstruction.[20] Their transnational cooperation mainly took place at the governmental level, especially in the context of the negotiations between the Netherlands and Belgium about a customs union and of the bilateral talks leading up to the Polish-Czechoslovak treaty of confederation of January 1942.[21] Moreover, the establishment of non-official transnational contacts was further complicated by the fluctuation in the personnel of the governments-in-exile. The Belgian government, for example, started its work in London with only four ministers. August De Schryver, who was to play a key role in transnational party cooperation after the war, only arrived in Britain at the start of August 1942. He was then on a mission to Washington and only returned to London in May 1943 to become interior minis-

18 Guiseppe Ignesti, "Momenti del Popolarismo in Esilio," in Pietro Scoppola and Francesco Traniello, eds, *I Cattolici tra Fascismo e Democrazia* (Bologna: Mulino, 1975), 75-183, 101; see also Lucia Ceci, *The Vatican and Mussolini's Italy* (Amsterdam: Brill, 2017).

19 Gabriele De Rosa, *Luigi Sturzo* (Turin: Unione Tipografico-Ed., 1977), 409; see also the chapters by Paolo Acanfora and Carlo Invernizzi Accetti in this book.

20 On the exile governments in London see, in a European perspective, Martin Conway, "Legacies of exile: the exile governments in London during World War II and the politics of postwar Europe," in Conway and Gotovitch, *Europe in Exile*, 255-274.

21 Pierre-Henri Laurent, "Reality not rhetoric: Belgian-Dutch diplomacy in wartime London, 1940-1944," in M.L. Smith and Peter M.R. Stirk, eds, *Making the New Europe: European Unity and the Second World War* (London: Pinter, 1990), 133-141; cf. Detlef Brandes, "Confederation Plans in Eastern Europe during World War II," in Michel Dumoulin, ed, *Wartime Plans for Postwar Europe 1940-1947* (Brussels: Bruylant, 1995), 83-94.

ter.[22] Shortly afterwards, in the early summer of 1943, Maurice Schumann, who was close to Charles de Gaulle and later played a prominent role in the MRP, left London when the Free French government moved to Algiers.

At the political level, the Christian Democrats in exile had no natural partners in the United Kingdom due to their predominantly secular, non-confessional party traditions and the resulting absence of comparable Catholic or "popular" parties. Catholicism formed a distinct minority culture in the United Kingdom, which still retained "something of the old ghetto mentality of a once-persecuted minority".[23] Despite significant rates of conversion, only 2,35 million citizens out of 40 million in England and Wales were Catholic in 1935. Some were so-called old Catholics and others recent converts, who were largely middle-class, but the vast majority were Irish immigrants or their descendants, who were almost exclusively working class.[24] The majority, especially of the Irish working class immigrants, supported the Labour Party – a preference that the Church leadership publicly condoned in 1924-25, referring to Labour's reform tradition and its lack of anti-clericalism and declaring it not to be socialist in the continental sense.

The profoundly disturbing experience of Catholic political refugees in the 1930s was the extent of initial political support for Mussolini and Franco and of philo-fascism among the Catholic communities in Britain. When Sturzo arrived in Britain, he was shocked by the support for Mussolini and attacks on him by prominent Catholics like the writer Hilaire Belloc.[25] Many British Catholics admired Mussolini for his staunch anti-communism. Their sympathy for the Italian dictator was further reinforced by the Catholic hierarchy, which toed the Vatican's line especially closely. Moreover, Mussolini as well as Franco seemed to guarantee the rights of the Church against a staunchly anti-clerical political Left in Italy and Spain. Finally, fascist and authoritarian states advanced concepts of a new social order that superficially aligned with Catholic social teaching, despite the muted criticism of fascist "state corporatism" in the 1931 papal encyclicals *Quadragesimo Anno* and (directed at fascist Italy) *Non Abbiamo Bisogno*.

22   Theo Luykx, "De rol van August De Schryver in het politieke leven tot en met de Tweede Wereld-oorlog," in *Veertig jaar Belgische politiek: Liber amicorum aangeboden aan Minister van Staat A.E. De Schryver ter gelegenheid van zijn 70ste verjaardag* (Antwerp and Utrecht: Standaard Wetenschappelijke Uitg., 1968), 121-211, 199.
23   Villis, *British Catholics*, 2.
24   Tom Buchanan, "Great Britain," in Tom Buchanan and Martin Conway, eds, *Political Catholicism in Europe, 1918-1965* (Oxford: Oxford University Press, 1996), 248-274, at 250.
25   Villis, *British Catholics*, 201.

These cleavages were accentuated further by the political debate about the Spanish Civil War. Following the atrocities committed by Republican troops against Catholic priests in the early phase of the war, the British Catholic press overwhelmingly supported the Nationalists.[26] The more intellectual *The Tablet* insisted, for example, that "all those Spaniards who wish to see the Church survive in Spain will have had to side with the insurgents".[27] Catholic writers like Belloc and Evelyn Waugh also supported Franco. Cardinal Arthur Hinsley refused to condemn Nationalist atrocities, such as the bombing of Guernica by German planes in the spring of 1937. He then congratulated Franco in March 1939 upon winning the war, praising him in a personal letter as "the great defender of the true Spain, the country of Catholic principles where Catholic social justice and charity will be applied for the common good under a firm and peace-loving government".[28] Among British Catholics, the religious cleavage largely overshadowed the class cleavage, with many Catholic Labour supporters being either neutral or hostile towards the Spanish Republic.[29]

In Britain, most Catholics also supported the Appeasement policy towards Nazi Germany and Italy during the 1930s. Catholics often caused the greatest trouble for anti-Appeasement politicians at the grassroots level, as the Scottish Conservative MP, the Duchess of Atholl, found when she started to support the Spanish Republic. The staunchest opposition to her political activism regarding the Spanish Civil War within her Scottish constituency party came from "very hot R.C.[s] [Roman Catholics]"[30]; opposition that led to the symbolic resignation of her seat and contributed to her narrow defeat in the ensuing by-election in December 1938.[31] However, small groups of articulate middle-class liberal Catholics and their Protestant friends tried to provide an alternative intellectual and political focus and to create a friendlier environment for Christian Democrats in exile.

26   James Flint, "'Must God go Fascist?' English Catholic Opinion and the Spanish Civil War," *Church History* 56, no. 3 (1987): 364-374, at 367.
27   *The Tablet*, 1 August 1936.
28   Hinsley to Franco, 28 March 1939, Westminster Diocesan Archives, Hinsley papers, HI 2/217.
29   Tom Buchanan, *The Spanish Civil War and the British Labour Movement* (Cambridge: Cambridge University Press, 1991), 107.
30   Duke of Atholl to G. Mickel, 31 May 1937, Blair Castle Archives, Atholl MSS 22/6.
31   On the by-election see, in more detail, Stuart Ball, "The Politics of Appeasement: the Fall of the Duchess of Atholl and the Kinross and West Perth By-election, December 1938," *The Scottish Historical Review* LXIX, no. 1 (1990): 49-83.

Catholic charitable and political support networks

Much of British charity work in the 1930s and during the Second World War was geared towards supporting refugees, and it was mainly carried out by women. One particularly pertinent case is Eleanor Rathbone, the Independent MP for Combined English universities from 1929 onwards. Rathbone inter alia became involved in supporting refugees from Republican Spain, especially from the Basque Country, which included the temporary relocation of children from there to France and the United Kingdom. She also worked tirelessly for persecuted German Jews and initiated the transport of Jewish children from Nazi Germany to the United Kingdom in 1938-39, which was to save their lives. Continuously engaging with a largely unsympathetic British government and quite hostile public, she also lobbied for improved conditions for German and Italian nationals – many of them refugees – who were interned as "enemy aliens" from 1940 onwards.[32]

Among those who specifically supported Christian Democratic refugees from continental Europe, Barbara Barclay Carter stands out. Together with her friend Cicely Marshall, Carter formed the core of Sturzo's "survival system" in London.[33] She first met Sturzo, who was under continuous pressure from the Vatican to refrain from statements and publications in exile, at a dinner in December 1924 organised by Catholic women from the St. Joan's Social and Political Alliance, who advocated women's rights and political participation. Eventually, in the spring of 1926, when Sturzo could no longer live in Church-owned accommodation, Carter and Marshall invited him and his twin sister to move in with them in their flat and from 1933 onwards, a semi-detached house.

Orphaned at the age of 12, Carter, a US citizen, had grown up in London and was 24 when she met Sturzo. She had converted to Catholicism three years previously. A graduate of the Sorbonne in Paris, she had taken a keen interest in the Italian writer Dante. She had also studied Scholastic philosophy at the Institut Catholique in Paris and was fluent in both Italian and French. The encounter with Sturzo reinforced her religious and intellectual conversion and her cooperation with him gave her a "sense

---

32 See Susan Cohen, "Eleanor Rathbone: MP for Refugees," in Grenville and Reiter, *Political Exile and Exile Politics*, 1-15; Susan Cohen, *Rescue the Perishing: Eleanor Rathbone and the Refugees* (London: Vallentine Mitchell, 2010).
33 Giovanna Farrell-Vinay, "The London Exile of Don Luigi Sturzo (1924-1940)," *Heythrop Journal* 45, no. 2 (2004): 158-177, here 163.

of purpose".[34] Crucially, however, Sturzo, shunned by the British Catholic hierarchy, depended even more on her, especially as he had knowledge of French, but no English at all when he arrived in London, which only served to reinforce his initial severe social and intellectual isolation.

Carter and Marshall played a crucial role in supporting Sturzo in multiple ways, which cannot be fully appreciated based on the limited surviving records. To begin with, they managed the household and made it possible for him to concentrate on his writing and correspondence. Moreover, Carter worked as his interpreter and translator – support that very few political exiles enjoyed and that was crucially important in view of Sturzo's language limitations. She also tirelessly propagated him and his political philosophy, for example in publications for the more liberal-Catholic Dominican publication *Blackfriars* and by drawing on her network to initiate reviews of Sturzo's books. Carter and Marshall also helped establish many of Sturzo's contacts with British citizens during the 1930s, such as with Henry Wickham Steed and Edward Ingram Watkin. Just how important Carter and Marshall were for Sturzo's physical and intellectual well-being became clear when he felt even more isolated in the United States after 1940, longing to return to London or at least to pass through it on his way back to Italy. Throughout the war, Carter remained personally committed to Sturzo. She also supported him in his patriotic campaign towards the end and after the war rhetorically to minimise the crimes of the fascist regime, establish Italy as a credible victim of Nazi Germany, secure "Free French" treatment by the Allies and protect Italy against territorial claims by Yugoslavia.[35]

In contrast with Carter, who became Sturzo's disciple, Virginia Crawford had long been a leading advocate of Christian Democracy in the United Kingdom. She also disposed of a wide network of contacts with continental Catholic institutions and individuals. She was received into the Catholic Church by Cardinal Henry Manning, who took a particular interest in the plight of the working class advocating social reform. Crawford was a key figure in the St. Joan's Alliance, where she later met Carter. In 1909 she also co-founded the Catholic Social Guild with the Jesuit Charles Plater, which had some 4,000 members by 1938.[36]

---

34 Farrell-Vinay, "The London Exile," 163. See also "Barbara Barclay Carter," *The Catholic Citizen*, 15 October 1951.

35 See, e.g., Giovanna Farrell-Vinay, "Viaggio nell'Italia del 1946: Quattro lettere di Barbara Barclay Carter a Luigi Sturzo," *Contemporanea* 13, no. 1 (2010): 79-102.

36 Joan Keating, "Looking to Europe: Roman Catholicism and Christian Democracy in 1930s Britain," *European History Quarterly* 26, no. 1 (1996): 57-79, here 64.

Wolfram Kaiser

Together with the Catholic Workers' College in Oxford, founded in 1921, the organisation promoted parliamentary democracy with equal rights for all adults as well as Catholic social teaching, not least via its monthly magazine *Christian Democrat*. Crawford knew continental European Christian Democracy inside-out and published many articles about its forms of organisation and intellectual traditions.[37] Like many left-Catholics in the United Kingdom, she supported Labour and served as a local borough councillor for the party in London for 14 years.

Although she did not share Carter's singular preoccupation with Italy, Crawford became secretary of the Relief Committee for Refugees from Italy founded in 1927 and, from 1929 to 1931, edited the anti-fascist publication *Friends of Italian Freedom*.[38] While supporting neutrality in the Spanish Civil War, Crawford, together with like-minded British Catholics, co-founded the British Committee for Religious Peace in Spain in January 1938 to temper the strongly pro-Franco opinion among the majority of British Catholics. When the People & Freedom Group was created in November 1936, Crawford became its chairwoman, with Carter as honorary secretary and several prominent corresponding members like Jacques Maritain, Alcide De Gasperi and Georges Bidault. Through 1944, Crawford and Carter largely organised its work and edited its publications, including a book, *For Democracy*, which came out in 1939.[39]

While Carter and Crawford were both middle-class converts with social and liberal Catholic preferences, the Duchess of Atholl was a Scottish Episcopalian (Protestant) aristocrat before joining the (also Protestant) Church of Scotland upon getting married, and she was an elected MP for the Scottish (conservative) Unionist Party from 1923 to 1938.[40] Even by the standards of this party, she held staunchly conservative views on some issues. Even after the introduction of the vote for women in 1918, for example, she continued to oppose franchise reform for an entirely equal footing with men, which was eventually implemented in 1928.[41] In 1935 she clashed with the National (Conservative-dominated) government when she opposed autonomy for India. Like several other Protestant Sturzo

---

37 See, e.g., Virginia Crawford, *Catholic Social Doctrine 1891-1931* (Oxford: The Catholic Social Guild, 1933).

38 See the obituary by Barbara Barclay Carter, Virginia Crawford, *People & Freedom* 108 (1948), 1; Barbara Barclay Carter, "Virginia Crawford," *The Catholic Citizen*, 15 November 1948.

39 People & Freedom Group, ed, *For Democracy* (London: People & Freedom Group, 1939).

40 See Shelia J. Hetherington, *Katherine Atholl 1874-1960: Against the Tide* (Aberdeen: Aberdeen University Press, 1989), xv and 35, for her and the family's religious beliefs and allegiance.

41 Cf. William W.J. Knox, *Lives of Scottish Women: Women and Scottish Society, 1800-1980* (Edinburgh: Edinburgh University Press, 2006), 165.

interlocutors and so-called "friends" of the People & Freedom Group, the Duchess therefore did not become associated with the Christian Democrats in exile and their Catholic supporters like Carter and Crawford through her religious beliefs, intellectual preoccupations or domestic political preferences. Instead, her main interests were in humanitarian relief work and foreign policy. Even more than other Protestant "friends", who were anti-Appeasement dissidents in the Conservative Party, the Duchess became obsessed about the need to change the course of British foreign policy. However, she is also an example of how getting in touch with Catholic exiles and Christian Democratic thought for these reasons nonetheless facilitated a limited interconfessional opening towards continental European politics after 1945, which led her briefly to represent British "Christian Democrats" within the newly founded Nouvelles Équipes Internationales during 1947-48.[42]

Employed as a junior minister in the Department of Education from 1924 to 1929, she was not initially interested in foreign policy. However, she had the unabridged German version of Hitler's *Mein Kampf* personally translated for her in 1935 and became a vociferous opponent of her own government's Appeasement policy.[43] She advocated drastic increases in defence spending early on and even sided with the Republic in the Spanish Civil War. She played a leading role in the All-Party Committee for Spanish Relief, where she worked closely with Rathbone and others. After a personal visit to Spain, her book *Searchlight on Spain* sold roughly 100,000 copies during the first week alone.[44] Inside the Conservative parliamentary party in Westminster she was considered an anti-fascist hawk and maverick, but she did have close relations with Churchill; Anthony Eden, who resigned as foreign secretary in February 1938; and other critics of Neville Chamberlain's policy. Many pro-fascist Catholics and other supporters of Appeasement in 1930s Britain called her "Red Duchess" for seeing fascism and Nazi Germany as a more imminent threat than communism.[45] However, she was just as strongly opposed to Stalinism. In 1944, for example, she

---

42 See Katherine Duchess of Atholl, *Working Partnership: Being the Lives of John George, 8th Duke of Atholl and of his wife Katherine Marjory Ramsay* (London: Arthur Baker, 1958), 251. See also Kaiser, *Christian Democracy*, chapter 5.

43 Katherine Duchess of Atholl, *Working Partnership*, 200.

44 Katherine Duchess of Atholl, *Searchlight on Spain* (London: Penguin, 1937).

45 See, e.g., Gavin Bowd, "Scotland for Franco: Charles Saroléa v. The Red Duchess," *Journal of Scottish Historical Studies* 31, no. 2 (2011): 195-209. See also for the larger context, Gavin Bowd, *Fascist Scotland: Caledonia and the Far Right* (Edinburgh: Birlinn, 2013).

published another book, *The Tragedy of Warsaw and its documentation.*[46] In it she resolutely attacked Britain's ally, the Soviet Union, for deliberately letting the Polish national Resistance be destroyed by German troops.

Carter, Crawford and the Duchess of Atholl, who tried to connect some British Conservatives with continental European Christian Democrats immediately after the war, gave Christian Democrats in exile in London crucial social support, built at least limited links to British politics for them and facilitated cooperation among themselves to discuss a postwar order for Europe. Through 1939 the People & Freedom Group had some transnational connections, for example with the French publication *L'Aube*, and Carter participated in a congress of Les amis de *l'Aube* in Paris in November 1937.[47] Guest speakers at this congress included, for example, Alfredo Mendizábal, a professor at the University of Oviedo, who was later in exile in the United States and had close contacts with Sturzo and Maritain, and Javier Landaburu, a Basque deputy of the Spanish Cortes.[48] Several Christian Democrats in exile, including De Schryver, attended meetings organised by the People & Freedom Group.[49] The Group's role in facilitating transnational contacts among Christian Democrats in exile is also corroborated by the fact that Crawford, Carter and Sturzo helped to lay the foundation of the ICDU at a People & Freedom Group meeting on 21 November 1940.[50]

The People & Freedom Group remained largely "isolated from mainstream [British Catholic] discourse",[51] and they had at best marginal influence on Catholic opinion on the Spanish Civil War and Appeasement policy.[52] The Group was usually far ahead of public opinion in the United Kingdom. In early 1939, for example, it passed strongly worded resolutions against anti-Semitism and the persecution of Jews in Germany and for a joint Western effort to restrain Franco and encourage him to grant a wide amnesty for Republicans.[53] Just after the British declaration of war the Group demanded the inclusion of the leading Conservative dissidents like Churchill and Eden

---

46 Katherine Duchess of Atholl, *The Tragedy of Warsaw and its documentation* (London: John Murray, 1945).

47 "People & Freedom," *People & Freedom* 1 (1938), 1-2.

48 See Leyre Arrieta's analysis of the exile of Basque Christian Democrats in this volume.

49 Philippe Chenaux, "Bijdrage tot de internationale christen-democratie," in Wilfried Dewachter et al., eds, *Tussen staat en maatschappij 1945-1995: Christen-democratie in België* (Tielt: Lanoo, 1995), 253.

50 "Reception for Leading Christian Democrats," *People & Freedom* 18 (1940), 4.

51 Villis, *British Catholics*, 203.

52 Tom Buchanan, *Britain and the Spanish Civil War* (Cambridge: Cambridge University Press, 1997).

53 "General Meeting," *People & Freedom* 4 (1939), 4.

in a new and "truly National Government".[54] Their politics of resolutions did very little to impress either Franco or Chamberlain, however.

Transnational contacts and cooperation among Christian Democrats in exile

The People & Freedom Group was an organisation for British and later also US citizens who wanted to uphold and develop the Catholic anti-fascist and pro-democratic tradition. It also facilitated transnational contacts among Christian Democrats in exile. Sturzo, Antonio de Onaindia, a Basque emigrant and several others felt, however, that this was not sufficient and that a separate organisation, the ICDU, was needed as a platform for common thinking about postwar Europe.[55] The ICDU's main aim was to create "permanent bonds of solidarity between the Christian Democratic movements in the various nations" and to organise them against "the forces of materialism and totalitarian oppression, and for the triumph of organic and parliamentary democracy".[56] The ICDU had the political backing of politicians from governments-in-exile like the Czechoslovak Prime Minister Jan Šrámek and General Józef Haller, chairman of the Supreme Council of the Polish Christian Labour Party and Minister of Education,[57] who, together with Sturzo, formed the ICDU's Committee of Honour. However, like many other leading politicians in governments-in-exile such as the former Belgian Prime Minister Paul Van Zeeland and the Polish minister Karol Popiel, they do not appear to have attended meetings or otherwise to have played an active role in the organisation.

Of those better-known ICDU members who did participate actively in the ICDU, most tended to be from East-Central Europe and the Basque Country, not Western Europe. They included František Hála, secretary general of the Czechoslovak Popular Party[58]; Michał Kwiatkowski, spokes-

---

54 "'White War'," *People & Freedom* 5 (1939), 1.
55 "International Christian Democratic Union," *People & Freedom* 20 (1941), 4 speaks of an "initiative" of Onaindia; see also, Antonio de Onaindia, *Capitulos de mi vida II: Experiencias del exilio* (Buenos Aires: Ed. Vasca Ekin, 1974), 216-218.
56 "International Christian Democratic Union," *People & Freedom* 22 (1941), 2.
57 See also Jarosław Rabiński, *Stronnictwo Pracy we władzach naczelnych Rzeczypospolitej Polskiej na uchodźstwie w latach 1939-1945* (Lublin: Wydawnictwo KUL, 2012), 285-295.
58 For more detail on the Polish exile see Stachura, *The Poles in Britain*; Halik Kochanski, *The Eagle Unbowed: Poland and the Poles in the Second World War* (Cambridge, Mass.: Harvard University Press, 2012), chapter 7; John Coutouvidis and Jaime Reynolds, *Poland 1939-1947* (Leicester: Leicester University Press, 1986).

man of the Polish Christian Labour Party and a member of the Polish National Council[59]; and Manuel de Irujo, acting president of the Basques.[60] The Polish and Czech exiles in particular treated the ICDU from the start as a forum for propagating their national war agendas like the annexation of German territory (in the case of Poland) or the expulsion of German speakers from their countries or from newly acquired territory after the war.

The ICDU was chaired by J.A. Veraart, a professor at the University of Delft, who had only rejoined the Roman Catholic State Party in 1939 and was quite marginal in Dutch exile politics. During the war, Veraart organised regular meetings with guest speakers.[61] Veraart himself gave several such lectures, mostly on economic and social policy. These meetings seem to have been quite well attended. From 1943, however, and especially after the 1944 Allied invasion, when concrete postwar planning became urgent, they increasingly seemed "too great a tax on their [the ICDU members'] time" and no longer took place on a monthly basis.[62] Thus, the ICDU did develop into a transnational forum for debate on postwar Europe, but it was a much more modest affair than Veraart had planned in early 1941.

The discussions at ICDU events and in associated publications focused mainly on three themes: the relationship between corporatism and liberal parliamentary democracy; plans for a world organisation to succeed the League of Nations; and possible solutions to the German question. The exile experience induced the political downgrading of corporatist concepts for an "organic" society. Compared to the Resistance, moreover, the Christian Democrats in exile put more emphasis on creating a modern world organisation than propagating European integration. They also disagreed fundamentally about Germany's economic and political future and territorial questions.

When many of these Catholic democrats arrived in Britain, their thinking on socio-economic reform had already long been shaped by notions of corporatism. They often regarded such corporatist institutions as the key to a European "third way" between liberal capitalism and Soviet communism. Their reform rhetoric was quite aggressively anti-capitalist and

---

59 Peter Heumos, *Die Emigration aus der Tschechoslowakei nach Westeuropa und dem Nahen Osten 1938-1945* (Munich: Oldenbourg, 1989).

60 The Basque exile is treated in the context of Spanish opposition to Franco after 1939 in Sergio Vilar, *Historia del Anti-Franquismo 1949-1975* (Barcelona: Plaza & Janes, 1984).

61 On the ICDU activities during 1941-42 see also, ICDU First Annual Report, Algemeen Rijksarchief (ARA), Collectie Veraart.

62 "International Christian Democratic Union," *People & Freedom* 48 (1943), 5.

sometimes retained anti-Semitic overtures. In one of his speeches, Veraart attacked the "parasitic finance that [is] strangling the finest enterprises", for example.[63] In another speech he demanded forcefully that "the empire of the money market over human life must be shattered".[64] Sturzo – by now in the US – also repeatedly attacked American capitalism with its "secret monopolies" and "capitalist speculation at the expense of the community".[65]

Christian Democrats in exile broadly agreed that the old capitalist system, which in their view had produced the world economic crisis and facilitated the rise of the totalitarian ideologies, had to be replaced with a non-socialist alternative. The actual experience with clerical and fascist forms of corporatism in the 1930s raised crucial questions, however. As Louis Terrenoire argued in his chapter in *For Freedom*, corporatism had to be reconciled with "the political regime founded on liberty".[66] Sturzo wrote in his contribution to the same book that corporatist institutions absolutely had to conform with "political democracy".[67] The 1942 manifesto *Devant la Crise Mondiale*, published by the Maison Française in the US in 1942, similarly argued against the "corporatist and paternalist state" and for a clear distinction between "the political structure of the state and the economic organisation of society".[68]

In the case of Christian Democrats in Britain, the relative shift from authority to liberty and – in the words of the ICDU's constitution – from "organic" to "parliamentary" democracy was enhanced by the experience of a liberal parliamentary democracy they came to respect and, sometimes, to admire. Sturzo, for example, valued what he saw as the pragmatism of the British, the non-ideological character of their social institutions and their tradition of international solidarity, reflected in their relatively liberal refugee policy.[69]

Their exile in Britain (as well as the United States) also contributed to a more Atlanticist view of postwar Europe among Christian Democrat

---

63 Veraart, "Christian Democracy: Economic and social programme," *People & Freedom* 28 (1941), 3.

64 "International Christian Democratic Union," *People & Freedom* 40 (1942), 4.

65 Luigi Sturzo, "The Bolshevist Peril," *People & Freedom* 37 (1942), 1.

66 Louis Terrenoire, "Corporatism and Democracy," in People & Freedom Group, *For Democracy*, 185-209, here 186.

67 Luigi Sturzo, "Democracy, Authority, and Liberty," in People & Freedom Group, *For Democracy*, 95-116, 105.

68 *Devant la Crise Mondiale* (New York: Ed. de la Maison Française, 1942); see also the report "Catholic Principles for the New Order," *People & Freedom* 39 (1942), 1 and 4.

69 David Forgacs, "Sturzo e la Cultura Politica Inglese," in Gabriele De Rosa, ed, *Luigi Sturzo e la Democrazia Europea* (Rome: Laterza, 1990), 342-347, here 346.

refugees than prevailed in the Resistance movements.[70] Most believed that a larger federal Europe was either unrealistic or even dangerous. Joseph Bech, the Luxembourg foreign minister argued, for example, that a regional customs union, such as the future Benelux, could be formed and later extended to other states bordering on the Atlantic, principally France, but – he implied – not Germany or Italy.[71] The inclusion of Germany in any new organisation was excluded more explicitly by Frans Van Cauwelaert, president of the Belgian Chamber of Deputies, in a speech he delivered in Washington in April 1942. Such a larger integrated Europe, Van Cauwelaert argued, would inevitably be dominated by Germany, and it was therefore crucial for the United States and Britain to play a leading role in the reconstruction of Europe and in any new organisations.[72]

When Christian Democrats in exile did advocate federalism after 1940, they applied the concept in a rather loose way to an imagined Atlantic community or even to the world. Not surprisingly, therefore, the Christian Democrat refugees greeted the 1941 Atlantic Charter and its promise of a better world order with great enthusiasm. The Anglo-American initiative appeared to take up demands also made by the People & Freedom Group for a more effective League of Nations, or what the ICDU called in a 1943 resolution, a new "Commonwealth of democratic nations".[73]

From mid-1943 onwards, however, members of the People & Freedom Group and the ICDU quickly became disillusioned with Allied great power politics. They rejected the inclusion of the Soviet Union and the veto envisaged for the great powers. The new organisation instead had to consist of democratic states only, who fully supported its principles, and should be principally concerned with protecting its smaller members against any hegemonic threat.[74] A "hegemony of the Big Three", the People & Freedom Group argued, would make the continental European countries mere "client states" of the new world powers.[75] Their disillusionment was com-

---

70   G.M.V. Mans, "Ideas of Netherlands Exiles on the Postwar International Order," in Walter Lipgens, *Documents on the History of European Integration. Vol. 2: Plans for European Union in Great Britain and in Exile, 1939-1945* (Berlin: de Gruyter, 1986), 451-475, here 453, makes this point comparing the Dutch exile and Resistance.
71   Quoted in Walter Lipgens, *Europa-Föderationspläne der Widerstandsbewegungen 1940-1945* (Munich: Oldenbourg, 1968), 471-472.
72   Frans Van Cauwelaert, "Dangers of a European Federation," 2 April 1942, reprinted in *Washington Post*, 10 May 1942.
73   "A New League of Nations Now. Proposal endorsed by International Christian Democratic Union," *People & Freedom* 46 (1943), 3.
74   This general view among Catholic refugees was expressed most coherently after the war by Luigi Sturzo, *Nationalism and Internationalism* (New York: Roy Publishers, 1946).
75   "The Voice of Europe," *People & Freedom* 53 (1943), 3.

plete when Churchill publicly exempted enemy states and colonies from the Charter's guarantees. In March 1944, the People & Freedom Group protested vehemently that his redefinition of the Charter, as they saw it, "knocks away the already frail foundations of a new international order".[76] Sturzo concluded in 1944 that the Charter, "after so many torpedos, is well and truly sunk".[77]

Churchill's public surrender of the universality of the Atlantic Charter seemed to make it necessary that each nation would have to fend for its own interests by lobbying the great powers directly. This need was in most cases linked to the German question, the third major theme in ICDU debates. Several ICDU members strongly supported notions of German collective guilt and its necessary dismemberment. For Paul Tschoffen, a Belgian councillor of state, for example, "Germany as a whole was behind Hitler and guilty with him".[78] Veraart in turn believed that National Socialism "responded to something in the souls of the German people".[79] Such views were often linked to anti-Prussian sentiments that were also prevalent among other political groups at the time. In Sturzo's view, for example, the greatest danger was "the Prussian mentality, as forged by the Teutonic Knights, the Brandenburgs, the Hohenzollerns and Bismarks [sic!], ... of whom Nazism is the heir".[80]

Others believed strongly in political securities which they did not yet see in some form of European integration. Instead, many ICDU members wanted to go beyond the imposition, if necessary, of fully-fledged federalism and saw the only real solution in the dismemberment of Germany. This country, Veraart argued, was an "artificially big unit" and had to be divided into at least five different states. Veraart's statement was followed by an animated discussion in which the German political refugees Karl Meyer and Franz Xaver Aenderl argued for federalism but opposed the division of Germany.[81]

---

76 "Downward Steps," *People & Freedom* 57 (1944), 1.
77 Sturzo, "The Shade of Wilson and the Atlantic Charter," *People & Freedom* 58 (1944), 1.
78 "International Christian Democratic Union: Annual General Meeting," *People & Freedom* 61 (1944), 4.
79 "International Christian Democratic Union: 'How to deal with Germany and the Germans'," *People & Freedom* 58 (1944), 3.
80 Sturzo, "A New Germany," *People & Freedom* 9 (1940), 3; see, the left-Catholic Centre Party refugee Carl Spiecker, *Germany – from Defeat to Defeat* (London: Macdonald, 1943) for a more differentiated assessment.
81 See also Meyer's speech on German political Catholicism: "German Catholics Yesterday and Tomorrow," *People & Freedom* 36 (1942), 4.

Wolfram Kaiser

Concerning changes in Germany's external borders, most Catholic politicians in exile were happy to go beyond the restoration of the pre-1938 situation. With the Italian situation in mind, Sturzo advocated minor territorial changes in Silesia and elsewhere. "Mass deportation", he argued, "would be a crime that the Allies cannot and must not commit".[82] On the other hand, the Polish ICDU representatives made the most far-reaching territorial demands even before the Soviet occupation and annexation of eastern Poland. Responding to a letter to the editor in *People & Freedom*, Kwiatkowski defended Polish demands for the annexation of East Prussia, "the sword of Damocles" hanging over Poland. In his view, the "expulsion of a few hundred thousand of Prussian Junkers who amply share the responsibility for all the crimes committed both in the first and the present world war" was perfectly justified.[83]

Throughout the war, British members of the People & Freedom Group consistently sought to moderate rabidly anti-German discourse and territorial demands in the ICDU. At a meeting of the People & Freedom Group in January 1945, Conrad Bonacina, Crawford's successor as chairman and a translator from German into English, insisted that "a Carthaginian peace would be no peace" and that any large territorial changes would mean either "huge transfers, with terrible human misery, or the incorporation of some millions of hostile people in the Polish State".[84] In March 1945, the People & Freedom Group then protested against the Polish border changes which reflected "a preoccupation with States rather than peoples – or, more basically, simply people – [which] implies an impenitent pursuance of the process that has made modern history a series of wars of ever more destructive range".[85] Moreover, the notion of Germans as a "guilty people" was "a myth". It made National Socialism seem like "no tyranny, rooted in terrorism, but as resting on general consent, as though subject to the control of free opinion. ... Discrimination between guilty and innocent vanishes. ... History has been fantastically twisted to prove the Germans a people of aggressors throughout the ages, creating an atmosphere of falsehood in which even Mr. Churchill's historical sense succumbs".[86]

These views on the future of Germany were highly unpopular with most British people who had a mental image of the destruction of Coventry or real experience with German V1 or V2 rockets. They were also

---

82 Sturzo, "What to do with Germany," *People & Freedom* 63 (1944), 1.
83 Michał Kwiatkowski, "Poland and East Prussia," *People & Freedom* 57 (1944), 3.
84 "Principles of Peace," *People & Freedom* 68 (1945), 4.
85 "States or Peoples," *People & Freedom* 69 (1945), 1.
86 "Victory and After," *People & Freedom* 71 (1945), 1.

incompatible with the majority view among the Christian Democrat exile community. Their pronouncements and resolutions had no impact on wartime reality either. When the Group spoke out against aerial saturation bombing, Churchill was about to consider the indiscriminate use of poison gas against German cities. When they opposed far-reaching territorial changes in East-Central Europe, Stalin had already decided, with implicit British and American consent, to annex eastern Poland. When, finally, the Group spoke out against large-scale resettlements, the expulsion of millions of Poles from eastern Poland and Germans from eastern Germany was already in full swing.

Conclusion

This chapter has focused on Christian Democrats in exile in London between October 1924, when Sturzo first arrived, and the end of the Second World War. Compared to socialists, this group was small and very isolated during their exile. To begin with, many of the refugees like Sturzo initially had no or limited English language skills, which made it difficult to engage with a political elite with a predominantly imperial, not European or cosmopolitan view of the world. As Catholics, moreover, the refugees were shunned by the Church hierarchy, which toed the Vatican's line and – as in the case of Cardinal Hinsley – even exceeded its enthusiasm for apparent defenders of the Catholic faith like Franco. The Christian Democrat refugees were also isolated in the wider Catholic community in the United Kingdom. As a minority culture, this community was still characterised to some extent by a fortress mentality due to the legacy of formal discrimination against their religion and ongoing social discrimination due to their predominantly Irish working-class immigrant background. Until the start of the war, many British Catholics were pro-fascist, for Franco, and they supported the Appeasement policy – views that were profoundly disturbing for the anti-fascist and pro-democratic Christian Democrats in exile.

In these bleak circumstances, a very small group of Catholic middle-class people, many of them women and converts to Catholicism like Carter and Crawford, formed a "survival system" for Catholic democrats from continental Europe. Sturzo especially benefitted from the personal support by Carter, who organised his life, translated his works into English and established contacts with pro-democratic Catholic media, writers and politicians. When they formed the People & Freedom Group in 1936, this support network not only constituted an anti-fascist and pro-democratic voice in the increasingly heated British political culture and media debate; it also made it easier for Catholic exiles from Germany after 1933, and from Austria and East-Central and Western European countries alike after 1938-40, to have some social contact with British citizens and like-minded continental European refugees sharing their fate. Making these connections constituted more of a social and intellectual than a political endeavour, however. The People & Freedom Group's meetings and resolutions had no impact at all on the policies of the Allied powers or, for that matter, on those of any of the governments-in-exile who were engaged in postwar planning.

The ICDU created in February 1941 and administratively coordinated by Carter constituted an additional forum for social and intellectual exchange for Christian Democrat exiles only. Contrary to Sturzo's and Veraart's hopes, however, it failed to establish an institutional trajectory for the postwar cooperation of Christian Democratic political parties, which was instead created by politicians who had been in domestic exile or in the Resistance, and then strongly supported by the United States and American foundations in the emerging new context of the Cold War.[87] One reason for this failure was that most ICDU participants were marginal within their parties, exile communities and national post-war politics; or they had some influence in exile, as in the case of some East-Central European refugees, but not on post-war politics due to the communist usurpation of power in their countries.

The members' policy preferences constituted the second reason for the failure of the ICDU to create a pathway for postwar Christian Democratic party cooperation. Their quite aggressive denunciation of capitalism – at times with anti-Semitic overtones as in the case of Veraart – was incompatible with the choice of a mixed economy and close economic ties with the United States after 1945. Their preference for a democratic world organisation was thwarted and in part replaced with Western European integration after the war. And their broad support – especially among East-Central European members – for a punitive peace settlement including the mass expulsion of Germans, large-scale territorial changes and the dismemberment of a defeated Germany became progressively substituted in the Cold War with the vision of (in the words of Thomas Mann) a "European Germany" to be shaped through its institutionalised integration in what is now the European Union. The united continental Western Europe

---

87   See, Kaiser, *Christian Democracy*, chapters 4-6.

that emerged after the Second World War was not made by Christian Democrat exiles in the United Kingdom or, for that matter, elsewhere.

2

LUIGI STURZO IN AMERICAN EXILE
Building a New Christian-Inspired International Order

Paolo Acanfora

Luigi Sturzo's experience in the United States lasted a little under six years (from October 1940 to August 1946), and was, for many reasons, a decisive episode in his political and intellectual biography. He arrived in New York on 3 October 1940, after a voyage of around twelve days – he had left Liverpool on 22 September – and in an extremely precarious state of health, although this had improved enough to allow him to tackle the move.[1] From an individual perspective this experience obviously comes in the context of the Sicilian priest's more than twenty years of exile, while from a generational perspective it fits into the wider theme of anti-fascism's political exile in the "New World": a veritable land of reference for the intellectual elites discriminated against and persecuted by European totalitarianisms between the two wars. This is a complex phenomenon characterised by an enormous variety of personal experiences. The topic has been dealt with historiographically in numerous ways, and there is now an imposing bibliography around it – although in the Italian case there remains much to reconstruct.[2]

This chapter aims to investigate the particularities of Sturzo's exile in the United States, considering the network of relationships he built among Italian anti-fascists and US Catholics, as well as the efforts undertaken to shape organisations capable of sustaining and promoting Sturzian positions and Catholic-democratic culture in generally unfavourable environ-

---

1   This, at least, was what Reverend H. A. Reinhold of Saint James Cathedral in Seattle wrote. See Francesco Malgeri, *Luigi Sturzo* (San Paolo: Cinisello Balsamo, 1993), 239; Vittorio De Marco, *Tempore belli: Sturzo, l'Italia, la guerra (1940-1946)* (Caltanissetta-Rome: Salvatore Sciascia Editore, 1995), 8-9.

2   Peter Burke, *Exiles and Expatriates in the History of Knowledge, 1500-2000* (Waltham, Mass.: Brandeis University Press, 2017).

ments. Clear testimony of this is provided by his dedication to the development of new branches of People and Freedom, along with the difficult search for political and intellectual interlocutors capable of influencing US choices regarding the war, the treatment meted out to Italy and the new post-war international order. Of course, this is not the first time that such themes – whether the exile of Italian anti-fascists taken as a whole,[3] or the specific case of Luigi Sturzo[4] – have been addressed. Nonetheless, insofar as the figure of the priest is concerned, there remain elements to examine in greater depth. As Pietro Scoppola, one of the most important historians of Italian political Catholicism, stated in 2001, "Sturzo in exile continues to be a land that is at least partly unexplored", something that is true "not just with regard to political themes, but also – and above all – with regard to religion and culture, which may prove even more significant in defining the contours of his character". As well as desiring to highlight the "psychological and moral price" of exile, this observation intended to underline the specific importance of the American experience in determining a configuration of the relationship between religion and politics "in new terms".[5] There is thus a firm belief that this is a crucial passage in Sturzo's life that has yet to be brought fully to light. This was, naturally, marked by the relationships Sturzo accrued over these years, as well as his direct familiarity with the situation in America. This analysis will draw on documentation from the personal archives of Luigi Sturzo, while simultaneously taking advantage of contributions from a literature that is already substantial.

This chapter aims, ultimately, to analyse how the Sturzian view of post-fascist Italy, of the new post-war international order and of the centrality of a Christian-influenced democratic political culture, may have been affected by the experience of exile, on a theoretical level as well as in more pragmatic and organisational terms. The relationships built both

---

3   A brief contextualisation may be found in Renato Camurri, "Idee in movimento: l'esilio degli intellettuali italiani negli Stati Uniti (1930-1945)," *Memoria e ricerca*, no. 31 (2009): 44-62. For an analysis of various studies see Paolo Acanfora, "L'esilio degli intellettuali italiani negli Stati Uniti tra le due guerre," in Davide Grippa, ed, *Oltreoceano: politica e comunicazione tra Italia e Stati Uniti nel Novecento* (Florence: Olschki, 2017), 105-230. An essential reference – albeit one shaped in large part around the political project of Carlo Sforza – is undoubtedly the study of Antonio Varsori, *Gli alleati e l'emigrazione democratica antifascista (1940-1943)* (Florence: Sansoni, 1982).

4   De Marco, *Tempore belli*; Gianni La Bella, *Luigi Sturzo e l'esilio negli Stati Uniti* (Brescia: Morcelliana, 1990); Francesco Malgeri, "Luigi Sturzo nel 'difficile' esilio americano (1940-46)," *Analisi storica*, no. 2 (1984). Also of interest is the section dedicated to the American exile in *Universalità e cultura nel pensiero di Luigi Sturzo* (Soveria Mannelli: Rubbettino, 2001), 521-617.

5   Pietro Scoppola, "L'esperienza dell'esilio: aspetti religiosi," in *Universalità e cultura nel pensiero di Luigi Sturzo*, 37, 60.

Paolo Acanfora

among American Catholics and in exiled anti-fascist circles were crucial in shaping Sturzo's efforts to try to influence the choices being made by the US government and steer American public opinion, starting with Italian émigrés. This unsparing work allowed him to come into contact with high-profile figures in politics, the Church and US academia, and even to build significant institutional links, beginning with the Anglo-American secret service organisations.

Democratic Catholicism in exile: the "People and Freedom" groups

Sturzo is unanimously considered to be one of the most important exponents of Christian Democratic thought. The years he spent in exile greatly contributed to making his work known beyond continental Europe, from England to the United States and even Latin America. His activity developed on various fronts, aiming at the construction of a robust network of relationships between political and intellectual figures tied to the world of Christian-inspired democracy. When Sturzo arrived in the United States, he already had quite considerable experience in dealing with international organisations and networks. In 1925 he had been the key protagonist in the creation of SIPDIC (Secrétariat International des Partis Démocrates d'Inspiration Chrétienne),[6] the initial form of international Christian Democratic cooperation, which had, however, experienced years of extreme political difficulty, with notable internal frictions during the inter-war period.[7] This experience was necessarily shaped by the "matrix" of exile,[8] which led to the establishment in November 1940 of another organisation: the International Christian Democratic Union.[9]

Sturzo was the principal organiser of the P&F group, established in London in November 1936, which laid the groundwork for a singular, al-

6   For an institutional analysis, see Roberto Papini, *The Christian Democrat International*, trans. Robert Royal (Lanham, MD: Rowman & Littlefield, 1997), 19-47.
7   Wolfram Kaiser, *Christian Democracy and the Origins of European Union* (Cambridge: Cambridge University Press, 2007), 72-118.
8   See Jean-Dominique Durand, "Exile as a Matrix of Christian Democrat Internationalism," in Jean-Dominique Durand, ed, *Christian Democrat Internationalism: Its Action in Europe and Worldwide from post-World War II until the 1990s*, Vol. 1: *The origins* (Brussels: Peter Lang, 2013), 145-157.
9   Kaiser, *Christian Democracy and the Origins of the European Union*, 145-162.

beit decidedly peripheral British path towards democratic Catholicism.[10] Its membership consisted of Catholics (although there were also relationships with Protestant figures) who aimed to spread Christian Democratic ideas with the goal of constructing an international order inspired by the teachings of Catholic social doctrine, and implemented within a framework of democratic modernity.[11] Sturzo was the most active propagandist of the group, which enabled the establishment of transatlantic links that gave impetus to the formation of small groups under the P&F banner on the American continent. These came into being not just in the United States,[12] but also in several Latin American countries, above all in Argentina, thanks to links with Father Silvio Braschi; Luigi Chiti, the manager and editor of the journal *Italia Libre*; and Miguel Guglielmino, one of the leaders of the small Argentine Christian Democratic party.[13] With the help of these contacts, and the involvement of other groups, "such as the 'Maritainians' [i.e. people inspired by Jacques Maritain's writings] of the *Orden Cristiano* or the *Pregoneros Social Cristianos*", he tried to form local P&F groups between 1942 and 1943.[14] This was a complicated effort, whose outcome was inevitably affected by the marginality of pro-democratic activists within the lay and ecclesiastical worlds in Argentina.[15] In

10   See Joan Keating, "Looking to Europe: Roman Catholics and Christian Democracy in 1930s Britain," *European History Quarterly*, no.1 (1996): 57-80. On the constitution of the P&F group, see especially Wolfram Kaiser's chapter in this volume. On Sturzo's London exile, see Giovanna Farrell-Vinay, "The London Exile of Don Luigi Sturzo (1924-1940)," *The Heythrop Journal* 45, no. 2 (2004): 158-177.

11   See Wolfram Kaiser, "No Second Versailles: Transnational Contacts in the People and Freedom Group and the International Christian Democratic Union, 1936-1945," in Michael Gehler, Wolfram Kaiser and Helmut Wohnout, eds, *Christian Democracy in 20th Century Europe* (Vienna: Böhlau Verlag, 2001), 616-641. On the overall ideological commitments of this milieu, see also Or Rosenboim, *The Emergence of Globalism: Visions of World Order in Britain and the United States, 1939-1950* (Princeton, NJ: Princeton University Press, 2017), 241-271.

12   See Corrado Malandrino, "L'iniziativa sturziana del People and Freedom Group of America nell'esilio di Jacksonville (1940-1944)," in Eugenio Guccione, ed, *Luigi Sturzo e la democrazia nella prospettiva del terzo millennio: Atti del seminario internazionale, Erice 7-11 ottobre 2000* (Florence: L.S. Olschki, 2004), 193-213; Alfred Di Lascia, "Luigi Sturzo nella cultura degli Stati Uniti," in Gabriele De Rosa, ed, *Luigi Sturzo e la democrazia europea* (Rome-Bari: Laterza, 1990), 119-145.

13   Archivio Storico Istituto Luigi Sturzo (ASILS), Archivio Luigi Sturzo (ALS), Box 134/605/606. For a reconstruction of Sturzo's influence in Argentina, see Diego Mauro, "I popolari en la Argentina: Luigi Sturzo y el antifascismo católico de entreguerras," *Anuario IEHS*, nos. 29-30 (2014-2015): 267-287.

14   Diego Mauro, "Católicos antifascistas en Argentina (1936-1943): Luigi Sturzo y las tramas locales de People & Freedom Group," *Itinerantes: Revista de Historia y Religión*, no. 7 (2017): 10-11.

15   For a recent long-term overview of Argentine Catholicism, see Miranda Lida, *Historia del Catolicismo en la Argentina entre el siglo xix y el xx* (Buenos Aires: Siglo Veintiuno Editores, 2015).

the spring of 1942, Braschi wrote a despairing letter to Sturzo stating that the lower clergy "is not democratic, but rather Nazi and fascist", and then adding, significantly: "some priests are only fascists because being Nazi carries a slight whiff of heresy".[16] In truth, the ecclesiastical hierarchy as a whole shared a similar orientation, and this above all was why Braschi had no illusions about attracting recruits to the local group of P&F that he and Guglielmino were putting together.[17] These were positions that were widespread in Latin American Catholicism, and substantially complicated the project of democracy promotion being undertaken by Sturzo.

Later, even less successful, attempts to construct a network of relationships were made by developing contacts in other Latin American countries using publishing channels for the translation and distribution of writings by Sturzo, from Venezuela to Mexico, from Cuba to Panama and San Salvador.[18] This is a crucial point. In the dense web of relationships woven by Sturzo during his years in exile, journalism and political-organisational activities often went hand in hand. In Latin America, the demand for the translation and re-publication of articles and essays written by Sturzo allowed the Italian exile to widen his influence and to try to initiate small groups of support. In Caracas, for instance, thanks to contacts with Francisco de Mardones (a businessman who ran a construction company, "*la Compañia anonima 'Concreto'*") and the young Rafael Caldera (future leader of the COPEI and president of Venezuela), the *P&F* bulletin arrived from London, sent by Barbara Barclay Carter, a close collaborator of Sturzo, and, together with Virginia Crawford, one of the key protagonists of the English group.[19]

During this period the foundations were thus laid for the strong influence of Sturzian thought on the groups that would give rise to the Christian-inspired parties that went on to play an important, albeit heterogeneous, role in the history of the continent during the second half of the twentieth century.[20] The works and thought of Sturzo and Jacques Maritain (who was also exiled, as is well known, in the United States) were

16 S. Braschi to L. Sturzo, 12 May 1942, ASILS, ALS, Box 134.
17 S. Braschi to L. Sturzo, 10 July 1942, ASILS, ALS, Box 134.
18 ASILS, ALS, Box 134/605/606.
19 F.G. Mardones to L. Sturzo, 27 December 1941, ASILS, ALS, Box 134/606. Regarding Barbara Barclay Carter and Virginia Crawford, see Kaiser in this volume; Farrell-Vinay, "The London Exile of Don Luigi Sturzo." On the role of Barbara Barclay Carter, see also Carlo A. Giunipero, *Luigi Sturzo e la pace: Tra universalismo cattolico e internazionalismo liberale* (Milan: Guerini Associati, 2009), 52-54.
20 For a general view, including also some specific case studies, see Scott Mainwaring and Timothy R. Scully, eds, *Christian Democracy in Latin America: Electoral Competition and Regime Conflicts* (Stanford, Calif.: Stanford University Press, 2003).

the two principal formative influences on the Latin American Christian Democratic ruling class.[21] In this sense, Sturzo has been called "the political thinker who has had the most profound influence on Latin American Christian Democracy".[22] A further channel of communication consisted of the committees for the liberation of Italy that had been founded on the American continent. This was the case, for instance, of the Comitato Nazionale Italia Libera (the National Committee for a Free Italy), led by Fulvio Cabella, and headquartered in San Salvador.[23]

These were thus the channels that Sturzo used to promote the creation of groups oriented towards Christian Democracy: journals like *Italia Libre*; relationships with pro-Italian committees; and contacts with ecclesiastical, lay and academic spheres in Latin America. While there is no doubt that the concrete results were rather modest, appeals for help from the Roosevelt administration, as well as US requests for Sturzo's involvement in their Latin American operations, indicate that the network that was put together had a degree of importance. In particular, the Italian anti-fascist and exile Max Ascoli, a "natural liaison between the anti-fascist émigrés and the American ruling class",[24] had taken on a significant assignment in the Department of State as a member of the Office for Coordination of Commercial and Cultural Relations, established in August 1940, and presided over by Nelson Rockefeller.[25] Its mission was to extend US influence in Latin America, with the aim of propagandising democratic ideas as a part of the anti-totalitarian initiative. Ascoli repeatedly asked Sturzo for advice and suggestions, but above all for contacts and entry points that would enable him to operate effectively in the complex world of Latin American Catholicism.[26]

---

21 See the chapter "Christian Democracy in the Americas: Periphery or Vanguard?," in Carlo Invernizzi Accetti, *What is Christian Democracy? Politics, Religion and Ideology* (Cambridge: Cambridge University Press, 2019), 280-316. On the influence of Jacques Maritain, see Olivier Compagnon, *Jacques Maritain et l'Amérique du Sud: Le modèle malgré lui* (Villeneuve d'Ascq: Presses Universitaires du Septentrion, 2003).
22 Gianni La Bella, "Latin America: Rafael Caldera, Eduardo Frei, Napoleone Duarte," in Durand, *Christian Democrat Internationalism*, 2: 267.
23 F. Cabella to L. Sturzo, 5 January 1943, ASILS, ALS, Box 134/606.
24 Varsori, *Gli alleati e l'emigrazione democratica antifascista*, 43.
25 Davide Grippa, *Un antifascista tra Italia e Stati Uniti* (Milan: Franco Angeli, 2009), 135-137. An account of the work in this role undertaken by Ascoli in Peru can be found in Sandro Gerbi, "Nelson Rockefeller e Max Ascoli: l'Office of Inter-American Affairs, la propaganda americana in America Latina e il caso del Perù," in Renato Camurri, ed, *Max Ascoli: Antifascista, intellettuale, giornalista* (Milan: Franco Angeli, 2012), 197-207.
26 M. Ascoli to L. Sturzo, 10 November 1941, ASILS, ALS, 561.

This was a sign both of the faith placed in Sturzo and the conviction that his network of contacts would be useful. The subsequent exchange of letters between the pair attest to the priest's efforts to supply names and methods that would contribute to the success of the US mission, which had met with notable difficulties due to the strongly pro-fascist and pro-Francoist orientation of the Latin American clergy – sympathies that meant they were not very receptive to the democratic orientation promoted by the Roosevelt administration.[27] In April 1942, Ascoli wrote to Sturzo expressing his pessimism about the results that had been achieved: "I really can say that the record of my first government experience is a succession of constant failures".[28] In spite of this, there are traces of attempts to agree on a programme of democratic proselytism or the development of concrete activities, for instance among trade unions. At the request of Mardones, Sturzo had worked to solicit, via Ascoli, the interest of the "Rockefeller committee" in financing South American trade unionism, within which there existed factions interested in building links with workers' organisations in North America.[29] The contacts with the "Committee" became, furthermore, a possible tool for developing business relationships or publicising scholarships for exiles.[30] These, however, were secondary concerns.

Naturally, the anti-democratic – if not openly pro-fascist – orientation of a large part of the clergy and laity was not a quality exclusive to the Latin American countries. The difficulties encountered by Sturzo within the world of US Catholicism showed the prevalence of a certain diffidence, if not open hostility towards him. Following his arrival in the United States, Sturzo encountered meagre initial support[31]; was directed into "confine-

---

27 On the efforts made by the Roosevelt administration from the perspective of the "good neighbor policy," see the classic study of Irwin F. Gellman, *Good Neighbor Diplomacy: United States Policies in Latin America, 1933-1945* (Baltimore: John Hopkins University Press, 1979). On the "missionary" role of Nelson Rockefeller, see the study of the Venezuelan case in Darlene Rivas, *Missionary Capitalist: Nelson Rockefeller in Venezuela* (Chapel Hill: University of North Carolina Press, 2003).
28 M. Ascoli to L. Sturzo, 9 April 1942, ASILS, ALS, 561.
29 L. Sturzo to F. de Mardones, 16 December 1941 and 3 March 1942, ASILS, ALS, Box 134/606; S. Braschi to L. Sturzo, 6 February 1942, ASILS, ALS, Box 134/606.
30 F. de Mardones to L. Sturzo, 13 August 1943, ASILS, ALS, Box 134/606; Domenico Angelini (exiled in Argentina from Portugal and Francoist Spain) to L. Sturzo, 22 September 1942, ASILS, ALS, Box 134/606.
31 For instance, Sturzo had to rely initially on a family of Sicilian emigrants, the Bagnaras, in Brooklyn.

ment" in Jacksonville, Florida[32]; and found his political positions misunderstood, coming to a head with the controversy that followed his article in a well-known journal, *The Protestant* – a controversy that provoked open remonstration from the Titular Bishop of Cyrene and Auxiliary Bishop of New York, Monsignor James Francis McIntyre.[33]

Encountering one disappointment after another demonstrated how difficult it was to make inroads in such an environment and create the conditions for the diffusion of Christian Democratic thought.[34] The exchange of letters between Sturzo and the apostolic delegate to Washington, Amleto Cicognani, is a revealing testament to these difficulties.[35] Italian-American milieus themselves were notoriously characterised by their largely pro-fascist sympathies. So far as the complex relationship between the Catholic Church and fascist totalitarianism is concerned, what remained stamped in the mind of the international public, whether Catholic or not, was the strong support given to the regime.[36] The consequence of this was that even in democratic countries there was a "wing of the Catholic Church infected by Maurrasian ideas, by Demaistrian traditionalism and by Mussolinian fascism", which looked with favour on "the end of the *Encyclop*édie and the French Revolution, of Rousseau and Zola, of liberalism and of democracy".[37] The United States was no exception. Quite the contrary – in figures like Charles Coughlin the country had an extraordinary exemplification of its capacity for mass mobilisation in a pro-fascist direction.[38] Sturzo's task was thus to mobilise progressive Catholics in the

---

32 See the letter from Sturzo to A. Cicognani, 20 April 1944 in La Bella, *Luigi Sturzo e l'esilio negli Stati Uniti*, 92. A significant contact in this context was Joseph Hurley, nominated Bishop of St. Augustine in Florida shortly before Sturzo's arrival in America. The sequence of events is narrated in Charles R. Gallagher, *Vatican Secret Diplomacy: Joseph P. Hurley and Pope Pius XII* (New Haven and London: Yale University Press, 2008), 170.

33 See the exchange of letters between Sturzo and Amleto Cicognani between March and April 1944; La Bella, *Luigi Sturzo e l'esilio negli Stati Uniti*, 79-91.

34 On the evolution of American Catholicism's position towards fascism, see Peter R. D'Agostino, *Rome in America: Transnational Catholic Ideology from the Risorgimento to Fascism* (Chapel Hill and London: The University of North Carolina Press, 2004), 197-315. For specific attention paid to the incidents related to the Italian war in Ethiopia of 1935-36, see also David Kertzer, *The Pope and Mussolini: The Secret History of Pius XI and the Rise of Fascism in Europe* (New York: Random House, 2014), 223-252.

35 La Bella, *Luigi Sturzo e l'esilio negli Stati Uniti*, 53-131.

36 On the complexity of this relationship, see in particular Emilio Gentile, *Contro Cesare: Cristianesimo e totalitarismo nell'epoca dei fascismi* (Milan: Feltrinelli, 2010); Emilio Gentile, "New Idols: Catholicism in the face of Fascist Totalitarianism," *Journal of Modern Italian Studies* 11, no. 2 (2011): 143-170.

37 Luigi Sturzo, *La mia battaglia da New York* (Rome: Edizioni di Storia e Letteratura, 2004), 55.

38 On the figure of Charles Coughlin, see Donald Warren, *Radio Priest: Charles Coughlin, the Father of Hate Radio* (New York: Free Press, 1996). See also Kertzer, *The Pope and Mussolini*.

Paolo Acanfora

United States, trying to challenge positions that he judged harmful to the Catholic Church and to the international order.

The propaganda work of the P&F groups responded, naturally, to these needs. Sturzo did all he could to speed up the formation of local groups that could serve as mouthpieces for Christian Democratic principles and positions. He had thus initiated a dense correspondence that already yielded some initial results. Academic milieus seemed to be the most sympathetic. In the state of Indiana, for example, guided by the German exile, Ferdinand Hermens, professor of economics at the University of Notre Dame, a group of intellectuals had formed that included the historian Nutting and the political scientist O'Hare, while the group's secretary, and later president, was Professor McCarthy. The P&F group in Indiana was formally established on 14 March 1942.[39] Its real influence was very modest, as were its promoted activities, which basically remained on paper. A case like this was hardly an exception. In California, in Pennsylvania, in Washington, in Boston, and even in Montreal, Canada, the network revealed itself to be rather flimsy, and consisted of intellectuals who had little involvement in social or political activities.[40] The only group that seemed to aspire to a truly active role was in New York. Sturzo availed himself in this initiative of the help of friendly figures like the lawyer Joseph Calderon; the young sociologist Alfred Di Lascia; Monsignor Francesco Lardone, professor of canon law at the Catholic University of America in Washington, DC; and the Italian economist Mario Einaudi, lecturer at Fordham University in New York. The relationship with Einaudi was crucial for Sturzo's activities, and has been exactly reconstructed,[41] with the aid of an intensive exchange of letters.[42]

Although the P&F initiative never really took off completely in the United States, the group in New York nonetheless enabled the formation of a solid network centred on the figure of Sturzo. Both P&F and the subsequent People and Liberty – aimed more at questions concerning Italy, and addressed principally to Italian circles in the United States – attempt-

39 F. Hermens to L. Sturzo, 15 March 1942, ASILS, ALS, Box 145/677.
40 See the correspondence archived in ASILS, FLS, Box 145.
41 See Corrado Malandrino, "I rapporti di Luigi Sturzo con Mario Einaudi negli anni dell'esilio americano," in *Universalità e cultura nel pensiero di Luigi Sturzo*, 551-596; Andrea Mariuzzo, *Una biografia intellettuale di Mario Einaudi: Cultura e politica da sponda a sponda* (Florence: Olschki, 2016), 87-150.
42 Luigi Sturzo and Mario Einaudi, *Corrispondenza americana (1940-1944)*, ed. Corrado Malandrino (Florence: Olschki, 1998). On the work of Mario Einaudi, see Peter J. Katzenstein, Theodore Lowy and Sidney Tarrow, eds, *Comparative theory and political experience: Mario Einaudi and the liberal tradition* (Ithaca, New York: Cornell University Press, 1990).

ed to influence the Roosevelt administration's policies concerning Italy and the international post-war order. Similarly to the case in England, in this group the role played by women – Ellie Calderon, Ellis Skinner, Mary Bagnara, Genevieve and Mildred Camera – was extremely active.[43] The topics the group's activities stressed the most concerned US policies towards Italy. The struggle for full recognition of the country's Allied status after armistice with the Anglo-Americans in September 1943 was undertaken partly with the goal of launching a policy of aid and support, but, more than anything else, aimed at legitimising post-fascist Italy. Sturzo wrote about it directly to the Italian section of the Office of War Information at the State Department, while the New York group sent its own resolutions to President Roosevelt.[44] Anthony Ullo, chairman of People and Liberty, wrote confidential letters to both the President and First Lady, soliciting greater support for Italy by means of the UNRRA funds.[45] This communication channel worked because the outline for planned aid arrived in the hands of Ullo and Sturzo, although the plan was judged insufficient, and correspondence on the subject was duly initiated.[46]

So far as international questions were concerned, it was a similar story. A key example was the work at Dumbarton Oaks on the organisation of the United Nations, a topic that was very close to Sturzo's heart. An ad hoc commission was formed within the P&F group to advance its proposals. The outcome of the study was communicated to the press, while a detailed report was sent to the State Department.[47] All the proposals that were advanced went in the direction of the democratisation of the system of international relations: from the elimination of the right to veto to the responsibilities regarding arms reduction, as well as the concrete integration of economic matters within peacekeeping policy with the development of the Economic and Social Council. Above all, the assembly should embody

---

43 For the case in England, see Wolfram Kaiser's chapter in this volume.
44 L. Sturzo to Mr. English (Italian Section – Office of War Information), 28 August 1944, with a copy attached of the P&F group's resolution of 22 August 1944, addressed to the President of the United States. ASILS, ALS, Box 145/678; see also the Telegrammemes from the chairman of the group, Anthony Ullo, addressed to Roosevelt on 25 and 27 September 1944.
45 A. Ullo to F. D. Roosevelt, 20 October 1944, ASILS, ALS, Box 145/678; and letter from A. Ullo to E. Roosevelt, 21 October 1944.
46 On behalf of Mrs. Roosevelt from Harry L. Hopkins to A. Ullo, 13 November 1944, ASILS, ALS, Box 145/678; and letter from A. Ullo to Hopkins, 28 November 1944.
47 L. Sturzo to E. Calderon, 16 November 1944, ASILS, ALS, Box 145/676; letter from L. Sturzo to E. Skinner, 18 January 1945; People and Freedom press release; letter from E. Calderon to L. Sturzo, 27 February 1945; letter from E. Calderon to L. Sturzo, 7 March 1945.

democratic principles and be conceived of as a "law-making body in the international field".[48]

Naturally, the actual efficiency of this pressure campaign on the US administration was rather limited. Nonetheless, there was no shortage of recognition and acknowledgements, above all where Italian matters were concerned; from the country's reinsertion into the international economic system to loans with the extension of the Lend-Lease mechanism, and from military support and coordination to delicate territorial matters, like Trieste. From the American documents one can infer that, at least in part, "the Sturzian views were greeted with interest among the planners in Washington working on post-war questions", and, in some cases, it was hypothesised that they may even lead to the modification of positions that had already been defined.[49]

The support from certain corners of the US Catholic world was also important in this pressure strategy. The relationship with Monsignor Luigi Ligutti, Executive Secretary of the National Catholic Rural Life Conference, was particularly active. This was a figure who after the war would go on to have significant connections with the Italian Christian Democrats and Coldiretti (the principal organisation representing the agricultural sector, guided by the Christian Democrat Paolo Bonomi).[50] It was precisely in order to finance this party that Ligutti proposed in the spring of 1944 to set up an ad hoc commission which, with great significance, he would call "Don Sturzo's Christian Democrats Committee", or "Don Sturzo's Liberation Committee".[51] In supporting the Italian cause, Monsignor Ligutti intervened directly with the White House, trying to exploit electoral politics; indeed, the imminence of the elections, in November 1944, enabled him to offer the non-negligible possibility of the Italian-American vote (traditionally linked to the Democratic Party, in spite of the community's generally pro-fascist orientation),[52] as well as Catholics.[53] Monsignor Patrick

48 E. Calderon to L. Sturzo, 27 February 1945, ASILS, ALS, Box 145/676.
49 Guido Formigoni, "Luigi Sturzo e la posizione internazionale dell'Italia nel secondo dopoguerra," in *Universalità e cultura nel pensiero di Luigi Sturzo*, 366.
50 On the links between Ligutti and these milieus, see Emanuele Bernardi, *Il mais "miracoloso": Storia di un'innovazione tra politica, economia e religione* (Rome: Carocci, 2014).
51 L. Ligutti to L. Sturzo, 22 May 1944, ASILS, ALS, Box 145/678.
52 For an overview of the problem and a relevant bibliography, see Antonio Varsori, "Gli Stati Uniti: paese di rifugio e l'emigrazione politica italiana fra le due guerre," in *L'émigration politique en Europe aux XIXe et XXe siècles: Actes du colloque de Rome (3-5 mars 1988)* (Rome: École française de Rome, 1991), 171-187. On the "alliance" between the Italian-American community and the Roosevelt administration, see Stefano Luconi, "Italian Americans and the New Deal Coalition," *Transatlantica: American Studies Journal*, no. 1 (2006).
53 L. Ligutti to L. Sturzo, 5 October 1944 and 13 October 1944, ASILS, ALS, Box 149/707.

A. O'Boyle, executive director of the War Relief Services of the National Catholic Welfare Conference, and Monsignor Howard J. Carroll (Assistant General Secretary of the NCWC) also mobilised to support the efforts of the Christian Democratic party in the middle of a civil war, and thus in an extremely thorny point in Italian history.[54]

There was, furthermore, a constant search for contacts across the Atlantic, and religious channels seemed fundamental. Organisations like the NCRLC, the NCWC or even the Church of Our Lady of Lourdes, were important in this initiative, which had in the figure of Sturzo a go-to person of great consequence.[55] Naturally, compared to the earlier part of Sturzo's American exile, many things had changed. The United States's entry into the war in December 1941, the collapse of fascism after 25 July 1943, the signing of the armistice on 3 September the same year and the evolution of the context in Italy, with the formation of a national unity government and civil war in the north of the country – all of this had significantly influenced the orientations of the US Catholic Church. Support for the Christian Democratic cause now appeared to be crucial for the fates of Italy and the Church. The moment had even arrived to propose a "merger" between the propaganda activities of the Pro Deo Centre of Information, guided by Father Felix Morlion, and those of the Sturzian P&F groups – a proposal that was rejected, and held impossible, but which nonetheless seemed symptomatic of the change in certain outlooks.[56]

Italian anti-fascism in exile: Sturzo's position

As well as going through US Catholic channels, the attempts to pressure and influence the US administration went through the network that had been built by Italian anti-fascists in exile. Among the many political and intellectual figures who had emigrated were persons of considerable stature, including the historians Gaetano Salvemini, Lionello Venturi, and Aldo Garosci; the historian of Italian literature Michele Cantarella; the literary critic Giuseppe Antonio Borgese; politicians like Carlo Sforza, Alberto Tar-

---

54 P.A. O'Boyle to L. Sturzo, 5 July 1944, ASILS, ALS, Box 147/690; L. Sturzo to H.J. Carroll, 25 August 1944, 691. The NCWC, established in 1919 as a means of coordination among the American bishops, played an important role in anti-communism starting in the 1920s. See Jonathan P. Herzog, *The Spiritual-Industrial Complex: America's Religious Battle against Communism in the early Cold War* (New York: Oxford University Press, 2011), 55-71.
55 Mons. J. Valdambrini to Sturzo, 1 November 1944, ASILS, ALS, Box 145/678.
56 Mrs. A.M. Bradley (of the CIP) to L. Sturzo, 11 December 1944, and reply from L. Sturzo on 13 December 1944, ASILS, ALS, Box 145/677.

chiani, Randolfo Pacciardi and Alberto Cianca; and many others. The most important organisation, which gathered together a majority of the anti-fascist exiles, was undoubtedly the Mazzini Society.[57] The peculiar position taken by Sturzo with regard to these circles has often been highlighted. He was never formally a part of the movements organised in exile, but can hardly be called a stranger to them. This failure to become a member was less the expression of some inflexible opposition than of a certain sense of otherness. Similarly, it would be misleading to claim that the arrival of as consequential a political and intellectual figure as Sturzo on American soil could pass unnoticed. On the contrary, as has been stated, "it was an event that was destined to effectuate profound change in the political and interpersonal equilibrium of a diminished and unstable group which, faced with swiftly developing events in Europe, was trying to define its character more precisely, and gain prominence in public opinion".[58]

Sturzo managed, therefore, to carve out for himself a decidedly distinctive space in these milieus. It was a relationship that played out at several levels, in which a degree of esteem came to exist between the different camps, marked though they obviously also were by radical differences. The most troublesome point concerned collaboration with groups and figures that were known to hold positions strongly critical of the Catholic Church and of political Catholicism. As Malgeri has observed, "the intense anti-clericalism of certain anti-fascist groups in America [...] made it particularly difficult for Sturzo to insert himself actively into organisations of Italian exiles in the United States".[59] None of this, however, prevented the initiation of various close collaborations.

Sturzo was very careful to maintain a certain balance in his relationships, contributing on one hand to particular intellectual activities – for example, his collaboration with the journal *Nazioni Unite*, from the 1942 in-house weekly of the Mazzini Society – and on the other, defending his profile as a Catholic intellectual, and his alignment with a particular political culture. There were certainly points of confluence between the two spheres, and, taken as a whole, common feelings of esteem. Nonetheless, hostile and malicious judgments were not lacking either, and the differ-

---

57 On the birth of the Mazzini Society, see Varsori, *Gli alleati e l'emigrazione democratica antifascista*, 38-43. See also Charles Killinger, "Fighting Fascism from the Valley: Italian Intellectuals in the United States," in Peter I. Rose, ed, *The Dispossessed: An Anatomy of Exile* (Amherst: University of Massachusetts Press, 2005), 143-146.

58 Mariuzzo, *Una biografia intellettuale di Mario Einaudi*, 88.

59 Francesco Piva and Francesco Malgeri, *Vita di Luigi Sturzo* (Rome: Edizione Cinque Lune, 1972), 383.

ences, which were significant, ultimately came to the surface. The former secretary of the Partito Popolare firmly stressed his democratic and Christian identity, and clearly used it to emphasise his distinctiveness. The letter written by Sturzo to Carlo Sforza in March 1941 regarding the priest's possible membership in the Mazzini Society was greatly significant in this regard. Although respecting the organisation and the legendary figure from whom it took its name, he wrote:

> As a Catholic I cannot attribute my activities to the historical name of an anti-Catholic, whatever his merits may have been, which I am not recognising just now, but have recognised all along. And while I agree with the programme [...] I do not accept the symbol or the name [...] I cannot fold away my flag of Christian Democracy after forty-six years of work and struggle to become, at the age of sixty-nine, a follower of Mazzini. All my past is bound up in this, as well as my political thought and my faith.[60]

This defence of belonging to a religious political culture was accomplished not only in full respect of the principled loyalties of others, but also with a clear appreciation of the historical figure and cultural and political legacy of Giuseppe Mazzini. Such a perspective would go on to be widespread in Christian Democratic culture in the post-war period, when Mazzinian thought would be in part adopted, in part refuted, in various ways within the ideological vision developed by the Democrazia Cristiana.[61]

Naturally, this feeling of otherness was entirely reciprocal. Many exiled exponents of anti-fascism regarded Sturzo with suspicion. The divisive factor was the deep-rooted anti-clericalism present in many of these circles. This anti-clericalism, heightened by the role played by the Catholic Church during the years of fascism, was cultural and political. Among the consequences, it was difficult, on the one hand, for Sturzo's insertion into anti-fascist organisations to be accepted, and, on the other, even to find the will for it to happen at all.

In spite of the undoubted respect and esteem accorded to Sturzo himself, there thus remained difficulties. A specific case is the relationship with Gaetano Salvemini, one of the most well-known and respected figures

---

60   *Luigi Sturzo e i Rosselli tra Londra, Parigi e New York: Carteggio (1929-1945)* (Soveria Mannelli: Rubbettino, 2003), 84, note 139; the letter is also cited in Piva and Malgeri, *Vita di Luigi Sturzo*, 382 and De Rosa, *Luigi Sturzo*, 409-410.
61   See Paolo Acanfora, "Myths and the Political Use of Religion in Christian Democratic Culture," *Journal of Modern Italian Studies* 12, no. 3 (2007): 307-338; Paolo Acanfora, "La Democrazia cristiana degasperiana e il mito della nazione: le interpretazioni del Risorgimento," *Ricerche di storia politica*, no. 2 (2009): 177-196.

of the exiled anti-fascist movement. To give an idea of the size of their differences, we might cite the reply that Sturzo gave to James Loeb, executive secretary of the Union for Democratic Action, who had asked the Sicilian priest to attend a meeting at which Salvemini would close his tour of lectures on Italy: "I appreciate very much the fighting qualities of Professor Salvemini, but I disagree with him for some of his religious and political utterances made in these lectures; so that I cannot give my adhesion [sic!] to a meeting where he will complete his lecture tour".[62] After all, as with other exponents of anti-fascism, Salvemini held positions on the Catholic Church's support of fascism, and, even more, on the incompatibility of Catholicism and democracy, that went in exactly the opposite direction from Sturzo. This was a political and cultural battle of key importance.

Further oppositions arose concerning the different strategies elaborated for the future of Italy and the tools to use in that regard, among them the Mazzini Society. It is no coincidence, for example, that the republican and future defence minister, Randolfo Pacciardi, complained to Salvemini about the instrumental use he claimed was being made of the Society, as well as the solutions proposed by its board of directors. The proposal to uphold special recognition of the Vatican in the future Italy and to maintain Catholicism as the state religion, as provided for in the "Albertino" statute (of the Italian constitution then in effect), was for Pacciardi, understandably, intolerable. The target of his diatribe, however, was Sturzo himself, who was not even a member of the organisation: "Poor Mazzini, triumvir of the Roman Republic! He is needed to cover up the collusive Anglo-Giolittian intrigues of Don Sturzo!"[63] The accusation was two-pronged: Sturzo's position was dominated by English strategy, and his politics practiced with the methods of the old Giolittian liberal class (whom Sturzo had in fact always railed against vehemently) – a repudiation, essentially, of the Mazzinian tradition in favour of Sturzian clericalism. Similarly, between the spring and summer of 1944, at an extremely difficult point in Italy's evolution, Borgese, commenting on Pacciardi's displeasure with Sturzo's assent to the policies of the Badoglio government that succeeded Mussolini, said: "I was cheered by the news that Sturzo is with Badoglio. It is a fine thing whenever a destiny achieves itself, and the atmosphere is

---

62 L. Sturzo to J. Loeb, 27 June 1944, ASILS, ALS, Box 149/704.
63 Alessandra Baldini and Paolo Palma, eds, *Gli antifascisti italiani in America (1942-1944): La legione nel carteggio di Pacciardi con Borgese, Salvemini, Sforza e Sturzo* (Florence: Le Monnier, 1990), 99.

calmer for it (I meant to say cleaner)".[64] Striking in both cases is the rather scornful way in which Sturzo is regarded, and the evident distance being taken not only from his specific positions, but from his identity, his origins and his political and cultural background.

In spite of these cases, overall relations with the anti-fascists in exile featured notable moments of commonality and convergence. Disagreements emerged, obviously enough, above all regarding the concrete political choices made about Italy during and after the war. The above is important in order to evaluate the elements of cohesion and unity among the various actors, but also, obviously, their differences, divergences and peculiarities. Without wishing to underplay the liberal aspects of a figure like Sturzo – a question that is not unique to the founder of the Partito Popolare, but applies more broadly to the complex relationship between Christian Democratic and liberal culture[65] – great care is needed not to reduce or marginalise actors' cultural, political and religious allegiances. Even so great an historian as Renzo De Felice has essentially assimilated Sturzo into the liberal-democratic camp.[66] However, it is certain that Sturzo did not feel he could be fully integrated into this camp, and furthermore he was not perceived as being suitable for integration.

Among the liberal figures with whom he had a relationship of esteem and collaboration was Max Ascoli, one of the most eminent Italian exiles.[67] Ascoli played a crucial role in academic circles through the New School for Social Research in New York – an institution founded in 1919, of notable repute because of the calibre of the students it attracted.[68] Presented as the "University in Exile", the school was "destined in a few years to become

---

64 Baldini and Palma, *Gli antifascisti italiani in America*, 336. On the relationship between Sturzo and Borgese, and the influence of Christian personalism on the latter, see also Rosenboim, *The Emergence of Globalism*.

65 As the German-American historian George Mosse has affirmed, after "the Second World War, the liberal camp came largely to coincide with the Christian Democratic movement". See George L. Mosse, *Intervista su Aldo Moro*, ed. Alfonso Alfonsi (Soveria Mannelli: Rubbettino, 2015), 11.

66 See Renzo De Felice, "Prefazione," in Baldini and Palma, *Gli antifascisti italiani in America*, viii-x.

67 See Paolo Acanfora, "L'esilio antifascista negli Usa e la ricostruzione nazionale: I rapporti tra Luigi Sturzo e Max Ascoli," in Grippa, *Oltreoceano*, 169-196.

68 One need only look at the directing committee, composed in large part of German social scientists, and which included Max Ascoli, Karl Brandt, Arnold Brecht, Gerhard Colm, Arthur Feiler, Eduard Heimann, Alfred Kähler, Horace M. Kallen, Emile Lederer, Fritz Lehmann, Rudolf Littauer, Carl Mayer, Albert Salomon, Hans Simons, Hans Speier, Hans Staudinger, Max Wertheimer and Frieda Wunderlich, not to mention Alvin Johnson, who "designed and built the new faculty"; Mariuccia Salvati, *Da Berlino a New York: Crisi della classe media e futuro della democrazia nelle scienze sociali degli anni Trenta* (Bologna: Cappelli, 1989), 67.

one of the most important refuges for intellectuals fleeing from Europe".[69] In addition to being a politically engaged academic, Ascoli was a militant anti-fascist and one of the presidents of the Mazzini Society. He was a man capable of developing important political contacts and even became directly involved in the activities of the Roosevelt administration.[70] The significance of his relationship with Sturzo is not simply due to the importance of Ascoli's political and academic network – which was of great consequence for Sturzo's activities and objectives – but also to the centrality of certain shared thoughts on Italian history, on the experience of fascism (the two men had been among the very few to grasp its totalitarian and politico-religious features), on the urgency of the post-war period and on the international responsibilities of the United States in the new world order.[71]

Ascoli was furthermore a fine example of the close relationship between exiled Italian anti-fascist circles, the US administration and the British government. The British Security Coordination had played an important role in "influencing" and "interfering with" the Mazzini Society presided over first by Ascoli, and then by Tarchiani, while the two countries' secret services had stipulated an agreement of close cooperation. Along with the BSC, the US Office of Strategic Services (OSS) made use of the expertise of the Mazzini Society and other exiles for its policies concerning Italy.[72] Among these, Sturzo played a significant role, following his endorsement by Ascoli and Sforza. The Sicilian priest became a constant point of reference for the Anglo-American organisations, which consulted him for information on on-the-ground realities in Italy and on particular Christian Democratic figures. The BSC, the OSS, the Office of War Information, the Division of Southern European Affairs and the Department of Education and Research of the Congress of Industrial Organisations all came to Sturzo for usable information on questions of interest to them: from

69 Renato Camurri, Introduction to "L'Europa in esilio: La migrazione degli intellettuali verso le Americhe tra le due guerre," *Memoria e ricerca*, no. 31 (2009): 5. On the New School, see Judith Friedlander, *A Light in Dark Times: The New School for Social Research and its University in Exile* (New York: Columbia University Press, 2019).
70 On the figure of Ascoli, and his various facets and activities, see Camurri, *Max Ascoli*. On his education, see Grippa, *Un antifascista tra Italia e Stati Uniti*.
71 Acanfora, "L'esilio antifascista negli Usa e la ricostruzione nazionale," 179-193.
72 See Lawrence Gray, "L'America di Roosevelt negli anni dell'esilio di Luigi Sturzo fra Jacksonville e New York: quale America ha conosciuto?," in *Universalità e cultura nel pensiero di Luigi Sturzo*, 521-549; Gabriele De Rosa, "Luigi Sturzo nei documenti dell'Office of Strategic Service," in Bruno Bertoli, ed, *Chiesa Società e Stato a Venezia: Miscellanea di studi in onore di Silvio Tramontin* (Venice: Edizioni Studium Cattolico Veneziano, 1994), 313-335.

"surviving labour leaders"[73] to the Christian Democratic Party itself,[74] as well as figures from Italy's lay and ecclesiastical worlds.[75] Maurice English, chief of the Italian section of the Office of War Information, asked Sturzo to intervene with messages and comments,[76] and sent him classified reports on Italy.[77]

The priest's most frequent interlocutor, however, was Anthony Moore, a British intelligence officer charged with managing the relationships between the BSC and the OSS.[78] The principal requests made to Sturzo were invitations to comment in regard to certain episodes or on the occasion of anniversaries related to the evolution of events in Italy. Thus he was asked for communiqués on the congress of anti-fascist forces in Bari,[79] on the liberation of Florence,[80] on the anniversary of the death of Mazzini,[81] or the occasion of Easter,[82] or even comments on the speech made by US Secretary of State Cordell Hull[83] (one of the contacts made by Sturzo thanks to the involvement of Ascoli).[84] At the same time, these relationships were used, together with the Catholic channels covered above, to put pressure on the Roosevelt administration and on the British government to reconsider, improve and elaborate political strategies regarding Italy. Memoranda and reports on various issues were sent to officials at the OSS and State Department, involving prominent figures in the Roosevelt administration with whom Sturzo was in direct contact, like Sumner Welles or Adolf Berle. Direct approaches were also attempted with the aim of conditioning US choices regarding Italy. Such was the case, for instance, of the meeting between Sturzo and Fiorello La Guardia, mayor of New York and future director of UNRRA. On 6 October 1944, at Sturzo's request, the two met to

73 J.R. Walsh to L. Sturzo, 29 July 1943. Raymond Walsh was the director of the Department of Education and Research of the Congress of Industrial Organisations, ASILS, ALS, Box 147/686.
74 A. Moore to L. Sturzo, 12 December 1943. Along with this letter, Anthony Moore sent a questionnaire about the DC on behalf of Earl Brennan, ASILS, ALS, Box 147/686.
75 Emmy Rado of the OSS to L. Sturzo on 10 December 1943 and 4 January 1944, ASILS, ALS, Box 147/686.
76 Letter from M. English to L. Sturzo, 2 August 1943, ASILS, ALS, Box 147/686.
77 See for example letter from M. English to L. Sturzo, 26 August 1944, ASILS, ALS, Box 149/705.
78 On Anthony Moore, see L. Gray, "L'America di Roosevelt," 529.
79 Telegram from A. Moore to L. Sturzo regarding the congress in Bari held on 28-29 January 1944, ASILS, ALS, Box 147/687.
80 Frances Keene (Office of War Information) to L. Sturzo, 4 August 1944, ASILS, ALS, Box 149/705.
81 Telegram from A. Moore to L. Sturzo, March 1944, ASILS, ALS, Box 147/687.
82 Frances Lanza (Special Events Section, Office of War Information) to L. Sturzo, 23 March 1944, ASILS, ALS, Box 147/687.
83 Paolo Sereno (Office of War Information – Special Events Section Overseas Radio Programme Bureau) to L. Sturzo, 20 April 1944, ASILS, ALS, Box 147/689.
84 See L. Gray, "L'America di Roosevelt", 529-530.

talk about the mission to Italy with which La Guardia had been charged.[85] The Sicilian priest had expressed his opinion on the needs of Italy and on the strategy that the US government, in his view, should adopt. Two days later, he sent his recommendations to the New York mayor for submission to Roosevelt.[86]

Conclusions

The anti-fascist and democratic Catholic networks were thus used by Sturzo in two basic ways: as a means to open communication channels with public authorities in order to try to condition their strategies, and as a means to influence public opinion and promote Christian Democratic principles, not just in reference to the Italian case, but with the view to building a new international order. The strongly negative opinion expressed by Sturzo about his "battle from New York" is well known.[87] There were four objectives on which he principally concentrated his energy: the promotion of non-fascist Italy; the affirmation of the ethical-political value of freedom in the face of totalitarianisms; the construction of an international order founded on law and people's rights; and the struggle for a fair peace settlement with Italy. In each case, the outcome was unsuccessful.[88] These subjects were all closely linked. The battle for a fair peace treaty for Italy and the promotion of its democratic elements were specific aspects of the democratisation of the international scene and the definition of a new world order. Aid to post-fascist Italy and a non-punitive peace agreement were supposed to be part of Roosevelt's strategy for the international mission from which the United States – unlike what had happened after the First World War – would be unable to absent itself.

Sturzo, like a significant number of the exiled Italian anti-fascists, had criticised many aspects of US policy, but at the same time understood its centrality, and valued the elements of liberal civic-mindedness within it. He had observed its characteristics first-hand, and he appreciated in, one might say, Tocquevillean fashion the country's role as a crossroads between religious consciousness and political democracy. In this sense, he was deeply convinced that the United States was the moral force and

85 L. Sturzo to F. La Guardia, 30 September 1944, ASILS, ALS, Box 149/706.
86 L. Sturzo to F. La Guardia, 8 October 1944, ASILS, ALS, Box 149/706.
87 Sturzo, *La mia battaglia da New York*.
88 Ibid., xv.

engine of the new international order, and the only country capable of advancing the principles enshrined in the Atlantic Charter. Without a moral basis, no new peaceful international order could be built, and the Atlantic Charter was the best possible expression of this.[89] Among the most recurrent themes of Sturzo's "American writings" was precisely this: the Atlantic Charter, its principles, its values and their continual betrayal by the political praxis of the great powers.[90] Similarly to Maritain "and many other left-Catholic refugees", the Sicilian priest was "enthusiastic about the 1941 Atlantic Charter, and its promise to build an international order that would defend human rights and the national self-determination of all peoples". Furthermore, the experience of exile in liberal democratic countries had nudged him towards favouring the idea that Great Britain and the United States should play "a leading role" in the new international system.[91]

In these ongoing appeals, there is no doubt that Sturzo's political concerns about the future of post-fascist Italy also played a clear role. The struggles for an equitable peace treaty, for an adequate assessment of Italy's place in the post-war international order and for open support of the Italian people and the country's democratic forces, were all explained with continual references to the system of values of which the Atlantic Charter was an utmost expression. The goal, clearly, was to shape public opinion and the Anglo-American political class in order to promote a less critical reading of events in Italy, aimed at separating the historical responsibilities of fascism from those of the Italian people. This was clearly a laboured and contrived operation, which sought the political legitimisation of post-war Italy.

If the goal of contributing beneficially to the Italian cause was plain, so too was the conviction that the same system of values ought to be the basis for the new international order. This call, after all, could be seen even in the manifestos of the Partito Popolare Italiano (and thus in a completely different political climate), which clearly took inspiration, as far as international affairs were concerned, from the idealistic Wilsonian statement

---

89 See Luigi Sturzo, "Gli scopi di guerra degli alleati," *New Europe* (September 1942), reprinted in Sturzo, *La mia battaglia da New York*, 86-94.

90 "La Carta atlantica," *People and Freedom* (March 1943); and especially "L'ombra di Wilson e la Carta atlantica," *Il Mondo* (April 1944), reprinted in Sturzo, *La mia battaglia da New York*, 102-104 and 171-175.

91 Giuliana Chamedes, *A Twentieth-Century Crusade: The Vatican's Battle to Remake Christian Europe* (Cambridge, Mass.: Harvard University Press, 2019), 216.

Paolo Acanfora

that had been salvaged by Roosevelt and incorporated into the Atlantic Charter.[92]

In the documents defining the ideological line of the P&F groups too, the profound mixture of religious inspiration and a hybrid Wilsonian-Rooseveltian perspective was evident. In the paragraph of the mission statement dealing with the "New Order", reference was made to two fundamental documents: the Atlantic Charter, whose principles had been reiterated in both the declaration of Washington and the conference in Rio de Janeiro in January 1942, and the five points expressed by Pius XII in his message on 24 December 1939.[93] The new international order, therefore, was to be constructed on the dual foundations of the moral influence exercised by the Holy See and the ethical-political role of the United States. These were two different missions, which would nonetheless converge in the new post-war world. It soon became evident how far this perspective departed from the strategies that were actually in development, and which, ultimately, would dictate the configuration of the Cold War.[94]

In these verdicts, there is probably also something of Sturzo's bitterness at not having been able to influence the Anglo-American decisions regarding post-war Italy in any significant way. The frustration he experienced in exile, whether during the years in London or those in America, both of which had been characterised largely by isolation,[95] found confirmation in the meagre results obtained by his efforts to condition the political choices made by the Allied governments. In this there is a significant continuity between the two different experiences of exile. The Sturzian struggles had been, indeed, those of a minority, and conducted within political and religious contexts that had generally been hostile or diffident. In the United States, however, by virtue of wartime dynamics, and of the peculiar evolution of the Italian front, it had seemed as though new scenar-

92 As regards the PPI programmes, see Giunipero, *Luigi Sturzo e la pace*, 25-26. On the theoretical planning, see Rosenboim, *The Emergence of Globalism*, 241-271.

93 See the appendix to the essay by Malandrino, "L'iniziativa sturziana del People and Freedom Group of America nell'esilio di Jacksonville," 208-213. The message of 24 December 1939 by Pius XII can be consulted at: http://www.vatican.va/content/pius-xii/it/speeches/1939/documents/hf_p-xii_spe_19391224_questo-giorno.html.

94 Sturzo wrote at the beginning of 1946: "Between the Atlantic Charter and the spheres of influence there is as great a distance as that between white and black"; Luigi Sturzo, "Anche in politica non durano l'equivoco, la menzogna, l'inganno," *The New Leader* (January 1946), reprinted in Sturzo, *La mia battaglia da New York*, 276.

95 In England, Sturzo had managed to build his own network of companions around the St. Joan's Alliance and the Catholic Social Guide; however, these were "small islands of dissent". See Farrell-Vinay, "The London Exile of Don Luigi Sturzo (1924-1940)," 162. On Sturzo's isolation, see also Kaiser's chapter in this volume.

ios might open up, in which the weight of Sturzo's personality might play some persuasive and influential role. As has been seen, though, the contacts he made, albeit significant and important, brought little in the way of concrete results. His relationships with the allied governments were effectively channelled into consulting activities, which usually resulted in requests for support, in public declarations and in signalling contacts and figures useful to Anglo-American aims. Real political decisions, however, largely eluded him.

Sturzo's difficulties were, furthermore, linked to the evolution of the Italian context, and to the birth of a new party of Catholic inspiration under the guidance of Alcide De Gasperi. It is clearly not mere chance that the end of the war did not coincide with the conclusion of Sturzo's exile. He faced many problems in coming back to Italy. Sturzo only succeeded in returning on 6 September 1946, around sixteen months after the end of the conflict, and, more particularly, three months after the institutional referendum on the form of government, which had been held on 2 June. Indeed, his republican orientation was an extremely problematic element to manage, and this may have intensified the internal divisions of the Democrazia Cristiana, compromising its relationship with a significant part of the electorate.[96] Given his substantial authority, the Sicilian priest's critical voice would have caused a number of problems for the leadership of De Gasperi and for the unity of the party. The invitation to postpone his return came directly from the Vatican.[97] Upon his return, he found an Italy that was very different from the Italy he had left, and an international context that was evolving towards a different equilibrium from the one he had desired during his stay in America.

---

96 Two-thirds of the Christian Democratic leadership were in favour of the republic, but the electorate had a strongly rooted monarchist orientation.
97 Even in October 1945, Amleto Cicognani wrote that "grave causes for prudence", of which "persons friendly to him" were convinced, advised against his return. See La Bella, *Luigi Sturzo e l'esilio negli Stati Uniti*, 129-130.

Paolo Acanfora

3
CHRISTIAN DEMOCRACY IN AMERICA AND VICE VERSA
Sturzo, Maritain and the United States

Carlo Invernizzi Accetti

This chapter looks at the way in which two prominent European Catholic thinkers and political activists who spent part of the Second World War in exile in the United States – Luigi Sturzo and Jacques Maritain – thought about their host country and how this inflected their political thought more broadly. Although the United States never had a significant Christian Democratic party or movement, it played an important role in the formation of the European Christian Democratic ideology, as the projected (and largely mythical) location of a form of politics in which Christianity and democracy were not held to be at odds with one another, but rather reciprocally sustaining.[1]

---

1   For the purposes of this analysis, I will be treating Christian Democracy as a distinct though internally differentiated ideological tradition, following the approach I also adopted in my book entitled: *What is Christian Democracy? Politics, Religion and Ideology* (Cambridge: Cambridge University Press, 2019). Building on Michael Freeden's seminal work on the study of political ideologies, I assume there – and here – that Christian Democracy amounts to a "constellation" of reciprocally defining concepts that have been appropriated and deployed in a variety of different ways by multiple political actors and thinkers over the course of the past century and a half; Michael Freeden, *Ideologies and Political Theory* (Oxford: Oxford University Press, 1996). Its unifying element is the attempt to reconcile Christianity (and, in particular, Catholicism) with modern democracy in the wake of their traumatic encounter in the democratic revolutions of the late 18th and 19th centuries. As such, Christian Democracy is not reducible to the ideology of the political parties – or even political actors – that explicitly employed this label as a self-description. It is a much broader set of ideas, united by a common historical purpose, but also compatible with significant internal differences and even disagreements. Thus, the sense in which Jacques Maritain will be treated as relevant to the Christian Democratic ideological tradition is different – and looser – from Luigi Sturzo's, since Maritain was never a member of any Christian Democratic party, and was indeed often critical of these political formations. Yet, both can be said to belong to it, since they played a decisive role in articulating the key concepts and ideas that were used by many Christian Democratic actors and thinkers who came in contact with them. Nor is this meant to suggest that either Sturzo or Maritain somehow capture a presumptive *essence* of Christian Democratic thought or practice, since it is evident that there are many other strands of this broad ideological tradition on which they had less influence – notably, the more "interconfessional" strands of Christian Democracy that developed in Germany and other Northern European countries in the second half of the twentieth century.

This is visible already in those strands of French liberal Catholicism of the middle part of the nineteenth century which ultimately led to the papal condemnation of "Americanism" in 1898. As Thomas McAvoy has noted, "if one were to examine carefully the writings on the subject of Americanism prior to 1898, one could easily see that the real heresy charge that the anti-Americanists were trying to hang onto the Americanists was that they held the liberalism condemned by the 'Syllabus or Errors' and the Encyclical *Quanta Cura*".[2] Thus, "the theological controversy over Americanism ... ultimately revolved around the question of the separation of Church and state".[3]

Far from being rooted out by Leo XIII's condemnation, the European progressive Catholics' fascination with the United States as the site of a different mode of articulation of politics and religion reached a peak during the middle part of the twentieth century, when many of those involved with the nascent Christian Democratic political movement were forced into exile there. Luigi Sturzo and Jacques Maritain are two of the most prominent examples. Although both had been rather critical of what they perceived as America's "materialism" and "individualism" in their youth, the experience of exile decisively affected their intellectual careers and political views, transforming the United States into a positive model – and indeed a "source of inspiration" – in their later writings.[4] Tracing the evolution of these two authors' views on this country before, during and after their exile in the United States therefore offers a useful lens through which to examine the effect of this experience on the development of European Christian Democratic thought more generally.

Luigi Sturzo's American battles

Luigi Sturzo was born in Caltagirone, Italy in 1871 and ordained into the Catholic priesthood in 1894. As of 1919 he contributed to founding the Italian Partito Popolare Italiano (PPI), which is widely regarded as the main historical antecedent of the post-war Democrazia Cristiana.[5] Obtain-

---

2   Thomas McAvoy, "Liberalism, Americanism, Modernism," *Records of the American Catholic Historical Society of Philadelphia* 63, no. 4 (1952): 22.

3   Ibid.; see Thomas McAvoy, *The Americanist Heresy in Roman Catholicism 1895-1900* (Notre Dame: University of Notre Dame Press, 1963).

4   See Luigi Sturzo, "L'Italia e L'Ordine Internazionale," in *Opera Omnia*, Prima Serie, Vol. VIII (Bologna: Nicola Zanichelli Editore, 1943) [1961], 423.

5   See Antonio Acerbi, *Chiesa e Democrazia: Da Leone XIII al Vaticano II* (Milan: Vita e Pensiero, 1991); Francesco Malgeri, *Luigi Sturzo* (San Paolo: Cinisello Balsamo, 1993).

ing around 20 per cent of the vote in its first elections, the PPI immediately became the second largest political force in the Italian Parliament. However, it soon split over the question of the attitude to adopt to fascism after Mussolini's rise to power in 1922. As leader of the "leftist" faction that opposed any collaboration with the fascist regime, Sturzo was forced to resign from the leadership of the PPI in July 1923 and finally fled to exile in the United Kingdom in October 1924.[6]

From London, Sturzo carried out an intense activity of political organisation and opposition to Italian fascism, collaborating among others in the formation of the People and Freedom Group and the International Christian Democratic Union (ICDU), which sought to mobilise international and especially Catholic public opinion against the continental authoritarian regimes of the inter-war period and in favour of a more progressive and democratically oriented Catholicism.[7] After Italy's entry into the war on the side of the Axis powers, Sturzo's position in the UK became increasingly precarious, not least in light of the British government's policy of internment of political refugees from Germany and Austria, as of the spring of 1940.[8] In September of that year, he therefore decided to leave the UK and to move to New York.

At the time, the United States was still nominally neutral, so Sturzo was initially perceived as an "uncomfortable" figure by the US authorities given his previous anti-fascist activities.[9] Owing also to his precarious health condition, after a brief stay in New York, he was transferred to Saint Vincent's Hospital in Jacksonville, Florida: a move he later described as an attempt to "isolate" him. Despite this, in the same interview, Sturzo also claimed that:

> The room at St Vincent's Hospital was quickly transformed into a sort of laboratory/press office from which I managed to activate a network of contacts with various worlds: the cultural and academic world in the United

6   See Gabriele De Rosa, *Luigi Sturzo* (Turin: Unione Tipografico-Ed. Turin, 1977). On Sturzo's exile in the United Kingdom, see Wolfram Kaiser's chapter in this volume.
7   See Martin Conway, "Legacies of Exile: The Exile Governments in London during World War II and the Politics of Postwar Europe," in Martin Conway and José Gotovitch, eds, *Europe in Exile: European Refugee Communities in Britain 1939-1945* (Oxford: Oxford University Press, 2000); Wolfram Kaiser, "Co-Operation of European Catholic Politicians in Exile in Britain and the USA during the Second World War," *Journal of Contemporary History* 35, no. 3 (2000): 439-465.
8   See Peter Gillman and Lenni Gillman, *'Collar the lot!' How Britain interned and expelled its Wartime Refugees* (London: Quartet Books, 1980).
9   See Nicolò Maria Iannello, "Sturzo in America: Idee in Movimento e Nuovi Progetti," 2004, at: http://www.centrosturzo.it/newsletter/conversazioni-popolari/17-sturzo-in-america-parte-2.html.

States, the diplomatic one, that of American Catholicism and of course the relations I already had with other Italian and European exiles ... I attempted, in other words, to transform my condition as an exile into an opportunity, an occasion to engage with new challenges and start new political projects.[10]

In another set of recollections, Sturzo further described these "American battles" as oriented towards three main goals: the public recognition of the "existence of a non-fascist Italy, on a par with non-Vichyist France"; the "affirmation of the politico-moral value of freedom in the face of totalitarian regimes"; and the defence of a conception of "the future international order founded on the principle of popular self-determination".[11] As Sturzo also admits in the same text, however, the immediate outcome of each of these battles was "practically null". Interest in Italian anti-fascism only really began to take root in the United States after the country's liberation, by which time Sturzo himself had already returned to Italy; the principle of anti-totalitarianism was severely compromised, throughout the duration of the war, by the Allied forces' cooperation with the Soviet Union; and the idea of a juridically constituted international regime founded on the principle of popular self-determination remained on the back-burner as long as the fighting continued.

Each of Sturzo's "American battles" became a central pillar in the construction of the post-war international (and particularly European) political order – which contributed to Sturzo's towering reputation as a leading Christian Democratic intellectual in the post-war period, even though he never returned to exercise the central position of leadership he had held in the PPI during the inter-war years. Running across Sturzo's American writings, however, there is also another unifying theme, which has so far received less attention. This is his changing estimation of the political standing and world-historical significance of his host country, the United States. Indeed, what we can observe in this respect is an important transformation in Sturzo's thought, which also contributed to laying the foundations for another central aspect of European Christian Democracy's post-war political orientation.

Prior to his experience in America, the references to the United States in Sturzo's writings are few and largely negative. In his 1938 monograph

10 See Nicolò Maria Iannello, "Sturzo in America: Idee in Movimento e Nuovi Progetti," 2004, at: http://www.centrosturzo.it/newsletter/conversazioni-popolari/17-sturzo-in-america-parte-2.html.

11 Luigi Sturzo, *La Mia Battaglia da New York* (Cernusco Sul Naviglio: Grazanti, 1949).

on *Politics and Morality*, for instance, Sturzo mentions that "the United States have celebrated the 150th anniversary of their democratic constitution" commenting that "their political experience is very different from ours", first and foremost because of the "issue of slavery", but also because of its "long-standing tradition of the separation of Church and state", which is said to have "isolated spirituality, culture and the finality of the human individual, dissociating modern society from its Christian roots and depriving the state of a higher finality than its merely institutional ends; that is, economic prosperity and political stability".[12] Later, in his 1939 monograph *Church and State*, Sturzo also explicitly refers to the nineteenth-century papal condemnation of "Americanism", describing the latter as a form of "modernism *avant la lettre*",[13] and even adding that "some of the tendencies that were implicit in it, which are all American in their spontaneity and not at all theological or philosophical [...] were tinged with heresy".[14]

These comments offer a marked contrast with what Sturzo wrote about the United States when he was there, between 1940 and 1945. In his 1943 treatise on *Italy and the International Order*, for instance, we read that: "The idea of a democracy founded on Christian principles ... is prevalent in America".[15] On this basis, Sturzo goes on to argue that the United States are an "indispensable ally" in the European Christian Democrats' struggle against "both anti-democratic regimes, and democratic but anti-Christian ones".[16] Later in the same text, Sturzo also draws a distinction between the "continental" and "American" ways of structuring the relations between politics and religion, manifesting a clear preference for the latter. To this effect, he writes that:

> The legal or *de facto* separation between Church and State has taken place in a variety of contexts and for a variety of different reasons, often with an anti-religious and anti-clerical intent. Only in North America has such a separation remained neutral and respectful, drawing its foundation from religious ideas which American politicians have, by and large, never abandoned or repudiated ... [For this reason], in the United States, the moral

---

12 Luigi Sturzo, "Political e Morale," in *Opera Omnia* Prima Serie, Vol. VI (Bologna: Nicola Zanichelli Editore, 1938) [1961].

13 Luigi Sturzo, "Chiesa e Stato," in *Opera Omnia* Prima Serie, Vol. VI (Bologna: Nicola Zanichelli Editore, 1939) [1961], 150.

14 Ibid., 149.

15 Luigi Sturzo, "L'Italia e L'Ordine Internazionale," in *Opera Omnia* Prima Serie, Vol. VIII (Bologna: Nicola Zanichelli Editore, 1943) [1961], 75.

16 Ibid.

relations between the federal state and the various churches existing in the different states have never ceased to exist, but have on the contrary contributed to maintaining a religious atmosphere, which the philosophical positivism and practical atheism of the European cultured class have almost entirely obliterated here.[17]

Along very similar lines, in his 1945 book *The Spiritual Problems of Our Time*, Sturzo advances a criticism of the kind of "secularism" (*laicismo*) that aims to put "democracy or the people in the place of God". Sturzo adds that: "the American constitution does not forget this origin, and the American tradition entrusts the Chief of State with the responsibility of fixing Thanksgiving day, in which citizens are expected to turn to God to thank Him for the benefits received during the year […]. Nor do American congressmen forget to begin their sessions with an invocation of God".[18] "In contrast", Sturzo also writes, "we [Italians] have become so secularised that both Parliament and the government regard religion as a private and personal affair".[19]

The key idea advanced in these writings therefore seems to be that the United States is home to a particular mode of articulation of the relationship between politics and religion, which is consonant with the core Christian Democratic principle of religious "inspiration" of politics.[20] Indeed, this point is made more or less explicitly by Sturzo himself in another pamphlet he wrote in 1943, entitled *Italy After Mussolini*, in which he states that: "All through the [Italian peninsula] … the starred flag of the United States is known and loved as a friendly flag",[21] later also adding that:

Some anti-fascists, even though they are not on the whole anti-religious, nevertheless suspect the "political" action of the papacy. They fight the concordat in the name of the separation of Church and State, and quote the example of the United States to show how well that system operates … But the United States never had a concordat; its government did not have to assume any ecclesiastical financial burden as a result of the expropriation of church property; and it never was called upon to abolish religious orders. On the contrary, the United States moved from several different colonial

17   Luigi Sturzo, "L'Italia e L'Ordine Internazionale," 115.
18   Luigi Sturzo, "Problemi Spirituali del Nostro Tempo," in *Opera Omnia*, Prima Serie, Vol. IX (Bologna: Nicola Zanichelli Editore, 1945) [1961], 236.
19   Ibid.
20   See Jean-Dominique Durand, *L'Europe de la Démocratie Chrétienne* (Brussels: Éditions Complexe, 1995); Invernizzi Accetti, *What is Christian Democracy*.
21   Luigi Sturzo, "Italy after Mussolini," *Foreign Affairs* 21, no. 3 (1943): 412.

regimes, based in some cases on civil and political discrimination against Catholicism, to a system based on religious freedom.[22]

The specific conception of "religious freedom" that is alluded to here was of course to become one of European Christian Democracy's key rallying points in the context of the Cold War – which, as many commentators have noted, almost immediately assumed religious overtones.[23] European Christian Democracy's "Atlanticism" was therefore widely construed at the time as having a "religious foundation" in the context of a world-historical conflict pitting "the god-fearing against the godless".[24] Alongside Sturzo's other "American battles", the normative re-valuation of the United States as home to a specifically Christian *and* democratic conception of "religious freedom" can therefore be seen as another key contribution he made to the post-war European Christian Democratic political project.

What is perhaps even more intriguing, however, is that in the period after his return to Italy, the references to the United States in Sturzo's writings acquire a distinctively less enthusiastic tone. As Wolfram Kaiser has noted, in fact, despite their clear choice in favour of the "western bloc" in the context of the Cold War, the attitude of most European Christian Democrats to the United States in the immediate post-war period remained rather ambivalent. To this effect, for instance, Kaiser writes that: "Many Christian Democratic leaders were frankly hostile to what they regarded as the liberal, competition-driven American system, a system in their view marked by excessive Protestant individualism and materialism".[25] Moreover, Kaiser adds, "the Christian Democrats were equally ambivalent about US political leadership in NATO and in international politics more generally".[26]

Sturzo seems to sound a similarly ambivalent note when, in a 1947 article on "The Philosophic Foundation of Christian Democracy", he writes that: "American democracy (which was not, in fact, conceived as true democracy until later) ... suffered the effects of rationalist and even positivist political philosophies, even though it maintained a deistic inspiration

22 Ibid., 423.
23 See Dianne Kirby, "The Cold War, the Hegemony of the United States and the Golden Age of Christian Democracy," in Hugh McLeod, ed, *The Cambridge History of Christianity, 1914-2000* (Cambridge: Cambridge University Press, 2006).
24 Ibid.
25 Wolfram Kaiser, "Trigger-Happy Protestant Materialists? The European Christian Democrats and the United States," in Marc Trachtenberg, ed, *Between Alliance and Empire: America and Europe During the Cold War* (Lanham: Rowman and Littlefield, 2003), 65.
26 Ibid.

in the Declaration of Independence and a widespread religious tradition among the people (a thing which, aside from anti-clericalism by a reaction connected with historic facts, was not lacking in France)".[27] Moreover, Sturzo's attitude with respect to the United States hardened further in the context of the debate over the ratification of the Paris peace treaty, which he strenuously opposed because he considered the Allies' proposal excessively punitive and insensitive to Italy's internal political dynamics. In an article published in the American edition of the *People and Freedom* news bulletin on 23 April 1948, Sturzo thus wrote that, "If the Americans, who have waited anxiously for the anti-Communist victory of the Christian Democrats in the elections of 18 April, will reflect on their actions, they will have to take the initiative of revising the military and economic clauses of the peace treaty, in order to free Italy from the shackles of international servitude ... For, our country will never truly be free from the risk of Bolshevik takeover as long as it remains under US domination".[28]

The comparison between these passages and those written while Sturzo was actually in the United States offers a means of isolating the specific effect of the experience of exile on his views with respect to that country. It shows that Sturzo's views on America were most appreciative during the period in which he was in exile there, whereas they tended to be far more ambivalent – if not explicitly critical – both before and after his stay in the United States. This suggests that the experience of exile had a profound impact on Sturzo's political attitude with respect to the United States, laying the conditions for his positive embrace of "Atlanticism" as one of the core features of Italian Christian Democracy's political outlook in the aftermath of the Second World War. At the same time, the fact that Sturzo later tempered – and to some extent even reversed – his political evaluation of the United States in the period after his return to Italy shows that the effect of exile on his political views was at its strongest during the period of exile itself, and later reabsorbed into Sturzo's complex and shifting engagement with the evolving political circumstances. Thus, even though the analysis above shows that exile had an important impact on Sturzo's political views, it would be an overstatement to reduce his complex views – even just on the topic of the United States – to it alone. Exile was a factor amongst a multitude of others in shaping the thought of as complex and context-bound a thinker as Sturzo.

27 Luigi Sturzo, "The Philosophic Background of Christian Democracy," *Review of Politics* 9, no.1 (1947): 6.
28 Luigi Sturzo, "Vittoria Italiana," in *Opera Omnia* Seconda Serie, Vol. X (Rome: Edizioni di Storia e Letteratura, 1948) [2004], 14.

Jacques Maritain's reflections on America

Born in Paris, France only eleven years after Luigi Sturzo, and originally raised in a Protestant milieu, but converted to Catholicism in 1906, Jacques Maritain is widely regarded as one of the most prominent Catholic intellectuals of the twentieth century.[29] As a young political activist, he had initially been associated with the nationalist anti-modernism of Charles Maurras's Action Française, which he however immediately repudiated after the papal condemnation of 1926.[30] Maritain's political views then increasingly moved towards a greater acceptance of modern democratic principles, starting with his 1936 book *Integral Humanism* and culminating with his wartime pamphlets on *Christianity and Democracy* and *Human Rights and Natural Law* – which are widely regarded as "pioneering works" of the post-war Christian Democratic intellectual and political tradition.[31]

To be sure, to associate Maritain with the Christian Democratic political movement as such is not unproblematic, since he never took up formal membership in a Christian Democratic political party, and towards the end of his life also advanced a rather stern judgment on the latter's achievements, contending that "the political parties that are called 'Christian' (which are in reality little more than combinations of electoral interests)" played an active role in the "frustration of the hopes for the realisation of a truly Christian politics".[32] In this respect, however, it is also worth noting that, in the immediate aftermath of the Second World War, Maritain had been closely connected and highly appreciative of the creation of the French Mouvement Républicain Populaire, arguing for instance as French Ambassador to the Vatican that "the fact that there is now in France a political party – alongside other parties – which is the manifestation of civic

---

29 See Roberto Papini, ed, *Jacques Maritain e la Società Contemporanea* (Milan: Massimo, 1978); Vittorio Possenti, ed, *Jacques Maritain: Oggi* (Milan: Vita e Pensiero, 1983).
30 See Philippe Chenaux, *Entre Maurras et Maritain: Une Génération Intellectuelle Catholique 1920-1930* (Paris: Cerf, 1999).
31 Paul Misner, "Christian Democratic Social Policy: Precedents for Third Way Thinking," in Thomas Kselman and Joseph Buttigieg, eds, *European Christian Democracy: Historical Legacies and Comparative Perspectives* (Notre Dame: University of Notre Dame Press, 2003), 77; Jean-Marie Mayeur, *Des partis catholiques à la démocratie chrétienne* (Paris: A. Colin, 1980); Durand, *L'Europe de la Démocratie Chrétienne*; Piero Viotto, *Introduzione a Maritain* (Bari: Laterza, 2000); *De Gasperi e Maritain: Una Proposta Politica* (Rome: Armando, 2013); Stathis Kalyvas and Kees Van Kersbergen, "Christian Democracy," *Annual Review of Political Science* 13 (2010); Invernizzi Accetti, *What is Christian Democracy?*.
32 Durand, *L'Europe de la Démocratie Chrétienne*, 125.

and social forces which had previously not found expression in French political life, seems to me of considerable historical importance".[33]

Moreover, in light of the unparalleled intellectual influence exercised by Maritain's thought on the political orientations of many of the leading figures in the post-war European Christian Democratic political movement – from Alcide De Gasperi, Giuseppe Dossetti and Giorgio La Pira in Italy, to Robert Schuman, Pierre-Henri Teitgen and Étienne Borne in France, up to (albeit to a lesser degree) Konrad Adenauer in Germany and Jean Duvieusart in Belgium – it seems justified to treat Maritain as an integral component of the Christian Democratic political tradition.[34] To this effect, Piero Viotto has written that, although Maritain was not "the philosopher of any Christian Democratic party", he was nonetheless "the Christian philosopher of democracy" for most European Christian Democratic leaders. Viotto cites as evidence a telegram written by the organisers of the 1947 Montevideo conference that led to the creation of the Christian Democratic Organization of the Americas, in which Maritain was explicitly saluted as "our teacher" and his *Integral Humanism* identified as the "ideal solution to our social and economic problems" – to which Maritain apparently responded by saying he was "proud that my book has received historical consecration in this act of political foundation".[35]

At the time of the outbreak of the Second World War, Maritain was already a prominent academic in the United States. He was in fact on visit there for a lecture tour when France capitulated to Nazi Germany in June 1940. Upon a recommendation from the French Ministry of Cultural Relations, and because Maritain's wife Raïssa had a Jewish heritage, he decided to remain in the United States for the duration of the war. Almost immediately, he assumed a central role in this country's academic and cultural life, taking up teaching positions at both Columbia University and Princeton between 1940 and 1942, and contributing to the foundation of the École Libre des Hautes Études, a university-in-exile for French academics, housed at the New School for Social Research in 1942.

At the same time, Maritain continued and even escalated an already intense intellectual and political activity in his home country, France. As soon as the United States entered the war, he began a regular radio broadcast criticising the Vichy regime and broadly supporting Charles de

---

33 Jacques Maritain, "Speech Delivered as Ambassador of the French Republic to the Holy See" (14 July 1947), in *Oeuvres Complètes*, Vol. VIII (Paris: Saint Paul Editions) [1984], 1136-1140.
34 See Papini, ed, *Jacques Maritain e la Società Contemporanea*; Mayeur, *Des partis catholiques à la démocratie chrétienne*.
35 Viotto, *De Gasperi e Maritain*, 9-10.

Gaulle's government-in-exile. By 1942, the broadcast's resonance was so great that Maritain was invited by De Gaulle to join the National Committee for a Free France – an offer he ultimately turned down on the grounds that he had more to offer the cause of Liberation by continuing in his role as teacher and broadcaster.[36] Raymond Dennehy even reports that "miniature editions of *Christianisme et Démocratie* were dropped by British Royal Air Force planes over occupied France in 1944".[37]

After the end of the war, Maritain briefly served as French Ambassador to the Vatican between 1945 and 1948. He then returned to the United States to take up a position as Professor of Philosophy at Princeton University between 1948 and 1952, later remaining at the same university as an Emeritus Professor until 1960. The effect of this experience of voluntary exile on Maritain's thought and writings was even more marked than on Sturzo – with whom he entertained a regular correspondence before, during and after their time in exile.[38]

The United States are barely mentioned in any of Maritain's writings prior to 1940. It therefore seems safe to assume that he took this country to fall within the purview of his early – although increasingly nuanced – critique of modern "liberalism" and "democratism". In his 1922 pamphlet entitled *Antimoderne*, for instance, Maritain had written that, "Since the end of the Middle Ages, modern history has been little more than the history of the agony and impending death of Christianity [...]. Man has progressively isolated himself from the supernatural life and become deaf to the revealed teachings, folding back on himself as all-powerful being and worshipping himself as if he were the author of truth".[39] A more or less explicit link between this overarching condemnation of modernity and America's growing cultural dominance is later established in the same text, when Maritain writes that: "One of the causes which have most severely weakened modern Catholics, aiding and abetting the spread of liberalism, Americanism and modernism, has been the infiltration in their souls of the masonic dogmas of necessary progress and humanitarian optimism: sentimental pseudo-ideas which answer the secret desire to put the individual before God and have no equal in clouding man's judgment".[40]

---

36 Marie Shannon and Tony Shannon, *Jacques Maritain* (London: Catholic Truth Society, 1983).
37 Raymond Dennehy, "The Return of Thomistic Political Philosophy," (2012) at: https://thomistica. net/news/2012/3/19/the-return-of-thomistic-political-philosophy-part-i.html.
38 John McGreevy, *Catholicism and American Freedom: A History* (New York: Norton, 2003), 374.
39 Jacques Maritain, *Antimoderne* (Paris: Éditions de la Revue des Jeunes, 1922), 198-199.
40 Ibid., 206.

Although Maritain's views on the moral and spiritual standing of modernity had already significantly evolved by the time he published *Humanisme Intégral* in 1936, his opinion of actually existing political regimes remained profoundly critical, as is evidenced by the following passage from this text:

> The world that has issued from the Renaissance and the Reformation has been ravaged by powerful and monstrous energies, in which error and truth are tightly intermixed and feed off one another ... It belongs to the lovers of wisdom to try to purify these abnormal and destructive productions, extracting and preserving the truths they contain and pervert.[41]

Following his move to the United States in 1940 we observe a marked shift in Maritain's evaluation of the moral, political, and spiritual standing of modernity, and of its modern democratic political form. Already in his 1943 pamphlet on *Christianity and Democracy*, for instance, he wrote that: "The very name democracy has a different ring in America and in Europe ... In America, where, despite the influence wielded by the great economic interests, democracy has penetrated more profoundly into existence, and where it has never lost sight of its Christian origin, the name conjures a living instinct stronger than the errors of the spirit that prey upon it in Europe, where it conjures an idea scoffed at by reality and whose souls has been devoured by these same errors".[42]

Later, in his 1951 treatise on *Man and the State*, he also added that: "A European who comes to America is struck by the fact that the expression 'separation of Church and State' does not have the same meaning here and in Europe. In Europe it means, or it meant, that complete isolation which derives from century-old misunderstandings and struggles, and which has produced most unfortunate results. Here it means, as a matter of fact, together with a refusal to grant any privilege to one religious denomination, a distinction between the State and the Churches which is compatible with good feeling and mutual cooperation ... That's an historical treasure, the value of which a European is perhaps more prepared to appreciate, because of his own bitter experiences".[43]

41 Jacques Maritain, *Humanisme Intégral* (Paris: Aubier, 1936), 7.
42 Id., "Christianity and Democracy," in *Christianity and Democracy and The Rights of Man and Natural Law* (San Francisco: Ignatius Press, 1943) [2011], 18.
43 Id., *Man and the State* (Chicago: University of Chicago Press, 1951) [1984], 182-183.

The text in which Maritain reflects most directly on the effect that the experience of exile had on his own intellectual development is, however, his 1958 volume *Reflections on America* – which, as Maritain himself concedes in the first chapter, is "in essence a statement of why I love America, that America which I have known and loved for almost a quarter of a century".[44] The overarching point he makes in this book is that there exists a "mysterious affinity, a strange and deep-rooted congeniality" between the moral and political ideals Maritain had developed in his previous writings and what he refers to as the "promise of America".[45] Given the pivotal role Maritain's ideas had in establishing the intellectual coordinates of the post-war European Christian Democratic political project, this is another way of saying that Maritain came to see in the United States a practical approximation – or at least a "promise" – of what a realised Christian Democracy would actually look like.

The various elements of "affinity" between the two which Maritain points to in his *Reflections on America* can be grouped in three broad categories. The first concerns the nature of American political society and its relationship to the state, with respect to which he writes,

> There is in this country a swarming multiplicity of particular communities – self-organised groupings, associations, unions, sodalities, vocational or religious brotherhoods, in which men join forces with one another at the elementary level of their everyday concerns and interests ... Such basic organic multiplicity, with the tensions involved and sometimes a kind of puzzling diversity which resembles a medieval feature ... is in my opinion a particularly favourable condition for the sound development of democracy ... The American mind still does not like the look of the very notion of the state. It feels more comfortable with the notion of community.[46]

The second element of "affinity" between Maritain's ideal of a society inspired by Christian values and American democracy concerns the socio-economic domain. In this respect, Maritain suggests that the United States are the site of an attempt to overcome the standard opposition between capitalism and socialism, by tracing a "third way" which preserves the sacred value of private property while at the same time ensuring dignified living conditions for all of society's members. To this effect, for instance, he writes that:

44 Jacques Maritain, *Reflections on America* (New York: Scribner, 1958), 17.
45 Ibid., 11-12.
46 Ibid., 162-163.

> This country has discovered the direction in which a new regime, both be-
> yond capitalism and beyond socialism will gradually take form – a regime
> which it does not seem inappropriate to describe, as I did in my book, as
> personnaliste et communautaire; that is, personalist and community-ori-
> ented at the same time.[47]

Finally, perhaps the most important element of "affinity" Maritain finds
between his ideal of a society inspired by Christian values and American
democracy concerns the way of structuring the relations between politics
and religion. In this respect, he begins by noting, "The United States is indeed a 'secular' state so far as any one denomination is concerned. But it is
at the same time a 'religious' commonwealth as concerns the general belief in the necessity of a truly religious basis of citizenship".[48] On this basis,
Maritain suggests that this is a country in which "religious inspiration is
at work in the temporal consciousness ... as a projection of religious belief
into the secular order".[49] This, in turn, leads him to the striking conclusion
that:

> From this point of view, we may believe that if a new Christian civilisation,
> a new Christendom is ever to come about in human history, it is on Ameri-
> can soil that it will find its starting point ... Then, the Atlantic Ocean would
> become the great inner lake of western civilisation, as the Mediterranean
> sea was for classical civilisation.[50]

Not unlike Marx – who famously prophesied that a communist revolution
would take place in England first, since he took the latter to be the most
advanced capitalist economy of the time – Maritain therefore does not shy
away from identifying the United States as a privileged site for the realisation of his Christian Democratic political ideal. In retrospect, this may also
help to alert us to the fact that – like Sturzo's – Maritain's views on America
were articulated from a very particular point of observation, which cannot
be separated from the Cold War context in which they were formulated.
But what is at stake here is not the empirical accuracy of their respective
views on this country, as much as the cultural and political significance of
the fact that they came to articulate such views at all. At a minimum, this
teaches us something about the role that the experience of exile had on the

47 Jacques Maritain, *Reflections on America*, 179.
48 Ibid., 181.
49 Ibid., 184.
50 Ibid., 188.

development of their thought. More broadly, it also gives a glimpse into the role that a largely mythical reconstruction of the way in which the relations between politics and religion are organised in the United States played in the historical elaboration of the Christian Democratic political ideal.

Sturzo's and Maritain's reciprocal influence during their time in America

A final issue that is also worth considering is the extent to which the personal relationship of friendship and collaboration that existed between Sturzo and Maritain during their years in America contributed to their respective re-valuations of this country's normative standing in light of their experience of exile there. This can help further isolate the latter's effect on the development of their political views from other concurrent influences that were also at work on them at the time.

The relationship between Sturzo and Maritain can be divided in two distinct periods. Up to the late 1920s and early 1930s they occupied almost diametrically opposed positions within the overarching ideological struggle that divided the Catholic world, with Sturzo pushing for greater acceptance of modern liberal and democratic principles, and Maritain expressing far more anti-modern – if not outright reactionary – positions. While there is no record of Maritain's views on Sturzo's work or political action at this time, the latter formulated some rather stern judgments on the former, in particular in connection with his adhesion to Maurras's Action Française. In a 1929 letter to his brother, for instance, Sturzo wrote that, "with the condemnation of the Action Française, Maritain's star seems to be setting … What a *mélange* of philosophy, politics and art! But, after all, this it is how it is always been amongst French reactionaries more than anywhere else".[51]

Beginning in the mid-1930s their political views began to converge, first of all over the Spanish Civil War, which they both opposed and whose religious significance they both rejected, and then in their common opposition to the fascist and national-socialist regimes in Italy and Germany. Although there is no record of this, it is probable they met for the first time in London between 1937 and 1938, where they were both involved in the

---

51 Émile Goichot, "I Maritain e gli Anni Americani," in *Luigi Sturzo e gli Intellettuali Cattolici Francesi: Carteggi (1925-1945)* (Soveria Mannelli: Rubettino, 2003), 413-415.

activities of a Catholic committee "for civil and religious peace in Spain".[52] The correspondence between them begins in 1939 and already clearly manifests a certain degree of familiarity and reciprocal appreciation.

Upon arriving in the United States, Sturzo solicited Maritain's help in having some of his works published in English and also asked for his endorsement of the New York chapter of the People and Freedom group that Sturzo immediately set about establishing; both of these requests were promptly granted.[53] There followed an assiduous and at times even impassioned correspondence, during which Sturzo and Maritain exchanged views on a wide variety of topics, ranging from the nature of fascism, to the conditions of international peace and the prospects for the realisation of a Christian conception of democracy.

During 1941-42 they also collaborated in drafting a "Manifesto of European Catholics sojourning in America", which Sturzo was later to describe as "one of the most important expressions of Catholic thought during the war years".[54] The degree of reciprocal trust and admiration that developed between them out of these exchanges is clearly manifest in the homage Maritain wrote for Sturzo after his death in 1959, where he describes the Italian cleric and political activist as "one of the greatest historical figures of Christian Democracy", later also adding that "in him, temporal activity and spiritual life were as perfectly distinct as they were harmoniously united, in love and service of Christ".[55]

What is most striking, however, about Sturzo and Maritain's correspondence during their years of exile in the United States (at least for our present purposes) is that it contains almost no reference to their host country. Apart from purely practical or logistical matters, the United States is only mentioned in passing, as one of the main strategic players in the context of the ongoing world conflict. But there is no sustained reflection on the nature and historical significance of this polity – whereas, as we have seen, this is something about which both Sturzo and Maritain were thinking rather extensively, in other contexts, at the time. It therefore appears that the normative re-valuation of the historical standing of the United States is something that Sturzo and Maritain elaborated separately, rather than jointly, during their time in exile there.

---

52 Francesco Malgeri, "Sturzo e Maritain," in Papini, *Jacques Maritain e la Società Contemporanea*, 268.
53 Goichot, "I Maritain e gli Anni Americani," 444-445.
54 Malgeri, "Sturzo e Maritain," 269.
55 Goichot, "I Maritain e gli Anni Americani," 417.

Conclusion

Analysing Sturzo and Maritain's relationship further confirms the main thesis I have sought to advance throughout this chapter: namely, that it is possible to isolate a specific effect of the experience of exile itself from the other concurrent historical and personal influences on Sturzo and Maritain's respective revaluations of the normative standing of their host country. This revaluation in turn helped to lay the conceptual foundations for Christian Democracy's profoundly revised attitude with respect to the United States as of the beginning of the Second World War.

Josef Maria Trias Peitx' French-issued *Carte de circulation temporaire* dated 9 December 1939.
[Document in the possession of the CRAI Bibliotheca Pavelló de la República, University of Barcelona, FP(Trias)2(1)a1(22), and reproduced with its permission]

SECTION II

EXILES FROM SPAIN IN WESTERN EUROPE AND THE AMERICAS 1937-1975

4

EXILE AND CATHOLIC POLITICS IN SPAIN
National Reconciliation, Europeanisation and the Contested Christian Democratic Alternative to Franco

Christopher Stroot

Spain is often seen as an outlier to Europe, and the common narratives of twentieth-century Christian Democracy are no exception. The success of European Christian Democracy in Western Europe after the Second World War plainly contrasts with the "national Catholic" dictatorship of Francisco Franco. Although late in arriving to the Iberian periphery, mass Catholic politics came of age in the interwar Second Republic (1931-36) with the Confederación Española de Derechas Autónomas (CEDA), founded in response to vehemently anticlerical policies. Many of its founders were not Christian Democrats per se, but rather what Juan Linz has called "semi-loyal" to the Republic, elevating confessional interests above those of democracy.[1] After the fall of the Republic and the Civil War (1936-39), many of them became Christian Democrats, however, endorsing democratisation and Europeanisation in opposition to Franco and coordinating domestic and international efforts leading to the fourth Conference of the European Movement in Munich (1962), and in the 1970s, the Transition itself.

Experiences of exile were crucial to this movement of Spanish Catholic politics away from "semi-loyalty" towards an authentic Christian Democratic movement. Nowhere is this shift more evident than in the two most prominent figures of the CEDA – José María Gil Robles and Manuel Giménez Fernández – who founded the principal parties of the Christian Democratic "right" and "left": Democracia Social Cristiana (DSC) and Izquierda Democrática Cristiana (IDC). With nearly two decades in France

---

1   Juan José Linz, *The Breakdown of Democratic Regimes: Crisis, Breakdown and Equilibration* (Baltimore, MD: Johns Hopkins University Press, 1978), 28.

and Portugal, Gil Robles, a legal scholar-turned-leader of the CEDA, had a more traditional exile, permitting him a more public role as a protagonist of the anti-Francoist opposition. Giménez, an academic-turned-agricultural minister, was restricted to internal exile; deprived of career and passport, he offered the intellectual inspiration for a more full-throated form of Christian Democracy. Both men mobilised significant domestic and international support around their efforts to unite the anti-Francoist democratic opposition and consolidate Spanish Christian Democracy.

The contours of this history follow three periods. In the aftermath of the Civil War (1939-50), the experience of exile helped to cure the partisan hatreds between leaders of the interwar Catholic right and anti-Communist left, culminating in the Treaty of St-Jean-de-Luz (1948) – a platform for the anti-Francoist opposition and manifesto for the restoration of democracy in Spain. From the ambiguities of monarchical restoration, based on the oppositional politics of the interwar Catholic right, Gil Robles increasingly adopted an anti-totalitarian language rooted in Christian human rights – a shift prompted in part by Giménez, whose vision of a "Catholic modernism" rooted in a Maritain-inspired Christian Democracy was fruit of his internal exile. The path towards Europe ending in the fourth Congress of the European Movement in Munich (1956-62), promised, in the words of Salvador de Madariaga, an "end to the Civil War" – the promise of a positive ideology, based on democratic principles and grounded in the European idea that would unite the anti-Francoist opposition. With the foundation of pro-European organisations like the Association for European Cooperation (AECE), incorporating followers of Gil Robles and of Giménez, Spanish Christian Democracy reached the point of greatest popular influence and maximal possibility for consolidation.

The Congress in Munich exposed the Spanish public to the existence of an authentic, Christian Democratic opposition; however, the subsequent Francoist repression and exile also aggravated internal and external tensions – some pre-existing, others new – which, in the period 1962-1976 led to the failure of consolidation. Within the DSC and IDC, the tensions were ideological and generational, mirroring not simply the particularities of Francoist Spain – the debate over the form of state – but also tendencies common to postwar European Catholicism, like the division between older, social Catholic and younger, Marxist-leaning supporters. Externally, these two parties formed a united front in European Christian Democratic organisations, seeking a unified Spanish representation against the resistance of older, exiled regionalist formations in Catalonia and the Basque

Country – a conflict rooted in the interwar experience. Spanish Christian Democracy did not endorse a common agenda that would have facilitated its political union; in the end, however, the ideas inspired by this plural and democratic "Catholic modernism" permeated post-Francoist democracy.

A contested narrative

The historiography on the exiled anti-Francoist politicians of the interwar CEDA is rather undeveloped – a consequence, I would argue, of the heated, ideologically oriented debate over the formation's role in the interwar Republic, the Civil War, and the rise of Franco. In the narrative of the Left, historians characterise the CEDA as anti-democratic, seeking the rise of authoritarianism and fascism.[2] In the narrative of the Right, historians blame the Left for the failures of the CEDA and the fall of the Republic.[3] Looking through the lens of Spanish Catholicism, Mary Vincent argues that Catholic republican options, initially strong, were progressively marginalised as the Republic became polarised.[4] In response to anti-clerical legislation, the emergence of a nominally confessional mass party like the CEDA increasingly made anti-Republicanism the only legitimate option for Spanish Catholics. Other historians note how Catholic extremism gained terrain after the unsuccessful revolutions in Asturias and Catalonia in October 1934, with organisations like the youth wing of the CEDA moving toward fascism.[5] Moderates like Giménez Fernández were sidelined, whereas some like Gil Robles became demagogic and authoritarian. The rise of Franco was supported by many adherents of the former CEDA, who in the words of Julian Casanova were "decisive in the institutionalisation of the New State".[6]

2   Gerald Brenan, *The Spanish Labyrinth: An Account of the Social and Political Background of the Spanish Civil War* (New York: Cambridge University Press, 2014); Paul Preston, *The Coming of the Spanish Civil War: Reform, Reaction and Revolution in the Second Republic* (London: Routledge, 1994).
3   Richard A.H. Robinson, *The Origins of Franco's Spain: The Right, the Republic and Revolution, 1931-1936* (Pittsburgh, Pennsylvania: University of Pittsburgh Press, 1970); Stanley Payne, *Spain's First Democracy: The Second Republic, 1931-1936* (Madison: University of Wisconsin Press, 1993).
4   Mary Vincent, *Catholicism in the Second Spanish Republic: Religion and Politics in Salamanca, 1930-1936* (Oxford: Clarendon Press, 1996).
5   Sid Lowe, *Catholicism, War, and the Foundation of Francoism: The Juventud de Accion Popular in Spain, 1931-1939* (Portland, Oregon: Sussex University Press, 2010).
6   Julián Casanova, *La Iglesia de Franco* (Madrid: Temas de Hoy, 2001), 273.

The CEDA was ultimately a coalition of various parties, oriented around traditional monarchist, authoritarian and proto-Christian Democratic elements. Giménez understood the party as an "anti-party", but he nonetheless counted himself, his colleague Gil Robles and thirty others among its "progressive" wing who sought to transform the CEDA into a party which endorsed democratic institutions and reforms centred on Catholic social theory.[7] The heterogeneity of the CEDA inhibited this development under the interwar Republic. However, divested of many of these internal contradictions, and brought together by the experiences of a multifaceted "permeable exile" – internal as well as external, with a presence in domestic, European and international Christian Democrat forums – they evolved towards a liberal, pluralist conception of the Spanish state and society, in cooperation with other exiled and domestic anti-Francoist forces with which they had been at odds in the interwar Republic.

Not to be understated are the theological shifts which fundamentally underwrote how these political actors understood the role of religion in their society. James Chappel writes in the pan-European context on how and why Catholics departed from the rejection of modernity characteristic of nineteenth-century ultramontanism and started conceiving of different forms of Catholic modernism.[8] Yet, even among its own historians, Spain is excluded from normative narratives of "European modernisation".[9] From the Reformation-era *Black Legend* to twentieth-century Francoist "national Catholicism", Spanish Catholicism appears anachronistic, immune to the *segni dei tempi*. To shift from an institutional focus towards actors outside the formal hierarchy, as Chappel does for Europe at large, illuminates how different forms of Catholic modernism arrived in Spain from elsewhere in the Continent. The emergence of the interwar mass Catholic CEDA, and the debate over corporatist ideas among Catholics under the Republic, are undoubtedly evidence of the reception of the transnational intellectual exchange through which Catholic modernism arose.

Yet, importantly, this evolution did not end with Francoist "national Catholicism". The Church was far from monolithic, and never represented

---

7   Cited in Javier Tusell, *Historia de la democracia cristiana en España*, Vol. 1 (Madrid: Cuadernos para El Dialogo, 1974), 199; Manuel Giménez to Carlos Seco Serrano, 21 January 1967, Archivo Municipal de Sevilla (hereafter AMS), Manuel Giménez Fernandez (MGF) Collection, B-XV-j-190.
8   James Chappel, *Catholic Modern: The Challenge of Totalitarianism and the Remaking of the Church* (Cambridge, Mass.: Harvard University Press, 2018), 12.
9   For a description of this "failure" narrative of Spanish modernisation, see Jordi Nadal, *El fracaso de la Revolucion industrial en España, 1814-1913* (Barcelona: Ariel, 1975).

the totality of Spanish Catholicism.[10] In the shift from an anti-democratic to an anti-totalitarian Catholic politics that Chappel broadly posits, I argue that these exiled politicians of the interwar CEDA conceived of a different form of Catholic modernism from their earliest opposition to Franco onwards. Their anti-totalitarian opposition, couched in religious terms, was doubly important because no dictatorship in Europe was more associated with the banner of religion that that of Franco. Their reliance upon a personalist rhetoric asserting individual rights against totalitarian monopoly was, as Samuel Moyn argues, part of the shift from authoritarianism to human rights present in the postwar European Church and one of its leading figures, Jacques Maritain.[11] In contesting Francoist "national Catholicism" they were contesting the character of an anti-democratic Spanish Church, centred on neo-Thomist ideals of order and authority, which they had defended. While the nature of their "permeable exile" aided extensive cooperation with other anti-Francoist formations inside and outside of Spain, the *raison d'être* of this cooperation was theological as well, nourished by the notion of "integral humanism" voiced none other than by Maritain, sketching out how those forces with different intellectual positions could cooperate towards shared practical goals.[12] The divisions which led to the fall of the interwar Republic were overcome by a new form of Catholic modernism which endorsed democratic pluralism as the answer to Francoist authoritarianism.

From anti-democratic to anti-totalitarian

For those exiled politicians of the interwar CEDA like Gil Robles who initially supported the coup d'état of Francisco Franco, the experience of exile precipitated an important shift from an anti-democratic to an anti-totalitarian Catholic movement. Installed in Estoril in Portugal, Gil Robles lamented to his former deputy Geminiano Carrascal how "so much precious blood was not shed for this" – the totalitarian character of the

---

10   Mary Vincent, "Religion: The Idea of Catholic Spain," in Javier Moreno Luzón and Xosé M. Núñez Seixas, eds, *Metaphors of Spain: Representations of Spanish National Identity in the Twentieth Century* (New York: Berghahn, 2018), 122-141, at 135.

11   Samuel Moyn, *Christian Human Rights* (Philadelphia, Pennsylvania: University of Pennsylvania Press, 2015), 58.

12   Jacques Maritain, *Integral Humanism: Temporal and Spiritual Problems of a New Christendom*, trans. Joseph Evans (New York: Scribner and Sons, 1968).

regime, and the Francoist cult of personality.[13] In fleeing from Spain, Gil Robles collaborated with other exiled anti-Francoist liberals and leftists, overcoming the intense political rivalries that had led to the failure of the interwar Republic. Much of his success was due to the intervention of his counterpart Giménez, well regarded among exiles and domestic opponents of Franco alike.

This shift, however, exposed conflicts within the broadly-construed Catholic Right as to the nature of Christian Democracy – the form of the state, the acceptance of liberal democracy, the status of basic human and civil rights and the degree of cooperation with other forces of the anti-Francoist opposition. The tensions over the form of the state and its ideological character were rooted in the history of the interwar Catholic Right – a coalition founded in opposition to the anti-clericalism of the interwar Republic, but which struggled to define itself beyond those terms.

In the case of interwar Spain, the issue of form centred on a negative, oppositional versus positive, reformist ideology. Giménez thus referred to the ideologically and generationally diverse CEDA as an "anti-party" – the "negation of the negation" – founded on a lowest common denominator of confessional defence. In seeking the restoration of the constitutional monarchy (1876-1930), Gil Robles sought an intentionally ambiguous position – a "double policy", similar to that of the CEDA, which was anti-Francoist, anti-Communist, and counterrevolutionary at the same time – to mobilise conservatives.[14] Many of these elements opposed negotiation with the exiled democratic Left – a legacy of the partisan Republic and bloody Civil War. The internally exiled Giménez, however, saw the younger core of the interwar CEDA – proponents of positive reforms oriented towards what they called the social question – as critical to anti-Francoist mobilisation and national reconciliation.[15] To Gil Robles, he worried how those monarchists "hated social doctrines that I profess" and would be manipulated by Franco.[16] While personally republican, Giménez sought a popular plebiscite to determine the form of the state. Substance was greater than form, as he argued to Gil Robles: "the ruin would not be in an accidental thing like a political regime, but the invisibility [*virtualidad*] of Catholic social

13 José María Gil Robles to Geminiano Carrascal, 28 May 1942, Archivo General de la Universidad de Navarra (hereafter AGUN), Pedro Beltrán de Heredia (PBH) Collection, 022/002/021.
14 Gil Robles to Salvador Madariaga, 25 June 1946, AGUN, PBH Collection, 022/002/321.
15 Giménez to Seco Serrano, 21 January 1967, AMS, MGF Collection, B-xv-j-190.
16 Giménez to Gil Robles, 25 June 1943, AMS, MGF Collection, B-xv-i-34.

Christopher Stroot

doctrine". The form of state was not fundamental, but its actions were important.[17]

Opposition to Franco was not enough; rather, the experience of exile propelled interwar Catholic political culture away from the ambiguities of monarchist restoration towards one linking anti-totalitarianism with a common project acceptable to all sectors of the exiled and domestic anti-Francoist democratic opposition. As elsewhere in Western Europe after 1945, the old formula of interwar political Catholicism was discredited in post-Civil War Spain.[18] Social reform was one pillar of this new strategy. For some, the Allied victory augured a quick end to the regime, yet Giménez and Gil Robles worried about what they saw as the proletarianisation of postwar Spain, intensified by international isolation, economic depression, staggering social inequalities and statist tendencies.[19] The Francoist minister-turned-monarchist dissident Sainz Rodríguez argued for a "progressive" social base rooted in Catholic principles and a "rightist" political base that enshrined both individual and corporate forms of representation as well as public and private liberties, providing a "transactional formula of *convivencia* [co-existence]".[20]

Another pillar of this strategy was linking anti-totalitarian opposition to Franco with the adoption of a distinctly Catholic idiom of human and civil rights. Pope Pius XI emphasised, starting with the anti-Nazi encyclical *Mit brennender Sorge* (1937), the hostility of all forms of totalitarianism towards religion, defending divine and human rights articulated in "Christian teaching". In Francoist Spain, governed according to "national Catholic" ideology, this effort furthermore contested the monopoly on religious identity. In citing the 1944 Christmas address of Pius XII, the followers of Gil Robles publicly petitioned Franco for the restoration of liberties of press, association and political organisation. At the same time, Gil Robles argued to the monarch-in-exile that his restoration depended on guarantees of "essential rights of the human person" and a truly "plural vote".[21]

---

17 "Accidentalism", as a political philosophy, argued that the faults of the interwar Republic were not due to the type of regime, but how it was run. Paul Preston, *The Spanish Civil War: Reaction, Revolution, and Revenge* (New York: W.W. Norton, 2007), 43.

18 Wolfram Kaiser, *Christian Democracy and the Origins of European Union* (Cambridge: Cambridge University Press, 2007), 163.

19 Giménez to Miguel Maura Gamazo, 19 January 1949, in Alfonso Braojos Garrido and Leandro Álvarez Rey, eds, *Epistolario Politico: Manuel Giménez Fernandez (1896-1968)* (Seville: Ayuntamiento de Sevilla, 2003), 172; Gil Robles to Juan José Giménez, 25 December 1943, AGUN, PBH Collection, 022/002/075.

20 Pedro Sainz Rodríguez to Gil Robles, 27 July 1945, AGUN, PBH Collection, 022/002/213.

21 Unknown senders to Franco, November 1945, AGUN, PBH Collection, 022/002/280; Gil Robles to Antonio Aranda, September 1945, AGUN, PBH Collection, 022/002/227.

The Francoist general Antonio Aranda, an important link between Gil Robles and the domestic leftist opposition, argued that this new "democratic and social" idiom would attract the masses.[22] A rhetoric of human rights and the dignity of the person was attractive to the diverse following of Gil Robles and Giménez on the Left and Right alike. For conservatives, it reinforced anti-Communist attitudes and reasserted traditional values, whereas for progressives it appealed to social justice and national reconciliation.[23]

The experience of exile diminished historic hatreds between the interwar leaders of the anti-Francoist Catholic Right and anti-Communist Left. The initial reunions of Gil Robles and Socialist Indalecio Prieto were facilitated by intermediaries like Sainz Rodríguez, exiled *cedista* deputy Félix Vejarano and Catholic layman Francisco Herrera starting in the fall of 1945. In contrast to the interwar Republican experience, the exiled Socialists, Republicans and even anarcho-syndicalists enshrined religious freedom, balanced their support for civil rights and freedoms with respect for public order, and heartily endorsed the social Catholic programme inspired by Giménez Fernández and echoed by Gil Robles.[24] Across the political spectrum, the exiled opposition increasingly agreed upon the criteria of social reform and political liberties, impossible under the hyper-partisan Republic.

The legacy of the interwar democratic experiment complicated negotiations over the form of the state. From the autumn of 1946 onwards, Prieto and Gil Robles initiated meetings in London and later Paris, agreeing on all major points except on the provisional state. This historically charged dispute was more about form than substance: Gil Robles argued that a constitutional monarchy would "placate [*tranquilizar*]" conservatives who had supported the *coup d'état*, whereas Prieto insisted on the legitimacy of the interwar Republic as successor.[25] This debate was also symbolic of divisions within the anti-Francoist factions. A sign of dire circumstances, those Socialists within Spain and even the anarchist National Worker's

---

22 Aranda to Gil Robles, 16 October 1945, AGUN, PBH Collection, 022/002/253.
23 For conservative interpretations, see Moyn, *Christian Human Rights*, 60; Marco Duranti, *The Conservative Human Rights Revolution: European Identity, Transnational Politics and the Origins of the European Convention* (Oxford: Oxford University Press, 2017), 402. Personalist rights-talk was not simply conservative; rather, derived from French personalism, it was used also by progressive Catholicism in its effort to become a viable Catholic political option in Communist Poland. Piotr H. Kosicki, *Catholics on the Barricades: Poland, France and "Revolution," 1891-1956* (New Haven, Conn.: Yale University Press, 2018), 174.
24 Francisco Herrera to Gil Robles, 15 November 1945, AGUN, PBH Collection, 022/002/271.
25 Gil Robles to Herrera, 28 December 1945, AGUN, PBH Collection, 022/002/272.

Christopher Stroot

Confederation (NWT) tacitly accepted the monarchy as a pathway to democracy, whereas the exiled Socialists – marked by the traumas of civil war and forced exile – fought for interim democratic rule and a later popular plebiscite.[26] The conflict within the anti-Francoist Catholic Right was also palpable. Anything less than monarchist restoration, Sainz Rodríguez worried, would split the conservative opposition – some of whom opposed negotiations – into two "bands".[27] Although the form of the state was left ambiguous, the substance was clearly plural and democratic in nature.

A product of the exile experience, the 1948 Treaty of St-Jean-de-Luz looked towards Europe in providing a coherent platform for anti-Francoist coordination and eventual democratic restoration. The negotiations elevated international recognition of the anti-Francoist democratic opposition, bringing together British Labour minister Ernest Bevin, French Mouvement Réplican Populaire (MRP) leader Georges Bidault and Belgian Socialist politician Paul-Henri Spaak.[28] Prieto sought the attendance of Gil Robles at the Congress of Europe in May 1948. Invited by Winston Churchill, he was ultimately unable to attend. Arguably, the congress, which focused on advancing European integration, would have provided a "tribunal of exceptional resonance" for the Francoist opposition.[29] Gil Robles also networked within the new transnational, postwar European framework.[30] Instrumental in coordinating earlier negotiations, the exiled liberal intellectual Salvador de Madariaga underlined the anti-Francoist "common labour", bound to the European project, which could capture conservatives and the moderate Left, bridging the ideological conflicts of the interwar Republic.[31]

Theological changes and the "Segni dei tempi"

The practically minded ambiguity of Gil Robles, as leader of the interwar CEDA and then *de facto* representative of anti-Francoist monarchism, contrasted with the forcefulness of Giménez's social Catholic politics. Yet, he

26 Aranda to Gil Robles, 6 November 1947, AGUN, PBH Collection, 022/003/088.
27 Sainz Rodríguez to Gil Robles, 8 November 1947, AGUN, PBH Collection, 022/003/092.
28 Gil Robles to Ernest Bevin, 6 October 1948, AGUN, PBH Collection, 022/003/159; Indalecio Prieto to Félix Vejarano, 15 November 1948, AGUN, PBH Collection, 022/003/159.
29 Prieto to Various Recipients, 25 May 1948, AGUN, PBH Collection 022/003/138; for reference to the invitation, see Gil Robles to Camilo Alonso Vega, 18 July 1962, AGUN, PBH Collection, 022/005/077.
30 Kaiser, *Christian Democracy and the Origins of European Union*, 191.
31 Madariaga to Gil Robles, 19 July 1946, AGUN, PBH Collection, 022/002/322.

included himself and Gil Robles among a minority of younger *cedistas* who sought Catholic integration into republican institutions – a Spanish *ralliement* after the model of French Catholics adhering to the Third Republic – and an end to the confessional "tower", the metaphor used to describe the German Catholic Right's religious exclusivity, which placed Church interests above those of democracy.[32] This vision was rooted in an understanding of Christian Democracy that responded to the social question, evinced in Giménez's devotion to Catholic intellectuals like Jacques Maritain critical to *aggiornamento* (updating) in the spirit of the Second Vatican Council. Overall, Giménez popularised a new form of Catholic modernism, tailored to the circumstances of Spain, among successors to the interwar CEDA.

Maritain was an essential figure for both Giménez and Gil Robles, because his evolution as a neo-Thomist thinker mirrored their own shift from anti-democratic to Christian Democratic. In his prior support of *Action française* leader Charles Maurras, Maritain had an integralist past, in which his suspicion towards modern liberal democracy was more evident. The interwar Maritain struggled with the issue of pluralism in modern political life, threatening social and particularly religious unity.[33] In 1928, Gil Robles presented on Maritain's notions of the political and the spiritual in *Primauté du spirituel* (1927), in which Maritain had argued that, in exceptional circumstances, Catholics could unite with other aconfessional forces in favour of the "common good", guided by religion and morals.[34] Trumpeted by Gil Robles, this precept would guide the political behaviour of the interwar CEDA. Both members of the National Council of Catholic Action, Giménez and Gil Robles invited the celebrated French thinker to the summer schools of Santander in 1934 and 1936; the latter, where was due to present on his "integral humanism", was cancelled due to the Civil War.[35] Thirty years later, Gil Robles praised in his memoirs how Maritain defined with his work a "real Christian political society"; however,

---

32 The *ralliement* was the effort of French Catholics to adhere to the Third Republic, responding to Leo XIII's *Au milieu des solicitudes* (1892). The "tower" was the metaphor used to describe the interwar German Catholic Right's religious exclusivity – a concept tied as well to the internal conflict over the "social question"; Maria Mitchell, *The Origins of Christian Democracy: Politics and Confession in Modern Germany* (Ann Arbor: University of Michigan Press, 2012), 21.

33 Joseph Evans, "Jacques Maritain and the Problem of Pluralism in Political Life," *Review of Politics* 22, no. 3 (July 1960): 307-323.

34 *Boletin ACNdP*, 20 February 1928.

35 *El Debate*, 5 August 1934, 5 May 1936. Maritain wrote extensively on Republican and Civil War-era Spain; Bernard Doering, *Jacques Maritain and the French Catholic Intellectuals* (South Bend, IN: University of Notre Dame Press, 1983), 85-90.

Christopher Stroot

Giménez was the first to openly identify with the views of Maritain that became central to Vatican II.[36]

In internal exile, Giménez found greater intellectual resonance in framing a distinctly Spanish vision of Christian Democracy. Far from endorsing the Francoist "crusade" [cruzada], he opposed the coup d'état, deploring the killing of Catholics by Catholics and the Church's entry into secular politics. Giménez firmly rejected "national Catholicism" – the mobilising ideology of Francoism – writing that the latest works of Pius XII proved that "Sturzo and Maritain were right, Eijo y Garay [Bishop of Madrid, ally of Franco] wrong".[37] In anonymously publishing his *Pontifical Doctrine against Contemporary Heterodoxy* (1944), Giménez highlighted the distortions in religious thought that produced Francoism, focusing on the role of Catholic integralism and the cosy relationship between ecclesiastical and civil power.[38] While accentuating the errors of liberalism, laissez-faire capitalism and unrestrained democracy, tracing a path from secularism and the French Revolution to totalitarianism, he outlines the compatibility of the Spanish philosophical tradition with democracy, starting with the work of the sixteenth-century School of Salamanca onwards. Concretely, the programme which Giménez sketched out to later-Francoist Minister (1951-55) Ruiz Giménez sketched out both political and socioeconomic goals: democratic freedoms and institutions, separation of Church and State and administrative decentralisation; but also public works projects, a universal minimum wage, agricultural reform, progressive taxation and free primary education.[39] His idea of a new Christian social order clearly relied on Maritain's integral humanism. As in Latin America, Maritain was translated through local intellectual, cultural and political traditions.[40] In referring to an "authentic Hispanic Christian Democracy" in correspondence with Venezuelan Christian Democracy's leader Rafael Caldera, Giménez Fernandez saw himself as one of Maritain's interpreters in Spain.[41]

36 José María Gil Robles, *Cartas del Pueblo Espanol* (Madrid: Afrodisio Aguado, 1966), 52.
37 Giménez to Angel Herrera, 15 June 1947, AMS, MGF Collection, B.xv.g/37.
38 He published this work through his friend, Sergio Méndez Arceo, a Mexican historian and liberation theologian (and Roman Catholic bishop) for whom Giménez Fernandez served as *peritus* in Vatican II.
39 Giménez to Joaquin Ruiz Jimenez, 19 February 1946, AMS, MGF Collection, B-xv-j/171. Ruiz Giménez was later the anti-Francoist founder of the magazine *Cuadernos para el Dialogo,* and Christian Democratic politician of the Transition.
40 Olivier Compagnon, *Jacques Maritain et l'Amerique du Sud: Le modèle malgré lui* (Villeneuve d'Ascq: Presses universitaires du Septentrion, 2003), 249.
41 Giménez to Rafael Caldera, 19 October 1959, in Braojos Garrido and Alvarez Rey, *Epistolario Politico*, 193.

For many exiled Catholic and even republican personalities, Giménez was the more authentic representative of Christian Democracy. A frequent correspondent with Maritain and Sturzo, the exiled Spanish political philosopher Alfredo Mendizábal endorsed Giménez to lead "an authentic movement of Christian inspiration", contrasted with Gil Robles's "authoritarian and anti-democratic past".[42] Giménez's social reformist ideals and profession of personal republicanism earned him the respect of exiled republicans and Socialists, and his friendship with exiled regionalist leaders like the Basque Manuel de Irujo opened up collaboration with regionalist parties such as the PNV. To the chagrin of some of these exiles, however, Giménez continued to collaborate deeply with Gil Robles, lending legitimacy to his anti-Francoist efforts outside of Spain. The product of his internal exile, Giménez saw himself as an intellectual inspiration and vanguard, not only for Gil Robles and his followers but also for a newer generation.

Europeanist trajectory and the road to Munich

The embrace of Europeanism provided a new means of mobilising a disparate and often conflicted anti-Francoist opposition around a positive, reform-oriented ideology. In providing an alternative outlet to still-prohibited democratic opposition to Franco inside of Spain, the idea of Europe was understood as an open, free, democratic, anti-Communist and ultimately Christian project around which the opposition could unite. Both domestically and internationally, the European project created sites of contestation against the Franco regime and for cooperation between allied forces.

Founded initially in 1954, the AECE united followers of both Gil Robles and Giménez – a mix of older, former *cedistas* and younger members like Fernando Álvarez de Miranda and Iñigo Cavero, later to become protagonists in the democratic transition. For Giménez, this organisation was the legitimate democratic alternative to the "pseudo-Christian Democrats who intend to manoeuvre around in Strasbourg", referring to Francoist attempts to enter the European Economic Community (EEC).[43] The AECE acted in concert with leading proponents of European integration like Robert Schuman in organising conference series like the "Europeanist Days" in

---

42 Alfredo Mendizábal to Giménez, 11 September 1946, in AMS, MGF Collection, B.XIV.a.12/1;
     Mendizábal to Luigi Sturzo, 5 January 1944, in Alfonso Botto, ed, *Luigi Sturzo e gli amici spagnoli: Carteggi (1924-1951)* (Bologna: Rubbettino, 2012), 378.
43 Giménez to Gil Robles, 21 November 1963, AMS, MGF Collection, B-XV-I/71.

Strasbourg (1960) or the 1st Spanish Europeanist Week in Mallorca (13 to 18 September 1961).[44] While seeking to represent the anti-Francoist opposition outside of Spain, the AECE was perhaps more effective in its domestic task of launching metropolitan seminars on European integration, supranational institutions, anti-Communism, federalism and the Catholic legacy – topics which, while touching upon democracy, were permitted within the confines of Francoist censorship. The level of coordination between the AECE and the European Movement (EM) for these conferences was substantial, with Robert Van Schendel, Secretary of the EM, bringing figures like Jean Monnet, the first Head of the High Authority of the European Coal and Steel Community (ECSC), to Spain.[45]

The pro-European campaign underlined some of the limitations of linking European integration exclusively with Christian Democracy. Under the direction of its president Madariaga, the Spanish Federal Council of the European Movement (SFCEM) secretary Enrique Gironella sought to limit the politicisation of seminars and conferences, restricting them to "Europeanist action and propaganda".[46] The AECE, portraying Europe and Christian Democracy as one and the same, sought to avoid framing the campaign as distinctly anti-Francoist. Socialists like Rodolfo Llopis saw the downplaying of a "democratic alternative" to that of "Europe and Spain" – a result of the Strasbourg conference (1960) of the EM, focused on the problem of Spain – as an attempt to "favour a monarchist and Catholic tendency".[47] Yet it was clear that both followers of Gil Robles and Giménez favoured a stronger democratic rhetoric, but were limited by political conditions in Spain. Since the Francoist regime regularly intervened to cancel conferences and other activities, Van Schendel counselled AECE secretary Álvarez: "let us do Europeanism… that is one of the serious things in which we can work without disappointments".[48]

In seeking entry into European Christian Democratic circles, the AECE faced opposition from other Spanish regionalist parties – a product of unresolved tensions from the Republic and Civil War. The central role of Gil Robles, a polarising figure whose exile gave him renewed prominence in Europeanist circles, complicated the organisation's efforts to join the

---

44 Fernando Álvarez de Miranda to Pedro Beltran de Heredia, 14 September 1960, AGUN, PBH Collection, 022/004/278.
45 "Carta de Robert van Schendel a Jean Monnet," Historical Archives of the European Union, ME-2157 1962, 10 May 1962.
46 Enrique Gironella to Beltran, 22 May 1959, AGUN, PBH Collection, 022/004/190.
47 Rodolfo Llopis to Giménez, 8 February 1961, AMS, MGF Collection, B.xv.k/35.
48 Álvarez to Beltran, 5 November 1960, AGUN, PBH Collection, 022/004/286.

Christian Democratic Nouvelles Équipes Internationales (NEI) in 1961. The regionalist Catalan Democratic Union (CDU) and PNV both questioned the participation of the AECE, with the exiled Basque leader Xabier Landáburu characterising Gil Robles as "barely democratic" and referring to Giménez as the leader of Christian Democracy.[49] The intervention of exiles like the Basque Christian Democrat Manuel de Irujo or Socialist leader Llopis – acquaintances of Giménez – facilitated the eventual accession of the AECE into the NEI. The tensions between newer, national and older, regional Christian Democratic entities would remain problematic, as the efforts progressed towards a unified Spanish representation in European organisations.

A product of his interwar past and internal exile, the reputation of Giménez was vital to not only the construction of Europeanist initiatives but also the coordination of exiled Spanish democratic forces. No less an Europeanist than Gil Robles, Giménez, thanks to his relationship with the Spanish and broader European Left, provided an important conduit for the embryonic Spanish Christian Democracy. The Belgian Socialist Spaak had invited him to the 1948 Congress at The Hague, and he was later asked by the socialist Gironella to join the SFCEM.[50] Known for his willingness to forge pro-democratic alliances, particularly with the anti-Communist Left, Giménez was invited to Catholic organisations like the NEI, Pax Romana and the International Confederation of Christian Syndicates (CISC).[51] His following grew significantly after the strikes of 1956. Giménez proved most influential in the construction of alliances with the Socialists – the Democratic Union (UD) in 1958, and the Union of Democratic Forces (UDF) in 1961, the latter bringing his followers in collaboration with the anti-Communist Left. Named president of the UDF, Giménez underlined the federative and autonomous nature of this alliance, stressing that it was not merely a "negative front" against Franco but positive, openly democratic and accidentalist.[52] Yet, he deferred to the former CEDA leader, offering even to resign from the presidency of the UDF "if it present[ed] an obstacle" to the consolidation of Christian Democratic forces.[53] For all of the recognition of his democratic credentials, he understood how his experience of exile – internal, intellectual and idealistic - complemented that

49 Rodolfo Llopis to Giménez, 13 February 1961, AMS, MGF Collection, B.xv.k/35.
50 Paul-Henri Spaak to Giménez, 23 September 1953, AMS, MGF Collection, B.xiv.i-11/49; Enrique Gironella to Giménez, 22 July 1952, AMS, MGF Collection, B.xiv.a.2/36.
51 Rafael Sánchez Mazas Ferlosio to Giménez, 6 July 1960, AMS, MGF Collection, B.xiv-c.6/6.
52 UDF Program, September 1959, AMS, MGF Collection, B.xiv.a.2/2.
53 Giménez to Gil Robles, 22 December 1959, AMS, MGF Collection, B.xv.i/51.

of Gil Robles – external, political and pragmatic – in growing the ranks and role of the anti-Francoist Catholic opposition both domestically and internationally. With its embrace of Europeanism, the movement moved towards his definition of Christian Democracy.

Most important in this notion of Europe as the "solution" to Spain was a deeply ingrained Christian notion of the European idea. Few Catholics agreed with the philosopher Jose Ortega y Gasset when, in 1910, he argued that the Continent was the answer to the "problem of Spain".[54] For them, Europe was revolution and secular modernity – not the regeneration of Spain. Yet, a half-century later, both younger and older opponents of Franco saw this European idea as central to a Catholic modernism. Gil Robles hoped that "Christian Democracy … the saviour of western Europe" would rescue Francoist Spain, whereas to French MRP co-founder Maurice Schumann he expressed faith in the idea of a "Christian Europe".[55] Echoing the conclusions of German Social Democratic member of the European Parliament Willi Birkelbach who, in his 1962 committee report, rejected Spanish accession to the EEC, Álvarez spoke to the Council of Europe of the power of the "European idea" among the opposition to Franco.[56] Like other European Christian conservatives, this Europeanist tendency went hand-in-hand with the earlier adoption of an idiom of "Christian" human rights.[57] The AECE vice-president Juan Luis de Simón Tobalina argued to the exiled Don Juan how Spain needed to join those organisations "cementing European unity" aligned with both Christian principles and the rights and freedoms in the European Convention on Human Rights.[58] In this formula, "Europe" replaced the monarchy as a unifying figure for Spaniards.

The major strikes in Asturias and Catalonia in the spring of 1962, spreading throughout Spain, provided an important prelude to what Madariaga called the "end to the Civil War", in his remarks to the fourth congress of the European Movement, held in Munich from 6 to 8 June 1962.[59] With clear coordination among the three largest European political movements

---

54 "La pedagogia social como programa político," in José Ortega y Gasset, *Discursos políticos* (Madrid: Alianza Editorial, 1990), 62.

55 José María Gil Robles, *Marginalia política* (Barcelona: Ariel, 1975), 131.

56 Committee on Non-Represented Nations, *Statement by Don Fernando Alvarez de Miranda, 5 September 1961* (Strasbourg: Council of Europe, 1961).

57 Samuel Moyn, *The Last Utopia: Human Rights in History* (Cambridge, Mass.: Belknap Press of Harvard University Press, 2010), 77-79; Moyn, *Christian Human Rights*.

58 Simón Tobalina et al. to Don Juan de Borbón, 27 May 1960, AGUN, PBH Collection, 022/004/247.

59 Joaquin Satrústegui and Fernando Álvarez de Miranda, eds, *Cuando la Transición se hizo posible* (Madrid: Tecnos, 1992), 188.

– Christian Democratic, liberal and socialist – the declaration promoted by French Socialist Maurice Faure and Van Schendel reinforced how the "European idea", as outlined in the Social Charter and Convention on Human Rights, was central to ending the conflict in Spain.[60] The conclusions of the Congress posited not mere opposition to Franco, but a positive ideology embodied in a Christian Europe and resoundingly embraced by Spaniards: "not the product of pacts with interior or exterior political forces; it is the scope of coincidence of criteria elaborated and sustained in Spain".[61]

The Francoist reaction to the "conspiracy [*contubernio*] of Munich" was repressive, and left the opposition fractured: Gil Robles departed again into exile, this time in Paris, whereas Giménez was sent with the majority of the younger attendees to internal exile on the Canary Islands.[62] The congress and Franco's harsh reaction revealed to a majority of Spaniards the existence of a significant democratic opposition, however, ushering in a re-politicisation of what the two former CEDA leaders called the "neutral masses", aided in part by the movement towards European integration. Yet, the events of Munich were almost anti-climatic: the intense cooperation among the three aforementioned political formations lost traction. Those forces of the Christian Democratic Left and Right would be incapacitated by internecine conflict, and the promise of representation in European and international Christian Democratic organisations would do little to aid the consolidation of these parties.

After Munich: optimism and disappointment over European institutions

The post-Munich development was one of pre-existing contradictions which translated into electoral failure in the transition. The Spanish Christian Democrats secured support for their cause in the fora of the European Movement and in continental and international Christian Democratic organisations. However, their promise to aid the consolidation of Spanish

---

60 Council of Europe. Consultive Assembly. Political Commission. *Resolution adopted by the Congress of the European Movement, in Munich, 8 June 1962* (Strasbourg: Council of Europe, 1962).

61 "Conclusiones aprobadas por la Asociación Española de Cooperación Europea en los actos del décimo aniversario de su fundación," 29 December 1964, Historical Archives of the European Union, ME-2158 1963-1964.

62 "Carta de Enrique Gironella a Robert van Schendel," 21 June 1962, Historical Archives of the European Union, ME-2157 1962.

Christian Democracy was fleeting and frequently stunted by the internal divisions which plagued both the Gil Robles and Giménez's formations.

The need to provide a "united front" was paramount in the post-Munich representation of a strong, vibrant opposition in European and Christian Democratic organisations.[63] That Spaniards were now aware of an alternative to Francoism was not enough. Both Gil Robles and Giménez combated Francoist efforts to form a "domesticated" Christian Democratic party, arguing that a "true Christian Democratic" force already existed and that Francoism was "not capable of evolution".[64] Yet the question of which leader would represent this "united front" was heavily disputed, creating a rift between the two interwar Catholic leaders. In internal exile again, Giménez complained that Gil Robles, in French exile, projected himself as sole leader of the movement outside of Spain.[65] This assertion, however, was not left uncontested. Carmelo Cembrero, a younger follower of Giménez who later worked as Spanish liaison to the EEC, appealed to future European Popular Party secretary general Jean Seitlinger to endorse Giménez as the "true" leader of Christian Democracy.[66]

Transnational contacts were regarded as central to the anti-Francoist effort, and particularly the consolidation of Spanish Christian Democracy. Seeing potential for growth in Spain, the Christian Democratic Union of Central Europe (CDUCE) liaison for Latin America Janusz Śleszyński advised Giménez's secretary Jesús Barros de Lis on the integration of Basque and Catalan Christian Democrats and collaboration with those disaffected followers of Gil Robles.[67] More often, however, these young Christian Democrats were the ones who sought attention for their cause. Looking to the German Christian Democratic Union (CDU) as a model, Barros sought informal contacts through the businessman and politician Johannes Schauff, later contacting CDU minister Bruno Heck for "moral" and formal economic help for the opposition led by Giménez.[68] For Barros, European Christian Democrats seemed unaware of the challenges – not only the difficulties

---

63 Rodolfo Llopis to Giménez Fernandez, 19 October 1963, AMS, MGF Collection, B-xv-i/184.
64 Manuel de Irujo to Giménez, 15 August 1964, AMS, MGF Collection, B-xv-i/126.
65 Giménez to Cembrero, 6 November 1965, AMS, MGF Collection, B.xv.k/210; Emilio Pardo Reina to Giménez, 6 June 1966, AMS, MGF Collection, B.xv.k/346.
66 Cembrero to Jean Seitlinger, 30 December 1964, AGUN, Jesus Barros de Lis (JBL) Collection, 038/004/142.
67 Barros to Janusz Śleszyński, 26 November 1964, AGUN, JBL Collection, 038/021/111. For Śleszyński's role in the broader work of the CDUCE's initiative, Piotr H. Kosicki, "Christian Democracy's Cold War," in Piotr H. Kosicki and Sławomir Łukasiewicz, eds, *Christian Democracy across the Iron Curtain: Europe Redefined* (London: Palgrave Macmillan, 2018), 221-256, at 241-243.
68 Barros to Bruno Heck, 14 September 1966, AGUN, JBL Collection, 038/002/021; Barros to Johannes Schauff, 5 January 1966, AGUN, JBL Collection, 038/002/026.

faced by the democratic opposition to Franco, but the unresolved internal cleavages within Spanish Christian Democracy – writing to NEI functionaries Karl Josef Hahn and Angelo Bernassola that their movement was "up to now forgotten".[69]

Heavily influenced by the experience of exile, the tensions with other Christian Democratic formations frustrated the formation of a unified Spanish representation in organisations like the NEI. While asserting their own cultural distinctiveness, the long-established exiled regionalist parties in Catalonia and the Basque Country feared that the newer, national formations would revive the centralising tendencies of interwar Catholic politics.[70] For their part, both Gil Robles and Giménez found common cause in the effort for joint representation.[71] Hahn and Bernassola, in particular, understood these difficulties, unique to Spain. After the first major meeting in July 1963, Barros and Cavero complained that the PNV and particularly the UDC rejected the "most elemental fraternity", denying the "spirit of Munich".[72] With the possibility of Francoist Spain's accession to the EEC, the exiled Basque leader (and friend of Giménez) Manuel de Irujo intervened, proposing a "new Munich" conference with the "real participation" of the six Christian Democratic parties from the EEC and a unified Spanish team.[73] The troubles over "particularisms", as Bernassola called them, continued unabated with the acrimonious internal debate of the NEI congress in Taormina in late 1965, when the organisation transformed into the European Union of Christian Democrats (EUCD).[74] The initial lack of agreement threatened, Hahn warned on a short visit to Madrid, the "high level" talks planned and the establishment of formal relations in

---

69 Barros to Angelo Bernassola and Karl Josef Hahn, 30 December 1964, AGUN, JBL Collection, 038/004/196.
70 Leire Arrieta Alberdi, *Estación Europa: La política europeísta del PNV en el exilio (1945-1977)* (Madrid: Tecnos, 2007). There are no in-depth works on its Catalan counterpart in exile. For a summary view, see Joan B. Culla i Clara, *Unió Democràtica de Catalunya: el llarg camí (1931-2001)* (Barcelona: Unió Democràtica de Catalunya, 2002). Giménez cited the Basque and particularly Catalan belief in the "differential fact" separating them from Spain. Giménez to Gil Robles, 6 November 1965, AMS, MGF Collection, B-xv-i-/77.
71 Gil Robles to Giménez, 4 November 1965, AMS, MGF Collection, B-xv-i/76.
72 Barros to Iñigo Cavero, 31 July 1963, AGUN, JBL Collection, 038/021/249; Barros to Bernassola, 16 September 1963, AGUN, 038/021/014.
73 De Irujo to Giménez, 16 March 1964, AMS, MGF Collection, B-xv-i/124.
74 For evolution of the NEI/EUCD, Wolfram Kaiser, "Transnational Christian Democracy: From the Nouvelles Équipes Internationales to the European People's Party," in Michael Gehler and Wolfram Kaiser, eds, *Christian Democracy in Europe Since 1945*, Vol. 2 (New York: Routledge, 2004), 194-208; Kaiser, *Christian Democracy*, 312.

Christopher Stroot

the EUCD.[75] Both functionaries were instrumental in bringing those forces into final agreement in December 1965, forming the Christian Democratic Team of the Spanish State (CDTSS).[76] In spite of internal tensions, the Venezuelan Caldera wrote to Giménez that the combined presence of the CDTSS in the World Congress in Lima in 1966 was "high[ly] symbolic".[77]

In this process of integration, there were forces opposed to this consolidation of Spanish Christian Democracy. International organisations like the Franco-sponsored European Centre for Documentation and Information (CEDI) clearly sought the acceptance of authoritarian Spain into the European and Atlantic framework, at the expense of the democratic opposition.[78] Yet, from inside the Christian Democratic organisations there was resistance as well. As early as 1963, Gil Robles lamented the lack of support from Italian Christian Democrats, with whom he had close contacts.[79] The more persistent example was the obstruction by the Bavarian Christian Social Union, closely linked to the Franco regime, at Taormina. Gil Robles wrote of the "manoeuvres of pseudo-democratic tendencies, shamelessly sponsored by the Germans and especially the Bavarians", whereas Giménez spoke of "continuists [of the regime supported by] ... Bavarians, crypto-Nazis or capitalists".[80]

Internal crisis and the fleeting promise of Christian Democracy

The promise of Christian Democratic organisations like the EUCD was limited by the internal conflicts in the movements of Gil Robles and Giménez. Ideological and generational in nature, these tensions reached their full-

---

75 Barros to various recipients, 1 November 1965, AGUN, JBL Collection, 038/005/018. For the invitation of Hahn and NEI president Mariano Rumor to Taormina, see "Procès-verbal de la ré-union du Bureau à Stresa, 2.8.1965," in Michael Gehler et al., eds, *Transnationale Parteienkoope-ration der europäischen Christdemokraten und Konservativen* (Berlin: de Gruyter, 2018), 97.

76 "Procès-verbal de la réunion du Bureau à Taormina, 9.-12-12-1965," in Gehler et al., *Transnatio-nale Parteienkooperation*, 119-120.

77 Caldera to Giménez, 6 May 1966, in Braojos Garrido and Alvarez Rey, *Epistolario Politico*, 345.

78 Birgit Aschmann, *Treue Freunde: Deutschland und Spanien in der Nachkriegszeit* (Stuttgart: Steiner, 1999), 425-434.

79 When Gil Robles argued the Italians did not want to upset relations with Franco, Remo Giannelli, DCI National Council member replied it was due to the threat of elections and provisional government (under Segni). Remo Giannelli to Gil Robles, 22 June 1963, AGUN, PBH Collection, 022/005/125.

80 Gil Robles to Giménez, 4 November 1965, AMS, MGF Collection, B-xv-i/76; Giménez to Gil Robles, 6 November 1965, AMS, MGF Collection, B-xv-i/77.

est expression after the congress in Munich. On the Christian Democratic Right situated around Gil Robles's DSC, the principal cleavage was between monarchists and accidentalists. Particular to Francoist Spain, this conflict pitted popular support for the constitutional monarchy against the notion that the substance of a Christian Democratic state – and not its institutional form – was more important. On the Christian Democratic Left oriented around Giménez's IDC, the tensions mirrored more closely the conflicts in 1960s European Catholicism: the ideological and generational confrontation between older, social Catholic and younger, more Marxist-leaning members.[81] There were also major generational differences in the practice of politics. After Munich, the experience of a "permeable exile" – internally, silenced by the Francoist authorities; externally, prevented from returning to Spain; or in a fluid state of semi-exile – was shared by both young and old, Christian Democratic Left and Right. Whereas the generation of Gil Robles and Giménez concentrated primarily on uniting the anti-Francoist opposition, those younger Christian Democrats who succeeded them were far more distinctly political in their interventions in domestic, European and international Christian Democratic forums, based in part on their expectations for regime change. These all-consuming internal issues prevented Spanish Christian Democracy from consolidating as a political force.

A movement initially defined by its support for the restoration of the constitutional monarchy, the DSC under Gil Robles progressively asserted the substance of Christian Democracy over the form of the state. Whereas alternatives like Satrústegui's Spanish Union (UE) were unambiguously conservative and monarchist, the DSC leadership asserted to Don Juan that his future as monarch depended on "Christian liberty and democratic form" and not a return to the "dead path" of traditionalism.[82] His ambiguity towards Franco pushed Gil Robles's followers to emphasise the Christian Democratic rather than monarchist orientation for the party. In this vein, Enrique Moreno Baez wanted to show Giménez's followers the "firmness" with which the DSC defended Christian Democracy and held the monarch-in-exile accountable for his behaviour.

Don Juan's rejection of the conclusions of the Congress in Munich further complicated the officially monarchist DSC's stance on the form of the state. In resigning from Don Juan's Privy Council, Gil Robles called

---

81 See Gerd-Rainer Horn, *The Spirit of Vatican II: Western European Progressive Catholicism in the Long Sixties* (Oxford: Oxford University Press, 2015), 50.
82 DSC Leadership to Don Juan de Borbon, 27 May 1960, AGUN, PBH Collection, 022/004/247.

Christopher Stroot

his attitude "absolutely intolerable".[83] None other than the Socialist Llopis revealed that his party's relationship with Gil Robles had improved significantly, with the latter no longer seeking declarations of "sympathy to the monarchy".[84] Yet Gil Robles tempered this distancing with a public campaign to frame the Congress not as a "conspiracy with the Lefts" but an effort to access the EEC and encourage a "slow and gradual" democratisation and monarchist restoration.[85]

Accidentalism was a double-edged sword, promoting greater interparty unity but also threatening internal cohesion. Some members of the DSC sought a more forceful approach, disavowing monarchist restoration and thereby paving the way for the consolidation of Spanish Christian Democracy. Lamenting the "suffering" of accidentalists in the DSC, Moreno wrote to long-time friend Giménez of the need to expel monarchist collaborationists "who do not accept Munich". For Moreno, the only impediment to the fusion of the DSC and IDC was "the monarchist-accidentalist dilemma".[86] The continued endorsement, however timid and formulaic, of the monarchy by Gil Robles and the DSC leadership into the mid-1960s provoked a response from those "progressives" to throw out monarchists like Álvarez, who formed a subsidiary of Satrústegui's UE.[87] Generational change was not immediately tied to ideological disposition. Whereas the younger left-wing so-called Buddhist group moved towards Barros de Lis's UDC, those committed monarchists who came of age under Franco largely followed Álvarez. Many older former *cedistas* like Gil Robles retreated from public life. The disaggregating effects of the conflict over the form of the state paralysed the Christian Democratic Right well into the 1970s.

Ideology and generational change were far more intertwined in Giménez's Christian Democratic "Left". Like Gil Robles's DSC, the internal tensions initially dealt with the form of the state: the official accidentalism of the IDC belied a significant republican sentiment among many of Giménez's university-age followers, threatening popular support among Spanish Catholics.[88] A friend of Giménez, the fascist intellectual-turned-social democrat Dionisio Ridruejo – an attendee of the Munich Congress –

83 Gil Robles to José María Peman, 24 July 1962, AGUN, PBH Collection, 022/005/079.
84 Llopis to Giménez, 6 December 1962, AMS, MGF Collection, B.xv.i/183.
85 Gil Robles to Camilo José Vega, 18 July 1962, AGUN, PBH Collection, 022/005/077. Vega was the Francoist Interior Minister who pursued the harsh repression against participants in the Munich Congress.
86 Moreno to Giménez, 4 December 1963, in Braojos Garrido and Alvarez Rey, *Epistolario Politico*, 324.
87 "Confidential: Situation of the DSC," 5 April 1966, AGUN, JBL Collection, 038/004/044.
88 Jaime Cortezo to Giménez, 4 March 1959, AMS, MGF Collection, B.xv.k/141.

complained of the "flaming Christian Democrat leftism" tending towards Marxism.[89]

These internal, generationally oriented tensions were magnified after the events in Munich. The Francoist repression moulded a new generation of anti-Francoist opposition leaders across the political spectrum; however, those on the Christian Democratic left like Barros de Lis returned from exile seeking a more radical ideological shift and greater militancy than that offered by Giménez. In the reorganisation of the post-exile IDC in May 1963, the IDC pushed for centrist policies and clear ideological lines in the sand. In response, the establishment by Barros in 1964 of the Christian Democratic Union (UDC) – an umbrella organisation for "authentic Christian Democrats" – was intended to absorb Giménez's IDC into a newer, younger and broader movement.[90] Giménez criticised the imprecision of Barros' political programme, which abandoned the moderation that "until here ha[s] united us".[91] This ambiguity further impeded any confederation with the DSC, with Gil Robles calling the move a "dangerous path" which opened Christian Democracy up to extremist tendencies.[92] The middle ground that the aging Giménez sought out was increasingly challenged, as he wrote to Caldera – not only by a monarchist Right whose democratic credentials were questionable, but also a left-wing Christian Democratic youth flirting with "Marxism".[93]

Generational and political differences collided in the last major effort to unite the Christian Democratic Left and Right. The unwillingness of the UDC's younger delegates to work with the DSC in the November 1965 summit in Madrid was patent, with the future minister Oscar Alzaga remarking that the discussions "gave them importance they did not deserve", and calling Gil Robles a "living cadaver".[94] Gil Robles saw his friend's presence as the only means of "impeding tensions and discrepancies", whereas Giménez viewed his attendance as counterproductive – a sign of his declining role and importance.[95] With the negotiations in Taormina at an impasse as well, these events were, for both of them, "demoralising and lamentable".

89 Dionisio Ridruejo to Barros, 2 March 1959, AMS, MGF Collection, B-xv.i/148.
90 Barros to Giménez, 30 April 1964, AMS, MGF Collection, B-xv-k/60.
91 Giménez to Barros, 23 October 1964, AGUN, JBL Collection, 038/005/115.
92 Gil Robles to Giménez, 16 November 1964, AMS, MGF Collection, B.xv.i/72.
93 Caldera to Giménez, 2 March 1966, AGUN, JBL Collection, 038/021/058.
94 Barros to Giménez, 24 November 1965, AGUN, JBL Collection, 038/006/028.
95 Gil Robles to Giménez, 4 November 1965, AMS, MGF Collection B-xv-i/76; Giménez to Gil Robles, 6 November 1965, AMS, MGF Collection, B-xv-i/77.

Christopher Stroot

The ideological chasm within the newer generations paralysed the Christian Democratic Left nominally led by Giménez. After the failed summit in Madrid, Cembrero warned against the "excessive and useless leftist snobbism" within the UDC, whereas Giménez reinforced the need for the party to "not accede to leftist accentuations nor shift to the right [*retornos derechistas*]".[96] Censured by his own movement, Giménez was *persona non grata* not only to the youth but to those like his once-time secretary Barros – together with Gil Robles, they were considered "expired leaders" who were "distanced from the humanist and Christian principles" of Christian Democracy.[97]

A failure of Christian Democracy?

After the death of Giménez in 1968, the octogenarian Gil Robles ran with the CDTSS in the first free elections after the death of Franco in 1977, with the movement winning less than one per cent of the vote. Despite this electoral failure, Donato Barba Prieto argues that the ideals of Christian Democracy permeated post-Francoist liberal democracy.[98] In political form as well, Christian Democracy survived and thrived in the transition. Charles Powell notes that, in the case of the young, reformist bureaucrats who participated the late-Francoist Christian Democrat-oriented Tácito Group, they initially belonged to associations like the AECE, the DSC or the IDC – all founded by Gil Robles and Giménez.[99] Many of these members were foundational to the Union of the Democratic Centre (UDC) – as Javier Tusell argues, the "functional equivalent" of Christian Democracy, albeit divested of the "essentialism" of Gil Robles's and Giménez's movements.[100] Their former collaborators like Álvarez de Miranda and Iñigo Cavero found relative success with the UDC, becoming ministers and *de*

---

96 Cembrero to Pedro Altares, 11 May 1965, AGUN, JBL Collection, 038/005/022; Giménez to Cortezo, 16 April 1965, AMS, MGF Collection, B.xv.k/190.
97 Barros to Alejandro Mon Munaiz, 2 May 1966, AGUN, JBL Collection, 038/004/071.
98 Donato Barba Prieto, *La democracia cristiana en España*, Vol. 2 (Madrid: Ediciones Encuentro, 2004), 291.
99 Charles Powell, "The Tacito Group and Democracy," in Paul Preston and Frances Lannon, eds, *Elites and Power in Twentieth Century Spain* (Oxford: Oxford University Press, 1990), 249-268, at 249-252.
100 "Prólogo" in Barba Prieto, *La democracia cristiana en España*, 11; Fernando Álvarez de Miranda, *La España que soñé: Memorias de un hombre de consenso* (Madrid: Esfera de los Libros, 2012), 141.

facto standard-bearers for Christian Democracy within the heterogeneous coalition led by Adolfo Suárez after 1977.[101]

The achievements of Spanish Christian Democracy cannot be understood without the experience of exile. Gil Robles overcame partisan hatreds in external exile, moving from an ambiguous monarchism modelled upon anti-democratic interwar Catholic politics towards an anti-totalitarian opposition to Franco, founded upon a language of Christian human rights and a positive ideology of social reform shared with other exiled anti-Francoist democrats. This movement towards Christian Democracy would not have been possible without the internal exile of Giménez and his understanding of a Catholic modernism. Both leaders identified this vision with the promise of Europe, which united the anti-Francoist opposition and brought Christian Democracy to the height of its popular influence and closest point to its consolidation.

The triumph of Munich, however, masked the ideological and generational conflicts that awoke (or revived themselves) after the dislocations of the Francoist repression and exile. Particular to Spain, the tensions between monarchists and accidentalists within the DSC weighed the form of state against the substance of Christian Democracy. The confrontation between the older, social Catholic and younger, Marxist sectors in the IDC was common to the experience of 1960s European Catholicism. These internal tensions belied any sense of unity on the European stage, as the newer, national formations of Gil Robles and Giménez fought with the older, regionalist Basque PNV and Catalan UCD over unified representation in the NEI and from 1965, the EUCD.

Lastly, the failure of consolidation was a product of the experience of interwar Catholic politics: the evolution from a negative, oppositional ideology rooted in anti-Francoism, towards a positive ideology, reformist and Christian Democratic in nature. European integration offered a basis for this unity; however, in the context of late-Francoist Spain, the organisationally heterogeneous and ideologically inchoate Christian Democracy could not come to agreement, either internally or externally. While electorally unsuccessful, however, the ideals of Spanish Christian Democracy, developed in exile, produced the consensus of the transition.

---

101 International Christian Democratic organisations, like the German CDU and the COPEI, did participate, supporting Álvarez. Wolfram Kaiser and Christian Salm, "Transition und Europäisierung in Spanien und Portugal," *Archiv für Sozialgeschichte* 49 (2009): 274-279; Natalia Urigüen López de Sandaliano, *A imagen y semejanza: la democracia cristiana alemana y su aportación a la transición española* (Madrid: Consejo Superior de Investigaciones Científicas, 2018).

5

A WINDOW OF OPPORTUNITY?
The Basque Nationalist Party
and European Christian Democracy in Exile

Leyre Arrieta

Basque nationalist, Catholic and democratic.[1] These three concepts, and in this order, defined the Basque Nationalist Party (PNV) when it went into exile in 1937 as a result of the Spanish Civil War. This exile would last for nearly forty years, the duration of Franco's dictatorship. The PNV had been created in the late nineteenth century as a reaction to the supposed loss of Basque identity caused by what was perceived as a Spanish "invasion". Its objective was to safeguard what it regarded as the essence of the Basque people, in which Catholicism played a key role. For the party's leaders, the defence of democracy derived naturally from Catholicism. Catholicism and democracy therefore became consubstantial with "being Basque". This axiom also caused the PNV to gradually move towards Christian Democratic positions.

The PNV was nevertheless not a Christian Democratic party at the time. Not all Catholic regionalists could be deemed to be Christian Democratic, not even those who were members of the PNV. In 1936 only a few PNV politicians had adopted key tenets of Christian Democracy. But those few people took control of the party during the years in exile. Their ideological affinity to that line of thought fostered contact with Christian Democratic leaders and bodies, particularly after the end of the Second World War.

This chapter has a twofold objective. Firstly, it intends to show when and how the PNV evolved from integralism towards a more moderate, modern approach to Catholicism. At the same time, it aims to establish to what extent this transformation influenced what was probably the most

1   Research for this chapter has been funded under the auspices of Project PGC2018-094133-B-100 (MCIU/AEI/FEDER, UE) and within the Communication Research Team of the University of Deusto.

important decision in the party's history, to support the Republic in the Spanish Civil War. The starting point for this development goes back to the years of the Second Spanish Republic (1931-36), when the main Basque nationalist leaders oriented themselves to the doctrines of the most modern European Catholic thinkers. This newly adopted social approach was one of the factors that explained the PNV's position during the war.

Secondly, this chapter analyses how the PNV connected with European Christian Democracy during the years in exile, as a way of gaining a foothold in Europeanist organisations and forums that could potentially cooperate in the overthrow of Franco's dictatorship. It argues that the Basque leaders used their contacts, which included Christian Democratic thinkers and politicians in Europe and in the United States, as a means of participating in European politics. They sought the help of Christian Democratic politicians and thinkers to justify to European Catholic public opinion – especially the Vatican – their decision to support the Republican Government and to oppose the Francoist regime; and to build alliances in their fight against Franco. In the years immediately after the Second World War, "Europe" became a key reference point in the PNV's discourse. Basque nationalists thought (perhaps in a somewhat utopian way) that the new Europe that emerged from the rubble of the war would be not be based on states, but "peoples". This led them to believe that it would become the perfect solution for stateless nations such as the Basques.

This chapter draws on many primary and news sources located mainly in the Archives of Nationalism and the Basque Historical Archives, as well as on other sources and literature. It is structured as follows. Firstly, it will briefly outline the reasons for the birth of the Basque nationalist movement, setting out how two political parties emerged in the Basque Country and in Catalonia, the PNV and the Unió Democratica de Catalunya (UDC), respectively, which adopted a Christian Democratic stance, and how this determined the decisions made by both parties in the Civil War. Secondly, the chapter will briefly discuss how Basque nationalists organised in exile and will then deal with the PNV's Europeanism. This will include an analysis of the pro-European discourse elaborated in the first years in exile, and the political proposals made in connection with how the Basque Country would fit within Spain and Europe. The chapter will move on to address the relations established by Basque nationalists with Christian Democratic political parties and organisations. The conclusion will explore the question of how the PNV's political ideas evolved beyond the exile years.

Catholic regionalisms and the Republic: going into exile

The Basque Country is a territory located on either side of the Franco-Spanish border. The relationship between the Basque Country and the Spanish government changed over time. At the end of the nineteenth century, a pro-independence movement emerged, and the PNV was founded by Sabino Arana in 1895.[2] The Basque nationalist movement took hold within a very specific context, as a reaction to the crisis of identity centred on values which many Basques shared, in a region which had experienced little change over the centuries. According to Sabino Arana, the Basque Country at this time was undergoing a critical turn caused by the arrival of people from other places, that is, the Spanish. Liberalism had resulted in modernisation and industrialisation, which had given rise to a massive influx of what at the time were often called "foreign elements". Their presence was believed to put traditional Basque society at risk. Thus, the new movement was a Catholic pro-independence movement whose political enemy was Spain and the Spanish.[3]

The emergence of Basque nationalism brought with it a new division within political Catholicism, which until then had been separated into traditionalists and fundamentalists, so named within the Spanish historiography. This situation caused problems within the Basque Church, which intensified during the Republican period from 1931 to 1936. By then, as Javier Tusell has pointed out, Basque nationalism was already a modern political movement, which had undergone significant changes in the 1920s that would be consolidated in the 1930s. A young generation of Basque politicians, led by José Antonio Aguirre, led the gradual modernisation of the party.[4] This modernisation was reflected in the identification between nationalism, democracy and Catholicism, and in a programme that was far more focused on social issues than was usual for most inter-war Catholic

---

2   For more on the figure of Sabino Arana, see José Luis de la Granja (Sabino Arana), *Ángel o demonio* (Madrid: Tecnos, 2015).

3   The best study on the history of the PNV is Santiago de Pablo et al., *El péndulo patriótico: Historia del Partido Nacionalista Vasco* (Barcelona: Crítica, 1999-2001).

4   For the ideological evolution of the PNV, see Javier Tusell, *Historia de la democracia cristiana en España*, vol. 2: *Los nacionalismos vasco y catalán: Los solitarios* (Madrid: Cuadernos para el diálogo, Edicusa, 1974), 9-119. The most comprehensive biography of José Antonio Aguirre is Lugder Mees et al., *La política como pasión: El lehendakari José Antonio Aguirre (1904-1960)* (Madrid: Tecnos, 2014).

parties.[5] It was precisely this increasing importance accorded to social issues by the PNV that marked its growing distancing from the conventionally understood Right, to which it had been closer in the first months of the Republic. The contrast between the two types of Catholicism became more visible: a more democratic form, sensitive to social issues, which was reflected in and strengthened by the creation of the Basque Association for Christian Social Action (Agrupación Vasca de Acción Social Cristiana, AVASC) chaired by Aguirre, and a more orthodox, authoritarian kind of Catholicism. This divide also characterised the ecclesiastical hierarchy, with the Seminary of Vitoria described by critics as a "hotbed of nationalism".[6]

In the November 1933 election campaign, the PNV voiced its clear commitment to freedom and democracy, in the face of the dictatorial tendency that was gathering increasing support among right-wing supporters. Also significant was the fact that the nationalist newspaper *Euzkadi*, which had a section entitled "social work", added a section called "Esprit Nouveau Basque" (in French), explicitly invoking French magazines such as *Esprit* and *Ordre Nouveau*, which were linked to currents of thought such as personalism and integral federalism.[7] The young generation of party leaders thus gradually moulded their Catholicism into a more modern, Christian Democratic form. These young people rejected both dictatorships and democracies that were characterised by a "tendency to atheism, and its tumultuous, and often demagogic and revolutionary manifestation", as described by José de Ariztimuño, also known as Aitzol. He perceived Christian Democracy as being organised around "institutions of natural and positive law, including the family, professional associations, municipalities and natural regions that form the State and were prior to that State".[8] When the war broke out, the PNV *stricto sensu* was not a Christian Democratic party yet, as it had not yet drawn up a new programme. Moreover, the leaders' convictions had not been totally accepted at the grassroots level. However, the party was very close to Christian Democracy at that

5   Antonio Elorza, *Ideologías del nacionalismo vasco (De los "euskaros" a Jagi Jagi)* (San Sebastián: Luis Haranburu Editor, 1978), 294-310.
6   Santiago de Pablo et al., *La diócesis de Vitoria: 150 años de historia (1862-2012)* (Vitoria: Editorial ESET, Diócesis de Vitoria, 2013), 327.
7   On integral federalism as a means of overcoming the nation-state, see José Luis De Castro, "El fundamento teórico y doctrinal: el federalismo integral superador del Estado-nación," in *La emergente participación política de las regiones en el proceso de construcción europea* (Bilbao: HAEE/IVAP, 1994), 63-104.
8   Note taken from the introduction to the book by José Ariztimuño, written under the pseudonym J. de Urkina, *La democracia en Euzkadi* (San Sebastián: Editorial Euskaltzaleak, 1935), 23.

point. In Javier Tusell's words, it was a "Christian Democratised" political party.[9]

The only political party that could be considered fully Christian Democratic in Spain in the 1930s was the Catalan UDC, founded in November 1931. From the beginning, the UDC expressly adhered to the principles of Christian Democracy. As in the case of the PNV in the 1930s, the UDC also combined (Catalan) nationalism, with a modern form of Catholicism and a concern for social issues.[10] Its radical nationalism was far from acceptable to other Spanish Christian Democrats. But, without a doubt, this was the party in Spain that was most steeped in Christian Democratic doctrine at the time. The UDC fully accepted democracy as a political system linked to Christianity, and its interpretation of the pontifical doctrine was reflected in its practice. The most important speeches given at the UDC's second congress, held in October 1933, were related to social issues.

The progressive character of the type of Catholicism advocated by the UDC and the PNV also explains the position of these two parties in the Spanish Civil War, which ran counter to that advocated by the vast majority of Spanish Catholics, who took the side of General Francisco Franco. Many Spanish Catholics considered the war to be a crusade.[11] There were some exceptions to these views among Spanish Catholics such as Ángel Osorio and Gallardo or Maximiliano Arboleya, as well as in the UDC and the PNV.[12] Both political parties supported the legitimately established power of the Republican government. This position can be – and has been – understood either as pure political opportunism to secure regional autonomy; or as a direct consequence of its doctrinal approach (in the case of the UDC), or of

9   Tusell, *Historia de la Democracia Cristiana*, 203.
10 Ibid., 138. According to Tusell, there were Christian Democratic sectors within the CEDA (Spanish Confederation of Autonomous Right – Confederación Española de Derechas Autónomas). All of the young leaders in the PNV were Christian Democrats, but the UDC was the only specifically Christian Democratic party.
11 The stance taken by the Catholic Church on the Spanish Civil War was analysed in detail in Hilari Raguer, *La pólvora y el incienso: La Iglesia y la guerra civil española (1936-1939)* (Barcelona: Península, 2001).
12 Tusell dedicated a chapter of his book to these Catholic personalities: Tusell, *Historia de la Democracia Cristiana*, 205-261.

its previous ideological evolution (in the case of the PNV); or as a mixture of both.[13]

In the case of the PNV, the decision was neither simple nor unanimous. There was reluctance within the party among those who preferred to support the insurgents commanded by Franco for religious reasons. In addition, a party as Catholic as the PNV could not support the religious persecution that was happening in the Republican zone. But a choice was ultimately made to support the Republic in late September and October 1936, when Manuel Irujo was appointed as Minister of the Republican government, the Statute of Autonomy agreed and the Basque regional government formed. From then on, the PNV became purposefully involved in the war. One of its objectives was safeguarding Catholicism and preventing religious persecution and indiscriminate killings.[14]

The quick decision to stand by the Republican government meant that the PNV was branded as opportunistic by right-wing Catholic Francoists. However, the PNV's democratic ideas and desire for social reforms also brought the party closer to the Republican side.[15] The decision to support the Republican government was in keeping with the party's distancing from the Catholic Right and the move towards Christian Democracy. The Republican anti-clericalism, either real or perceived by Catholics, was not a strong enough reason for the PNV to oppose the Republic or support the rebels. They could not separate their firm religious beliefs from democracy and the established order.

Yet it was far from an easy decision. In fact, the situation placed the PNV in a real moral dilemma, since the ecclesiastical hierarchy gave its support to Franco's new order. As José Azurmendi has noted, it was difficult to understand "that Basque Catholics fought alongside communists against

---

13 Fernando de Meer, for example, emphasised the achievement of autonomy: Fernando de Meer, *El Partido Nacionalista Vasco ante la guerra de España* (Pamplona: Ediciones de la Universidad de Navarra EUNSA, 1992). Hilari Raguer, when discussing Catalonia, and Tusell for both Catalonia and the Basque Country, analysed how the two parties evolved: Hilari Raguer, *La Unió Democràtica de Catalunya i el seu temps (1931-1939)* (Monserrat: Publicacions de l'Abadia de Monserrat, 1976); Tusell, *Historia de la Democracia Cristiana.* However, as far as the PNV is concerned, both the immediate achievement of autonomy and the modernisation of the party must be taken into account: Leyre Arrieta, "Dilemas del nacionalismo vasco en la guerra civil," in Sergio Valero and Marta García Carrión, eds, *Desde la capital de la República: nuevas perspectivas y estudios sobre la guerra civil* (Valencia: Universitat de Válencia, 2018).

14 On the stance taken by the Basque Church on the Spanish Civil War, see Alfonso Botti, "La Iglesia vasca dividida: Cuestión religiosa y nacionalismo a la luz de la nueva documentación vaticana," *Historia Contemporánea* no. 35 (2007): 451-489.

15 Tusell, *Historia de la democracia*, 119.

Franco's Catholics".[16] In fact, on 6 August 1936, the bishops of Pamplona and Vitoria, Marcelino Olaechea and Mateo Múgica, published a joint pastoral letter ordering the PNV not to oppose a movement that included "the traditional love of our sacrosanct religion" among its objectives.[17]

However, for José Antonio Aguirre, president of the Basque government since October 1936, the Civil War had nothing to do with religion. It was a conflict between "a legitimate craving for social justice and an outdated conservatism that was clinging to its privileges". Aguirre wondered how it was possible that international public opinion was mostly favourable to Franco's side. He found the answer in the belief (which he deemed to be false) that the Spanish war was a conflict between "communism and order".[18]

The Catalan Christian Democrats adopted a similar position. Of course, the Catalan situation was different from that in the Basque Country. The UDC was eclipsed by anarchism, on the one hand, and by the conservative Catholicism of the Lliga Regionalista, or Regionalist League, on the other. The party was reduced to a small group of people who, at first, chose not to go into exile and collaborate with the Generalitat, the Catalan government. During the war, the UDC's main objective was to maintain the Republic as a democratic political system that defended public liberties, and they did their best to prevent reprisals against Catholics.[19]

In July 1937, after the loss of the Basque territory, a new stage began for the Basque government. It first moved from Bilbao to Santander, and then, in October 1937, to Barcelona. The exodus of members of the Basque government, political leaders and ordinary refugees accelerated. It was essential for the leaders to maintain contact and establish a network of relations with all the Basques scattered around the world. To this end, they made use of the autonomy gained during the Civil War and exercised powers that they did not constitutionally have, such as foreign affairs. At that stage, the Basque government established delegations in different parts of Spain, Europe and America. These delegations were the first evidence that they were acting not as a party, but as an institution. Although they

---

16 José Azurmendi, "Pensamiento personalista," *Revista internacional de estudios vascos*, RIEV 41, no. 1 (1996): 80.

17 Pablo et al., *La diócesis de Vitoria*, 342. The leaders of the PNV initially believed the news of the pastoral letter to be false, as they could not believe that Bishop Múgica had taken that position. The truth is that the bishop was disconcerted because he couldn't bring himself to extol either the rebels or the PNV.

18 "Nuestro pueblo ante la sublevación fascista," *Euzkadi*, 23 December 1936: 1-2.

19 For further details on the position of the UDC, see Tusell, *Historia de la democracia*, 121-204; Raguer, *La pólvora*, 331.

were not embassies of an independent state and did not enjoy the usual diplomatic treatment, they did win political recognition.

The Basque nationalist exile was structured around these delegations, notably including those in Paris, London and New York. The Basque government, which during those years was practically restricted to nationalist counsellors, used those offices to weave a network of relationships with Christian Democratic political parties and intellectuals in order to justify their support for the Republic, and seek alliances in their struggle against Franco's regime. It was the experience of exile, moreover, that caused the Basque Nationalist Party to embrace the notion of a united Europe, around which its political discourse was structured.

The Europeanist discourse of the PNV in exile

From the PNV's birth, "Europe" had become increasingly more important in the ideological repertoire of Basque nationalism. The political hopes of the PNV had gradually become linked to international relations and, specifically, to contacts established at the European level. The international conjuncture that emerged at the end of the First World War favoured nationalism in Europe. The PNV was aware of the demands of other European nations and minorities that had not been met by the conflict's resolution through peace treaties, and of the significance of some of these minorities. Therefore, the perception within the party was that "Europe" could be the solution for the Basque Country to achieve international recognition.[20] The Allied victory in the Second World War aroused enormous expectations among Basque nationalists. On the one hand, it fuelled their dream of returning to a democratic Spain, and, on the other hand, it encouraged them to rely on a new European space where Basque aspirations could materialise. "Europe" was seen by Basque nationalists as a window of opportunity, a world full of potential not to be missed.

The basis of the PNV's pro-European discourse was the so-called Aguirre Doctrine, an international demand for a free Basque Country, which would contribute to the construction of a federal Europe made up not of states, but of peoples or nations. This approach was based on the alleged crisis of the liberal nation-state and on the need for a European "suprastate" solution, which did not preclude stateless nations from becoming

---

20 Alexander Ugalde, *La Acción Exterior del Nacionalismo Vasco (1890-1939): Historia, Pensamiento y Relaciones internacionales* (Oñati: HAEE/IVAP, 1996).

independent. It defended the right of those peoples with enough political will and capacity to be free and autonomous. This perspective was already outlined by Aguirre in 1945 in an article entitled "L'homme et la Nationalité: Bases de la Paix future" ("Man and Nationality: Fundamentals of a Future Peace").[21] The Aguirre Doctrine combined classic ideas of Basque nationalism with concepts such as the crisis of nation-states and the notion of a united and federal Europe.[22] These were all typical outcomes of the atmosphere caused by the Allies' victory, and, therefore, allowed the PNV to fully embrace the notion of European integration.

An integrated Europe offered the PNV a suitable framework for the achievement of several objectives. Firstly, Europe became the ideal platform from which to publicise and propagate the will of the Basque people, disseminating their claims of being a statelessness "nation". If the new Europe was to be a federal Europe, it could protect and reinforce Basque identity.[23] Reduced state sovereignty might offer new opportunities for stateless nations such as the Basques. While international recognition was sought for the Basque Country and, therefore, for Basque nationalism, the aim was also to dispel the accusations of introspective isolationism made against both:

> Those who think we want to close ourselves off in our own world of songs and dances are not well informed. What we want is to retain and love what is ours, protecting our essence and our full personality, while openly showing it to others and learning whatever we should learn, without ever forgetting who we are. We are an old tree that grows new and robust young branches, a tree that must not and will not break loose of its roots, because then it would die.[24]

Many of the efforts championed by Basque nationalists in their early years in exile were also focused on explaining their support for the Republican government in the Civil War. The PNV refused to accept that European Catholic public opinion, and especially the Vatican, regarded the war as a "crusade" and generally defended the Francoist side. Europe was also an

21 *Euzko Deya* (Paris), no. 211 (31 March 1945): 1-2; It can also be found in José Antonio Aguirre, "El problema de las nacionalidades ante la Federación Europea," in *Obras Completas*, vol. 2 (San Sebastian: Sendoa, 1981), 791-793.
22 "Coordinación de Nacionalidades Europeas," in Aguirre, *Obras Completas*, 2: 463-479.
23 "Europe was born as an anti-totalitarian, anti-imperialist symbol, as a defensive redoubt of human personality, of natural collectivities, as the rectification of a long series of secular errors and historical crimes". "Nacimiento de Europa," 1949, in Landaburu, *Obras Completas*, 2: 287.
24 Letter from Iñaki Unceta, Secretary of National Council of the Basque Nationalist Party, to Javier Landaburu, Bayonne, 14 October 1949, AN, EBB Fund, 120–3.

excellent framework to incite the political hostility of Western states towards Franco's regime. The PNV tried to isolate the regime by preventing it from having any contact with European and American governments or other agencies, and it attempted to be a link between Basque and Spanish democrats. The aim was to unite the Spanish Republican forces to demonstrate to the North American and Western European governments that a viable, solid, non-communist democratic alternative was possible in Spain.

In short, for Basque nationalists, Europe was the ideal framework within which to achieve their aspirations. Nationalist leaders were keen (in a somewhat utopian way) to become directly and independently integrated into Europe, and they did not want to achieve this objective through Spain. They advocated a federal Europe in which the Basque Country could gain at least a similar level of self-government that many of the states that were part of a future European supranational organisation would enjoy, on an equal footing.

In this new Europe, the Basque Country would not participate as a Basque state in the classical way, which would make no sense in a federation composed of nations. This would avoid the historical fracture that could lead to the creation of a state and the consequent border alterations. The Basque Country would operate as a nation, and therefore a European union or federation of nations would be the appropriate ground to rebuild and consolidate Basque identity.[25]

Only if direct participation in Europe was not possible could Spain serve as a gateway to Europe. The more moderate and advanced leaders of Basque nationalism – those who held the reins of the party during exile – did not discard the Spanish option, but their condition for agreeing to participate in Europe through Spain was that it should be a democratic and federal country. In these circumstances, the Basque Country could continue to be linked to Spain, but would retain its own political organisation:

> The Basque people consider it necessary to implement a supranational form of federalism that must be based on an intrastate federalism, as this is the only way to guarantee that the Iberian Peninsula will seriously be part of the European federation, and that the Madrid Government will cease to apply its oscillating policies whereby one day the peoples in the Peninsula are granted some rights, and then they are taken away the next day.[26]

25 For the Europeanist politics of the PNV in exile, see Leyre Arrieta, *Estación Europa: La política europeísta del PNV en el exilio* (Madrid: Tecnos, 2007).
26 Report by the Basque Delegation on the 2nd Congress of the UEF, November 1948, AN, EBB Fund, 52-11.

At that time, however, Spain was under the yoke of the Franco dictatorship, and Europe was the only window of opportunity, which the PNV relied on by taking two linked ideological paths: federalism and Christian Democracy. These were the major principles on which the Europeanist policy of Basque nationalism was based. The modernisation of the party's Catholicism during the Second Republic had given it a Christian Democratic tinge. This in turn had created fertile ground for Basque nationalists to identify with the Christian Democratic proposals that were popular in Western Europe after the Second World War.

The second path for Basque nationalism to enter "Europe" was federalism. After the war, the PNV was able to play a role in federalist media in search of new channels of participation in European forums, which would allow it to strengthen its presence in the European Movement and in the European construction process. During the 1930s, nationalist leaders, including Aguirre, had already accepted the ideas of integral federalism and personalism, as propounded in the personalist texts by authors such as Alexandre Marc, Emmanuel Mounier and Denis de Rougemont, precisely because their principles were aligned with the PNV's ideological corpus. The prominent role given to the individual, the high value conferred on so-called natural communities that acted as mediators between the State and the individual, and the defence of a federal Europe based on incorporating nations and not just states were all fully accepted by Basque nationalism.

Christian Democracy and federalism were not merely ideological trends that supported the PNV's Europeanist discourse. They also constituted channels for applying discourse to political practice. These two paths allowed Basque nationalist leaders to become involved in the European Movement and organisations of Western European Christian Democrats.

The PNV's involvement with the European Christian Democratic movement

After the Basque government's delegation was formally established in Paris in November 1936, it approached some political leaders who were favourable to the Basque and the Republican cause. Aguirre saw the potential for change that Christian Democracy could have for the Basque people if they were well-positioned in those circles:

It is worth exalting our future role as genuine representatives of a Christian Democracy that has not become a political reality anywhere outside of the Basque Country. This focal point, which to me is like a small spiritual metropolis, should be known, respected and given the opportunity to manage its life, as it is a civilisation of its own that can serve as an example to larger peoples (from a geographical point of view). These ideas have been very well understood by Maritain, for example, and should be conveyed to as many people as you meet there. They should be repeated, day in, day out, without fear of exhaustion.[27]

The Basque government's delegation also sought to contact intellectuals like François Mauriac, Georges Bernanos, Paul Vignaux and Jacques Maritain himself. These thinkers became indispensable supporters of the Basque cause, and a communication channel with the Vatican, as well as informal spokespersons for Basque views in the world.[28] Although the influence of European moderate Catholic thinkers had been seen in nationalist writings for years before the Spanish Civil War, it was during the conflict that a closer connection was established between these European thinkers and Basque nationalists. At first, most European Catholic intellectuals were supportive of the rebels. However, this unanimous support soon dissolved, and some thinkers such as Mauriac, Luigi Sturzo, Emmanuel Mounier and Maritain changed their minds.[29] They criticised both the errors committed by the Republicans and those made by the Francoists, and strongly advocated peace. Above all, they discarded the idea that the Civil War was a crusade, as Franco's side claimed.

This position chimed with the views held by politicians and thinkers who had taken steps towards Christian Democracy in Spain. One of those intellectuals was Alfredo Mendizábal, who had been dismissed from his university chair in Oviedo by both sides in the Civil War.[30] In the prologue to Mendizábal's book *Origins of a Tragedy*, Maritain claimed that turning

---

27 Letter from José Antonio Aguirre to F.J. Landaburu (unknown location, May 1938), AN, GE Fund, 120-10.

28 I have outlined the contacts between Basque nationalists and Jacques Maritain in Arrieta, "El nacionalismo vasco y Jacques Maritain," *Ayer*, no. 113 (2019): 189-215.

29 In 1937, Sturzo and other Catholic refugees published the text entitled "Reflections on Spain," in which they criticised Franco and advocated Catholic neutrality in the conflict. Wolfram Kaiser, *Christian Democracy and the Origins of European Union* (Cambridge: Cambridge University Press, 2007), 134.

30 See Alfredo Mendizábal Villalba, *Pretérito imperfecto: Memorias de un utopista* (Oviedo: Real Instituto de Estudios asturianos, 2009) (the original manuscript dates from 1974); Alfredo Mendizábal Villalba, *Los orígenes de una tragedia: Edición, introducción y traducción del original de Xavier Iturralde* (Madrid: Centro de Estudios Políticos y Constitucionales, 2012).

Leyre Arrieta

war into something sacred was committing blasphemy. However, he also did not support the Popular Front and criticised its abuses, such as the burning of churches and the assassinations of priests.[31]

As anxiety and doubts played havoc with the conscience of nationalists, Maritain's statements probably had a calming effect on them, since he saw how the choice that they had made on the grounds of their deep Catholic beliefs had been publicly condemned by the ecclesiastical hierarchy. The constant monitoring of the reactions of European Catholic individuals and media against Franco on Basque media such as the Basque government's Paris publication, *Euzko Deya*, and the repeated publication of articles, manifestos and opinions expressed and published by Catholic figures in favour of the Basque cause were clear signs of the importance accorded to their positions.

During the Second World War, relations with European Christian Democracy had been maintained in two ways: by Aguirre with important leaders of the Christian Democratic movement, and by the priest Alberto Onaindia after his arrival in England in July 1940. From their New York headquarters, Aguirre and his team tried to maintain contact with European Christian exiles through all available means. In 1942, during his trip to Latin America, Aguirre launched the idea of holding a congress for South American Catholics. Also, in December of that year, he was one of the signatories, together with Maritain and Sturzo, of the *Devant la crise mondiale* manifesto, a document that underlined the Christian values on which any future society should be based. Aguirre and his collaborators also sought the support of the American government by collaborating with their information services.[32]

In August 1940, on the other side of the Atlantic, Onaindia began talks with the European democrats from Poland, Czechoslovakia, Belgium and the Netherlands who were exiled in London. The aim of the talks was to form a body of Catholic democrats which, "in addition to studying current issues through the lens of Christian Democracy, could be presented to Catholics in other countries as an organisation that defends democracy within Catholic standards". The International Christian Democratic Union

---

31 Preface by Jacques Maritain in Mendizábal, *Orígenes de una tragedia*, 3-37.
32 A Spanish version entitled "Ante la crisis mundial: El manifiesto de los intelectuales católicos europeos" was published in *Euzko Deya* (Buenos Aires) 129, no. 6 (30 November 1942). On relations in the USA, see David Mota Zurdo, *Un sueño americano: El Gobierno Vasco en el exilio y Estados Unidos (1937-1979)* (Oñati: IVAP, 2016); Juan Carlos Jiménez de Aberásturi and Rafael Moreno Izquierdo, *Al servicio del extranjero: Historia del Servicio Vasco de Información (1936-43)* (Madrid: Antonio Machado Libros, 2008).

(ICDU) was thus born on 28 January 1941.[33] Jan A. Veraart, the former Rector of the University of Delft, was elected president, and the leaders of the Czech, Polish and Italian parties (Sturzo) were vice-presidents. The Basque group formed part of the IUCD with the same rights as the other national groups.[34]

After the Second World War, Christian Democratic parties experienced much electoral success in continental Western Europe. The idea of a united Europe was a common denominator in these parties' visions and a mobilising element for their voters. Christian Democrats came to dominate the governments of the six founding member states of the European Coal and Steel Community founded in 1951-52. For the PNV, Christian Democracy constituted the best guarantee of democracy and the best way to fight fascism, and it was also a suitable channel for disseminating the aims of social justice and solidarity. For this reason, when the war ended, the PNV tried to maintain and develop its relationships with European Christian Democrats. The parties with which the PNV had closer relationships were the French Mouvement Républicain Populaire (MRP) and the Italian Democrazia Cristiana (DC).

During the war, contacts with French Christian Democracy had been established through Ernest Pezet, the inter-war deputy of the Popular Democratic Party and secretary of the International League of Friends of the Basques (LIAV), which had been founded in the delegation of the Basque Government in Paris in 1938 with the support of prominent Frenchmen.[35] After the war, Aguirre and the members of the Basque delegation in Paris continued to maintain friendly relations with Georges Bidault, in particular. Basque representatives were invited to the MRP's third national congress, held in Paris from 13 to 16 March 1947. Five PNV members attended the congress. This event was of great value to the PNV because it enabled contacts to be established with other European Christian Democratic parties, as well as reinforcing relationships with prominent representatives of the MRP.

Basque politicians also attended the fourth national congress of the MRP, which took place in Toulouse from 6 to 9 May 1948. At this Congress,

33 See also the chapter by Wolfram Kaiser in this book.
34 Letter from Onaindia to Maritain, London, 30 July 1941, Labayru Institute, Onaindia Fund, 31-4; "International Christian Democratic Union," May 1942, Labayru Institute, Onaindia Fund, 31-8. On Onaindía's thoughts, see Iñaki Goiogana, "Alberto Onaindía: Ideas y contenidos de un demo-cristiano precursor de la Europa de la posguerra," in Dos vascos humanistas en la UNESCO: Alberto Onaindia, José Miguel de Azaola (Bilbao: UNESCO Etxea, 2016), 18-34.
35 Jean Claude Larronde, Exilio y Solidaridad: La Liga Internacional de Amigos de los Vascos (Bilbao: Bidasoa, 1988).

communism was strongly denounced, and Francoism described as a totalitarian regime. But above all, it was important for Basque nationalists insofar as it provided a platform for connecting with outstanding public figures such as Maurice Schumann, then leader of the MRP; Pierre-Henri Teitgen, the Defence Minister; Pierre Dumas, editor of the newspaper *La Victoire*; and André Colin, secretary general of the MRP. Aguirre and two other Basque representatives also joined the fifth congress in June 1949.[36]

The PNV also had quite close connections with the Italian DC. Representatives from the PNV attended the DC's first congress in Rome from 24 April to 4 May 1946. At this event, Basque representatives spoke with the Italian Prime Minister Alcide De Gasperi three times. They also met Giovanni Gronchi, Italian Minister of Industry and Commerce. In addition, they had meetings with Maritain, who was French ambassador to the Vatican at that time; the Marquis of Cavaletti, a high-ranking official of the Italian Ministry of Foreign Affairs; and several Basque priests who lived in Rome.

The PNV's aim at the DC congress was to provide information about the Basque case, as they considered that there was a lack of objective information in Italy. They were very warmly welcomed, and they thought that relations in Italy should be strengthened even further after the success of the DC in the 1948 Italian elections. Therefore, participation in study events organised by the DC, its youth branch and the NEI in Fiuggi in July of 1948, was considered indispensable. However, despite these efforts, except in some specific cases, the DC remained under the influence of the Spanish Catholic Church and press, and the PNV was not invited to the congress in 1949. Relations between Italy and Franco's Spain became closer again at this point in the emerging Cold War.[37]

Without a doubt, however, the main link between the PNV and the European Christian Democratic movement were the Nouvelles Équipes Internationales (NEI).[38] The growth of the Christian Democratic parties after the Second World War reinforced their desire to create an effective organisation that would support their transnational cooperation. This resulted

---

36 Details about the 1947 congress in *Euzkadi*, no. 46 (April 1947): 43-44; Javier Landaburu, "El Congreso Nacional del MRP francés," in *Obras Completas*, 1: 36-37. Details about the 1948 Congress in "La representación del PNV en el Congreso del MRP," May 1948, AN, EBB Fund 174-1; Informe del EBB a la segunda Reunión Consultiva, Baiona, November 1948, AN, EBB Fund, 26-13. Also, in several issues of *OPE*, *Euzko Deya* and *Alderdi*.

37 Report by José Eizaguirre on the Congress of Democrazia Italiana, Saint Jean de Luz, May 1946, AN, EBB Fund, 172-9; on the 1948 Congress, Landaburu, "Viaje de la Delegación Vasca a Italia," in *Obras Completas*, 3: 45-49.

38 Kaiser, *Christian Democracy and the Origins of European Union*, chapters 5-6.

in the creation in 1947 of the NEI, later transformed into the European Union of Christian Democrats (EUCD) in 1965. From 1945 onwards, when discussions about the possibility of creating an international party organisation began, the PNV made a great effort to participate actively. It managed to do so, not only as co-founder of the NEI, but just as importantly, in a notable role as a member of the main committees. This was an outstanding achievement for the aspirations of a small party in exile.

The NEI held their first congress in Chaudfontaine, near Liège, in Belgium from 31 May to 3 June 1947. The main aim of the new organisation was to coordinate European Christian Democratic leaders and political parties. Two Basque representatives took part in this first congress. The members of the congress approved a message of sympathy to Basques that had been proposed by the Basque delegation. Participation in this first congress was very important for the PNV, because it enabled the Basques to be recognised as a founding member, and, as a consequence, as a national équipe with full rights, not a "team in exile". In fact, Aguirre was named member of the Honorary Committee, and Javier Landaburu was chosen to represent the PNV on the executive committee. Some of the meetings of the NEI were even held at 11 avenue Marceau, the Parisian seat of the Basque government-in-exile.[39] For the PNV, which participated autonomously, not as part of a Spanish group, the NEI constituted the most important gateway to European Christian Democracy. This status provided the PNV, which participated in all NEI congresses from 1947 to 1965, with privileges that the party retained until 1960.

However, apart from receiving a warm welcome at the NEI meetings and congresses, the only practical PNV achievements were a few statements against Franco's regime. The party also encountered the difficulty that the NEI increasingly became dominated by more liberal-conservative parties like the German Christian Democratic Union and Christian Social Union, compared to the strong French influence in the beginning. Thus, the NEI over time adopted a strongly anti-communist position, which under the impact of the Cold War confrontation led to a more lenient attitude towards Franco's Spain. The more influential the centre-right and anti-communist parties were, the weaker the presence and voice of the Basque nationalists became.

---

39 "Reunión en la Delegación Vasca del Consejo ejecutivo de los NEI" (Meeting of the Basque Delegation of the Executive Council of the NEI), in Landaburu, *Obras completas*, 2: 404-407; also some articles published in *OPE, Euzko Deya* (Paris), *Euzko Deya* (Buenos Aires) and *Euzkadi*.

The NEI nevertheless continued to be the main link between the PNV and Christian Democracy both in the 1950s and the 1960s. However, the PNV ceased to be the only Spanish group, as new Christian Democrat groups from Spain such as José María Gil Robles's Democracia Social Cristiana (DSC) also became established. Initially, the Basque nationalists attempted to prevent these Spaniards from accessing the group, but eventually they had no choice but to accept the situation. The PNV ultimately preferred to take the initiative and promote the creation of an all-Spanish NEI *équipe.*

The negotiations among the Spanish Christian Democratic parties were not easy. In the end, the PNV lost its independent representation within the NEI, which it had enjoyed since its creation. The Spanish Christian Democratic équipe was officially formed at the NEI Congress in Taormina in December 1965. Reflecting the PNV's historical importance and role, however, the Basque Joseba Rezola, vice-president of the Basque Government, became its first secretary.

This strategy of enabling collaboration with other Spanish political forces that the PNV adopted in the 1960s was a strategy for the future. The Basque Autonomous Government was still alive in exile, but its existence was more symbolic than real. The young nationalists began to criticise the ineffectiveness of their elders. Some of them founded the ETA (Euskadi ta Askatasuna, the Basque Country and Freedom) in 1959. In the meantime, the leaders of the PNV had grown old; some of them had died in exile. In this context, the party continued to maintain its eminently nationalist discourse, but its tactics were based on a pragmatic and moderate approach, with a view to repositioning itself when the dictatorship ended.

If they wanted to remain in European organisations, they now had to do so through state-level organisations. PNV leaders resigned themselves to the need to work with Spanish political parties to secure a solution for the Basque Country in a future transition to democracy in Spain, which they expected to be imminent. In particular, they hoped for the restoration of Basque autonomy within Spain.

Conclusion

The PNV ultimately did not achieve its main objectives while in exile, the most important of which was to overthrow the Francoist regime. However, Franco's Spain seemed to be a lesser evil for Western European democracies in the Cold War, as it was perceived to be critical to stopping the expansion of communism. The initial optimism felt by the Basque exiles due to their connections with important politicians and intellectuals, and the PNV's status as founding member of the NEI ultimately shifted to disillusionment with Christian Democratic party cooperation. After observing that the Europe being formed was not the Europe of peoples which they had advocated, but – at least initially – a Europe of states, the goal of the Basque leaders in exile was little more than to survive as a recognised political group. In this situation, they clung by their fingernails to the democratic and federalist organisations in which they participated.

Nonetheless, when Franco died in November 1975, the situation of the autonomous Basque government-in-exile was critical. It was not operational and the parties that formed it were more virtual than real. However, it had great symbolic value. That small government-in-exile symbolised the only legitimate Basque authority, derived as it was from the Republican legal order and the will expressed by the Basques. They had managed to keep it alive for forty years, and this helped the Basque Country regain its self-government in the new democratic Spain. On 25 October 1979, the new Statute of Autonomy was approved in a referendum by the Basque electorate, and the new autonomous Basque Government was formed.

An additional legacy from the exile years was the political discourse conceived since then. The ideas that the PNV had developed in forty years in exile have remained at the core of their political ideology and programme. In the party's National Assembly held in Pamplona in March 1977, which marked the beginning of a new stage, the PNV was presented as a Basque, democratic, popular party with mass appeal. Its political orientation remained intact, although two new elements were added: the abandonment of confessionalism and the defence of the integration of immigrants into the Basque community. Therefore, of the three distinguishing features of the 1937 PNV introduced at the beginning of this chapter, nationalism remained intact, its "Catholic" orientation in the traditional form disappeared, and the adjective "democratic" was strongly emphasised instead. At this important meeting in Pamplona, the PNV particularly stressed the democratic path of the party and the continuation of its political project. It stressed its anti-Francoist struggle in exile, as a guarantee of credibility within the new democratic environment.

The PNV has continuously declared itself strongly in favour of Europe and European integration. In fact, its programmatic and rhetorical goal remains focused on the creation of a Europe of the peoples in which the

Basque Country can participate autonomously. This approach is merely an updated form of the Aguirre Doctrine, the political project that emerged during exile. However, in practice the PNV is aware that its participation in European institutionalised forums must principally be through Spanish organisations, although the region is directly represented in the European Union's Committee of the Regions.

In the specific case of the Christian Democratic movement, the participation of the PNV in the Christian Democrat International continued until 2000. By then, the Spanish Partido Popular (PP) under the leadership of José Maria Aznar had already been in power in Spain for four years. The PP and the Spanish Socialist Party included in the preamble to their 2000 Anti-Terrorist Agreement the claim that the PNV (as well as Eusko Alkartasuna, another Basque nationalist and social democratic party) were no longer to be considered democratic parties, as a result of the pro-independence pact that they had reached two years before. This confrontation with the PNV reached the international arena when in October 2000, the PP successfully pursued the PNV's expulsion from the Christian Democrat International, now the Centrist Democrat International. The PP argued that the PNV after all had already left the European People's Party to avoid being a member of the same organisation as the PP, which had joined it in 1991. This (self-)exclusion from European and international political party organisations has had a strong psychological impact on the PNV's leaders ever since, as the party had co-shaped transnational cooperation in exile and co-founded the NEI after the Second World War.

6

A CATALAN CATHOLIC REGIONALIST FLEEING FRANCO
Josep Maria Trias Peitx's Exile in France

Gemma Caballer

On 24 January 1939, Josep Maria Trias Peitx arrived at the port of Port-Vendres, in the south of France, aboard the Sirocco, a ship belonging to the French Embassy. Trias Peitx was one of approximately 440,000 refugees who left Spain during that winter.[1] He had been a member of Unió Democràtica de Catalunya (UDC) since 1931, when he had broken with the family's political tradition of Carlism and its advocacy of a confessional state, and was the party's secretary-general during the Spanish Civil War. He worked intensely for the rescue of those persecuted for reasons of conscience during the conflict, and he also mediated between the Republican government and the Holy See to re-establish relations and to guarantee religious freedom. His trip to Port-Vendres was the beginning of an exile in France that would last until his death in August 1979. Trias Peitx called these 40 years the "Solitude of freedom".[2] Freedom had a price, and in his case, the price was solitude.

Based on fresh research in libraries and archives in Catalonia, France and the United States,[3] this chapter will explore Trias Peitx's voluntary ex-

---

1   Francesc Vilanova, *Exiliats, proscrits, deportats: el primer exili dels republicans espanyols: dels camps francesos al llindar de la deportació* (Barcelona: Empúries, cop. 2006), 69.
2   Josep Maria Trias Peitx to Maurici Serrahima, 28 August 1955, National Archive of Catalonia, Personal archive of Maurici Serrahima, Box 96. All translations from correspondence in Catalan are the author's, unless otherwise noted.
3   This study is part of the Proyecto I+D del Programa Estatal de Fomento de la Investigación Científica y Técnica de Excelencia, subprograma Estatal de Generación del Conocimiento del Ministerio de Economía y Competitividad: "La Guerra Civil española y tres décadas de guerra en Europa: herencias y consecuencias" (1914–1945/2014) (HAR2013-41460-P).

ile spanning 40 years. It draws on the literature on the history of Christian Democracy in Catalonia and Spain, and more particularly, on the history of the UDC and Trias Peitx's role in Catalan politics between 1931 and 1939.[4] It also assesses sources related to Trias Peitx's experience in exile and the history of his political party after 1939. In fact, the UDC was a very small party, and it has not attracted much attention from researchers in the Catalan historiography, especially not for the party's clandestine period. As a result, apart from brief overviews, there is no history of the UDC between 1939 and 1975. This chapter draws primarily on sources such as oral history interviews recorded in the 1970s, which also found their way into Trias Peitx's memoirs.[5] Research for this chapter has also included his private papers and those of some UDC party colleagues, as well as sources of the relief agency American Friends Service Committee (AFSC) and the French authorities.

We should begin with an important caveat. Trias Peitx's humanitarian activities and projects during 1939-44 were carried out against the backdrop of war, and as a result the documentation is fragmented and incomplete. His relations with the UDC as a clandestine party are also marked by a shortage of sources. As the academic literature dedicated to anti-Franco underground activities highlights, those who lived clandestine lives needed to keep their houses "clean" in case of a police search; in other words, much of the documentation was read and then destroyed, and as a result it is not available to researchers.[6]

This chapter will focus on two key issues of Trias Peitx's exile. The first is the difficulty he faced as a Catalan Christian Democrat during his exile in France from 1939 to 1945, by following the fortunes of two projects that he led: the Comité national catholique de secours aux réfugiés d'Espagne and the project Pour la renaissance des villages abandonnés. These two ventures provide new insights into the interaction of the Catalan Christian Democrats with the French authorities and French society before and during the Second World War, as well as the relations that they established with other religious groups, in particular the Quakers (a topic unexplored

---

4   The key study for the role played by the UDC and Trias Peitx during the Spanish Second Republic and the Spanish Civil War is: Hilari Raguer, *La Unió Democràtica de Catalunya i el seu temps: 1931-1939* (Barcelona: Publicacions de l'Abadia de Montserrat, 1976).
5   Gemma Caballer, Imma Tubella and Eduard Vinyamata, eds, *La Solitud de la llibertat: memòries de Josep M. Trias i Peitx, secretari general d'Unió Democràtica de Catalunya durant la Guerra Civil* (Sant Cugat del Vallès: Símbol, 2008).
6   Ivan Bordetas and Anna Sánchez, *L'antifranquisme oblidat: de la dissidència al comunisme revolucionari, 1953-1972* (Barcelona: Base, 2019), 14.

up to now). Furthermore, the leading role of this Catalan Christian Democrat in two humanitarian initiatives of an internationalist nature, under the auspices of groups as different as Catholics and Quakers, forged an apprenticeship that would be paramount for the establishment at the end of 1944 of the Secours catholique international. This organisation was the embryo of the present-day Secours catholique français, the main charity arm of the Catholic Church in France.[7]

The second issue is the evolution of Trias Peitx's political ideology and his relations during his exile in France with his political party, the UDC. The chapter's biographical approach will shed some light on the problems faced by the clandestine UDC and on the fragility of its relations with members like Trias Peitx who decided to remain in exile. Trias Peitx also exemplifies how the experience of exile can lead to diminishing return for political commitments that are maintained in exile. However, in the case of Trias Peitx, the causes underlying his transition from exile to emigrant were more linked to external factors – such as the party's ideological evolution and the resulting struggles for power, which moved him away from the ideological mainstream of his party – than to Trias Peitx's express desire to distance himself from the UDC. Until his death, Trias Peitx felt part of the UDC, despite the obvious ideological discrepancies.

The Catalan Christian Democrats in France: a history of mistrust

During the Spanish Civil War, the Catalan UDC members had remained faithful to the Republican government, and when Franco's army entered Barcelona, they decided to flee in order to avoid reprisals. They arrived in a country, France, where the role that they had played in Spain was not well understood.[8] Ferran Ruiz-Hébrard, a member of the Federation of Young Christians of Catalonia, expressed this clearly in a letter he sent from France after crossing the border: "Here, nobody understands us .... What a strange thing, those Catholics who flee from Franco".[9] Franco's campaign

7   Gemma Caballer, "Secours catholique international, una iniciativa catalana a França?," in Teresa Abelló, Giovanni Cattini, Víctor Gavín, Jordi Ibarz, Carles Santacana, Queralt Solé and Antoni Vives, eds, *Postguerres/Aftermaths of War* (Barcelona: Universitat de Barcelona/Ventall, 2020), 335-349.
8   See Leyre Arrieta's chapter in this volume.
9   Ferran Ruiz-Hébrard to Josep Maria Trias Peitx, 2 February 1939, Pavelló de la República CRAI Library (University of Barcelona), Personal archive of Josep Maria Trias Peitx, Box FP(Trias)3(1) bl.

to denounce the religious persecutions in the Republic-controlled parts of Spain had been reported all over the world. The Spanish Catholic Church had been practically unanimous in supporting Franco and his "national crusade". Why were these Catalan Christian Democrats fleeing at a time when Franco was winning the Civil War?

The idiosyncrasies of Catalan Christian Democracy were largely unknown in France. Javier Tusell has talked of the movement as an "environmental Christian Democracy".[10] In his view, Catalan Catholicism was "modern" in the first third of the twentieth century, in the sense of combining the principles of Catalan nationalism, political democracy and the social doctrine of the Church.[11] It dispensed with traditional clericalism and was much more open-minded than most Catholics elsewhere in Spain, with the notable exception of the Basque Country. A good example of the difference between Catalan and Spanish Catholics can be found in their distinct reactions to the fall of the monarchy. In Madrid, the more progressive Catholics, understood here as pluralist, forward-looking and favouring social reform, followed the doctrine of Leo XIII and were indifferent to the advent of the Republic, but the vast majority of Spanish Catholics were opposed to the new Republican regime. Indeed, the most extreme among them very soon began to conspire against it. In contrast, only one day after the proclamation of the Republic, on 15 April 1931, the editor of the Catalan newspaper *El Matí*[12] wrote: "We breathe with satisfaction [...]; A legitimate power has emerged [...]. Do not let this be or seem to be the regime of others. The Republic [...] must, of course, belong to all of us. Therefore, it is also ours".[13]

Why this difference? According to Hilari Raguer, in Spain the opposition between Right and Left coincided almost completely with that between Monarchy and Republic, as well as clericalism and anti-clericalism. In Catalonia, possibly due to the influence of France, neither clericalism nor anti-clericalism existed to the same extent. Rather, indifference prevailed. However, the persecution of Catalanism (a movement based on Catalan language, culture, identity and self-government) and of any kind of expression of Catalan identity under the dictatorship of José Antonio

---

10 Javier Tusell, *Historia de la democracia cristiana en España* (Madrid: Cuadernos por el diálogo, 1974), 128.

11 Isidre Molas, *El sistema de partits polítics a Catalunya, 1931-1939* (Barcelona: Edicions 62, 1972), 65.

12 *El Matí* appeared in 1929 and became the newspaper of the most open-minded sector of Catalan Catholicism.

13 "La nostra actitud," *El Matí*, 15 April 1931.

Gemma Caballer

Primo de Rivera (1923-31) had strengthened republican attitudes among Catalan Catholics, both among the clergy and the faithful. During those eight years, the dictatorship dissolved organisations like Els Pomells de Joventut, a youth organisation that promoted the Christian spirit and the purity of the Catalan language. The regime had also made it more difficult to preach in Catalan.

Through these forms of repression, Primo de Rivera's dictatorship strengthened the support for democracy and republicanism among Catalan Catholics, which led to a widening of the gulf between Catalan and Spanish Catholics generally.[14] With the exception of a very active but small fundamentalist Catholic group, Catalan Catholics were broadly liberal, something that explains the positive reception of the Republican regime reported in *El Matí*. Thus, as Raguer has emphasised, most Catalan Catholics welcomed the proclamation of the Republic and saw in the new regime the most effective way to protect Catalan liberties.

This was the background to the creation of the UDC on 7 November 1931. It was a Christian Democratic party and, above all, a Catalan nationalist party, decidedly republican and in favour of social reform. As such, it was the only specifically Christian Democratic party in Spain in the 1930s. Adopting the political language used elsewhere in Western Europe during the 1920s by groups like the short-lived Partito Popolare Italiano or the German Centre Party, its members referred to it as "a party of Catholics, but not *the* Catholic party".[15] Trias Peitx explicitly placed the non-confessional UDC in this broader Western European context: "There was the German Zentrum, which we considered to be of a strong bourgeois and capitalist character. In France there had recently been the Sillon incident, and thereafter there was the Jeune République. In Italy there was Sturzo, a Christian Democrat, but we didn't like the fact that the party was led by a priest".[16] Thus, while the UDC followed the doctrine of the Church, particularly its social doctrine, it did not maintain the characteristically close relations of confessional parties with the ecclesiastical hierarchy (as it happened, neither did the Italian priest Sturzo, who thereby incurred the Vatican's ire). Crucially, the UDC did not defend the political principles of the ecclesiastical hierarchy in exchange for electoral support. In fact, the UDC never had any relationship with the hierarchy at the level of the episcopate, the Nunciature or the Holy See, nor did it receive ecclesiastical

---

14 Hilari Raguer, *Escrits dispersos d'història* (Barcelona: Publicacions de la Presidència, 2018).
15 Raguer, *Escrits dispersos d'història*, 81.
16 Caballer, Tubella and Vinyamata, *La Solitud de la llibertat,* 74.

blessing. In fact, in Catalonia the Church never recommended voting for the UDC.

As Raguer has argued, the emergence of the UDC was thus the result of a process of evolution of Catalan Catholicism that had been seeking to free itself from what it saw as the reactionary fundamentalism widespread elsewhere in Spain, and to move towards a form of intellectual and political modernisation that allowed it to dissociate itself from the monarchist and unionist parties which for a long time had seemed to be the only political and electoral options open for all practising Catholics.[17]

In the light of these developments in the 1920s and 1930s, it is not surprising that the UDC, despite the revolutionary circumstances in the Republican area, opted to support the Republican government when the Spanish Civil War broke out in 1936. This did not prevent the party from criticising the religious persecution and uncontrolled violence unleashed on the Republican side. Due to its combination of Catholicism and Catalanism, the UDC incurred the wrath of both sides; its militants were harassed by the Republicans, while one of its main leaders, Manuel Carrasco i Formiguera, was shot in Burgos by the Franco authorities.[18] Although Franco's military uprising had no religious motivation, within days religion had become an important factor in the war, and in the areas where the insurgents failed to gain control, religious persecution began almost instantly. In this revolutionary context, the majority of Spanish bishops supported the Francoists in a war that they termed a "crusade", and Franco made clever use of these religious overtures for the propaganda war he waged within Spain and abroad.[19]

The most significant actions carried out by Trias Peitx within the UDC took place during the Spanish Civil War and were related to the aid, protection and rescue of people persecuted for reasons of conscience within the Republican zone, actions described as heroic by the historian Hilari Raguer.[20] Trias Peitx also stood out under the orders of the Minister of Justice Manuel de Irujo – of the Basque Nationalist Party – for his efforts to re-establish the cult in the Republican zone, as well as his attempts to re-establish diplomatic relations between the Republic and the Holy See. Trias Peitx and his UDC colleagues played a prominent role during the

---

17 Raguer, *La Unió Democràtica de Catalunya i el seu temps*, 80.
18 Astrid Barrio López, "Les arrels de Convergència Democràtica de Catalunya," in Joan B. Culla i Clarà, ed, *El pal de paller: Convergència Democràtica de Catalunya, 1974-2000* (Barcelona: Pòrtic, 2001), 13-39, at 20.
19 Raguer, *Escrits dispersos d'història*, 174.
20 Raguer, *La Unió Democràtica de Catalunya i el seu temps*, 393.

Spanish Civil War in attempting to control the arbitrary acts, murders and other violence perpetrated against the Catholic Church, which Francoist propaganda used to try to project a uniform view of a "red" Spain.

The success of that propaganda largely explains why, upon their arrival in France, Ruiz-Hébrard and others were surprised that no one there understood why Catalan Catholics were actually fleeing from Franco. The news that reached French Catholics concerning the murdered priests and the burned-down churches caused great indignation, and it seemed impossible that there could be Spanish Catholics who had fought beside the "reds".[21] René Rémond has stated that, initially, all French Catholics manifested such a right-wing reaction.[22] Little by little, however, discordant voices began to be heard, such as exiles from fascist Italy like Sturzo or, later, Jacques Maritain. Maritain was not the only French Catholic who criticised the "crusade", but he was the most prominent and influential among those Catholic critics; he managed to mobilise considerable support but also attracted criticism for his moderate position. As Maurice Duverger has argued, to be for or against Franco became a dividing line between the Right and the Left in French politics for years to come.[23]

Humanitarian work in France, 1939-45

In addition to widespread ignorance of the political situation in Catalonia, there was a deep general mistrust of refugees in France. More generally, French society was divided between those who defended the right of Spanish refugees to asylum at any cost and, on the other hand, those who demanded a policy of immediate repatriation. France had many domestic problems – national security, the economy and the state of maintaining public order in a deeply divided society – and so refugees were not a priority. In fact, France in 1939 teetered on the edge of a precipice: the electoral victory of the Popular Front in March 1936 had increased unrest among conservatives, and at the same time, it had no forceful response to the aggressive foreign policy of Nazi Germany. Surrounded by three fascist re-

---

21 Hilari Raguer, "Maritain i la guerra d'Espanya," *Qüestions de vida cristiana,* no. 67 (1973): 111-125, at 112.

22 René Rémond with Aline Coutrot, *Les catholiques, le communisme et les crises, 1929-1939* (Paris: A. Colin, 1961).

23 Maurice Duverger, *Cours de vie politique, en France et à l'étranger: rédigé d'après les notes et avec l'autorisation de M. Maurice Duverger, ... Diplôme d'études supérieures de science politique 1956-1957* (Paris: Les Cours de droit, 1957).

gimes – Germany, Italy and now Spain – the French government was keen to generate as little conflict as possible in its response to the Spanish refugee crisis.[24] Moreover, the Third Republic officially recognised Franco's Nationalist government on 26 February 1939 pursuant to the Bérard-Jordana Accords. As Jordi Guixé has pointed out, "with these pacts, France sealed the fate of the Spanish Second Republic".[25] From that moment on, events accelerated, and the consequences of the pact for the Spanish exiles were profound: they were *personae non gratae* both in their homeland and in the country where they sought refuge. As the title of Francesc Vilanova's study reflects, the Spanish exiles were "entre la espada y la pared": that is, between the devil and the deep blue sea.[26]

Amidst these adverse circumstances, two internationalist humanitarian projects practically unknown to this day were launched – one led by Catholics, the other by Protestants. Trias Peitx played a leading role in both. The first began in February 1939. With the support of the French ecclesiastical hierarchy, Trias Peitx and other exiled members of the UDC set up the Comité national catholique de secours aux réfugiés d'Espagne, under the umbrella of the Comité national catholique de secours aux Basques, founded in 1937. This committee had the same honorary presidents – Cardinal Jean Verdier and Maurice Feltin, Archbishops of Paris and Bordeaux respectively – and the same president, Clément Joseph Mathieu, Bishop of Aire and Dax. Beyond the ecclesiastical hierarchy, the Committee also received the support of French Catholic intellectuals like François Mauriac, Jacques Maritain and Marc Sangnier.[27] It was organised by two UDC members – Trias Peitx and Maurici Serrahima – and the president of the Federation of Young Christians of Catalonia, Ferran Ruiz-Hébrard, with three objectives in mind.[28] Firstly, it sought to re-unite Spanish families who had been separated by the French authorities after crossing the

24 Francesc Vilanova, "Entre la espada y la pared: el franquismo, la III República Francesa y los exiliados republicanos en 1939-1940," in Abdón Mateos, ed, *¡Ay de los vencidos!: el exilio y los países de acogida* (Madrid: Eneida, 2009), 13-40.

25 Jordi Guixé Coromines, *La República perseguida: exilio y represión en la Francia de Franco, 1937-1951* (València: Universitat de València, 2012), 88.

26 Vilanova, "Entre la espada y la pared," in Mateos, *¡Ay de los vencidos!*, 13-40.

27 The names of François Mauriac and Jacques Maritain appear on the official stationary of the Committee. Marc Sangnier, who during the war had been vice-president of the Comité d'action pour la paix en Espagne (with links to international circles sympathetic to the Republic) would host Catalan intellectuals and UDC politicians such as Pau Romeva at the Bierville castle near Paris.

28 The writer and politician Maurici Serrahima (1902-1979) and Ferran Ruiz-Hébrard (1903-1984) arrived in France on board the Sirocco with Josep Maria Trias Peitx on 24 January, 1939, but their exile was shorter: both returned to Spain in 1940.

Gemma Caballer

frontier. Working with a list of more than 150,000 names, by June 1939 the committee had managed to bring together more than a thousand refugee families. Secondly, the committee worked to relocate children living in camps into colonies with better accommodation and living conditions.

The committee's final goal was to organise work contracts for the Spanish internees which would allow them to leave the camps. This step marked the origins of the Labour Service, of which Trias Peitx became the director. On the eve of the Second World War, as more and more French nationals were mobilised, the refugees began to be seen as a pool for filling jobs that fell vacant as the French were enlisted. Thus, the committee established close relations with French businesses, and in the different refugee camps they organised a system of practical tests and exams to ensure that jobs were offered to people with suitable professional qualifications. As time passed, French companies were more prepared to take on former UDC militants and sympathisers on seeing that they could be trusted and that they did not associate with the anarchists and communists who had also fled Spain.[29] The committee's extreme caution in its role in finding jobs for its members is also strongly reflected in its correspondence. Its letters often include exhortations not to "send a bandit" or requests to "send me information about very trustworthy people".[30]

The committee operated between February 1939 and June 1940, when it ran out of funds. It is estimated that, due to its work, 26,350 Spaniards received work contracts and were able to leave the camps.[31] The committee's work proved useful for the French economy, but it remained hampered by the continued suspicion among French authorities that it had "red" political leanings, despite its links with members of the French Church hierarchy. Those who worked for the committee continually complained of interference from the French civilian and military authorities: difficulties in obtaining safe-conduct documents,[32] pressure to return refugees to Spain, or threats to force Spanish refugees to work in camps or

29 Gemma Caballer and Queralt Solé, "El Comitè Nacional Catòlic de Socors als Refugiats d'Espanya, una aproximació," in *Catalans du Nord et languedociens et l'aide à la République Espagnole, 1936-1946: actes de la Journée d'études de l'Association Maitron Languedoc-Roussillon...* (Perpignan: Presses universitaires de Perpignan, 2009), 109-134, at 124.
30 Josep Maria Trias Peitx to Joan Sabaté, 15 June 1939, Pavelló de la República CRAI Library (UB), Personal archive of Josep Maria Trias Peitx, Box FP(Trias)3(1)bI; Josep Maria Trias Peitx to the Committee, 30 August 1939, Pavelló de la República CRAI Library (UB), Personal archive of Josep Maria Trias Peitx, Box FP(Trias)3(1)bI.
31 Josep Maria Trias Peitx, Report [June 1940], Pavelló de la República CRAI Library (UB), Personal archive of Josep Maria Trias Peitx, Box FP(Trias)3(1)c(21).
32 Ferran Ruiz-Hébrard to Josep Maria Trias Peitx, 8 March 1939, Pavelló de la República CRAI Library (UB), Personal archive of Josep Maria Trias Peitx, Box FP(Trias)3(1)aI.

to send them to the colonies.[33] Indeed, to quote Guixé, "the French Sûreté Nationale closely surveyed and controlled the Spanish refugees".[34]

The second initiative in which Trias Peitx played a leading role was Pour la renaissance des villages abandonnés (For the Rebirth of Abandoned Villages). This was actually a Quaker-supported project that began in late 1940 and ended in 1944. The collaboration started in the French refugee camps, where Trias Peitx worked closely with the Quakers as the head of the committee's Labour Service. The Quakers played a very important role in refugee camps in southern France, and they maintained strong relationships with all kinds of humanitarian organisations.

Thus, the fact that Trias Peitx was a Catholic was not a problem and did not prevent him from becoming supervisor of the project Pour la renaissance des villages abandonnés and Delegate Manager of the SÉCAL (Société d'études et de coopération artisanale Lorraine), the organisation in charge of managing the instructions for production sent out to villages.[35] This ambitious plan aimed to repopulate semi-abandoned villages in France with displaced people from Alsace-Lorraine, but Spanish refugees also participated. People from Alsace-Lorraine were chosen for the project because of the vast numbers of refugees from that area: it is estimated that, during the so-called "phoney war" of 1939-40, the French government evacuated half a million people from that border region to the south and west of France. Following the armistice and the annexation of Alsace-Lorraine by Nazi Germany, many of these evacuees saw no hope of returning to their homes. The French authorities were especially generous towards refugees from Alsace-Lorraine – a reaction which, as Frédérique Barbara has suggested, may have reflected collective feelings of guilt regarding the fate of this refugee group.[36]

The two villages that were repopulated – Puycelsi and Penne – were situated in the Tarn Department, near a forest that would provide wood. The aim of the project was to start a furniture industry in Puycelsi and a wooden toy industry in Penne. The initiative began in the free zone of France but continued after the Nazis responded to the Allied landing in

33 Lluís Trias Peitx to Josep Maria Trias Peitx, 4 August 1939, Pavelló de la República CRAI Library (UB), Personal archive of Josep Maria Trias Peitx, Box FP(Trias)3(1)bI.

34 Guixé Coromines, *La República perseguida*, 133.

35 Alice Resch, *Over the Highest Mountains: a Memoir of Unexpected Heroism in France during World War II* (Pasadena, Calif.: International Productions, 2005), 90; Rapport du Gérant Délégué, 26 June 1943, American Friends Service Committee Archive, Box 30, Folder 33, 53-65.

36 Frédérique Barbara, *Les populations réfugiés dans le Tarn pendant la seconde guerre mondiale*, mémoire de maîtrise (Toulouse: Université de Toulouse Le Mirail, 1990), 65.

Gemma Caballer

North Africa by taking over the whole of the country in November 1942. In both periods, relations with the authorities and with the inhabitants of the zone were difficult: many locals were wary of the plan, and the local authorities were obstructive, both economically and administratively. Despite the expressly apolitical nature of the Quakers' activities, the French authorities and many inhabitants were suspicious of their intentions; their reticence towards the Quakers was exacerbated by the presence of Spaniards. Howard E. Kershner, who coordinated the Quaker aid, later observed in his memoirs that "any organization engaged in helping Spaniards was looked upon with suspicion".[37]

Moreover, Trias Peitx and the Quakers also had to face the problem of lobbying by the radical Right at the local level. As Javier Cervera has pointed-ed out, pro-Nazi or pro-fascist French organisations and groups provided information to the local authorities not just about Jews, but also about people and groups whom they considered to be leftists or "Spanish reds".[38] This also occurred in Puycelsi: one of the reports from members of the Légion française des combattants, sent to the Prefect of the Tarn Department and dated 19 May 1943, described the Quakers as a "sect" and their activities as "sinister".[39] The report defined Trias Peitx as a "communist" and alleged that he was romantically involved with (not married to) Clara Candiani, daughter of Pierre Mille, a well-known writer and journalist with left-wing political views, when he had in fact married her in 1939. Thus, the French authorities and radical Right organisations continued to make the lives of Trias Peitx and the Quakers difficult even though their activities were clearly well-intentioned and arguably had positive effects not just for the refugees, but for the local French population as well.

The balance of the two initiatives was clearly positive. At the head of the Labour Service of the Committee, 26,350 Spanish refugees were able to leave the camps to be integrated into the French economy, thus avoiding compulsory repatriation to Franco's Spain or conscription into the French Foreign Workers' Companies (or subsequent Foreign Workers' Groups), or deportation to the colonies. Leading the project "Pour la renaissance des villages abandonnés", he gave to refugees of different nationalities a chance to start a new life in war-torn France: Puycelsi tripled its population during this period, and Penne doubled in size. Meanwhile, little

37 Howard E. Kershner, *Quaker Service in Modern War: Spain and France, 1939-1940* (New York: Prentice-Hall, cop. 1950), 176.
38 Javier Cervera, "De Vichy a la liberación," in Mateos, *¡Ay de los vencidos!*, 41-70, at 49.
39 Légion française des combattants, Report, 19 May 1943, Archives départementales du Tarn, Fonds du Cabinet du préfet, File 506 W 179.

more than 250 kilometres from these two towns, 50,000 Spaniards were interned in the Rivesaltes camp in the summer of 1940; two years later, the deportation of Jews began from that same camp. In spite of all these difficulties, between 1941 and 1944, the initiative of Trias Peitx and the Quakers created a small oasis in the middle of the Second World War. Furthermore, the learning process in these two initiatives served as the basis for the formation of the Secours catholique international in 1944, an organisation that was born with the goal of growing into an international Catholic charity that would facilitate global Catholic collaboration in the service of postwar reconstruction, both material and spiritual.[40]

Trias Peitx and the UDC: exile versus clandestine activity

When the Second World War ended, Trias Peitx decided not to return to Catalonia. He continued his life in Paris with his wife, where he founded the teaching movement Le Musée à l'École and edited the *L'Amour de l'art* magazine. He launched businesses linked to the world of discography and was one of the founders of the Association des journalistes pour l'information sur le développement (vaincre la faim). Moreover, from the middle of the 1960s until his death in 1979, he held the position of Technical Adviser of the Comité Français pour la Campagne Mondiale contre la Faim, which promoted efficient protein consumption in the Third World.[41]

Trias Peitx also worked on projects directly related to Catalonia, including his project for the creation of a Universitat Lliure Mediterrània Ramon Llull. He hoped to organise a university based in France but of a Catalan, European, Mediterranean and above all international profile, with close contacts with the countries of the Arab Mediterranean. In the early 1970s, he believed that the importance of Arab countries and hence of learning Arabic would grow very fast: "In 10 years' time [...] you will have to know Arabic, like today, French, English or Spanish, and it will probably be more useful for you than Russian or Chinese [...]. What I am proposing", Trias Peitx continued, "is that we, Catalans, address this neglect with a bold

---

40 Caballer, "Secours catholique international, una iniciativa catalana a França?," 335-349.
41 Queralt Solé and Gemma Caballer, "Aproximación biográfica a Josep Maria Trias Peitx (Barcelona, 1900 - Prada de Conflent, 1979): un hombre de Unió Democràtica de Catalunya (UDC) clave para el exilio republicano en los campos de internamiento franceses," *Pasado y memoria: revista de historia contemporánea*, no. 12 (2013): 163-178, at 176.

initiative".[42] However, despite establishing contact with influential Catalan and French leaders, Trias Peitx's university project eventually came to nothing.

Throughout his life in exile, full of projects and activities, the correspondence with his friend and party colleague Maurici Serrahima reveals that his close emotional identification with Catalonia never waned. In 1955 he complained, "Give me news of yours, of your wife, whom I remember [...] ... and of our friends. I am living in a chilling silence of voices of my homeland".[43] In spite of his attempts to keep himself informed of developments in Catalonia and to participate in projects from the outside, he was unable to maintain close relations with people who had stayed in or returned to Spain. From the late 1940s onwards it was difficult to re-establish contacts with former UDC party colleagues who were still alive. During the Civil War and the early stages of exile, some leading UDC members had come to dislike Trias Peitx, criticising him for trying to dominate the party and usurping powers for himself as its General Secretary during the Spanish Civil War. Joan Baptista Roca i Caball, for instance, a co-founder of the UDC who returned to Spain in 1942 and then participated in the party's clandestine reconstruction, and Miquel Coll i Alentorn, who had joined the UDC in 1932 and much later became president of the Parliament of Catalonia after the transition to democracy, both attacked Trias Peitx for adopting a form of personal rule in the party.

During the war Trias Peitx also began to work as an intermediary between the Basque Catholics, especially the Basque minister in the Republican government, Manuel de Irujo, and the Church hierarchy. Trias Peitx worked to save individuals in danger and to arrange the exchange of hostages. At the same time, through the Archbishop of Paris, Cardinal Jean Verdier, he helped to set up informal diplomatic relations between the Holy See and the Republican government. However, Irujo put an end to Trias Peitx's diplomatic role as he believed that the Catalan UDC politician had overstepped his role as a mere intermediary.[44]

Similarly, when he left Spain in January 1939, some of Trias Peitx's activities in the Comité national catholique de secours aux réfugiés d'Espagne had a markedly political character. Other UDC colleagues in exile

---

42 Report "Per la fondació [sic] d'una Universitat Lliure Mediterrania Raymond Llull: missatge als catalans", [circa 1970], Pavelló de la República CRAI Library (UB), Personal archive of Josep Maria Trias Peitx, Box FP(Trias)2(1)cI(1).

43 Josep Maria Trias Peitx to Maurici Serrahima, 31 July 1955, National Archive of Catalonia, Personal archive of Maurici Serrahima, Box 96.

44 Raguer, *La Unió Democràtica de Catalunya i el seu temps*, 497.

disapproved, as they had decided that Pau Romeva should instead take the lead in establishing political relations in exile; Romeva, a Catalan educator, writer and politician was after all the only UDC member who had been a member of the Catalan parliament.[45] Finally, Trias Peitx's marriage to Clara Candiani, a left-wing journalist working for *La Dépêche* and a divorcee and single mother, did little to endear him to the socially conservative UDC members.

Trias Peitx's initial decision to remain in France, added to all the preceding factors, contributed to create a huge barrier for cooperation with other party members who returned to Spain upon receiving guarantees that they would not be imprisoned. To a large extent thanks to his marriage, unlike many other exiles Trias Peitx was able to restart his professional and social life in France. After the end of the Second World War, it became clear that the Franco regime would not collapse as fascist Italy and Nazi Germany had done; in fact, the dictatorship consolidated power and subsequently overcame its international isolation. The Franco regime eliminated the use of fascist rhetoric but remained totalitarian in character; in this situation, Trias Peitx preferred to remain in exile in France.

Additionally, the changing dynamics within the party in Catalonia also sped the rupture between Trias Peitx and other UDC members. The Law of Political Responsibilities of 9 February 1939, which forbade political activity, explicitly included the UDC among the 23 prohibited parties and organisations, and the party's clandestine activities thereafter were ridden with difficulties. The UDC leaders Miquel Coll i Alentorn, Joan B. Roca i Caball, Pau Romeva and Maurici Serrahima had to reorganise the party in order to secure its survival in Franco's Spain. With the return of the exiled leaders, party activities started once more in 1942, but were aimed mainly at strengthening cultural resistance to the Franco regime. In the 1950s, the UDC became more active, and an internal debate eventually generated two currents within the party. The majority, led by Miquel Coll i Alentorn and Anton Cañellas, supported Jacques Maritain's notion of integral humanism and advocated more prudent clandestine action. Meanwhile, Maurici Serrahima and Josep Benet favoured more active opposition and, advocating Emmanuel Mounier's personalism, considered the strategic option of establishing contacts with non-Christians, even to the extent of "breaking the taboo of non-cooperation with communists".[46] As Joan B.

---

45 Vilanova, *Exiliats, proscrits, deportats*, 69.
46 Oriol Olivé, "Unió Democràtica de Catalunya durant el franquisme," *Diàlegs* no. 32-33 (April-September 2006): 53-66, at 59.

Culla has shown, all these disagreements placed Benet and Serrahima on the margins of the party.[47]

Trias Peitx's relations with the clandestine UDC were affected by its internal divisions within Catalonia. Trias Peitx had close ties with Serrahima, which made his position in exile even more peripheral. Moreover, he received young sympathisers in Paris who were keen to know his views on the situation in Catalonia. One of those was in fact Benet, who subsequently opposed the party's more conservative wing in his attempt to play a central role in the party.[48] The leaders of the UDC majority, Coll and Roca, were suspicious of Trias Peitx's links with Serrahima and Benet. The wounds from this internal conflict remained open, and Trias Peitx was never again able to play a central role in his party from his exile in France. However, despite the fact that being relegated to the fringes for the UDC had a negative influence on his political activity, with his biography coming to resemble that of an emigrant rather than an exile, Trias Peitx continued to work and collaborate with anyone who asked for his help in highlighting – from exile – the repression faced by Catalonia.

When Trias Peitx did play a leading role in a major project in exile, it was in fact thanks to the much younger Benet. In July 1960 they created the Comité de défense du Dr. Pujol et des catholiques persécutés de Barcelone in France, which organised a solidarity movement that emerged following the court-martial of Jordi Pujol i Soley, later to be leader of the Convergència Democràtica de Catalunya from 1974 to 2003, and Francesc Pizón, following the Fets del Palau. At this festival, the singing of the Catalan poet Joan Maragall's *El cant de la Senyera* by some of the audience in the presence of Francoist ministers led to severe reprisals, including the prosecution of Pujol, who had organised the festival.

The subsequent trial triggered a strong solidarity movement in support of the prisoners, both within Catalonia and throughout the Catalan communities in exile, and Benet asked Trias Peitx to organise it from Paris. The committee sent circulars to key politicians and intellectuals in France, including François Mauriac and Robert Schuman, to inform them of the suffering of Spanish Catholics under the Franco regime.[49] The creation of this committee generated a strong reaction in Spain, where the journalist

---

47 Joan B. Culla i Clarà, *Unió Democràtica de Catalunya: el llarg camí, 1931-2001* (Barcelona: Unió Democràtica de Catalunya, 2002), 22.

48 Jordi Amat, *Com una pàtria: vida de Josep Benet* (Barcelona: Edicions 62, 2017), 251.

49 Leaflet from the Comité de défense du Dr. Jordi Pujol et des catholiques persécutés de Barcelone, 1960, Pavelló de la República CRAI Library (UB), Personal archive of Josep Maria Trias Peitx, Box FP(Trias)4(1)cI(3).

José Ricart Torrens published an aggressive article in *Arriba* (the ideological organ of the fascist movement Falange Española de las JONS)[50] which was fiercely critical of the initiative.[51] The article sparked a great deal of controversy, so that Trias Peitx translated it into French and circulated it in France with the aim of further internationalising the conflict.[52] He also maintained correspondence on the subject with Josep Maria Batista i Roca, another Catalan politician in exile, head of the Consell Nacional Català established in London. In a letter to Trias Peitx, Batista i Roca stressed that "it is a good tactic to highlight the Catholicism of all these young people to help undo the great lie of Franco's 'Crusade' fighting only against the communist opposition".[53] These words by Batista i Roca highlight a particularly relevant aspect: with the consolidation of Francoism, a confessional state was being established, where once again the Christian Democrat elements of the UDC were to be marginalised and persecuted.

The common denominator of this repression – marked, for example, by the tragic fate of the UDC member Carrasco i Formiguera, shot in Burgos by the Franco authorities – was Trias Peitx's defence of the culture and freedoms of Catalonia. The persecution of any kind of manifestation of Catalan culture and identity was one of the pillars of Franco's regime – and not only the fight against the communist opposition, as regime propaganda was keen to suggest.[54] For many Catalan exiles of different political tendencies, highlighting this reality and defending the freedoms wrested away from Catalonia became the driving force behind their exile. At this point, we can establish a certain parallel with the Basque nationalists and their demands for a free Basque Country – a central concept of the Aguirre Doctrine – although in the case of the Catalan Christian Democrats this demand could not be articulated as early as in the Basque case, nor did the Catalans have the backing of a strong political party, aspects that adversely influenced their efforts.[55]

50 Spanish fascist party, founded in February 1934.
51 Amat, *Com una pàtria*, 237.
52 The Personal archive of Josep Maria Trias Peitx contains many typed copies of the article in French, as well as lists of the people to whom he sent the translation.
53 Josep Maria Batista i Roca to Josep Maria Trias Peitx, 19 June 1960, Pavelló de la República CRAI Library (UB), Personal archive of Josep Maria Trias Peitx, Box FP(Trias)4(1)aII.
54 Josep Benet, *L'intent franquista de genocidi cultural contra Catalunya* (Barcelona: Publicacions de l'Abadia de Montserrat, 1995).
55 See Leyre Arrieta's chapter in this volume.

The 1976 UDC Congress: the voice of the homeland from exile

On 20 November 1975, Franco died, leaving Spain to face an unclear future. The political parties took advantage of the resulting uncertainty and quickly established their positions in the new scenario. On 12 June 1976 in Barcelona, the UDC held the first congress of any Catalan political party since the Spanish Civil War. At what it counted as its fifth congress, the UDC sought to develop a structure and programme for the forthcoming legalisation of political parties. Although the party's statutes established that only delegates could attend congresses, in this exceptional case all members were invited to participate.

Trias Peitx was also invited to the congress, but he remained faithful to his promise only to return to Catalonia when the Generalitat, the highest governing body of Catalonia, had been re-established following the re-enactment of the 1932 Statute of Autonomy. Trias Peitx sent a long speech to the congress, however, which began with the words, "I bring to the congress the voice of the homeland from exile". In his speech he focused on the political situation in Spain, the internationalisation of Catalonia, the role of Barcelona as its capital for Catalonia's projection abroad, the challenge of integrating immigrants and the question of freedom of association.[56]

Beyond reflecting on these general problems, Trias Peitx was especially concerned about the definition of the UDC as a Christian Democratic party. In his speech, after recalling the UDC's founding reference points – movements such as the Jeune République of Marc Sangnier, or Italy's Partito Popolare – he opposed the UDC's new Declaration of Principles, which he considered to be too conservative. In his opinion, Christian Democracy was in decline in Europe because of what he regarded as its confessionalism and connivance with the Catholic hierarchy. Trias Peitx was especially critical of the strong opposition of the Church to the western Communist parties. Pointing to the example of the Italian Eurocommunists, he claimed that the Italian Catholic hierarchy's opposition to it "accentuates the decline of Italian Christian Democracy". Trias Peitx claimed that the Church's structures were anachronistic, that it sought merely to preserve its prerogatives, and that it was necessary for "the poorest and most religious popular masses to abandon the bosom of the Church if they wish to follow

---

56   Report "Intervenció d'en Josep Maria Trias Peitx al Ve. Congrés d'Unió Democràtica de Catalunya," June 1976, Pavelló de la República CRAI Library (UB), Personal archive of Josep Maria Trias Peitx, Box FP(Trias)4(1)dII(1).

the path of better collective well-being". He concluded: "Today, Christian Democracy is the most conservative democratic political force in Europe".

Consequently, Trias Peitx believed that the UDC should not define itself as a Christian Democratic party nor that it should associate forms of Spanish Christian Democracy centred on Madrid. However, with these views, especially the notion of rapprochement with the Left (including the communists) Trias Peitx once more found himself in an ideological limbo, opposed to the clear majority in the UDC. As Barberà has pointed out, the UDC's main challenge at its 1976 Congress was precisely to define what role it would play in Spanish politics. Most members strongly favoured cooperation with what they hoped would be a strong Christian Democratic political force at the national Spanish level.[57] The minority in the UDC subscribed to the approach of the Basque Nationalist Party: to focus on Catalan politics, and not to prioritise participation in Spanish politics. Trias Peitx personally went so far as to affirm the total independence of the Catalan parties from those of Madrid. In his memoirs, put together with the help of interviews conducted in Paris between 1973 and 1976, he concluded, "If I were to come to Barcelona now, I could not be a member of Unió Democràtica de Catalunya. I would have to be from far beyond".[58] He kept his promise and did not return to Catalonia. He died on 7 August 1979 in Prades, in France – paradoxically, on the day of the agreement on the Statute of Catalonia, which paved the way for the restoration of Catalan autonomy.

Conclusion

As the historian Josep Maria Figueres has put it, from 1931 to 1975 the UDC and Trias Peitx navigated between resisting the anti-clerical tendencies of anarchism, republicanism and later, totalitarianism as well.[59] Following Trias Peitx's exile in January 1939, we can identify two different periods. The first lasted from 1939 to 1945, when he, a Catalan Christian Democrat living in exile in France, embraced humanitarian work in spite of the prevailing socio-economic and political circumstances that became

---

57 Òscar Barberà, *Unió Democràtica de Catalunya (1976-1978): CiU-El pacte amb Convergència Democràtica de Catalunya* (Barcelona: Mediterrània, 2000), 52.
58 Caballer, Tubella and Vinyamata, *La Solitud de la llibertat*, 81.
59 Josep M. Figueres Artigues, "Hilari Raguer, historiador," in Raguer, *Escrits dispersos d'història*, 17-27, at 20.

increasingly hostile during the Second World War.[60] The second period began in 1945 and lasted until his death in 1979.

The two humanitarian aid initiatives to help refugees that he headed from 1939 to 1945, to which we can add his role as ideological force behind the genesis of the Secours catholique international, highlights "one of the major interpretative problems that face the historian of refugee movements, for they imply that the status of a person as forced migrant, evacuee or refugee may well depend more on their attitude of mind and their decision-making capacity – their inner world – than on their classification by state administrative bodies".[61] Trias Peitx was a refugee in France, a politician in exile who was in a much better position than the hundreds of thousands of anonymous refugees who arrived in the country, but it is clear that his main objective in January 1939 was to work – together with his wife, Clara Candiani – to help the other refugees who were not in such a privileged situation. This made the first period of his exile different, and also led to the emergence of the leader described by Phryné Pigenet: "Derrière sa personnalité exubérante, Trias Peitx révèle des grandes qualités d'organisateur et de meneur d'homme".[62]

After the war he settled in Paris and started a new life, but always tried to remain in touch with his party and with Catalonia. Increasingly, however, it proved difficult to keep up relations with the clandestine UDC. Initially, the UDC's activities were very much limited by the political repression after the war and the lack of freedom of speech and political organisation.[63] Moreover, the deep internal conflicts in the UDC affected Trias Peitx's activities in exile: the fact that his contacts in the party were mainly among the minority on the Left marginalised him still further.

Although the archival sources consulted for this chapter have revealed much about Trias Peitx's activities in France and his links with UDC members who remained in Spain or returned there, they shed little light on his contacts with French politicians and parties. It appears that these links were not especially significant. This is noteworthy because Astrid Bar-

60 Tusell, *Historia de la democracia crisitiana en España*, 149. According to Tusell, social concerns were a very important part of the UDC programme, so it is natural that Trias Peitx, as one of its main representatives, should have focused on humanitarian work during those years.

61 Sharif Gemie, Fiona Reid and Laure Humbert, with Louise Ingram, *Outcast Europe: Refugees and Relief Workers in an Era of Total War, 1936-48* (London and New York: Continuum 2012), 6.

62 Phryné Pigenet, *Les catalans espagnols en France au XXème siècle: exil et identités à l'épreuve du temps*. PhD Thesis (Paris: Université de Paris Ouest La Défense – Laboratoire IDHE, 2014), 191.

63 Natalia Urigüen López de Sandaliano, *A imagen y semejaza: la democracia cristiana alemana y su aportación a la Transición Española* (Madrid: Consejo Superior de Investigaciones Científicas, 2018), 119.

rio has claimed that "one of the most characteristic aspects of the UDC throughout the years of Franco's regime was the richness of its international contacts resulting from its affiliation to Christian Democracy, one of the strongest ideological currents after the Second World War".[64] Indeed, the UDC soon established contacts with other European parties and, from 1951 onwards, repeatedly applied to join the Nouvelles Équipes Internationales (NEI).[65]

From the freedom of his exile in France, Trias Peitx could potentially have played a key role in these relations, as the French Mouvement Républicain Populaire played a leading role in transnational networks at least until 1958. It may be, however, that Trias Peitx's role in the internal party strife meant that the UDC leadership did not take advantage of his contacts.[66] It is also plausible that his marriage with Candiani, linked to the political Left in France, shaped his contacts and networks in Paris after 1945; according to Jaume Lorés, the UDC leadership regarded Trias Peitx "exiled and in permanent contact with the French Catholic Left, with suspicion".[67] This caution attributed to his party may help us to understand the paltry political gain that the UDC obtained from Trias Peitx during his exile, an assessment that may lead us to consider him more an emigrant than an exile.

And yet, this was never Trias Peitx's perception of his situation. Trias Peitx felt alienated from the party against his will, but he carried out the actions of a political exile when demanded. He continued to think of himself like an exile, as is clear, for example, in the words with which he began his participation in the 1976 UDC congress: "I bring to the congress the voice of the homeland from exile". These conflicts in turn may well have strengthened his critical attitude to European Christian Democracy as expressed in his speech sent to the 1976 UDC congress and in his memoirs. In any case, although Trias Peitx still felt part of the UDC community until the end of his life, by the 1970s his political thinking had undergone a

---

64 Barrio López, "Les arrels de Convergència Democràtica de Catalunya," 22.
65 The UDC was not accepted because Spain already had a representative, the Basque Nationalist Party. The UDC would be finally integrated in December 1965, when the NEI became the European Union of Christian Democrats.
66 For more on the UDC's relations with European Christian Democracy, see Miquel Coll i Alentorn, *Escrits polítics, cívics i religiosos* (Barcelona: Curial Edicions Catalanes/Publicacions de l'Abadia de Montserrat, 1993), 103-107.
67 Jaume Lorés, "Aproximació al pujolisme," *Taula de canvi*, no. 23-24 (September-December 1980): 5-37, at 11.

Gemma Caballer

shift to the left which could not easily be reconciled with the majority view either in the UDC or in the broader context of western European Christian Democracy.

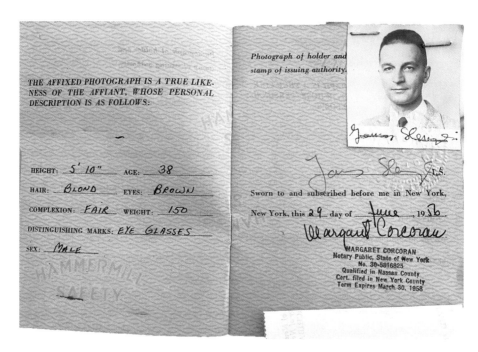

THE AFFIXED PHOTOGRAPH IS A TRUE LIKE-
NESS OF THE AFFIANT, WHOSE PERSONAL
DESCRIPTION IS AS FOLLOWS:

HEIGHT: 5' 10"   AGE: 38

HAIR: BLOND   EYES: BROWN

COMPLEXION: FAIR   WEIGHT: 150

DISTINGUISHING MARKS: EYE GLASSES

SEX: MALE

Photograph of holder and
stamp of issuing authority.

Sworn to and subscribed before me in New York,

New York, this 29 day of June 19 56

MARGARET CORCORAN
Notary Public, State of New York
No. 30-5816825
Qualified in Nassau County
Cert. filed in New York County
Term Expires March 30, 1958

Janusz Śleszyński's United States-issued Affidavit of Nationality dated 29 June 1956.
[Document in the possession of the Sleszynski family and reproduced with permission]

SECTION III

EXILES FROM EAST-CENTRAL EUROPE IN WESTERN EUROPE AND THE AMERICAS 1944-1989

7

POLISH CHRISTIAN YOUTH IN THE COLD WAR
A Generation's Potential Lost in Exile

Sławomir Łukasiewicz

Without an influx of young activists, a political party will sooner or later start losing its potential and its position. One of the mechanisms that allows a political party to retain its freshness and periodically revive its political capacity is to create and maintain so-called youth wings. A study carried out in the years 1960 to 1989 showed clearly that, among the organisations affiliated with European political parties, the largest numbers of members were found in those that brought together young people and women.[1] Youth organisations, in which the age criterion applies, by default perform auxiliary political functions,[2] yet they have a wider range of roles to play. They are an area of competition between parties, they reinforce socialisation processes, they help in recruiting future leaders and party experts, and they allow for staff substitution, especially of the leaders.[3]

This state of affairs is confirmed by research concerning young Polish Christian Democrats, who are the subject of this chapter. Although Christian Democracy is a political formation whose roots go back to the late nineteenth century, the emigration wave across Europe and the Cold War divide emerging in the wake of World War II led to the emergence of completely new types of activism by Christian Democratic youth wings. Operating under conditions of exile, the Christian Democratic youth organisations had to adapt to three political systems: a system in their native

---

1   Thomas Poguntke, "Political parties and other organizations," in Richard S. Katz and William Crotty, eds, *Handbook of Party Politics* (Los Angeles and London: Sage, 2014), 396-405, at 400.
2   Knut Heidar, "Party membership and participation," in Katz and Crotty, *Handbook of Party Politics*, 301-315, at 303.
3   Piotr Prokop, "Analiza działalności i rozwoju polskich młodzieżówek partii politycznych w latach 2001-2007," *Zeszyty Naukowe Uniwersytetu Szczecińskiego Acta Politica*, no. 28 (2014): 97-106.

country, from which they were pushed out; a diasporic emigration system, which was a form of residual continuation of the inter-war and war-time Polish political structures; and finally the systems of their host countries. At the crossroads of these political realities, young Christian Democrats quickly discovered tempting opportunities for international activities – with the support of their countries of settlement – by creating transnational exile initiatives or by joining international organisations. The common feature of these projects was their reference to Christian values and the fight against their principal political antagonist, communism.

In this chapter, we reconstruct the structures and the main qualities, as well as vectors of activism, of young Polish Christian Democrats in the conditions of Cold War exile. The first section deals with the tradition of Polish Christian Democratic parties and their exile structures, since overlooking these facts makes it difficult to understand the phenomenon of youth organisations as such. Christian Democracy – in the institutional form of the Polish Christian Labour Party (Stronnictwo Pracy, SP) – was one of the strongest Polish political groups during World War II, but it suffered disintegration after 1945. The consequences of its fragmentation, the social composition of its component groups, the goals they pursued and actions they undertook are studied in a subsequent part of the chapter. Next, we scrutinise different types of international activities of the young Christian Democratic exiles, including participation in Cold War youth campaigns, cooperation with other emigrant youth organisations from Central Europe, international cooperation for the cause of the unification of Europe or international cooperation projects in Latin America.[4]

The outline for this study was constructed on the basis of my research in private collections and conversations with Stanisław Gebhardt, one of the most prominent and active young Christian Democrats (b. 1928) in the 1940s and 1950s.[5] Equally important is the collection of correspondence discovered in the archives of the Polish Institute of Arts and Sciences of America (PIASA), which I had an opportunity to re-examine in January 2018. In this chapter, I quote documents from the Institute's own collec-

---

4   This chapter draws in part on an earlier study published in Polish over fifteen years ago: Sławomir Łukasiewicz, "Młodzi polscy chadecy na emigracji," *Zeszyty Historyczne (Paris)*, no. 163 (2005): 50-99. In the interim, the source base has been dramatically expanded, leading to new conclusions and this new text.

5   A record of conversations with Stanisław Gebhardt in the author's archive. "Stanisław Mieczysław Gebhardt," in Ewa Prządka, ed, *Świadectwa: Testimonianze*, Vol. 4: *Pro publico bono: Polityczna, społeczna i kulturalna działalność Polaków w Rzymie w XX wieku* (Rome: Fondazione Romana Marchesa J.S. Umiastowska, 2006), 321-322.

Sławomir Łukasiewicz

tion, but also from the bequest of Karol Popiel, President of the Polish Christian Labour Party, without whose consent no binding decision could have been made in the group.

The new sources show how throughout the 1940s and 1950s the potential of young Polish Christian Democrats grew in virtually all political contexts (home country, exile countries, international politics), and then how it dispersed and finally waned. Individual politicians gradually ceased to be "young" Christian Democrats, and thus youth organisations as such disappeared – a process that played out over the course of the 1960s. Only a few individuals were able to continue playing significant roles after reaching political "adulthood". After the collapse of the communist system, and after half a century of functioning in extreme exile conditions, Christian Democrats lacked adequate young staff that could provide fodder for the renewal of the party's presence in Poland.

Polish Christian Democratic parties in Cold War exile

In interwar Poland, Christian Democratic formations made up a diverse mosaic. It was only in 1937 that they managed to unite under the banner of the Polish Christian Labour Party. For this new Christian party, the outbreak of World War II was a turning point. Previously in opposition, marginalised by the ruling elites under Piłsudski, forced to emigrate, it suddenly became a pillar of the emigration government led by General Władysław Sikorski. After 1939, the Polish Christian Labour Party was among the most significant political groups both in exile and in Poland.[6] This period of relative consolidation of the party and its increased influence ended with the close of World War II. Three main factions emerged from the London-based exile SP structures. The first split resulted from the decision taken by the party leaders to return to Poland. This was, above all, the decision of Karol Popiel, a legendary figure and a former political prisoner in interwar Poland, a minister in the war-time government in exile and undoubtedly one of the most prominent politicians of this formation.[7] On the other hand, the so-called SP Foreign Committee,

---

6   Jarosław Rabiński, *Stronnictwo Pracy we władzach naczelnych Rzeczypospolitej Polskiej na uchodźstwie w latach 1939-1945* (Lublin: Wydawnictwo KUL, 2012).
7   Ryszard Gajewski, *Karol Popiel 1887-1977* (Suwałki: Wyższa Szkoła Służby Społecznej im. Księdza Franciszka Blachnickiego, 2008); Karol Popiel, *Od Brześcia do "Polonii"* (London: Odnowa, 1967).

headed by General Józef Haller, a veteran of the struggle for independence in World War I, stayed in exile.[8]

Furthermore, following Popiel's departure, the Christian Social Movement (Ruch Chrześcijańsko Społeczny, RCS) was founded in London in 1946. It focused on trade unionism and educational initiatives. Looking for sources of funding, its leaders turned to, among others, the American bishops of the National Catholic Welfare Conference (NCWC) in Washington, DC, declaring that, in the face of the growing impact of communist ideology on the youth, the RCS prioritises the issue of education "among the young generation in which the main fundaments [*sic*] are scouts and young Catholic workers".[9] The formation presented itself as a movement, the implication being that establishing a political party – with its "essential drive [...] towards effective power struggle" – does not make sense in the context of emigration.[10] Many other young emigrants, including those who founded political movements, thought similarly, although sooner or later all these formations joined the mainstream of political competition and transformed into formal political parties.[11]

The founders of RCS intended it to be a youth movement. In 1948 it even had its own youth representation within the organisation Jeunesse Éuropéenne "Juventus".[12] However, in terms of members' age, we can at best talk about a movement of thirty- and forty-year-olds. Moreover, the statute of the organisation provided for the so-called elders' supervision of the work of the RCS; these elders held on to their posts for life.[13] Among the members of the RCS, we find Konrad Sieniewicz, the right-hand man of Karol Popiel, suggesting that the RCS was in fact a political youth wing of the SP.[14]

Successive splits within Polish Christian Democracy coincided with the political divides within the Polish émigré community, caused by the

---

8 Marek Orłowski, *Generał Józef Haller 1873-1960* (Krakow: Arcana, 2007).
9 A copy of a letter from RCS to NCWC, 5 March 1948, PIASA, col. 17/1650.
10 A protocol of an organisational meeting of the Unionists [members of the clandestine organisation "Unia"] in exile, held in Paris, 2-5 February 1946, PIASA, col. 17/1650. Also therein, a document entitled "Christian Social Movement: Preliminary outline of basic progamme", 27 May 1946. The communist security apparatus undertook an unsuccessful approach to infiltrate the movement, as reported by Witold Bagieński, *Wywiad cywilny Polski Ludowej w latach 1945-1961*, Vol. 2 (Warsaw: Instytut Pamięci Narodowej, 2017), 34-38.
11 For more detail on these issues, see Sławomir Łukasiewicz, "A Shadow Party System: The Party Politics of Cold War Polish Exiles," *Journal of Cold War Studies* [forthcoming, 2021].
12 A copy of a letter from RCS to the General Secretariat of Jeunesse Européenne "Juventus", London, 27 September 1948, PIASA, col. 17/1650. These were Franciszek Gałązka, Karol Balon and Zygmunt Jędryka.
13 The Statute of the Christian Social Movement, art. 12, PIASA, col. 17/1650.
14 Letter of Konrad Sieniewicz to Msgr Iliński, July 1948, PIASA, col. 17/1650.

Sławomir Łukasiewicz

dispute over the succession to president-in-exile Władysław Raczkiewicz, who died in 1947. Within three years, three opposing exile decision-making centres emerged. In response to these splits, a smaller group of Christian Democrats led by Stanisław Sopicki and Hugon Hanke broke away from General Haller's faction in the autumn of 1951. The attempts undertaken by the remaining minority of Haller's group to reach an agreement with Karol Popiel's SP ended in fiasco. Young Christian Democrats, including Stanisław Gebhardt, took an active part in these talks, too.[15]

In subsequent years, individual factions of the SP were subject to further re-grouping. There were both splits and attempts at unification.[16] An important turning point was the scandal surrounding Hugon Hanke, who represented the third faction of the Christian Democrats, supporting the government in exile.[17] Hanke was successfully recruited by the intelligence services of the Polish People's Republic, and he decided to return to Poland. This incident caused a real political earthquake, mainly due to the fact that he had been prime minister in the government in exile. Yet his repatriation also had significant consequences for the functioning of Christian Democracy in exile. First of all, it cast a shadow of suspicion on his faction and dashed the prospects for reconciliation among the various factions. As far as Haller's faction is concerned, it was only when he died that the remains of the faction united with Karol Popiel's group at the Rome Congress in 1965.[18]

The splits among the Christian Democrats were fastidiously fuelled by the security apparatus of the People's Republic of Poland throughout the Cold War era. For example, the communists exploited a crisis triggered by the early 1956 trip to Poland by an important member of the SP leadership, Seweryn Eustachiewicz.[19] Deluding himself into thinking that it was

---

15 Handwritten copy of an anonymous report (source: informant "Literat") on the Polish Christian Labour Party, prepared for Ministry of Interior, Archives of the Institute of National Remembrance in Warsaw (AIPN) 01136/642, D4-D5.

16 The documentation presenting the split can be found in PIASA, Karol Popiel Papers, col. 9/64.

17 The case of Hanke's escape has recently been explored by Bagieński, *Wywiad cywilny Polski Ludowej*, Vol. 2, 52-55, 61-62, 65-66. See also Krzysztof Tarka, "Powrót premiera: Emigracja o sprawie Hugona Hankego," *Przegląd Polonijny*, no. 3 (2001): 19-33; Sławomir Cenckiewicz, *Oczami bezpieki: Szkice i materiały z dziejów aparatu bezpieczeństwa PRL* (Krakow: Arcana, 2004), 78; Krzysztof Tarka, "Hugo Hanke premier-agent," *Zeszyty Historyczne*, no. 152 (2005): 26-44. According to Janusz Zabłocki, Hanke and Sopicki "used" the banner of the SP unlawfully. Janusz Zabłocki, *Chrześcijańska Demokracja w kraju i na emigracji 1947-1970* (Lublin: Ośrodek Studiów Polonijnych i Społecznych PZKS, 1999), 86.

18 For more detail, see Orłowski, *Generał Józef Haller*, 483, 502-514; Zabłocki, *Chrześcijańska Demokracja w kraju i na emigracji*, 68-69, 83-87, 99-100, 189-190.

19 Paweł Ziętara, "Seweryna Eustachiewicza przypadki," *Zeszyty Historyczne*, no. 158 (2006): 35-71.

possible to enter into a reasoned debate with the leaders of the People's Republic of Poland regarding the reactivation of Christian Democracy in (communist) Poland, Eustachiewicz decided to embark on a trip to Poland. Despite substantial efforts at secrecy, the journey was discovered and publicised. This put the entire SP in a troublesome situation, irrespective of the fact that Eustachiewicz had relinquished his post in the party before his departure for Poland. The story had an adverse impact on the whole party, but Eustachiewicz's problems and his imminent death were particularly detrimental for the young Christian Democrats, for whom he served as liaison with the "adult" SP.

Christian Democratic youth

Young Christian Democrats were part of a larger phenomenon, i.e. of the Cold War emigration from Poland. This emigration settled mainly in the countries of Western Europe and the USA, and it had a specific gender, age and social structure. Owing to demographic trends in the wake of World War II, the core of the emigration were young men, most often soldiers of the Polish Armed Forces in the West. Despite the fact that it were predominantly men who died on the fronts of World War II, women were a minority in the gender structure of the Polish Cold War emigration. It is estimated that, out of 600,000 emigrants who stayed in the West after 1945, about 70% were men, most of whom were twenty or thirty years old.[20]

When we refer to emigrant youth, we mean primarily those who were born in the 1930s and who made their escape in a variety of manners and contexts (e.g. with their families) to the West, where they then completed their schooling. In the late 1940s, they were about twenty years old. According to the estimates of the security apparatus of the People's Republic of Poland, in the early 1960s, there were over 62,000 Polish young people aged between fifteen and thirty living in Western Europe, most of them in Great Britain, Germany and France. In the first fifteen years after the war, over 11,000 Polish émigrés studied and graduated from Western European universities. Communist intelligence also estimated that the political involvement of these young people was minimal, as evidenced by the fact

---

20 Rafał Habielski, *Życie społeczne i kulturalne emigracji* (Warsaw: Biblioteka Więzi 1999); Janusz Wróbel, *Na rozdrożu historii: Repatriacje obywateli polskich z Zachodu w latach 1945-1949* (Łódź: Instytut Pamięci Narodowej, 2009), 30.

Sławomir Łukasiewicz

that the youth organisations (including scouts) reportedly counted about 4,500 people.[21]

But even those young Polish emigrants who had a strong motivation to succeed had a difficult time finding their own place in émigré political life. Certainly, the soldierly character of the emigration was not conducive to successful assimilation. It was also difficult to create effective mechanisms of political engagement in the émigré party system. This in turn led to the deepening of the generation gap and to the ageing of the particular parties. Young people drew attention to the fact that the activists of the Polish political exile community belonged mainly to older generations. According to estimates from the end of 1949, "for over 1,500 Polish students in London, little more than 10% actively participate in the work of political organisations".[22]

One must keep in mind that London hosted the largest number of Polish post-war emigrants at that time, and was likewise the most politically active centre of the émigré community. It was also the seat of Poland's government in exile. It was home to many organisations in exile and to the headquarters of the most prominent Polish political parties. The majority of émigré political leaders were aware that a well-prepared young generation would likely grow into a future political resource, both in case of return to the country, or in the circumstances of prolonged exile. However, there were also exceptions, as evidenced by the striking example of the SP Foreign Committee. Its leader, Stanisław Sopicki, deliberately limited the size of his faction, which never exceeded 20 members. Thanks to this move – contrary to the logic of party politics – he effectively defended his position, opposing the admission of new, younger members. Only under strong party pressure did he eventually agree to create a youth club, which quickly outnumbered the party membership itself: after a few months the club could boast of about 50 members, two-and-a-half times more than the SP Foreign Committee.[23] This case illustrates how young people actively sought opportunities for development in political structures.

By 1949 several distinct Polish Christian Democratic youth organisations had formed. The first, connected with General Haller's faction,

21 *Polska emigracja polityczna: Informator* [a reprint from 1962], ed. Sławomir Cenckiewicz (Warsaw: Adiutor, 2004), 125-126.

22 Konrad Studnicki, "Parę uwag o ruchach politycznych na emigracji," *Zjednoczenie Chrześcijańsko–Społecznych Organizacji Młodzieżowych* [henceforth: *Zjednoczenie CSOM*], no. 2 (December 1949): 10.

23 A handwritten copy of an anonymous report (source: informant "Literat") on the SP, prepared for the Ministry of the Interior of the People's Republic of Poland, AIPN 01136/642, C11-C12.

was the Polish Christian Social Youth Association (Związek Młodzieży Chrześcijańsko–Społecznej).[24] Established in London in December 1947, it changed its name to the Christian Democratic Youth Association (Związek Młodzieży Chrześcijańsko–Demokratycznej) three years later. The second group of Christian Democratic youth based in London was called the Christian Social Youth Group (Chrześcijańsko–Społeczna Grupa Młodzieżowa). It was closely related to Karol Popiel's SP. The third group was formed in Paris under the name Christian-Social Youth Movement (Chrześcijańsko–Społeczny Ruch Młodych). Seeking their place on the political scene in exile and striving to overcome existing divisions, the first two formations established the Polish Christian Social Youth Federation on 6 May 1949 (Zjednoczenie Chrześcijańsko-Społecznych Organizacji Młodzieżowych, CSOM or the Federation). The third group joined them at a convention that took place six months later in London.[25]

The Federation was headed by Edward Bobrowski, represented the Christian Social Youth Movement in Paris, who jointly performed the function of president and a delegate responsible for the Nouvelles Équipes Internationales (NEI) Youth Section. Born in 1928, Bobrowski stood out from other colleagues in terms of his activism, his mastery of languages and his extensive contacts. These quickly made him a leader among young Christian Democrats. In his activities, he could also count on the support of the SP elders. Although he was the same age as Stanisław Gebhardt, he was much better prepared for international activism, having spent his childhood in Turkey and France, as well as having completed a law degree. He also had experience in journalism.[26] Until the end of his active participation in political life, he was consistently the first to be invited to cooperate with international organisations.

Meanwhile, Stanisław Gebhardt quickly grew to be the second figure in the Polish Christian Democratic youth movement. In the Federation, he was in charge of the Research Office, and was soon promoted to one of Bobrowski's deputies. When, in 1953, Edward Bobrowski became head of the International Union of Young Christian Democrats (IUYCD), it was agreed that his resignation as President of the Board of the Federation would be

---

24 *Zjednoczenie CSOM*, no. 6(8) (October 1950): 16.
25 "Zjazd," *Zjednoczenie CSOM*, no. 1(3) (January 1950): 2; Stanisław Gebhardt, "Korzenie," *Unia&Polska*, no. 21 (September 1999), at http://www.unia-polska.pl/archive/98-99/9909_1/17_f.html; Stanisław Gebhardt, "Zjednoczenie Młodzieży Chrześcijańsko–Społecznej," *Tygodnik Warszawski*, 18 June 2006: 8-9.
26 Polish Library in Paris, collection of Kajetan Morawski, Vol. 15.

necessary in order to avoid conflicts of interest.[27] Gebhardt became Secretary General of the Federation and later moved to Paris to become more active on the international arena.[28] Bobrowski's position, including the post of delegate to the International Union of Young Christian Democrats, was taken over by Jan Kułakowski from the Christian Social Youth Movement's Belgian branch. Kułakowski held this position until 1955, when he was replaced by the son of the exile government's Ambassador in Paris; Maciej Morawski then remained in this position until 1965.[29]

Among these individuals, Kułakowski's life offers the only example of a brilliant, long-standing political career. Born in 1930 in Warsaw, he fled in 1946 with his mother to her home country – Belgium. A breakthrough in his political career came when he met the leader of the International Federation of Christian Trade Unions, August Vanistendael.[30] Eventually, he would succeed his Belgian mentor, in 1976 becoming secretary general of the re-christened World Confederation of Labour.[31] Stepping down in 1989, he became one of the rare examples of an émigré who was able to put to good use his extensive experience and network of contacts during Poland's democratic transition communism, appointed first Poland's ambassador to the European Communities and then chief negotiator for Poland's accession to the European Union.[32]

The aim of the CSOM Federation was to coordinate the activities of all Polish youth organisations openly identifying with social Catholicism (in

---

27 Stanisław Gebhardt, telephone conversation, 8 February 2008.
28 A circular of the Board of the CSOM Federation of 9 June 1953, Stanisław Gebhardt Archive (ASG). See also Report by Stanisław Gebhardt sent to the USA, n.d. "Walny Zjazd Zjednoczenia CSOM w Tours (Francja)," *Zjednoczenie CSOM*, no. 15 (1954): 15-17. The initiators of bringing Stanisław Gebhardt to Paris were the leaders of the SP, and the main executors of the plan were Seweryn Eustachiewicz and Edward Bobrowski. PIASA, Karol Popiel Papers, col. 9/73, letter from Edward Bobrowski to Konrad Sieniewicz, 19 May 1953; letters from Seweryn Eustachiewicz to Konrad Sieniewicz, 6 and 20 May 1953; see also PIASA, Karol Popiel Papers, col. 9/75, letters from Stanisław Gebhardt to Konrad Sieniewicz, 4 and 8 October 1952.
29 A copy of a note by the Board of the Federation to Edward Bobrowski, 11 October 1955, ASG; Teresa Masłowska, *Łącznik z Paryża* (Leszno: Instytut im. Gen. Stefana "Grota" Roweckiego, 2007), 36.
30 Jan Kułakowski, "Chrześcijańskie związki zawodowe, Akcja Katolicka i stronnictwa polityczne," *Zjednoczenie CSOM*, no. 18/19 (1955): 5-7.
31 Jan Kułakowski, *Spotkania na Bagateli* (Warsaw: Wydawnictwo Rhetos, 2004); Patrick Pasture, *Histoire du syndicalisme chrétien international: La difficile recherche d'une troisième voie* (Paris: L'Harmattan, 1999).
32 Patrick Pasture, "Jan Kułakowski: From Exile to International Trade Union Leader and Diplomat," in Michel Dumoulin and Idesbald Goddeeris, eds, *Intégration ou représentation? Les exilés polonais en Belgique et la construction européenne* (Louvain-la-Neuve: Academia-Bruylant, 2005), 99-120; Leszek Jesień, "The Social Virtues of Christian Democracy, European and Polish: The Case of Jan Kułakowski," in Piotr H. Kosicki and Sławomir Łukasiewicz, eds, *Christian Democracy across the Iron Curtain: Europe Redefined* (London: Palgrave Macmillan, 2018), 277-290.

Polish movement parlance, the "Christian" in "Christian social" almost always meant "Catholic"). Young Christian Democrats seemed to show more courage than their older colleagues when, in December 1949, they wrote that "the conflicts among the various émigré factions are becoming – contrary to appearances – more and more fierce, thus weakening the strength of the émigré structures and discrediting them in the eyes of our western allies, who in this way find confirmation of the claim 'two Poles, three political views'. As these misunderstandings stem less and less from ideological motives, their spurious character becomes more and more obvious. Unfortunately, the Christian Democratic camp has not escaped the dramatic process of destruction of the émigré [political] communities. Fortunately, this process has been staved off in the youth section".[33]

Nonetheless, independence came at a price. As an independent organisation, the Federation could not count on the direct support of individual factions of Polish Christian Democracy, which were roiled by conflict. Stanisław Gebhardt emphasised that youth structures "are organisations independent of the Party [SP]. Therefore, their members cannot jointly perform leadership duties in youth organisations alongside similar duties in the SP".[34] A year later, he was also explaining that stance to the SP secretary: "Being an independent organisation, the Federation has a better chance of attracting young people who, having learned the ideology and methods of our movement, will have an open path to the SP. In this way, the SP gains informed members who have already passed through the political kindergarten. [...] Besides, there is a trail of unwritten cooperation with the SP, which I certainly do not need to assure you of".[35] In the long run, it was not possible to maintain the independence of youth organisations from the party structures. It was Popiel's SP that had the greatest influence on the Federation and could count on it for the recruitment of new party members.

The Christian Democratic youth groups became an important part of the portfolio of Karol Popiel's SP as its members went about building an

---

33 "Zjazd," *Zjednoczenie CSOM*, no. 1(3) (January 1950): 2.
34 Letter from Stanisław Gebhardt to Konrad Sieniewicz, 19 September 1952, PIASA, Karol Popiel Papers, col. 9/75.
35 Appendix to the letter from Stanisław Gebhardt to Konrad Sieniewicz, 10 September 1953, entitled "Youth matters: The Political Council [sic] of East-Central European Youth," PIASA, 17/1652.

Sławomir Łukasiewicz

international position for the faction.[36] It was the CSOM Federation that represented young Polish Christian Democrats at the NEI as the Polish Youth Team. The working programme adopted at the convention obliged the leadership of the Federation to intensify their engagement in the NEI International Youth Section and to introduce the Federation into the structures of the Union of Polish Federalists.[37] The plan was to maintain contacts with the World Federation of Liberal and Radical Youth, the People and Freedom Group and other international youth organisations.

In October 1950, the CSOM Federation announced an ideological declaration emphasising the coordinating role of the organisation and a need for its members' adherence to the principles of Christian ethics in public life. The principles governing social life were drawn directly from the papal encyclicals – *Rerum Novarum* and *Quadragesimo Anno* – considered to be the foundations of Catholic social teaching. The declaration was crowned with slogans characteristic not only for "adult Christian Democracy", but also for the entire political emigration of that time: striving for Poland's independence and introducing a truly democratic system in the home country. These slogans, with minor adjustments, reproduced the position expressed three years earlier in the ideological declaration of the Christian Social Youth Association.[38]

However, the postulates in the area of international relations were really novel for the time. They represented a new direction not only for young Christian Democrats, but also for a large part of the Polish political emigration. These included the following:
(a) creating a federal structure of East-Central Europe as a constituent part of United Europe and, later, a universal world federation organisation,

---

36 Zabłocki, *Chrześcijańska Demokracja w kraju i na emigracji*, 71-72, 80-83, 92-93, 95-99, 101-103, 105, 177-179, 202-204; Paweł Machcewicz, *Emigracja w polityce międzynarodowej* (Warsaw: Biblioteka "Więzi," 1999), 52; Stanisław Gebhardt, "Międzynarodowe organizacje chrześcijańsko–demokratyczne," in Tomasz Piesakowski, ed, *Materiały do dziejów polskiego uchodźstwa niepodległościowego 1945-1990*, Vol. 4: *Akcja niepodległościowa na terenie międzynarodowym* (London: Polskie Towarzystwo Naukowe na Obczyźnie, 1999), 115-139; Krzysztof Tarka, *Emigracyjna dyplomacja: Polityka zagraniczna Rządu RP na Uchodźstwie 1945-1990* (Warsaw: Rytm, 2003).

37 Sławomir Łukasiewicz, *Polacy w europejskim ruchu federalnym po II wojnie światowej* (Warsaw: Centrum Europejskie Natolin, 2006).

38 *Deklaracja Ideowa Związku Młodzieży Chrześcijańsko–Społecznej*, London, 19 December 1947, ASG.

(b) working closely with the rest of the world to build and consolidate the peaceful co-existence of peoples on the foundation of Christian ethics, (c) opposition to totalism and dictatorship in all its forms.[39]
On various occasions, the young Christian Democrats in the Section emphasised that their presence should be a reminder of the existence of East-Central Europe.[40] They also rejected the 1939 Molotov-Ribbentrop division of Poland and regarded the postwar Western Territories, reaching the Oder and Neisse rivers, as an integral part of Poland's territory. At the same time, young Polish Christian Democrats attempted to communicate and cooperate with their peers in Germany. In line with this objective, a joint meeting was held in the autumn of 1951.[41] The Polish side was represented by Edward Bobrowski, Stanisław Gebhardt and Jan Kułakowski, among others. The German side – i.e. the Junge Union Deutschlands der CDU/CSU – was represented, among others, by its leader Ernst Majonica, who later became a member of the Bundestag representing the CDU and a member of the European People's Party. This unofficial meeting took place thanks to the fact that both organisations belonged to the International Union of Young Christian Democrats, which in fact was behind the meeting. Ambitiously outlined projects, aimed at learning about each other's views and laying the foundations of good neighbourly cooperation, immediately provoked criticism from the émigré community and the press back in the home country.[42] A tangible outcome of these disputes was the with-

---

39 "Deklaracja ideowa Zjednoczenia Chrześcijańsko–Społecznych Organizacji Młodzieżowych," *Zjednoczenie CSOM*, no. 7(9) (November 1950): 15.

40 J. Kułakowski, "Kongres młodych chrześcijańskich demokratów belgijskich," *Zjednoczenie CSOM*, no. 1(14) (June 1952): 13-15; " Z życia innych organizacji," *Zjednoczenie CSOM*, no. 1(14) (June 1952): 28.

41 Details of the preparation of the Polish side for the meeting are contained in "Circular" no. 5 issued by the CSOM Federation, [February 1951], ASG.

42 These reactions were discussed by a person writing under the pseudonym of "Parisian Beaver", "Przegląd prasy tej... i tamtej," *Zjednoczenie CSOM*, no. 1(14) (June 1952): 23-26; see also "Komunikat prasowy (wydany po spotkaniu młodzieży chrześcijańsko–społecznej polskiej i niemieckiej)," *Zjednoczenie CSOM*, no. 1(14) (June 1952): 7; Edward Bobrowski, "Rok obfity w wydarzenia," *Zjednoczenie CSOM*, no. 1(14) (June 1952): 5-7. Bobrowski provided critical information – first of all concerning the technical detail of organising the whole meeting – in the internal "Circular" no. 9 of 4 January 1952. The whole of issue no. 14 of *Zjednoczenie CSOM* focused around that problem; it came out after almost a year-long hiatus. See also the comprehensive text: Stanisław Gebhardt, "Uwagi na temat przygotowania spotkania polsko-niemieckiego," 10 January 1952, PIASA, Karol Popiel Papers, col. 9/75. These announcements echoed in the home country in the form of a chapter entitled "Bieg do Bonn" [A run to Bonn], included in a propaganda attack on the emigration by Stefan Arski, *Targowica leży nad Atlantykiem* (Warsaw: Książka i Wiedza, 1952), 47. For the propagandist Arski, the meeting proved the treacherous character of actions undertaken by the émigrés, Germans and the Vatican. The role of the young Christian Democrats in the plot played nothing but a marginal role in this narrative.

Sławomir Łukasiewicz

drawal of the Association of Christian Democratic Youth from the CSOM Federation.[43]

The power of the young Polish Christian Democrats can be seen in the numbers. In 1955, the Federation counted approximately 8,000 young Polish émigrés scattered among Belgium, France, Germany, Great Britain, Australia, Canada and Venezuela.[44] This number probably included at least 7,000 people connected with the Catholic Association of Polish Youth (Katolickie Stowarzyszenie Młodzieży Polskiej), with which the Federation closely cooperated.[45] These figures served to build the image of the Federation as an organisation that was representative of the Christian Democracy youth movement in exile. If we juxtapose these numbers against the membership data in the "adult" SP at that time – in early 1957, the SP's branch in Great Britain only had 15 members[46] – it becomes clear that Christian Democratic youth constituted a real power in the postwar decade.

The events of 1956 – Khrushchev's "Secret Speech" and the political thaw in Poland, but also the failed Hungarian Revolution – affected the political strategy of young Christian Democrats. Cooperation ceased with the (émigré) Catholic Association of Polish Youth, as new opportunities emerged for contacts in communist Poland. In 1958, it was decided that the name of the Federation be simplified, and since then it has been known as the Christian Social Youth Federation.[47] However, the most serious change that the year 1956 brought to young Christian Democrats was Edward Bobrowski's decision to assume French citizenship and resign from all SP-related duties.[48] A matter of contingent circumstance rather than

---

43 A letter from President Adam Praun and Secretary General Teresa Fallenbüchl of the Christian Democratic Youth Association to President Edward Bobrowski, 20 December 1951, ASG. The letter was then reprinted in Circular no. 9 of 4 January 1952. The issue was also mentioned by Edward Bobrowski in his letters to Konrad Sieniewicz of 31 December 1951 and 11 January 1952, PIASA, col. 17/1652.

44 This data was included in a note on Polish young Christian Democrats published in the IUYCD magazine *Jeune Démocratie Chrétienne*, nos. 4-8 (May-September 1955): 11. See also Gebhardt to Jean Degimbe (then Secretary-General of the IUYCD), 24 June 1958, ASG.

45 Gebhardt, "Zjednoczenie Młodzieży Chrześcijańsko–Społecznej," 8. The highly confidential report by Seweryn Eustachiewicz to the representative of the FEC in Paris, Constance A. Dulles, (23 February 1955), gave the number of 8,000 members and the French name: Association de la Jeunesse Catholique Polonaise, PIASA, Karol Popiel Papers, col. 9/204.

46 Report of the SP's Branch in Great Britain for the first quarter of 1957, PIASA, Karol Popiel Papers, col. 9/64.

47 According to an internal informant of the Ministry of the Interior, reporting in 1962, the name changed in July 1958, *Polska emigracja...*, 153.

48 A copy of a letter from S. Gebhardt to Konrad [Sieniewicz?], 16 January 1957, ASG.

geopolitics, Bobrowski's departure nonetheless represented a body-blow to the otherwise-ascendant Polish Christian Democratic youth.

Transnationalism under the umbrella of Free Europe

Young Christian Democrats did not limit their activities to their own émi-gré environment. Adopting a programme that drew on both Catholic social teaching and European federalism, they focused most of their energy on building up their position across the international Christian Democratic youth movements – first on the European level, then globally. The creation of the Christian Democratic Union of Central Europe (CDUCE) in 1950 and its Youth Section on 2 February 1951 opened new horizons.[49] The main rationale behind launching both organisations is reflected in the words of Konrad Sieniewicz, Secretary General of the "adult" SP: "I am a great supporter of a united Europe. In my opinion, however, the road to it leads through smaller federations, e.g. a Central European federation. Thus, Europe will be a bag of diversity, or it will not be at all [...]. That is why I am working on bringing the possibility of a federation in our region of Europe closer [to reality]. [...] it is for that purpose that we have established here the Christian Democratic Union of Central Europe".[50]

The youth section gathered representatives of young Christian Democrats – analogically to the "adult" CDUCE – from Czechoslovakia, Hungary, Latvia, Lithuania, Poland and Yugoslavia (Slovenia).[51] Its main governing body was the Central Committee, composed of twenty representatives. Individual posts, vital for the functioning of the organisation, were distributed on the basis of a "gentlemen's agreement" concluded among the national delegations. The agreement assumed that the president would be a representative of the Czechoslovakian group, the "general delegation" would go to the Hungarians, and the general secretariat would be run by

---

49 Peter Van Kemseke, *Towards an Era of Development: The Globalization of Socialism and Christian Democracy, 1945-1965* (Leuven: Leuven University Press, 2006), 172; Roberto Papini, *The Christian Democrat International*, trans. Robert Royal (Lanham, MD: Rowman & Littlefield, 1997), 76; Sławomir Łukasiewicz, *Third Europe: Polish Federalist Thought in the United States 1940-1970s*, trans. Witold Zbirohowski-Kościa (Budapest: Helena History Press, 2016), 88; Stanisław Gebhardt, "The Christian Democratic Union of Central Europe," in Kosicki and Łukasiewicz, *Christian Democracy across the Iron Curtain*, 411-424.

50 A copy of a letter from Konrad Sieniewicz to Iga (surname unknown), 2 December 1950, PIASA, Karol Popiel Papers, col. 9/86.

51 J. Renner, Report of the Youth Section to the First International Congress of the Christian Democratic Union of Central Europe, New York, 13 March 1953, ASG.

the Poles.[52] Of the Poles, Edward Bobrowski was appointed Secretary General, and Stanisław Gebhardt became a member of the Central Committee.[53]

In September 1952, at a meeting in Florence, the CDUCE Youth Section was admitted to the European Youth Council, which undoubtedly strengthened its position.[54] The Section also published a monthly in French entitled *Bulletin d'Information de la Section des Jeunes de l'UCDEC*, and from 1955 onward, a separate French-language monthly entitled *Nouvel Horizon*.[55] The section maintained contact with Radiodiffusion Française and Radio Free Europe, where it was particularly supported by the Hungarian "desk".[56]

Bobrowski estimated that, in early 1953, the number of section members totalled around 400 or 500, the majority of whom lived in France.[57] The CDUCE Youth Section Regional Committee established in London was practically inactive.[58] In 1953, regional groups were established in Belgium (Brussels-Louvain), Strasbourg (at the Free Europe University in Exile, which educated students from behind the Iron Curtain under the auspices of the US-funded Free Europe Committee), Munich and Rome.[59] The CDUCE Youth Section also had an American branch.[60]

The emergence of the CDUCE Youth Section had a negative impact on the relations among Polish Christian Democratic youth organisations in exile, and it did not inspire their cooperation.[61] This potential cooperation was hampered by the fact that the CDUCE Youth Section was composed of representatives of youth from those Christian Democratic parties which

52 Letter from Edward Bobrowski to Konrad Sieniewicz, 10 December 1952, PIASA, col. 17/1652.
53 *Zjednoczenie CSOM*, no. 3(13) (March-April-May 1951): 22-23; a report by Stanisław Gebhardt for the USA, n.d., ASG.
54 Renner, Report of the Youth Section.
55 The flagship CDUCE journal – *The Christian Democratic News Service* – was published in English.
56 In April 1950, the group of elder Polish émigré leaders prepared a dedicated document entitled, "The comments on the radio programs in the Polish language", with a need of targeting some of the broadcast content to the youth issues "demonstrating the conditions of life of the free youth working and studying: the aims and the functioning of social, educational, international youth organisations, recreations, sport, touring etc". The document was signed among others by Karol Popiel (SP). PIASA, Karol Popiel Papers, col. 9/43.
57 A report by Stanisław Gebhardt for the authorities of the SP in the USA, n.d., ASG.
58 Letter from Edward Bobrowski to Konrad Sieniewicz, 26 May 1952, PIASA, Karol Popiel Papers, col. 9/75.
59 Edward Bobrowski, Rapport: L'activité de la section des jeunes de l'Union Chrétienne–Démocrate d'Europe Centrale durant ses premières deux années de fonctionnement, Paris, 15 February 1953, ASG.
60 "Formation of American Branch CDUCE Youth Section," *Christian Democratic New Service*, nos. 12-13 (30 July 1953): 2.
61 *Zjednoczenie CSOM*, no. 3(13) (March-April-May 1951): 23.

belonged to the "adult" CDUCE. As Konrad Sieniewicz admitted in a letter to his colleague Seweryn Eustachiewicz, "It is the SP and not the CSRM [Christian Social Youth Movement] that is a member of the CDUCE Youth Section, so if we turn a blind eye to the fact that in the Polish group not everyone is a member of the SP, we cannot agree that the key position [Secretary General of the CDUCE Youth Section] would be filled by a non-SP member, or by someone without the full confidence of the Party Council".[62]

As a politician in charge of youth matters in the SP, Eustachiewicz read these words with caution. His role was paramount, especially when the relations between "young" and "old" Christian Democrats did not turn out well. A case in point was the incident when the "young" Christian Democrats were not invited to the "adult" CDUCE congress, scheduled for the beginning of 1953 in New York. This incident was a source of frustration for the "young", and it even created an impulse to seek independence.[63] Equally frustrating were attempts to convince the "adult" Christian Democrats to organise a CDUCE congress with a dedicated youth section. In the end, these all came to nothing.[64]

In order to prevent further misunderstandings, Stanisław Gebhardt, who was gradually moving closer to the "adult" SP, suggested in the autumn of 1953 that the Federation be incorporated into the CDUCE Youth Section. To dispel the doubts of the SP leaders, Gebhardt proposed an appropriate modification of the section's statute, so that the admission of new members would be decided by the CDUCE "elders".[65] Under the auspices of implementing this plan, in December 1953, the Federation submitted an official request to be admitted to the CDUCE Youth Section.[66] However, the SP leaders were sceptical about this idea, and the matter remained unsettled until the end of February 1955. On Stanisław Gebhardt's intervention, the Federation was finally accepted.[67]

The CDUCE Youth Section was divided into five committees, which dealt with political and information activities, federalist matters, econom-

---

62 A copy of a letter from Konrad Sieniewicz to Seweryn Eustachiewicz, 20 March 1952, PIASA, Karol Popiel Papers, col. 9/85.

63 Letter from Edward Bobrowski to Konrad Sieniewicz, 10 December 1952, PIASA, col. 17/1652.

64 A relevant project was submitted by Stanisław Gebhardt in an appendix to his letter to Konrad Sieniewicz, 10 September 1953, entitled "Youth matters: The Political Council [sic] of East-Central European Youth," PIASA, col. 17/1652.

65 Ibid.

66 "Z życia organizacji międzynarodowych," *Zjednoczenie CSOM*, no. 15 (1954): 24.

67 The accession took place at a meeting of the enlarged Central Committee in Paris. PIASA, Karol Popiel Papers, col. 9/204, letter from Stanisław Gebhardt to Konrad Sieniewicz, 3 January 1955; PIASA, col. 17/1652, a letter from Stanisław Gebhardt to Edward Bobrowski, "Komunikat Zjednoczenia CSOM," *Zjednoczenie CSOM*, nos. 18/19 (1955): 27.

Sławomir Łukasiewicz

ic and social affairs, cultural and educational matters, as well as youth organisations and political training. The unanimously adopted declaration
assumed that the section's main objectives consisted in the coordination
of "the activities of the Christian social youth movements of the countries
behind the Iron Curtain"; drawing the "attention of the Western world to
the problems and needs of the emigrant youth;" publicising and defending
the interests of youth subjected to physical and moral terror by "godless
communism behind the Iron Curtain"; helping youth and informing them
about the struggle of the free world against "Soviet imperialism"; providing them with works of contemporary Christian and democratic thought;
promoting "the principles of political, economic and social organisation
of Central and Eastern Europe and a genuine Christian social ideology
in partnership with the corresponding centres in the free world and in
cooperation with the elders of the Christian Democratic Union of Central
Europe"; and preparing the young generation to take responsibility for political and social matters in the future.[68]

Compared with previous (and subsequent) documents, including the
ones developed by the CDUCE, this declaration spoke in much sharper anti-communist language.[69] In the following years, this rhetoric lost its edge
and, for example, in 1956 the "ultimate goals" were defined as seeking
"freedom, social justice, peace and prosperity, as well as international cooperation".[70] Of these four points, international cooperation increasingly
gained prominence in the context of the emerging new world order. It
was intended to reach several wildly different audiences at the same time:
both the exile youth in the West and youth behind the Iron Curtain, but
also any and all young Christian Democrats the world over who were willing to listen, or even young people in general, especially those exposed to
communist indoctrination.[71]

The international dimension of the activities of young Christian Democrats was immediately recognised by the management of the Free Europe Committee. When the CDUCE Youth Section was founded, Konrad
Sieniewicz announced this fact to Mary Augustine, responsible for FEC
contacts with the Polish Christian Democrats (at that point, still formally

---

68 *Zjednoczenie CSOM*, no. 3(13) (March-April-May 1951): 23.
69 The assumptions of the CDUCE working programme were discussed e.g. by Papini, *Christian Democrat International*, 77.
70 UCDEC Section des Jeunes, Programme of work [1956], ASG.
71 Ibid.

known as the National Committee for a Free Europe).[72] From mid-1951 on, the FEC provided the Youth Section of the Central European Christian Democrats with a permanent budget.[73] Undeniably, the FEC also attempted to influence the political line and actions of young Christian Democrats, just as the Americans sought to do with the "adult" CDUCE.[74]

FEC exile coordinator John Foster Leich apparently financed the German-Polish meeting with the sum of $500.[75] Young Christian Democrats were a promising strategic partner for the FEC: not only did they refer to Christian values and anti-communism, but they were also open to contacts with their German peers. With the Cold War American strategy, part of which rested on the assumption that West Germany was a natural ally against the Soviet Union, a partner organisation among the war-affected émigré communities was priceless. There are also some indications that the moment when the FEC's interest in young, politically active European Christian Democrats (or émigré Christian Democrats in general) grew considerably was Konrad Adenauer's second election victory in 1953.[76]

The FEC leaders grew to believe that the activities of young Christian Democrats stood out from other youth organisations – socialist or federalist. In October and November 1955, a series of meetings were held between FEC and CDUCE Youth representatives, including Gebhardt and Maciej Morawski. As the talks progressed, the admiration of the FEC representatives for the actions of young Christian Democrats grew. FEC vice-president Bernard Yarrow, hoping to keep the momentum going, and at the same time planning to exercise greater control over the exiles, promised, among other things, an increase in the salary of the Section Secretary General. He also suggested that the correspondence sent from the section

72 Letter from Konrad Sieniewicz to Mary Augustine, 26 February 1951, PIASA, Karol Popiel Papers, col. 9/43. At the same time, the relations between the Polish Christian Democrats and Mary Augustine were not always positive, as evidenced by e.g. her statement on the issue of withdrawing funding for the Christian Democratic Trade Unions, where she wrote, "in the future, we [NCFE] will not support any organisation, whether organised according to the Christian ideal or according to any other ideological concept". Letter from Mary Augustine to Konrad Sieniewicz, 22 October 1953, ibid.

73 Bobrowski, Rapport.

74 The rationale behind the support of the "adult" CDUCE by the FEC is outstandingly reconstructed by Piotr H. Kosicki, "Christian Democracy's Global Cold War," in Kosicki and Łukasiewicz, *Christian Democracy across the Iron Curtain*, 221-256, at 229. The relations between the FEC and the CDUCE are explored in Anna Mazurkiewicz, *Uchodźcy polityczni z Europy Środkowo-Wschodniej w amerykańskiej polityce zimnowojennej 1948-1954* (Warsaw: Instytut Pamięci Narodowej/Uniwersytet Gdański, 2016), 348-351.

75 Letter from Edward Bobrowski to Konrad Sieniewicz, 11 January 1952, PIASA, col. 17/1652.

76 That it was the case with the "adult" CDUCE is reported by Janusz Śleszyński in his letter to Konrad Sieniewicz, 10 September 1963, PIASA, col. 17/1652.

Sławomir Łukasiewicz

should be directed to the New York FEC, bypassing CDUCE headquarters. Gebhardt loyally reported on these meetings to his SP superiors,[77] but he also admitted that the activities of the CDUCE Youth Section clearly intensified as a result of the meetings.[78] Representatives of the section prepared materials on the situation of the youth on both sides of the Iron Curtain for the Assembly of Captive European Nations session in Strasbourg (12-15 April 1956). A few days later, they participated in the meeting of the Executive Committee of the International Union of Young Christian Democrats, and in May in the Congress of the Free Youth Council.

Free Europe Committee bureaucrats pinned their hopes on young Christian Democrats as future leaders. Observing their behaviours and reactions to a very "hot" 1956, on 8 October the chief of Free Europe Exile Relations (FEER) James McCargar indicated in a policy paper "that the older leaders of the emigration are less and less in touch with the issues of the day, and that youth-in-exile, while equally as devoted to the objective of independence for their countries as their elders, find themselves less and less in sympathy with the elder leadership. What is occurring within the emigration is a perfectly natural change of leadership from one generation to another, but precisely because this change takes place in exile, it can be more than normally disruptive. The preservation of the cohesion and integrity of the various emigrations as a component of the emigration as a political force is obviously in the interest of FEC objectives".[79]

As time passed, it became clear that the opportunities for generational exchange and party promotion in exile were practically non-existent, which gave rise to conflicts. In December 1957, the CDUCE Youth Section experienced a crisis which resulted in the establishment of a Working Committee, composed exclusively of representatives of the Hungarian, Latvian, Polish and Czechoslovak youth.[80] The crisis was partly caused by the splits that occurred between the national groups in the adult CDUCE

---

77 [S. Gebhardt], Internal report on the conversation held between Messrs. Yarrow and Brown and the officers of YS/CDUCE, [1955], ASG.

78 In a letter to Stanisław Wiśniewski (who used the name of Joseph Cherryson when in Great Britain), President of an SP centre in Great Britain, 20 March 1956, PIASA, Karol Popiel Papers, col. 9/64.

79 James McCargar, "The Function and Mission of Free Europe Exile Relations," 8 October 1956, Boston University Archives, James McCargar papers, Box 19/21.

80 A foundation declaration (in French) for the Executive Committee of the CDUCE Youth Section, 14 December 1957, ASG. Georges [György] O'svath was appointed president and was in charge of external relations. Stanisław Gebhardt was head of administration, Georges Volozinskis was responsible for the budget and finance, and Jaroslav Vrzala was editor-in-chief of *Nouvel Horizon* and other press publications. Meeting of the Working Committee, 30 Dec[ember] 1957, ASG.

in the spring of that year.[81] However, the main reason for the changes was that the young activists were gradually growing out of their twenties, which should have resulted in their natural transition to the "senior ranks" of the CDUCE. But it did not. To complicate matters even more, there was the issue of the diversity of youth representations at the CDUCE, and in the spring of 1960, a meeting of the Ad Hoc Committee of the CDUCE Youth Section, decided to settle the issue. The starting point was, among others, Stanisław Gebhardt's position that the International Union of Young Christian Democrats should take care of all youth matters, and therefore there is no need to maintain a separate exile international. Finally, in July 1960, at a meeting in Paris, Polish delegates withdrew from the Central Committee of the CDUCE Youth Section, which certainly weakened the organisation.[82] We lack data on when the CDUCE Youth Section formally ceased to exist, but it certainly was long gone by 1989. A lack of new membership, the "aging" of the "young" Christian Democrats, a lack of promotion prospects, personal and organisational conflicts, lack of funding opportunities from the FEC funding, problems in the "senior" CDUCE – these factors together led to the decline of the Youth Section.

Towards European and global affairs

The young Polish Christian Democrats refused to confine themselves to the émigré ghetto or to a narrowly focused cooperation with other exiles. They searched for a broader forum of activity, and the one they found was that of European Christian Democracy, flourishing with the progress of European integration. However, research on this topic is considerably hampered by the fact that the history of Christian Democratic youth in Europe since World War II has thus far apparently escaped the attention of scholars.[83]

---

81 Letter from Walter Grzegorzyca to Karol Popiel, 12 May 1957, PIASA, Karol Popiel Papers, col. 9/64.
82 The information can be found in an untitled document of 13 July 1960, Paris. Its most probable author was Stanisław Gebhardt, ASG.
83 For example, Jensen and Van Hecke only signal the existence of organisations that are precursors to the Youth of the European People's Party, without exploring their history in depth: Thomas Jensen and Steven Van Hecke, *At Europe's Service: The Origins and Evolution of the European People's Party* (Berlin: Springer, 2011), 18, 176. The same is true of Papini, *Christian Democrat International*, 57. Mentions of future Christian Democratic leaders in the early days of the NEI youth section can be found in Wolfram Kaiser, *Christian Democracy and the Origins of European Union* (Cambridge: Cambridge University Press, 2007), 212.

Sławomir Łukasiewicz

The documents produced and collected by the Polish émigrés come to our aid. The first commission whose task was to coordinate the cooperation of the Christian Democratic youth organisations was established during the NEI Congress in September 1948; its chair was Franciszek Gałązka, a Pole.[84] An important event in the history of the section was the congress in Villach, Austria, which was held in September 1952 and brought together at least 12,000 young Europeans.[85] It was then that the section was transformed into the IUYCD.[86]

It is estimated that in 1954, the International Union of Young Christian Democrats was able to attract around 1.5 million young people of different nationalities, making it one of the most powerful youth organisations in Europe. Its representatives took the floor during the NEI's proceedings, sitting, among others, on its steering committee. In 1953, Edward Bobrowski became Secretary General of the IUYCD and held this position until the end of 1956.[87] The delegates to the IUYCD working committees were the successive presidents of the CSOM Federation, including Gebhardt, who was in charge of Asian and African affairs. In the years 1962-68, he held the position of Secretary General of the IUYCD. Taking into account the nationalities in the IUYCD authorities, the Poles had an unquestionably strong position, although available documents fail to explain why. In 1957, for example, the countries of East-Central Europe were represented by only one Hungarian as Vice-President (Arpád Raksányi) and four Poles,

---

84 A document entitled "Międzynarodówka chrześcijańsko–społeczna," September 1948, which relates the conclusions drawn from the NEI Congress in The Hague, held on 17-19 September 1948, ASG.

85 See e.g., "18,000 młodzieży manifestuje za Zjednoczoną Europą," *Narodowiec*, no. 204 (28 August 1952); B. Braine, "20,000 Christians on the march," *Evening News* (27 August 1952); "Europa ojczyzna przyszłości," *Narodowiec*, no. 203 (27 August 1952).

86 The documents mainly used the names and abbreviations created in English, e.g.: International Union of Young Christian Democrats (IUYCD), or French, e.g.: Union Internationale des Jeunes Démocrates Chrétiens (UIJDC). In 1952, the president was the Swiss Leo Schurmann, and the general secretary was the Austrian Rudolf Lewandowski. Papini, *Christian Democrat International*, 57.

87 "Z życia organizacji międzynarodowych," *Zjednoczenie CSOM*, no. 15 (1954): 23. Bobrowski replaced the former president, the Austrian student and journalist Rudolf Lewandowski, PIASA, col. 17/1652, letter from Edward Bobrowski to Konrad Sieniewicz, 10 December 1952. For that reason, he resigned from the posts of the President of the Board of the CSOM Federation and of the Secretary General of the CDUCE youth section. ASG, letter from the President of the IUYCD, Franco Nobili, 23 November 1956, informing of a need to elect a new secretary general. At the same time, Bobrowski remained a member of the Presidium of the Executive Committee of the IUYCD.

who were members of the Central Committee – including, first and foremost, Bobrowski and Gebhardt.[88]

The activities of young European Christian Democrats were also part of the Campagne Européenne de la Jeunesse (CEJ), whose aim in the years 1950-58 was to respond to communist youth propaganda in Western Europe. The CEJ was financed by the American Committee for a United Europe,[89] and the International Union of Young Christian Democrats also benefited.[90] The main slogan of the campaign was the unification of Europe, and the course of its implementation was supervised by the European Movement.

One of the CEJ's first initiatives was the European Political Youth Assembly (Assemblée Européenne des Jeunesses Politiques), a kind of parliament held in The Hague at the Ridderzaal Palace in October 1952. It opened with speeches by eminent European federalists and declared advocates of European unification: the Dutch socialist Hendrik Brugmans – then rector of the College d'Europe in Bruges – and the Swiss intellectual Denis de Rougemont. The fact that the secretariat was headed by a Pole, Jerzy Rencki (future Director of the Directorate-General for Regional Development Policy in the Commission of the European Communities), and was assisted by Edward Bobrowski, among others, should be considered the Polish émigrés' huge success.[91] The Christian Democrats were undoubtedly among the most active and effective participants of the assembly: out of the eighteen representatives of East-Central Europe, seven were Christian Democrats. They also had half of the eight positions of delegates with voting rights.[92]

The model was then reproduced in the Political Council for East-Central European Youth founded at a meeting in Paris in June 1953 and intended to serve as a forum for exchange and cooperation among émigré youth. It also created an opportunity to seek consensus on a common political position, necessary in the event of the collapse of communism in

---

88 Procès-verbal de la réunion du Comité Directeur de l'U.I.J.D.C. tenue à Paris, le 30 Mars 1957, ASG.

89 For more on ACUE and its relations with NCFE, see Łukasiewicz, *Third Europe*, 70.

90 Created by Bobrowski, Document de travail [IUYCD] no. 21, DOC-TR-21, confidential, Note sur la Campagne Européenne de la Jeunesse, December 1953, ASG.

91 A leaflet dedicated to the assembly, the Polish Library in Paris, col. of Tadeusz Parczewski, acc. sign. 3231. Detailed reports on the conference and the members of the Board were included in the appendix to a letter from Stanisław Gebhardt to Konrad Sieniewicz, 10 September 1953, entitled "Youth matters: The Political Council [sic] of the East-Central European Youth," PIASA, col. 17/1652.

92 Renner, Report of the Youth Section; see also letter from Stanisław Gebhardt to Konrad Sieniewicz, 23 October 1952, PIASA, Karol Popiel Papers, col. 9/75.

Sławomir Łukasiewicz

Europe. This was by no means a trivial task, given that the views of individual national and political groups ranged from enthusiasts of pan-European unification (e.g. representatives of Hungary, Romania, Bulgaria and Yugoslavia), to supporters of regional unions and finally outright opponents of integration. Sixteen Polish delegates participated in the work of the Council, nine of whom represented the Polish National Committee of the European Movement, while six represented international youth political organisations.[93]

The formation of this entity created another opportunity for young Christian Democrats to extend further their political influence and promote their political agenda. Bobrowski, who was the rapporteur for one of the committees, was able to "influence the course of affairs to a greater extent" and hence managed to invite more Christian Democrats to Paris.[94] Jan Kułakowski was the person whose growing prominence in the international community made him the man of the hour. His speech on the Council's programme, which he gave at the beginning of the meeting, won him the favour of representatives of other exile groups, as well as non-Christian Democrats. Thanks to this, as well as to the efforts and negotiations of his colleagues, Kułakowski was elected a member of the Central Committee. In time, he replaced Arpád Raksányi, leader of the Hungarian Christian Democratic Youth, in the position of Secretary General of the Executive Committee, when Raksányi got more actively involved in internal Hungarian émigré issues.[95] For Kułakowski to achieve such a position was not easy in view of the fact that the Christian Democrats in the Polish delegation could only count on the support of the Polish Peasants' Party, as

---

93 S. Gebhardt's report sent to New York, ASG. Talks between the representatives of the exile youth organisations, which were held in the autumn of 1952, were discussed by Edward Bobrowski in a letter to Konrad Sieniewicz, 10 December 1952, PIASA, col. 17/1652; see also report by Kajetan Morawski for Minister [Sokołowski?] of 4 June 1953, The Polish Library in Paris, col. 1/101, temp. sign. 6, Vol. 2.

94 Appendix to a letter from Stanisław Gebhardt to Konrad Sieniewicz, 10 September 1953, entitled "Youth matters: The Politcal Council [sic] of the East-Central European Youth," PIASA, col. 17/1652.

95 Raksányi was Hungarian Undersecretary of State in the government of Imre Nagy, chief of the Political Department of the Hungarian Revolutionary Council in exile. See the note created by Kułakowski as Secretary General of the exile youth organisation: Note concernant le Conseil de la Jeunesse Libre de l'Europe Centrale et Orientale, Paris, le 2 Août, 1954, Historical Archives of European Union, sign. ME 239. Bobrowski and Gebhardt were also members of the Council; Stanisław Gebhardt, "Rada wolnej Młodzieży Europy Środkowej," *Zjednoczenie CSOM*, no. 16 (1954): 8-12.

well as the socialists, while the majority of youth delegates looked on their successes with disfavour.[96]

The activities of the young Polish Christian Democrats in Europe and their cooperation with the "senior" CDUCE sometimes yielded unexpected results. An "area of operation" identified by the CDUCE Youth Section in their working agenda in 1956 was to address "Young Christian Democrats in the world".[97] These included "UIJDC [...]; young Christian Democrats from Latin America; young Christian Democrats from Indonesia, Vietnam, India, Madagascar and Ghana; young spiritualists from Asia and Africa".[98] This trajectory was clearly inspired by the FEC, which conducted an operation to build alternatives to communist influences in Latin America. Both "senior" and young Christian Democrats were central to the pursuit of this objective. The latter, however, appeared to take precedence as the ideal choice for this mission, as they were genuinely interested in the region.[99] Catholic social thought was seen as the foundation for bold opposition to communist agitation. On the other hand, as Piotr H. Kosicki notes, "Christian Democrats like Gebhardt, Sieniewicz and Śleszyński became not only proxies for the American Cold War effort, but also empowered, independent political agents making use of American funds to pursue their own distinctly transnational, self-styled Christian Democratic agenda".[100]

Janusz Śleszyński, one of the leaders of the SP,[101] played a certain role in the development of Christian movements in Latin America. The fact that his wife – of French nationality – worked for the United Nations, among other factors, aided him in building a network of acquaintances among representatives of Latin American Christian Democratic movements. In 1953, Śleszyński reported to Sieniewicz that he had made contact with Venezuelan Christian Democratic leader Rafael Caldera.[102] Śleszyński tried to convince the Americans that the path to victory over communism led not through aggressive anti-communism, but instead support for democratic centres; Christian Democrats seemed poised to become the ex-

---

96 Appendix to letter from Stanisław Gebhardt to Konrad Sieniewicz, 10 September 1953, entitled "Youth matters: The Politcal Council [sic] of the East-Central European Youth," PIASA, col. 17/1652.

97 UCDEC Section des Jeunes, Programme of work [1956], ASG.

98 Ibid.

99 The most accurate description-to-date of this direction of the FEC's action and cooperation with Polish Christian Democrats is in Kosicki, "Christian Democracy's Global Cold War," 238.

100 Kosicki, "Christian Democracy's Global Cold War," 223.

101 This fact is elaborated upon by e.g. Konrad Sieniewicz and Stanisław Gebhardt in their memoirs published in Prządka, Świadectwa, vol. 4, 232, 281.

102 Letter from Janusz Śleszyński to Konrad Sieniewicz, 25 September 1953, PIASA, col. 17/1652.

emplar of such pro-democratic, anti-communist commitments in Latin America. Śleszyński crafted this strategy so effectively that he managed to obtain funds from the FEC, American trade unions and private industrial foundations, which had their own interests in the region, but which were also interested in a strict anti-communist campaign. His cooperation with the FEC, and his work in the CDUCE Secretariat, where Śleszyński was responsible for Latin America, opened up a new field of activity for him.[103] In time, young Christian Democrats started to take part in this action, especially Stanisław Gebhardt.[104]

The involvement of Polish Christian Democrats in global, and especially Latin American, affairs gradually came to dominate the movement's agenda, due to what has been perceived as an incredible success of Christian Democracy in these fields. The report for the years 1958-60 stated, "Whatever the future brings, whether a prompt return to the country, a long-lasting activity in exile or the limitation of our activity by the atrophy of financial possibilities at our disposal, one thing is certain, and that is that we can repeat after the poet [Horace]: *Non omnis moriar*... [I shall not wholly die], we will not disappear without a trace, the memory of us will not disappear, because we have created something new, something on a global scale, which will remain as a testimony to the fruitful functioning of the SP for a long, long time".[105] In time it became the main rationale of their exile.

Paradoxically, the young Christian Democrats, who undertook political activities with a view toward returning to their homeland, were increasingly involved in these activities in regions that were geographically remote from Europe. Lively cooperation among organisations from Latin America and Western Europe and the East-Central European émigrés resulted in the creation of a youth organisation on a global scale, parallelling the case of the "senior" Christian Democrats.[106] For the young Christian

---

103 Report, CDUCE Mission to Latin America, 21 June-24 July 1956, New York, August 1956, ASG.

104 Janusz Śleszyński, Raport o Stronnictwie Pracy w Chrześcijańsko–Demokratycznej Unii Środkowej Europy odczytany na Radzie SP w dniu 18 November 1956, Biblioteka Uniwersytecka Katolickiego Uniwersytetu Lubelskiego (BU KUL) rkps 2009, k. 235-239; Sprawozdanie: Działalność Stronnictwa Pracy w Chrześcijańsko–Demokratycznej Unii Środkowej Europy 1958-1960, BU KUL rkps 2008, k. 145-149.

105 BU KUL rkps 2008, k. 160.

106 By-laws of the Christian Democratic World Union (Union Mondiale Démocrate Chrétienne) UMDC, c. 76, BU KUL rkps 2021; see also Janusz Śleszyński, "Stronnictwo Pracy i Łacińsko–Amerykańska Chrześcijańska Demokracja," in Zygmunt Tkocz, ed, *Chrześcijańska myśl społeczna na emigracji* (London and Lublin: Odnowa, 1991), 251-254; Konrad Sieniewicz, "Chrześcijańska Demokracja na świecie," in Tkocz, *Chrześcijańska myśl społeczna na emigracji*, 242-250; Van Kemseke, *Towards an Era of Development*, 176.

Democrats, the first step was to set up an ad hoc Committee for World Questions in 1959 to draft the organisation's future statute, gather the opinions of its member organisations and take charge of the international contacts of the International Union of Young Christian Democrats. Yet the Committee's primary task was to prepare the first international congress, after which the Committee could be dissolved. Its president was the Swiss Laurent Butty, and among its five deputies were, among others, the Italian Angelo Bernassola and the Venezuelan Hilariòn Cardoso. Stanisław Gebhardt was appointed secretary.[107]

The congress was planned to take place in Caracas. Originally, it was hoped that holding the congress would be possible as early as the second half of 1960, but it was not until 1962 (8-16 May) that the efforts finally succeeded. The list of the Honorary Committee members was impressive. There were many prominent figures associated with Christian Democracy, such as Konrad Adenauer, Rafael Caldera or Amintore Fanfani. They were accompanied by Popiel and Sieniewicz, as well as other Central Europeans, mainly connected with the CDUCE: the Hungarians József Közi-Horváth and István Barankovics, the Slovene Miha Krek, and the Czechoslovak Adolf Procházka.[108] Gebhardt was Congress Secretary, and he was then elected Secretary General of the International Union of Young Christian Democrats until December 1968. In his three-year report submitted in 1965, Gebhardt estimated that the IUYCD had a total of nearly one million members worldwide.[109] He treated this as one of the greatest successes of the Polish exiles, in the wake of which they could actively participate in the shaping of the global Christian Democratic movement through the end of the 1960s. It was a plan carried out effectively by the Polish Christian Democrats who worked on the assumption that youth matters should be guided by a global organisation.

107 IUYCD ad hoc Committee for World Questions, A recapitulation of the decisions taken, CIR/INF M/59/I, [1959], ASG.
108 Based on the brochure *IUYCD. 1st World Congress*, ASG.
109 Stanisław Gebhardt, Informative report on the activities and perspectives of IUYCD from 15th May, 1962 till 15th May, 1965, prepared for the Second IUYCD Congress in Berlin (10-18 June 1965), ASG.

Sławomir Łukasiewicz

Decline and dispersal of the political potential of youth organisations

Although the International Union of Young Christian Democrats long outlived the CDUCE Youth Section, the participation of Polish Christian Democrats in its activities was on the wane already in the 1970s, in conjunction with the rise of détente in US foreign policy.[110] However, the decline of the political potential of the Christian Democratic youth organisations was caused by a number of factors – first and foremost, biology. Intra-emigration conflicts were also a significant issue. In the case of the Polish Christian Democratic youth groups, one cannot ignore the effects of the activities carried out by the communist authorities and the security apparatus of the People's Republic of Poland. They were supposed to weaken or destroy the Christian Democrats, suspected, among others, of maintaining contacts with their colleagues in the home country. The effectiveness of these actions was undermined by the lack of accurate data, since tracking Christian Democrats, who were constantly on the move around the world, was beyond the budget of the communist secret service. Therefore, the information obtained was often inaccurate.[111] Individual activists were stalked and approached. Attempts were made to recruit Edward Bobrowski, counting on the possibility of penetrating the Polish segment of the exile Christian Democrats, as well as the French Christian Democratic community. These attempts failed, although it cannot be ruled out that they partially influenced Bobrowski's decision to withdraw from political life.[112] From 1955 onwards, Jan Kułakowski was under surveillance,[113] and in the 1960s, an attempt was made to recruit Stanisław Gebhardt.[114] The question of what impact these attempts had on the activity of these exile politicians remains unanswered to this day.

In a symbolic sense, the potential of Polish youth organisations was absorbed by the elder Christian Democrats in the early 1960s. As noted in a circular letter after Seweryn Eustachiewicz's resignation from all duties, subsequent meetings were to be held in accordance with two principles, among others: respect for the support enjoyed by Karol Popiel in Poland

---

110 Kosicki, "Christian Democracy's Global Cold War," 231.
111 See, e.g., AIPN 01136/642, mf 1970-II, C2-C3.
112 The file of the information-operative case, codename: Zagończyk, conducted by Section V, Department I, of the Ministry of the Interior in the years 1957-63 against Bobrowski is stored in AIPN under AIPN 01227/680.
113 AIPN 01168/106.
114 AIPN 01168/248.

after World War II and invitations to these meetings of members of the General Secretariat, among whom we find the names of the "young" Christian Democrats: Stanisław Gebhardt and Jan Kułakowski, as well as the young publisher and bookseller Jerzy Kulczycki (1931-2013), who would play an increasingly important role in the organisation over time.[115] In the early 1960s, this was already a generation of thirty-year-olds, and it was difficult to call them "young" Christian Democrats. They did not have any successors either – and this is how the time of youth organisations came to an end.

The history of young Polish émigré Christian Democrats has several dimensions. Firstly, it shows how difficult it was for young ambitious politicians to find a place in a system of old political parties, seemingly frozen in time. Being a member of a youth movement did not open any prospects for promotion. Beliefs and ideas, Christian values, Catholic social teaching, Poland's independence, anti-communism and the unification of Europe opened a platform for cooperation and activism, but the conditions of exile quickly verified the scale and durability of the undertaken initiatives. As time passed, returning to Poland proved to be a mirage. It took a great deal of determination to survive until then, and over time this determination diminished drastically, as did available financial resources and the pool of willing partners. Eventually, on the battlefield there remained only a few individuals, even though they still stood fast under the banner of once thriving organisations.

The lack of chances for the return to the home country and scarce opportunities for achievement in the émigré party system meant that young politicians sought other outlets for their energy. First, they tried something extraordinary: uniting young Christian Democrats in flagrant disregard of the splits among their older colleagues. This was a partial success, which led to the formation of the Federation of Christian Social Youth Organisations. The Federation opened up new horizons, especially for activities on an international arena. For this purpose, the Federation used its connections with the NEI, via the International Union of Young Christian Democrats, and its relationship with the Christian Democratic Union of Central Europe, via the Youth Section. The Federation was actively involved in initiatives such as the European Youth Parliament, or the Free Youth Council of East-Central Europe.

One may also wonder why the potential of Central European, European and global projects was not maintained. With respect to European uni-

115 A circular by the SP Presidium, December 1962, PIASA, Karol Popiel Papers, col. 9/220.

Sławomir Łukasiewicz

fication, young Polish Christian Democrats drew ideas from their older colleagues and watched with fascination the continuing process of unification of the western part of the continent. Whenever they could, they raised the postulate of pan-European integration, which was inseparably connected with the liberation of East-Central Europe from the Soviet regime. Fulfilling this postulate would open a way to the political unification of the entire European continent. The young Polish Christian Democrats spoke unequivocally in favour of federal solutions.[116] They also realised that the international initiatives in which they participated gave them an opportunity to hone their communication skills and provided a good basis for cooperation in the future, united Europe.

At the same time, the division of Europe into two halves also contributed to growing differences between the émigré parties and their West European partners. According to Papini, in the mid-1970s Christian Democratic parties in Western Europe experienced a crisis manifested in the loss of historical memory and a collapse of the system of moral signposts upon which they had based their activities.[117] Changes initiated by the Second Vatican Council also contributed to the crisis in Christian Democratic parties. In the 1970s, the situation was complicated by the creation of the European People's Party. All of these nuances, however, were happening beyond the reach of the Poles and their fellow Central European Christian Democrats, who could only observe the changes and chronicle them as did the Centro Esperienze Internazionali, founded by Stanisław Gebhardt and his colleague Stanisław August Morawski in 1962 in Rome.

The young Polish Christian Democrats tried to get wherever they could by labouriously building up their positions. Edward Bobrowski, Jan Kułakowski and Stanisław Gebhardt became natural youth leaders, and with time, they should have earned a place in the structures of the SP. However, in the Polish exile party, there was no room for a change of leadership. As time went by, this deficit became more and more acute, and young Christian Democrats had to take this into account. So they found directions which did not threaten the elders, in which they could prove themselves. From 1956 onward, they played a role in funding grants for Poles visiting Western countries and cooperated with their Western colleagues as advisers, but it was far from their expectations and ambitions. Bobrowski, the great hope of the Polish Christian Democrats of the time, ultimately

---

116 See, e.g., Stanisław Gebhardt, "O współpracę międzynarodową," *Zjednoczenie CSOM*, nos. 18/19 (1955): 13-18.
117 Papini, *Christian Democrat International*, 99, 145.

withdrew from political life and took up a job in the French film industry. Kułakowski made his way beyond the Polish circles and became a leader of the global Christian trade union movement. Gebhardt remained an important go-to figure for prominent leaders of transnational European Christian Democracy; in spite of many years of involvement in European, and also Latin American, affairs, the many contacts and opportunities for action that he accumulated did not translate into any spectacular political success.

Yet Gebhardt's activities in the global structures of the Christian Democratic youth movement should nonetheless be considered the most important achievement of the Polish young Christian Democrats. Nothing of the kind was attained either earlier or later. Polish Christian Democrats ultimately failed to consolidate or properly exploit this position. Gebhardt also failed in his attempts to reactivate Christian Democracy in Poland after 1989.

Changes underway in Western politics, limited contacts with Catholic groups in the home country, the passing away of the "old guard" of Christian Democracy, the aging of the "young" and intimidation by the government of the People's Republic of Poland – all of these factors rendered it impossible to form modern East-Central European Christian Democratic parties capable of taking on new challenges.[118] Between May 1968 and January 1969, the RFI conducted a survey on a representative sample, which showed that Christian Democrats in Poland could still count on considerable public support (34%) in the hypothetical event of free elections. Although theoretically there was still a need for a Christian Democratic party in Poland, there was no way to create one. Young Christian Democrats could not play a significant role in home country national politics, and the party life of the émigré community was fading. There was a lack of tools that would make it possible to maintain the potential built on international activities in exile. The revolutions of 1989 opened a new chapter, but no instrument available to the Poles proved effective in rebuilding the Polish political scene with a strong Christian Democratic Party. Today, hardly anyone remembers the potential that was built outside the country in the quarter of a century after the war, but which was lost irretrievably.

---

118 *Party preferences in hypothetical free elections in Poland, Hungary and Czechoslovakia*, March 1969, PIASA, Karol Popiel Papers, col. 9/43.

Sławomir Łukasiewicz

8

CULTURAL VERSUS POLITICAL CHRISTIAN DEMOCRATS
Debating the Idea of (Christian) Democracy in Lithuanian Exile

Justinas Dementavičius

To talk about Lithuanian Christian Democracy in exile is to talk about the history of Lithuanian Christian Democracy writ large.[1] The two are inseparable, because more than a century's worth of history of the Lithuanian Christian Democratic movement was marked by close links with the Lithuanian diaspora.

At the beginning of the twentieth century, due to vast economic emigration to the USA and studies of Lithuanians in Western European and Russian universities, a vivid Lithuanian culture was forming outside the area of ethnic Lithuanian lands. As a result, many important events took place, and seminal political works were written by intellectuals treated as Lithuanians in exile. This holds true when one speaks about the first political programme of Lithuanian Christian Democrats written in 1905 by the priests Jonas Mačiulis-Maironis and Pranciškus Būčys, both lecturers at the Imperial Roman Catholic Theological Academy in Saint Petersburg,[2] prior to the so-called All-Lithuanian assembly, the first meeting of national political leaders,[3] on the eve of the 1905 Russian Revolution.[4] Even

---

1   This research was funded by a grant (No. MOD-17008) from the Research Council of Lithuania.
2   It is worth mentioning that the Lithuanian Christian Democratic Party was established by Catholic priests and followed Catholic social teaching; most (if not all) members of the party were Catholics. The same was true for other Christian organisations in interwar Lithuania and in Lithuanian exile. Therefore, in the Lithuanian case, *Christian* presupposes *Catholic* and vice versa.
3   Tomas Balkelis, *The making of modern Lithuania* (London: Routledge, 2009), 50-68.
4   It is worth noting that this programme was not supported by the Catholic Church's hierarchy. Even though it followed the social teachings of Leo XIII, it was written by Lithuanians and devoted only to Lithuanians, thus ignoring the claims of Polish and Belarussian Catholics. Later, this programme was cited and referred to in social work, but no party structures were built at the time. This happened only a decade later, in 1917.

though it did not lead to the formation of a party due to resistance from the Church hierarchy, it was remembered in 1917 when the Lithuanian Christian Democratic Party (LCDP) was established in German-occupied Lithuania. In the same year, a party of the same name was formed among war refugees in Russia. This émigré branch of the party played an important role in developing a more socially radical party programme. The most prominent Lithuanian Catholic intellectuals and future members of the LCDP were studying at universities in Western Europe (most of them in Louvain, Belgium, or Fribourg, Switzerland) before and after the establishment of the Lithuanian Republic in 1918, and played an important role in casting the nascent Lithuania for an international audience to see as a democratic and independent state.

The history of Lithuanian Christian Democracy is especially inseparable from the experience of exile during the Soviet occupation of Lithuania from 1944 to 1990. On the one hand, a large number of LCDP members fled the country, which led to the re-establishment of the LCDP in Germany in 1946.[5] From that time, the party acted as an autonomous political movement in Europe and the United States, up until Lithuanian independence. On the other hand, another influential political movement appeared in exile: the Fellows of Lithuania Front (FLF), led by Christian intellectuals. Criticising both authoritarian and liberal tendencies in Lithuanian politics, they called for a democratic politics based on Christian values but, at the same time, attacked the LCDP for being too passive, lacking responsibility, and misrepresenting the idea of (Christian) democracy. After escaping from the Soviet Union in 1944, they developed specific ideas on democracy, which they publicly presented as rooted in Christian tradition. Even though internal debates of Lithuanian émigrés about the true meaning of Christian Democracy and Christians in politics had already been exhausted in the 1960s, some intellectuals remained active up until the 1980s. Since then, their activity mostly boiled down ideologically to the repetition of old theses, focusing on the abstract idea of a free Lithuania, but lacking in deeper debate about its future political form or about the Christian concept of "democracy". After 1989, both organisations established contacts with intellectuals and politicians in Soviet Lithuania that later figured in the political activity of the LCDP and the cultural activity

---

5   In the 1950s, the LCDP moved its headquarters to New York and renamed itself the Lithuanian Christian Democratic Union (LCDU, Lith. Lietuvių krikščionių demokratų sąjunga) because American laws did not allow an ethnic non-American party.

Justinas Dementavičius

of the organisation Į laisvę (Toward Freedom) and the journal *Naujasis Židinys-Aidai* (New Hearth-Echoes).

Despite the historical importance of Lithuanian Catholic émigrés, the legacy of Christian political movements in Lithuanian exile is still under-researched. For example, broad transnational histories of the modern political thought of Central and Eastern European nations pay no attention to this subject – for Lithuania, the multi-volume *History of modern political thought in East Central Europe* mentions only, and only briefly, the influential thinkers usually linked to the Lithuanian liberal tradition Vytautas Kavolis, Tomas Venclova and Aleksandras Štromas, with Lithuanian Christian Democratic intellectuals presented only as a part of interwar political debates in Lithuania.[6] The same is true of the account of Lithuanian political thought in exile written by Leonidas Donskis.[7] Even Lithuanian national historiography remains insular. Mostly focused on other political and social organisations,[8] it gives only a broad overview of politics in exile,[9] at best introducing important documents and texts written by Catholic authors without providing a clear analytical narrative.[10]

The goal of this chapter is to reconstruct the ideological imaginary and debates of Lithuanian Christian Democracy in exile during the Soviet Lithuania period (1944-1990). While analysing Lithuanian Christian Democrats in exile, this contribution will focus on several issues. First, I will present the structure of Lithuanian Christian Democracy in exile, its genesis, development and relations to other political organisations. Second, I

---

6   Balázs Trenscényi et al., *A history of modern political thought in East Central Europe*, vol. 2, Pt. 1*: Negotiating Modernity in the "Short Twentieth Century" and Beyond* (Oxford: Oxford University Press, 2018), 183-184. For a broader presentation and interpretation, see Leonidas Donskis, *Identity and Freedom: Mapping Nationalism and Social Criticism in Twentieth Century Lithuania* (London: Routledge, 2002).

7   Donskis, among liberal thinkers, briefly mentions important figures in the FLF – Juozas Grinius as a kind of liberal Catholic and philosopher, Antanas Maceina as a cultural philosopher – but he does not take into account their interpretation of democracy. Leonidas Donskis, *Loyalty, dissent and betrayal: modern Lithuania and the East-Central European moral imagination* (Amsterdam: Rodopi, 2005), 97-118.

8   Ilona Bučinskytė, *Idealų vedami: Ateitininkai išeivijoje XX a. 5-7 dešimtmečiais* (Vilnius: Versus aureus, 2008); Daiva Dapkutė, *Lietuvių išeivijos liberaliosios srovės genezė* (Vilnius: Vaga, 2002); Kristina Ūsaitė, *Pasaulio lietuvių jaunimo sąjunga XX a. 6-9 dešimtmečiais* (Vilnius: Versus Aureus, 2013); Juozas Banionis, *Lietuvos laisvinimas Vakaruose 1940-1975* (Vilnius: LGGRTC, 2010).

9   Egidijus Aleksandravičius et al., *The Cultural Activities of Lithuanian Émigrés* (Vilnius: Versus aureus, 2002); Egidijus Aleksandravičius, *Karklo diegas: lietuvių pasaulio istorija* (Vilnius: Versus aureus, 2002); Linas Saldukas, *Lithuanian diaspora* (Vilnius: Vaga, 2002).

10 Pranas Povilaitis and Audronė Škiudaitė, eds, *Lietuviai krikščionys demokratai išeivijoje: 1946-2008 m.* (Vilnius: Baltijos kopija, 2013); Kęstutis Girnius et al., eds, *Lietuva, kurios nebuvo: pilnutinės demokratijos svarstymai ir vertinimai* (Vilnius: VU leidykla, 2016); Adolfas Damušis, *Žvilgsnis, nukreiptas į idealų aukštumas: Adolfo Damušio tekstai* (Vilnius: Versus aureus, 2009).

will focus on their political attitudes and try to explain the basis for their political thought. Finally, I will zero in on a specific discussion about the meaning of democracy.

The main focus of this chapter is not the institutional history of Christian Democrats (although this will be briefly discussed in the first section), but rather the ideological positions defining two versions of the political imaginary of Lithuanian Christians in exile, which were labelled as "political" and "cultural" forms of democracy.[11] I will argue that both of these versions can be called forms of Christian Democracy and in agreement on the imperfection of contemporary (liberal) democracy, which, thus, had to be *Instaurare in Christo*, restoring all spheres of human life – political, social, cultural, economic and international – according to Christian values. Both of these political views can be seen as a critique of the "narrow" understanding of democracy and the development of an alternative, "broader" Christian version. But, at the same time, they differed in their treatment of personal freedom and freedom of conscience, the role of the Christian worldview and Christian political parties in political life and other important matters. Therefore, from an ideological standpoint, it is possible to speak not about one Christian Democracy, but about several Christian Democracies in Lithuanian exile or, to be more precise, about Christian Democracy as a party and confessional political programme and Christian democratic ideals as a worldview, which do not have to be manifest in state or party politics, but rather be present as a respectful treatment of every person by other persons and institutions.

These perspectives will be presented by focusing on the works of two key political and intellectual figures of Lithuanian exile: philosopher and FLF ideologue Antanas Maceina (1908-1987), and the priest Mykolas Krupavičius (1885-1970), longtime leader of the LCDP. Krupavičius was already actively engaged in social activism and politics at the beginning of the twentieth century and an important figure in the creation of the LCDP in 1917. He wrote the first official programme of the party and subsequently established himself as one of its leaders. As such, he took an active part in governmental initiatives and parliamentary matters, at least until the military *coup d'état* of 1926 that led to a nationalist government headed by Antanas Smetona.[12] As the Catholic Church attempted to have good relations with this new authoritarian regime, Krupavičius retired

---

11 Antanas Maceina, "Kultūrinė demokratija," *Aidai*, no. 8 (1947).

12 Alfonsas Eidintas, *Antanas Smetona and his Lithuania: from the national liberation movement to an authoritarian regime* (Boston: Brill, 2015).

Justinas Dementavičius

from politics and for some time lived and studied in France. He returned in 1930 and worked as a priest in small Lithuanian parishes. During the first Soviet and the Nazi occupations, as a recognised public figure he protested the totalitarian politics that were directed against the rights of Lithuanian citizens. As a result, during the Nazi occupation in 1943, he was imprisoned and deported to Germany. After the war, he was not willing to return to Soviet Lithuania and stayed in Germany until moving to the US in 1956. Considered a founding father of the LCDP, he remained one of the leading figures in the party and was one of the most influential Lithuanian politicians in exile. Despite his age, he was active in public life and wrote several books and a number of articles on Christian Democracy and actively participated in political debates.

Maceina belonged to a younger generation of lay Christian intellectuals who were mostly educated in independent Lithuania, but also for some time studied in Western universities (in 1932-35 he visited Fribourg, Louvain, Strasbourg and Brussels). A gifted student, he became a pupil of the leading Christian intellectual of the older generation, the philosopher Stasys Šalkauskis. After finishing a dissertation on pedagogy (1935), Maceina worked at the main Lithuanian university as a professor of philosophy and cultural studies. During the years 1936-40, he became one of the most productive social thinkers dealing with questions of social Catholicism and education. In 1938, after publishing the book *Social Justice*, he became a target of critique from prominent priests who considered him too "socialist".[13] For some time, this distanced Maceina from Catholic social thought and instead led him to a more nationalistic secular discourse, mostly expressed in the text *Nation and State* (1939).[14] As a result of this and his activity in Lithuania during the Nazi occupation, some critics treat him as a proponent of nationalist ideology.[15] But his political thought, especially beginning in 1943, became anti-nationalistic in a political sense, even though he still defended the need for a solid national culture. As early as 1943, the article "Toward Reformed Democracy" appeared in the journal *Į laisvę*, articulating the ideas of a new kind of democracy that was

---

13 In this book, Maceina attempted to show that a certain measure of nationalisation of goods is important for public welfare. As he also spoke about the need for the Catholic Church to dispose of part of its property (lands, non-secular buildings etc.) the book was seen as having communist undertones.

14 Maceina, "Tauta ir valstybė," *Naujoji Romuva*, no. 11 (1939): 227-230. In this text, Maceina presented ideas of eugenics and claimed that the state should seek improvement of the nation not only culturally, but also physically.

15 Donskis, *Loyalty, dissent and betrayal*, 98.

to overcome the errors of liberal democracy; simultaneously, he criticised the Lithuanian authoritarian regime. After escaping to Germany in 1945, he and his colleagues further developed this idea in the periodical *Mažasis Židinys* (Little Hearth). From that time until his death, Maceina lived in Germany, where he taught at the universities of Freiburg and Münster, wrote a number of books dealing with questions of philosophy and Christianity in the modern world and also contributed to the political programme of the FLF known as "Toward Integral Democracy" (1957). Although most members of the FLF lived in the US, Maceina could be seen as an influential ideologue of the FLF. His democratic convictions were based on the social teachings of the Catholic Church, and his papers constantly referred to Christian intellectuals and papal encyclicals. But his milieu avoided being linked with the "narrow party politics" of the LCDP and called for integral (*pilnutinė)* democracy, which can be real only if based on Christian respect for the person.

The main sources of this chapter's analysis will be the personal papers, writings and letters of Maceina and Krupavičius. Both intellectuals can also be easily linked to a broader pool of documents kept in the archives of the Christian Democratic party as well as the personal papers of their various associates. It is worth noting that Christian Democrats and intellectuals were the most active group in publishing among Lithuanian political groups in exile. Dozens of journals, newspapers and books can be linked to their activity, but the most important among them are *Aidai* (Echoes) and *Į laisvę* (Toward Freedom), edited by intellectuals close to Maceina; the official magazine of the Christian Democrats, *Tėvynės sargas* (Guardian of Fatherland); and the daily *Draugas* (Friend), which was edited by members of the LCDP. These were the main platforms for presenting and discussing political ideas, analysing the conditions of Soviet Lithuania and Lithuanians in exile and offering a Christian interpretation of political questions. *Į laisvę* and *Tėvynės sargas* were the most political among them, but probably the most widely read by Lithuanians in exile were the cultural journal *Aidai* and the daily *Draugas*. Nonetheless, all of them are illustrative as representing intellectual trends and framing public opinion in Lithuanian exile.

Justinas Dementavičius

The institutionalisation of Christian political movements in exile

Unlike Christian Democratic movements and parties in Western Europe, the main reason for establishing the Lithuanian Christian Democratic party in exile was not the Nazi, but the Soviet occupation. True, from the early 1930s the right-leaning Lithuanian authoritarian regime had already been implementing policies directed against Christian social and youth movements, which reached the highest point of authoritarian oppression in 1936 with the banning of all political parties, including the LCDP.[16] But even despite these policies, politicians and intellectuals linked to the LCDP were not prosecuted and acted moderately, because they saw the main geopolitical threats as arising from territorial disagreements with Germany and Poland. Indeed, the Soviet Union was interpreted not as a geopolitical (at that time Lithuania did not have a border with the Soviet Union), but as a social and cultural threat, all the more so because Lithuanian Christian intellectuals considered communism as an ideology totally incompatible with Christianity.[17] These fears became particularly relevant after the 1939 Molotov-Ribbentrop Pact, which led to the so-called first Soviet occupation of Lithuania in 1940-41. This was interrupted by the relatively short Nazi occupation of 1941-44, which by some Lithuanians was treated as a lesser evil and an opportunity to restore Lithuanian statehood with the help of Germany. Not only did these naïve hopes not come true, but in 1944 Lithuania was incorporated into the Soviet Union as the Lithuanian Soviet Socialist Republic (LSSR), which by those in exile was considered to be the second Soviet occupation, or re-occupation.[18]

In 1940-41, during the first Soviet occupation, prominent Catholic intellectuals and priests were already fleeing to Germany in hopes of escap-

16 It is usually presented as authoritarian nationalist; for example, see Stanley Payne, *A History of Fascism, 1914-1945* (London: UCL Press, 1995). Until the 1930s, it was ideologically ambiguous, but some of the leading intellectuals of the regime (e.g. Izidorius Tamošaitis) were clearly sympathetic to Italian fascism. Militant politics and the racist ideology of Nazi Germany were not popular, mostly because Nazism considered the Lithuanian nation as inferior, and Germany threatened to take back Klaipėda (Memel), which was part of Prussia prior to World War I and governed by Lithuania only since 1923.

17 Communism was criticised following the lines drawn by Pope Pius XI in the encyclical *Divini Redemptoris*, but Lithuanian Christians experienced close encounters with Bolshevism much earlier – while attempting to have a Lithuanian Christian party in Russia in 1917 and during the Soviet seizure of Vilnius in 1919. Likewise, a communist coup was presented as an imminent threat to Lithuanian society throughout the entire interwar period.

18 Vytautas Stanley Vardys, *The Catholic Church, dissent and nationality in Soviet Lithuania* (Boulder, Colo.: East European Quarterly, 1978).

ing onward to the USA. In 1941 some of them returned to Lithuania with eastward-moving German troops and tried to establish independent, or at least semi-independent, political and cultural institutions. In some cases, these attempts were not in line with German interests and politics, so some of the disloyal activists were imprisoned, deported to Germany and stayed there because they did not want to return to Lithuania once it was re-occupied by the Soviet Union (as in the case of Krupavičius). In some cases, mild resistance remained unpunished by the German government, but the activists involved decided to leave the country to escape possible persecution by the Soviets in 1944 (as in the case of Maceina).

Around 60,000 citizens fled the country in 1944-45 and were located in displaced persons (DP) camps in Germany. According to the prominent Lithuanian scholar of exile Egidijus Aleksandravičius, this exile can be described as an exile of poets and soldiers, because a number of them were former military personnel or intellectuals.[19] In fact, it is quite hard to have an accurate description of the social structure of Lithuanian refugees in Western Europe, but it would be fair to claim that it was an exile of elites – university scholars, intellectuals and politicians. Therefore, the first years of exile already saw attempts to re-establish cultural (for example, journals, schools, even a university), political (for example, parties) and social (for example, youth and charitable) organisations, which were repressed by both Soviet and Nazi authorities in Lithuania. Having divergent ideological views, these people were nonetheless united by their anti-Soviet and pro-independence stance, which manifested itself in the activity of the Supreme Committee for the Liberation of Lithuania (SCLL; in Lithuanian – Vyriausiasis Lietuvos Išlaisvinimo Komitetas, VLIK).[20]

During the first years of exile, through the beginning of the 1960s, there was still hope of returning to a free Lithuania, but hopes of independent statehood vanished as the Lithuanian guerrilla resistance weakened, and the Soviet regime remained preponderant even after the death of Stalin in 1953. As a result, more than fifty percent of the Lithuanian refugees located in DP camps in Europe resettled to the USA. The main reason for this was the fact that the Lithuanian diaspora there was already large and active from the beginning of the twentieth century, and it actively participated in resettlement to the US according to the so-called DP Act 774 of 1948.

19 Aleksandaravičius, *Karklo diegas*, 411-556.
20 The first meetings of the SCLL as an anti-Nazi movement uniting all the main Lithuanian parties had already been held in 1943, in Kaunas. In 1944, most of its active members were arrested and imprisoned by German officials. Beginning in 1945, already as an anti-Soviet movement, its main office was located in Germany: Würzburg and later Reutlingen.

Justinas Dementavičius

Only a relatively small percentage of Lithuanians stayed in Europe (around 8,000 in Germany, around 4,000 in the UK, Italy and Sweden, with the numbers much lower for other important destinations) or immigrated to South America (around 2,000 to Venezuela) and Australia (around 5,000).[21] Accordingly, most of the organisations that had been (re-)established in Europe were relocated to various parts of the Americas (for example, the main political institution SCLL moved its headquarters to New York in 1955), while only individual party member branches remained in Europe. As a consequence, Lithuanians in exile were scattered around the globe. For example, if speaking about Christian institutions, it is worth mentioning that, even though some intellectuals remained in Germany, the most active publishing and intellectual work was done in various places in the US. One of the most important intellectual centres for Catholic studies, a seminary for Lithuanian priests called the Collegium of Saint Casimir, was located in Rome.

An influential segment of the exiled population consisted of Catholic intellectuals and ex-Christian Democratic party members, both laymen and priests, who played an active role in social and political life in interwar Lithuania and, later, in Lithuanian exile. Two groups became the main proponents of political Catholicism in the postwar era – the Lithuanian Christian Democratic Party and the Fellows of the Lithuanian Front (FLF, Lietuvos fronto bičiuliai). This Christian Democratic institutional structure can be explained by attempts to maintain continuity, which ultimately became not a unifying, but instead a fracturing element. Traditionally, at least since 1917, the main proponent of political Catholicism in Lithuania had been the Lithuanian Christian Democratic Party (LCDP), which was banned by the authoritarian regime in 1936. Most of its (ex-)members were not prosecuted and even took up high positions in administrative or Church institutions, but were not allowed to take part in political life; it was forbidden to join political parties or criticise the government for un-democratic behaviour. This intensification of authoritarian practices and lack of action to the contrary from the Church hierarchy led to political passivity, which was later criticised by the younger generation of Christian intellectuals, including Maceina. Loyal, however, to the democratic Lithuanian state of 1918, many of the ex-LCDP members fled Lithuania after the Soviet occupation in 1944.

The LCDP officially reappeared on 26 October 1946, in Scheinfeld, Germany. The LCDP declared a "traditional" attitude, that the party is a politi-

21 Eidintas, *Lietuvių kolumbai*, 96.

cal force of the centre, a third way between liberal individualism and left- or right-wing collectivism, aiming to reform society according to Christian Democratic principles: "only by reaching the goals [of our party] can a person enslaved by both radical left- and right-wing ideologies of modern civilisation liberate himself. The party's traditional line is progress and attempts to reform life in accordance with the principles of Christianity. [...] only this will guarantee individual liberty, economic and cultural well-being for every citizen".[22]

However, Catholic political activity in the public sphere did not take one form only, i.e. the form of a political party, but was also visible in the communities of intellectuals not related to the LCDP. The most active among them (Antanas Maceina, historian Zenonas Ivinskis, literary critic Juozas Ambrazevičius-Brazaitis, sociologist Pranas Dielininkaitis) were part of the so-called "generation of '36" – the younger generation of Catholic activists, mostly born in the first decade of the twentieth century.[23] They took their name from the collective declaration "Towards the creation of an organic state," published in 1936.[24] Formally, this declaration sought to avoid politics, and the scholars presented themselves as engaged in cultural and not political work. But in reality, its aim was to chart a third way between liberal parliamentarism and nationalist authoritarianism, and it was therefore harshly criticised by supporters of the existing authoritarian regime. At the same time, this younger generation of lay Catholic intellectuals attacked the LCDP for its inability to resist authoritarian tendencies, and for its lack of initiative. These younger intellectuals, in turn, wanted to reform Lithuanian society in accordance with Christian teaching.[25]

In 1940, the Soviet Union moved its troops into Lithuanian territory and forced it to join the Soviet Union. As a result, more than 10,000 non-Soviet social and political leaders were persecuted, but a number of the prominent figures of the "generation of '36" either managed to avoid repression (e.g. the historians Juozas Ambrazevičius and Zenonas Ivinskis) or fled to exile in Germany (then a neighbouring country) with the hope of escaping

---

22 LCDP, "Atkuriamosios Amerikiečių zonos LKDP konferencijos 1946-10-26 Schenfelde rezoliucijos," in Povilaitis and Škiudaitė, *Lietuviai krikščionys demokratai išeivijoje*, 52.

23 Ramūnas Labanauskas, *The young Catholic movement: genesis, ideological principles and putting them into practice (1919-1940)* (Kaunas: Lithuanian Academic Libraries Network, 2011).

24 Antanas Maceina et al., "Į organiškosios valstybės kūrybą," *Naujoji Romuva*, 8, August 1936: 169-175.

25 It is worth mentioning that, during the *coup d'état* of 1926 organised by the military and nationalists, the LCDP stayed relatively silent because it was directed against the left-wing majority in parliament and not parliamentarism or democracy itself. But, as it soon became clear, these convictions were naïve.

to the USA (like Maceina himself, or the Rev. Stasys Yla).[26] In 1941, some of them (Ambrazevičius, Maceina, the chemist Adolfas Damušis) joined the Lithuanian Activist Front (LAF), which was a movement uniting different prewar political parties ranging from social democrats to the radical Right, as well as non-partisan activists.

The LAF is known for organising an uprising against the Soviets on 23 June 1941. In fact, this revolt was quite limited, as the Red Army was withdrawing from Lithuania because of advancing German troops, and after several months of cooperation with the Nazi regime, the LAF was dissolved in September 1941. But those months were crucial for the "generation of '36" in establishing itself as a separate political movement – the Lithuanian Front (LF). Formally, the Lithuanian Front attempted to become a broad unifying movement, but was actually led by Catholic intellectuals and seen as a Christian political force both by parties of the Left and Christian Democratic party members.

The divide between these two Christian movements became clear as early as 1946, when this younger generation of politically active Christians remained separate from the LCDP and organised a meeting of LF members in Bad Cannstatt in 1948. They tried to avoid any links to party politics, and it became popular to speak about an organisation without any formal institutionalisation: "The Lithuanian Front must remain a movement [but not an organisation]. Frontmen are not united by statute: we don't have those [...] Frontmen are united by unity of ideas, their view on the state".[27] Even though some of the leading figures of the movement, including Maceina, called for remaining a movement and not an institutionalised party, after founding conferences that took place in the USA in 1951-52, they established the FLF (Fellows of the Lithuanian Front; Lietuvių fronto bičiuliai). This was reminiscent of the ideologically ambivalent LAF, but despite calls for the unification of all political forces for the sake of Lithuanian independence, the leaders of the FLF were Catholic intellectuals of the "generation of '36" (Brazaitis, Maceina, Damušis, Ivinskis, *etc.*) and were treated with suspicion, or even as enemies of Christian Democracy, because they opposed the political union of Christians in the structures of the LCDP.[28] For their part, the FLF criticised the LCDP for its lack of initia-

26 Antanas Maceina, *Antano Maceinos laiškai prel. Pranciškui Jurui* (Vilnius: Katalikų akademija, 1997), 13-16.
27 Antanas Maceina, "Lietuvių fronto organizacija ir taktika," National Library of Lithuania (NLL), F181-97, 2.
28 Central Committee of the LCDU, "Krikščioniškoji demokratija ir Lietuvių frontas," in Povilaitis and Škiudaitė, *Lietuviai krikščionys demokratai išeivijoje*, 111-119.

tive in the interwar era, the un-Christian lifestyle of some of its leading figures (e.g. belonging to masonic organisations and living in concubinage) and also for dogmatic party politics, which were closed to outsiders and did not help to consolidate Lithuanians in exile for the sake of Lithuanian freedom.[29] As an alternative, the FLF projected a broad movement that sought to bring together all Lithuanians devoted to the goal of an independent Lithuania and devoted to the principles of Christian morality.[30]

This divide raised a question about the political leadership of all Lithuanian Christians in exile, which remained relevant up until 1990. At least formally, the LCDP claimed to be the only real political party of Christians,[31] while the FLF tried to avoid the label of a party and presented itself as a unifying force based on Christian moral and cultural values.[32] To some degree, this self-representation was visible in practical initiatives. The LCDP first of all acted as a political party, setting itself the goal of becoming the leading political force of Lithuanians in exile. As such, it became the most influential member of the SCLL, which remained one of the most important institutions in the struggle for independence up until 1990.[33] In 1950 it became a member of the Nouvelles Équipes Internationales (NEI),[34] and it contributed in the same year to the establishment of the Christian Democratic Union of Central Europe (CDUCE). The LCDP was also the most active Lithuanian party in launching the Assembly of Captive European Nations in 1954.[35] While participating in various international organisations, the LCDP together with other Central and Eastern European countries also raised the issue of independent statehood, which became the most important question on the LCDP's international political agenda.[36] But this international cooperation with both Western and East-Central European Christian forces was a matter of secondary importance compared to the

---

29 Maceina, *Antano Maceinos laiškai prel. Pranciškui Jurui*, 36; Mykolas Krupavičius to Antanas Maceina, NLL, F181-170.
30 Būtėnas, "Atsišaukimas į politinę sąžinę," *Į laisvę*, no. 1 (1953): 1-4.
31 LCDP, "Krikščionys demokratai ir Lietuvių frontas," 111-119.
32 Brazaitis, "Srovė ir uola: Mūsų politinės diferenciacijos kelias," *Į laisvę*, no. 1 (1953): 6-15.
33 Banionis, *Lietuvos laisvinimas Vakaruose 1940-1975*; Juozas Banionis, *Lietuvos laisvinimas Vakaruose po Helsinkio akto 1975-1994* (Vilnius: LGGRTC, 2017).
34 After the decision of the NEI to accept parties in exile, Krupavičius wrote that the LCDP "decided to accept this admission. It will be a new international *cathedra*, from which we can shout to the world about wrongs done to our fatherland and ask for justice". Mykolas Krupavičius, "Krikščionių demokratų internacionalas," Lithuanian Institute of History (LIH) F54-649, 722.
35 See Katalin Kádár Lynn's chapter in this volume.
36 Idesbald Goddeeris, "Exiles' Strategies for Lobbying in International Organisations: Eastern European Participation in the Nouvelles Équipes Internationales," *European Review of History / Revue européenne d'histoire* 11, no. 3 (2004): 383-400.

Justinas Dementavičius

most urgent cultural and political issues of the dispersed Lithuanian exile community. The LCDP were following the international initiatives of the broader Christian Democratic movement, but the party's ambitions did not aim at an active role in this process, instead aspiring only to remind Western allies about threat of communism.[37]

The FLF took a different course of action than the LCDP. It claimed to be not a party, but, first of all, a cultural movement united by the Christian worldview with its main focus on cultural work among Lithuanians. In the words of its formal leader Juozas Brazaitis: "We grew up in the atmosphere of Christian principles, which are universal treasures of the Western spirit. Christian morality for us is the irrefutable norm, which should be followed in all human actions, including the political. We know that, even in the era of democratic Lithuania, the human person, so highly valued by Christianity, was overshadowed [by the state]. [In a cultural democracy we have to] respect the person's freedom and to create conditions for his free actions".[38]

True, like all other Lithuanian political groups, the FLF had representatives in the SCLL, but, as in the interwar period, their activity was more visible not in the political, but in intellectual fields. Philosopher Juozas Girnius became editor-in-chief of the multi-volume Lithuanian encyclopedia published in exile. A number of intellectuals began teaching in Western universities,[39] from which they wrote for the cultural journal *Aidai* and the more politically inclined magazine *Į laisvę*. They took an active role in the Scientific Academy of Lithuanian Catholics that united Catholic intellectuals working in various scholarly fields, and they presented their academic work to the Lithuanian public in exile. "Toward freedom" (the translation of *Į laisvę*) became an important motto and the name of a foundation established in 1960. It was engaged in publishing and supported the organisation of annual scientific and cultural symposiums.

But this formal divide between political and cultural work was not so perfect in reality. A number of Catholic organisations were re-established in exile, including the influential Lithuanian Catholic Federation movement Ateitis (Future), the Lithuanian Catholic Academy of Science (LCAS) and Caritas centres for Lithuanians. Both the LCDP and the FLF competed to have representatives on the managing boards of these organisations.

---

37 Vaclovas Zakarauskas, "Krikščioniškoji demokratija tarptautinėje veikloje," *Tėvynės sargas*, no. 1 (1963): 74-78.

38 Brazaitis, "Srovė ir uola. Mūsų politinės diferenciacijos kelias," 14-15.

39 For example, Maceina taught in Freiburg and later Münster, historian Zenonas Ivinskas in Bonn. After 1953 both of them were members of Baltisches Forschungsinstitut.

This cleavage was even more pronounced in the face of disagreements among the prelates of the Lithuanian Catholic Church. In 1946, as part of a Vatican mission to DP camps, Pope Pius XII entrusted the pastoral care of Lithuanian refugees to the so-called Lithuanian National Delegation (Lith. Tautinė Delegatūra; active until 1949),[40] but as some acting Lithuanian priests and bishops also escaped to Western Europe, there was disagreement as to who should have the higher rank and the last word in Church and Catholic Action matters among Lithuanians. As it happens, the LCDP had good relations with bishops, while the FLF was more inclined to listen to the National Delegation.[41] Last but not least, this competition for influence between the FLF and the LCDP was at least partly based on the worldviews of both organisations and their disagreement about the meaning of being a socially active Catholic in exile. For the LCDP activists, confessional party politics was an important part of realising Christian Democratic ideals, while the FLF believed that it was wrong to ascribe a democratic ideal to one party or one confessional view, and campaigned for cultural, but not political, activity on the part of Lithuanians.

Despite attempts to consolidate one Lithuanian Catholic movement in exile, the debate remained active, and disagreements were visible through the end of the 1960s.[42] In the first years of exile, the main reason for the debate was probably that there was still a certain (and naïve) hope that Soviet domination in Lithuania would not last long and that Western countries would fight the Soviet Union. Therefore, the debate about the future Lithuanian state, its leadership, political structure and the role of the Christian worldview in that state was an important issue. Gradually, however, they realised that Soviet domination would not be short-lived, and this led to a streamlining of the main political programme, by committing to the struggle for Lithuanian independence and projects to maintain a national identity (especially for the younger generation) in exile.

---

40 Paul Weidling, "'For the Love of Christ': Strategies of International Catholic Relief and the Allied Occupation of Germany, 1945-1948," *Journal of Contemporary History* 43, no. 3 (2008): 477-492; Indrė Vitkuvienė and Kęstutis Žemaitis, "Lietuvių išeivių pastoracijos modelis Vakarų Europoje 1946-1949 metais," *Soter*, no. 94 (2018): 25-49.

41 Jurgita Blažytė, "Religinis lietuvių gyvenimas DP stovyklose 1945-1950," *Oikos: lietuvių migracijos ir diasporos studijos*, no. 1 (2008): 83-103; Gudonis, "Vatikano tautinės delegatūros vaidmuo," *Aidai*, no. 26 (1949): 237-239; Maceina, *Antano Maceinos laiškai prel. Pranciškui Jurui*, 28-32. This tendency could also reflect interwar tensions between young Catholics and Archbishop Skvireckas, as the latter was critical in regard to initiatives of the younger generation and tried to privilege relations with Lithuanian nationalists.

42 Povilaitis and Škiudaitė, *Lietuviai krikščionys demokratai išeivijoje*, 91-119.

Several factors can be identified that fostered political routinisation and ideological ambiguity. First, two reasons led to the belief that the Soviet Union was stable and a strong political power in Lithuania: (a) the end of Lithuanian guerrilla fighting in 1953 and (b) the successful transition of power to Khrushchev after the death of Stalin, also in 1953. The absence of support from the Western powers for the Lithuanian cause also helped to foreclose the hope of independence. Second, as was mentioned earlier, the dispersal of Lithuanians across the globe made it difficult to coordinate actions effectively. Even though most of the exiles were located in the US, they lived in different cities – mainly Cleveland, Boston, Chicago and New York. This dispersal eased the tensions between different political parties, but at the same time made it difficult to have an active party organisation, especially because the party members, especially the younger generation, gradually integrated into the societies of their adopted countries.[43]

The heated debates of the first decades in exile gave way to political and cultural routine: annual conferences of the LCAS, scientific and cultural forums, meetings with Western politicians, *etc.*[44] This work constituted the main political activity up until 1989. A few years after announcing *perestroika*, attempts to liberalise the Soviet Union's administration of the Lithuanian Soviet Socialist Republic (LSSR) allowed for the founding of independent civic and political organisations, creating in turn the possibility of re-establishing old Lithuanian Catholic institutions in Lithuania. Therefore, in 1989 the LCDP was (re-)established by the anti-Soviet resistance, who then sought to reach out to the "Western" LCDP.[45] FLF initiatives were gradually transferred to Lithuanian soil; for example, *Į laisvę* opened a

---

43 For the broader stakes of choosing between "integration" and continued "representation", see, e.g., Michel Dumoulin and Idesbald Goddeeris, eds, *Integration or representation? Polish exiles in Belgium and the European construction* (Louvain-la-Neuve: Academia Bruylant, 2005).

44 Conceptually, this trend can be seen in the shift in self-representation of those in exile. During the first decades, it was more common to speak about *tremtis*, or forced deportation, because it was impossible to return to Lithuania safely. Later it became more common to speak about *išeivija*, or émigrés.

45 Audronė Škiudaitė, ed, *Krikščionys demokratai Lietuvoje 1989-2015* (Vilnius: Baltijos kopija, 2015), 22-23, 72-75. For a broader overview, see Artūras Svarauskas, "The Restoration of Christian Democracy in Lithuania, 1989-1990: Continuities and Ruptures," in Michael Gehler, Piotr H. Kosicki, Helmut Wohnout, eds, *Christian Democracy and the Fall of Communism* (Leuven: Leuven University Press, 2019), 275-286. Leaders of the "post-Soviet" LCDP attempted to have contacts with the LCDU in exile from the moment of the party's launching. Even though the Lithuanian LCDP split into two parties (a small faction led by Viktoras Petkus formed the LCD Union, while others claimed to be the true LCD party), in the first month of existence, both had already asked for the support of the "Western" LDCU. The LCDU in exile was rather lost as to which party was the most important, and so for some time, maintained contacts with both of them.

branch in Lithuania,[46] and *Aidai* transferred its name to the new magazine *Naujasis Židinys-Aidai* in 1991. The LCAS executive board was relocated to Vilnius in 1992. Consequently, all the main political, social and academic institutions were transferred from exile to Lithuanian soil, and the history of Lithuanian Christian Democracy entered a new phase.

On two ideologues: the intellectual inspirations and political aspirations of Maceina and Krupavičius

When considering continuities and shifts in the political and ideological imagination of Christian Democrats in exile, one should consider two important dimensions. The first is the reaction to the changing political and social environment. The experience of exile revealed new problems and reshaped political thinking. As the main problems changed over time, political practices, and even to some extent goals, also changed. Second, as I will show later, reactions to these challenges were different in the sense that their interpretation depended on the specifics of the worldview of a given Catholic group.

These factors make exile a multi-layered phenomenon not only in a temporal, but also a spatial sense – and not only for different political parties, but also for intellectuals representing similar political convictions. Therefore, it is important to understand how these practical issues reflected the broader tradition of Lithuanian Christian Democracy and Christian political movements, which were institutionalised in two main organisations, the LCDP and the FLF. Both can be treated as seminal for (re)shaping the political imagination of Lithuanians in exile. To understand these practical attempts by Christians to act, in the words of Jacques Maritain, *en chrétien* (in keeping with Christian teaching) and *en tant que chrétien* (in the name of Christianity) I would like to turn to two important Christian Democratic exiles: Krupavičius, leader of the LCDP, and Maceina, one of the main ideologues of the FLF.[47]

Krupavičius and Maceina represent two different traditions of Christian Democratic thought in Lithuania, but, despite generational and political differences, their theoretical inclinations and practical stance to some degree overlapped. First of all, in exile one finds oneself in totally new

---

46 Vidmantas Valiušaitis, ed, *Gairė - pilnutinė demokratija: "Į Laisvę" fondo dešimtmetis Lietuvoje* (Kaunas: Į Laisvę fondo Lietuvos filialas, 2001), 6.
47 Jacques Maritain, "Structure de l'action," *Sept*, 12 April 1935.

existential circumstances, where opportunities to cherish older political and social identities are limited. It was clear that there was no possibility of any meaningful influence in Soviet Lithuania or to take part in the country's political development. Thus, all that was left was to simulate Lithuanian state institutions in the West, with the goal of re-establishing Lithuanian statehood. All political declarations and party programmes began by stating this goal: "The LCDP [...] thinks that the ongoing fight for Lithuanian freedom is the most important matter, and all other goals should be connected to it".[48] Or, as Maceina put it, "the ideal of an independent state is shining brightly as the highest one [...] re-establishment of an independent Lithuanian state is a goal that unites all attempts by exiles".[49] This was the most important precondition for unity not only among Christian parties, but also with secular organisations. Institutionally, it was embodied in the SCLL, which was seen as the prototype of a democratic parliament where different party groups could meet and coordinate their approaches.

The LCDP's and FLF's respective goals and practical activities regarding Lithuania or the Soviet Union were more or less in concert. Both of these parties published their journals and took part in the activities of national and international organisations that were used to raise the question of Lithuanian independence. Indeed, this was a feature of all Lithuanian political movements in exile, excluding communists. There were only slight differences regarding their stance towards the Soviet Union, as right-leaning parties were very sceptical about any official contacts with representatives of Soviet Lithuania, even if it was just a concert or sporting event. Meanwhile, left-leaning parties tried to maintain contacts with the intellectuals of Soviet Lithuania, following the thesis of known interwar exile and social democrat Steponas Kairys to "turn to Lithuania", i.e. to have as many contacts with Lithuanians living in Soviet Lithuania as possible.[50] Eventually this led to a possibility for liberals to build solid relations with the intellectual elite of Soviet Lithuania, while the influence of Catholic thinkers spread to underground movements via *samizdat*, because the Soviet-based Catholic underground illegally republished books

---

48 LCDP, "LKDP atstovų suvažiavimo, įvykurio 1948 m. balandžio mėn. 20-21 dienomis Fellbach'e prieš Stuttgart'o, Vokietijoje, Rezoliucijos," in Povilaitis and Škiudaitė, *Lietuviai krikščionys demokratai išeivijoje*, 71.

49 Maceina, "Kuri paskirtis įprastmintų lietuvių buvima laisvajame pasaulyje dabar?," NLL, F181-53, 11. State sovereignty as the main goal is repeated in 1978 in the Credo of the FLF: FLF, "Lietuvių fronto bičiulių Credo," *Į laisvę*, no. 74 (1978): 43-46.

50 Steponas Kairys, "Visu veidu į Lietuvą," *Darbas*, no. 1 (1959): 1-4.

written in exile by Lithuanian authors such as Maceina and Girnius.[51] Still, in both cases exile was seen as the leading front against the Sovietisation of Lithuania.

Only in the middle of the 1960s, due to the lack of support from Western powers, the end of guerrilla resistance in Lithuania and the institutionalisation of the Soviet system, did the exiles shift to conceiving of independence instead as merely the goal of a distant future. Those in exile had to deal with the more immediate issue of keeping the commitment to this goal, which meant not only efforts to coordinate all initiatives, but also the need to keep Lithuanian identity Lithuanian. Already in the first years of exile there was a certain dispersal of Lithuanians across other states and societies, which was seen as a threat to the nation's future because of the greater possibility of assimilation into the receiving cultures – what historians Michel Dumoulin and Idesbald Goddeeris have labelled the dilemma of "integration or representation".[52] There was a wish among Lithuanians to cooperate not only on a party-political, but also on a broader societal level. The main institutional framework for this project was the World Community of Lithuanians (WCL), initiated by the LCDP and Krupavičius, which aimed to "keep alive [the nation's] vitality, language, and national and state traditions".[53] Despite these attempts, it was impossible to escape integration into Western societies, especially in the case of younger generations, who were educated in Western schools and universities. This visible shift in the national self-identity of Lithuanians in exile led to discussions on how to remain Lithuanian and what political parties should do to consolidate national identity.

The relationship between the nation and Christianity was another important question for different Lithuanian Catholic movements in exile. The political discourse of exile was mostly state- and nation-centred. All of the relevant political parties stressed Lithuanian independence and the preservation of national culture as common goals. Having in mind that this manifestation of political and cultural nationalism had worrisome connotations in post-Nazi Germany and in the US, parties used different strategies to avoid the accusation of being nationalist. Lithuanian left-leaning parties (the Union of Peasant Populists and the Lithuanian Social Democratic Party) and even former right-wing nationalists (the Union of Na-

---

51 For example, as is evident from personal interviews, Girnius's "Man without God" and Maceina's "Church and the World" were among the best known.
52 Dumoulin and Goddeeris, *Integration or representation*.
53 WCL, *Pasaulio lietuvių bendruomenė* (Augsburg, 1949), 9.

Justinas Dementavičius

tionalists and the Nationalist Party) emphasised the rights of man and nations as their main principles. Only that approach, they claimed, could safeguard the human person from oppressive nationalism and at the same time let every individual express his true national identity.

In both cases, Christianity was met with suspicion, seen either as an oppressive social power (and thus a threat to the individual) or as universalistic (and thus a threat to a nation). Christian organisations attempted to avoid this critique by presenting religion as an integral part of national identity and also by trying to synthesise Christian universalism with national particularism. But still, it was the importance of faith that made Christians an exception compared to other forms of Lithuanian democratic parties. In the words of Krupavičius: "Our highest goal at the moment is the fatherland. We don't have and can't have any higher goal than this, except only God".[54] That is, Christian faith should be treated as more important than narrow national or state interest. But, at the same time, Christians should respect the nation as the natural social order and thus seek full realisation of national culture and freedom – in other words, to fight for independent statehood.

The FLF shared this credo. In the pages of *Į laisvę*, Maceina stated that the formation and maintenance of the (Christian) worldview was as important as the national question: "Inclusion of Lithuania into the Soviet Union was not just an inclusion into the Russian empire, but also her inclusion into communistic ideology. That is why we were worried not only about the political freedom of Lithuania, but also about her Christian spirit and culture".[55]

This Christian stance was especially important in relations with secular parties and organisations – socialists, liberals and nationalists. All of them expressed frustration that Lithuanian Catholics divided only *pro forma* into different movements, while actually they shared the same "illiberal" worldview, merging religion with political institutions. In fact, in real political life the first statement was wrong (there were disagreements among Lithuanian Catholics), and the second was only partially true. Only the LCDP spoke about the importance of religion in political life, even though it did not mean direct involvement of the Church – for example, in a memo for Christian Democratic study clubs, that the "state lacks any principles which would safeguard it from unilateralism; it needs religion

---

54 Mykolas Krupavičius, "Žodis vytautininkams," LIH, F54-80.
55 Antanas Maceina, "Nuo ko mes bėgom?," in Antanas Maceina, *Raštai*, vol. 12 (Vilnius: Margi raštai, 2007), 308-332.

as a life-directing force".[56] For that matter, there was also a certain simplification in the treatment of secular organisations by Christian intellectuals. Socialists, liberals and nationalists (even to some extent communists) were seen only as different shades of one overarching enemy: liberalism.[57]

There are some important similarities not only in Krupavičius's and Maceina's political aspirations, but also in the nature of their devotion to Catholic social teaching. The first articles by Krupavičius were written under the influence of Leo XIII's social thought, and up until his death the Lithuanian priest constantly referred to *Rerum Novarum* (1891), *Quadragesimo anno* (1931) and, later, *Mater et Magistra* (1961) as the main intellectual inspirations for his political ideas.[58] On the other hand, he not only recognised the importance of modern Christian intellectuals (Mauriac, Chesterton, Guardini, Péguy, Mounier, etc.), but also acknowledged that Maritain is an important "theoretician and ideologue of Christian Democracy, probably the greatest authority in this field of our times. Lithuanian Christian Democracy has used his writings extensively".[59] Still, Krupavičius rarely interpreted or referred to other political thinkers in his texts and political speeches.

Meanwhile, Maceina and his fellows were active in the Ateitis (Future) movement, a Catholic organisation founded in 1911. Its main slogan, following Pius X, was: "To renew all things in Christ". But despite that pope's campaign against modernism, for Lithuanian Catholics this slogan became an impulse to talk about the brand-new secular world that needed to be renewed in conjunction with Christianity. That is why modern Christian thinkers of Western Europe were actively cited and invoked, starting with the pages of Mounier's *Esprit*, which served as inspiration for a critique of all modern ideologies. After World War II, Maceina also engaged more and more with the social and political thought of Jacques Maritain, who for Maceina was "the most loyal and zealous Thomist of our times".[60] Maceina did not encounter him in person, but read his works and clearly followed some of his ideas regarding the relationship between Christianity and democracy, even though his main references were the social teaching of popes.

56 Mykolas Krupavičius, "Krikščioniškosios demokratijos studijų klubams," LIH, F54-1024, 1-2.
57 Antanas Maceina, "Liberalizmo kelias į bolševizmą," *Aidai*, no. 13 (1948): 156-162.
58 Mykolas Krupavičius, "Enciklika *Mater et Magistra*," in *Visuomeniniai klausimai* (Chicago: Popiežiaus Leono XIII fondas, 1983), 371-384.
59 Mykolas Krupavičius, "Ryškieji veidai," *Tėvynės sargas* 1, no. 16 (1959): 81.
60 Antanas Maceina to Pranciškus Būčys, NLL, F181-140, 2. In the interwar period, Maceina mentioned him in his texts as an interesting French-speaking philosopher of culture.

At the same time, both Krupavičius and Maceina actively engaged in the political tradition of Lithuanian Catholic social thought, which was subject to influences not only from Western Catholicism, but also from Russian political and cultural traditions. Krupavičius's political involvement was stimulated by Russian politics and social conditions at the beginning of the twentieth century. First of all, as a child of the Lithuanian national awakening of the early twentieth century, he problematised questions of nationality, treating it with great care and recognising its importance and its perils at the same time.[61] Second, he wanted to improve the social condition of Lithuanians worldwide and in this regard maintained contacts with Jurgis Matulaitis and was keen to cite his social ideas. The latter was an alumnus of the University of Fribourg (attended 1898-1902), an activist and promoter of Christian social action in Poland and Lithuania alike and the first chair of sociology at the Catholic Theological Academy in Saint Petersburg (1907-11). Even though Krupavičius attended the Academy only after 1911, he followed Matulaitis's social convictions and consulted with him regarding the LCDP programme in 1918, when Matulaitis was already a bishop in Vilnius. This commitment to national and social integrity remained an important part of Krupavičius's convictions until his death, and especially during his years of exile, since the Soviet Union, as the successor state to Russia, once again posed a threat to Lithuania in both these senses.

As for Maceina, he was a child of interwar independent Lithuania. But even if he was educated in Lithuania, he clearly trended towards following in Western footsteps, drawing in part on his experience in 1932-35 auditing lectures at several Western universities, including Fribourg, Strasbourg and Louvain. Maceina also synthesised the thoughts of Western authors with the social thought and theology of Russian religious intellectuals like Nikolai Berdyaev, Sergei Bulgakov, Vladimir Solovyov and Fyodor Dostoyevsky. But his Lithuanian texts and writings dedicated to questions of political regime mostly referred to his teacher Stasys Šalkauskis and other Lithuanian Christian thinkers including Būčys, the first author of the LCDP programme project.[62] Therefore, even though the idea of integral democracy was developed in exile, in reality it could be treated as a continuation of political programmes developed by older generations of

---

61 This is clear from his memoirs and recollections about the first years of the twentieth century, when tensions between some Lithuanians and Polish priests were at their height; Mykolas Krupavičius, *Atsiminimai* (Chicago: Draugo spaustuvė, 1972), 9-225.
62 FLF, "Į pilnutinę demokratiją," in Girnius et al., *Lietuva, kurios nebuvo*, 382.

Lithuanian Catholic intellectuals. In other words, the political thought of Lithuanian Christians in exile was more concerned with preserving Lithuanian tradition and publicising the Catholic roots of their thinking, than in engaging in and presenting discussions of Western Christian Democratic thought.

Ideological debate: Christian confessional democracy and integral democracy

As we can see, fundamentally, the attitudes of Maceina and Krupavičius regarding the most important goals of exile were the same. Both of their organisations fought for the renewed national independence of Lithuania, criticised communist ideology and sought to protect and preserve the Christian worldview among Lithuanians in exile. But, as long as there was hope of once again having an independent state, the most important element of their political thought was the shape of the future political regime (held in trust in the meantime by the SCLL). At least in official declarations, all political parties, including former supporters of national authoritarianism, were pro-democratic. But, in reality, there were significant differences between them regarding ideas of democracy; even formally close allies could have a different understanding of the meaning of *democracy*. This was true for the LCDP and the FLF, as both featured influential intellectuals who did not hesitate to fight over the real meaning of (Christian) Democracy – both Christian, both anti-totalitarian, but also diverging in their perceptions of Church-state relations and the role of Christianity in political life.

These two interpretations seem similar, especially when one is talking about the procedural aspects of democracy. There was no doubt that democracy should express the will of the people; be based on the separation of legislative, executive and judicial powers; and create an equal opportunity to take part in political life and debate. Their ideas of democracy were seen as alternatives to the old and inefficient liberal parliamentarianism. The basis for that was the interpretation of liberalism as being exclusively focused on the question of individual freedom and welfare, while ignoring questions of social responsibility and common good. For example, in the early 1950s Maceina claimed that, "for liberalism, the individual embodies the highest value, and this grows into narrow self-interest. Trying to escape the social chaos that follows it, liberalism has to call for a 'common will' and thus becomes a dictatorship of the majority".[63] At the same time, Krupavičius expressed the same critical interpretation while describing the genesis of Christian Democracy.[64] A similar critique was elaborated regarding the question of a parliament. Formally speaking, he recognised it as an important democratic institution, but in liberal regimes and developing societies, parliaments were torn apart by demagogy and the factionalism of individual and party interests.[65]

However, while these basic principles and historical interpretations coincided, the theoretical grounding for their arguments and even some of the practical implications diverged. This can be attributed to the differences between cultural and political interpretations of Christian Democracy. The first dreamt about the Christianisation of social life from below by means of everyday cultural work, avoiding the use of enforced political power; the second treated political power as an important tool for strengthening Christianity. Referring to this debate, one can speak about a discussion between worldview-neutral politics on the one hand, where worldview pluralism is respected as a crucial choice of free persons and thus the basis for real democracy, and Christian party politics on the other. The latter claims to be "doing the work of the Church"[66] as was said in exile in 1948 – between full, or integral, and partial or (Christian) democracy.[67]

As leader of the LCDP, Krupavičius represented a confessional understanding of Christian Democracy. The basis for his interpretation of democracy was politics understood as, first of all, the ability to rule according to prudence. In a programme for Christian Democratic study clubs in exile, prudence was treated in a Catholic light, and Krupavičius, following Thomas Aquinas, claimed that it is based on three principles: (a) the goal of human life should be salvation reached through following Christ; (b) only the Catholic Church, as the representative and mystical embodiment of Christ, fully expresses this knowledge; and (c) the sacred matters of man should be more important than secular ones.[68] In the practical sphere, this meant that politicians first of all should take into account divine and

---

63 Antanas Maceina, "Pilnutinės demokratijos pagrindai," in Girnius et al., *Lietuva, kurios nebuvo*, 313.
64 Mykolas Krupavičius, "Darbininkas ir darbas," in *Visuomeniniai klausimai*, 206-221.
65 Antanas Maceina, "Politinis katalikų susiorganizavimas," NLL, F181-7, 9-12.
66 Mykolas Krupavičius, "Lietuvos krikščionių demokratų partijos pagrindai," LIH, F54-649.
67 Maceina uses the term *confessional democracy* while criticising the politics of the LCDP and quoting Maritain. Ironically, the quotation is borrowed from Maritain's treatise *Christianity and Democracy*, from which excerpts were published in the official magazine of the LCDP *Tėvynės sargas*.
68 Krupavičius, "Lietuvių krikščioniškosios demokratijos studijų klubas," 4.

Church commandments, the most important among them (as motives for any political and social action) being love for another person.[69]

These presuppositions are the basis for an idea of democracy in two senses. First of all, Christian citizens are obliged to go out into the world and, invoking Leo XIII, "to come out of the sacristy".[70] As everyone has natural social duties, it is not only those in positions of political power who shape social and political realities, but everyone, the people as a whole: "Christian democracy is a social order where all social groups – higher and lower – are working for the common good, but firstly for the abandoned and abused poorest [...] a social order where everybody should follow justice, truthfulness and love, which leads to brotherhood and equality before God for the children of God".[71]

In a Christian democracy, everyone has a certain power to effect change while striving to be just, foster peace and seek the common good, or, in other words, contribute to implementing an ideal political, social and economic regime. Any betterment of the political, social, economic or cultural situation of all society is an expression of love, so it is a duty of Christians, and especially of those in power, to act as "servant of servants of God (*Servus Servorum Dei*) [because] those who have more should give more; and those who have less should receive more".[72] The most important authority, the master, the only sovereign, is God. Second, this idea is broad in that it speaks about all aspects of social life: politics, economy and culture; after all, injustice can be seen in every sphere. Democracy amounts to an equal opportunity to take part in all those modes of life: to be a good citizen, to be a responsible worker, to develop one's own culture. In 1961, probably reflecting the mindset of Lithuanian émigrés in the US, Krupavičius wrote that, at the time, only political democracy was prevailing, while other forms of democracy had yet to be created.[73] And he contended that, by claiming the brotherhood of all man, protecting the freedom of man from worldly oppression, and trying to achieve social justice, the Church sets out the most fundamental principles for true democracy in all spheres of life – political, social and cultural.[74]

From a procedural point of view, it is not so important how political, social or cultural justice is reached. It can be attained in a democratic re-

---

69 Krupavičius, "Lietuvių krikščioniškosios demokratijos studijų klubas," 49.
70 Krupavičius, "Enciklika *Graves de communi*," in *Visuomeniniai klausimai*, 159.
71 Ibid, 155.
72 Mykolas Krupavičius, "Kas yra krikščioniškoji demokratybė?," LIH, F54-649, 639, 642.
73 Krupavičius, "Enciklika *Mater et Magistra*," 378.
74 Krupavičius, "Lietuvių krikščionių demokratų partijos pagrindai," 680.

Justinas Dementavičius

public or even in a monarchy, as long as the state cares about the common good, peace and justice.[75] On the contrary, it is a mistake to think that formal institutions can change human behaviour, while the opposite is true: it is wilful and responsibly humane behaviour that makes an institution work for the sake of the common good. Political agreements should be respected because "the essence of democracy is 'who can [do] more, should [do] more; who can [have] less, should receive more' – this is the essence, and everything else is just an accidental feature [...] Politically, democracy should not be related to any concrete regime or order, though order can help to achieve democratic goals. The most democratic state is the one that regards the good of the society and the interests of the majority in the best way".[76] In other words, true democracy does not merely equate to a man-made constitutional republic, but rather derives from actual consideration of people's fundamental needs, of which the most important are spiritual. Once again, the role of Christian politics is not only to remind people of that but, first and foremost, to try and implement the politics of real democracy in public and social life.

Therefore, according to Krupavičius, Christian Democracy is the only real form of democracy and should thus be a universal idea. This is so, not only because Christian Democracy aims to harmonise all social interests and spheres of human life, but also because its basic ideas are in accord with Christianity, in accord with the "[God-given] laws of brotherhood, love and justice", and not only the relative laws of men or the secular state.[77] As there is only one true God and one true Christianity, there should be one true form of social interaction, expressed by Christian Democrats who are following Church teachings. As devoted Catholics, they should aim to reform all political life in accordance with Christ and must act as a real political and social power. Once again recalling and commenting Leo XIII's *Graves de communi* in the 1960s, he suggested that "social order can be stable and lead to happiness only if it is following the natural order of things. And this natural order should be identified with duties to God, to the person himself and to other persons".[78]

Just as Krupavičius embodied the Christian Democratic party, so Maceina can be seen as a non-partisan Christian democrat, or, more concretely, a Christian and democrat not by name, but by conviction. In general,

---

75 This thought is present in a long commentary on Leo XIII's *Graves de communi*: Krupavičius, "Enciklika *Graves de communi*," 143-166.
76 Krupavičius, "Kas yra krikšioniškoji demokratybė?," 638-639, 645.
77 LCDP, "Lietuvos krikščionių demokratų partijos pagrindai," 680.
78 Krupavičius, "Enciklika *Graves de communi*," 151.

his intellectual trajectory can be described as a move from the "moderate democratisation" of authoritarianism in the form of an organic state in the 1930s to an integral democracy, renewing an older concept in exile in the 1950s and 1960s. By 1936, he and his associates had already been referring to "liberal democracy" as having done a lot of good for Lithuania, yet at the same time too mechanical and neglectful of "the common good of the nation in the name of party interests".[79] But while discussing the problems of the Lithuanian authoritarian regime in the 1930s, Maceina and his colleagues were proposing to restore parliamentary institutions and, following Western personalist critics of the liberal order such as Maritain and Mounier, to prioritise personal (but not individual) interests over state interests. They therefore called for social justice that would help to overcome narrow self-interest.[80] In 1943, during the German occupation, Maceina openly argued that modern democracy can and should be reformed. It is true that the essence of previous evils was party politics, which was too focused on religious and worldview issues. Meanwhile, in a *reformed* democracy, political parties should not represent one class or social group, but instead work for the benefit of all, "seek a common good".[81]

Maceina further elaborated these views throughout the decades that he spent in exile. In the first years, Maceina argued that "democracy is the most perfect and highest form of the life of the state".[82] But what did he really mean by such an *illiberal* integral democracy? The fundamental principle of integral democracy echoes the essential idea of an organic state, but its democratic character and references to Maritain's personalism were more explicitly stated in the 1960s: "In a democracy, the person is the highest principle, whom everything should serve, but which does

---

79   Maceina et al., "Į organiškosios valstybės kūrybą," 169-170.
80   It is worth noting that some of the prominent books written by Maceina at that time, *Social Justice* and *Fall of the Bourgeoisie*, contain in their premise a repetition of ideas expressed by Mounier, even though there is only scant reference to his texts. In this regard, Maceina can and should be seen as a promoter of "theocentric humanism" and compared to similar trends seen in France, Poland and elsewhere; see Piotr H. Kosicki, *Catholics on the Barricades: Poland, France and "Revolution," 1891-1956* (New Haven: Yale University Press, 2018), esp. ch. 1. That being said, Maceina's, his associates' or Lithuania's intellectual history is not so organically intertwined with the French personalistic tradition as in the case of Polish intellectuals. For example, after the Second World War there was still a need to explain to readers of *Aidai* and *Tėvynės sargas* who Maritain was, and the first Lithuanian translation of Maritain appeared as a separate book only in 1975, and of Mounier only in 1996. So it should not be a surprise that Juozas Girnius stated that Maritain, among Lithuanian Catholic intellectuals, "was not read by a lot, but at least known by name and respected". Juozas Girnius, "Jacques Maritainui mirus," *Aidai*, no. 9 (1973).
81   Maceina et al., "Į reformuotą demokratiją," in Girnius et al., *Lietuva, kurios nebuvo*, 224.
82   Maceina, "Demokratijos principai," NLL, F181-85, 1.

not serve anything. [...] The basis of democracy is the priority of the personal over the collective, over matter, over idea".[83] Maceina attempts to present a better form of democracy while criticising the traditional – in his words, "liberal" – idea of democracy for: (a) the domination of party interest over common good; (b) the denial of a person's privilege in favour of the state or majority; (c) the exaltation of material needs instead of fostering the human spirit; and (d) the restriction of the scope of democracy while speaking only about politics, but denying the democratic ideal in social, economic and cultural issues.

Maceina's revision is based on the Thomist philosophical conviction that every person is capable of expressing free will and thus acts as an image of God. This autonomy, and not a parliament or any form of popular sovereignty, is the main principle of democracy, and all other freedoms and rights are only derivative of this principle. It is universal, so freedom of will should be recognised for every human person or group, which is nothing more than the conglomeration of human persons expressing a certain "collective personhood", that is common features allowing different persons to be treated as one group.

That is why, in every true democracy, the person is always more important than the collective. Meanwhile, a "totalitarian state does not help man, but immerses him in a nameless crowd – class, nation, race – until he loses all personhood. Instead of serving man it dominates him. It ceases to be merely an instrument, and instead becomes a goal of human life. It takes away all human life goals and all human life itself", writes Maceina, criticising fascist and Soviet politics alike, treating both as equally evil.[84] This utterance can be interpreted as a critique of state totalitarianism, and that is true, but Maceina goes further. Not only can the state suppress personhood, but so can any collective entity, be it cultural, economic, social or ideological. Even the Church and family can act as oppressive forces that contradict human nature.[85] Therefore, the most important precondition of democracy is the protection of personhood from any social and political violence. This violence can take different forms and be expressed by different actors, but with a consequence of diminishing human will, it is always undemocratic.

---

83 Ibid, 4.
84 Maceina, "Pilnutinės demokratijos pagrindai," 308.
85 The critique of false usage of Christian principles is expressed in his study "The Grand Inquisitor," based on an interpretation of Dostoyevsky and written during the Second World War: Antanas Maceina, *Didysis inkvizitorius* (Weilheim: Atžalynas, 1946).

In Maceina's understanding, which clearly correlates with the ideas of Maritain and the early writings of Šalkauskis, the main goal of human nature is the so-called integral man: a man who tries to develop all of his capabilities and talents to the fullest potential. As he takes part in very different social interactions (political, economic and cultural), he must develop all of them, having in mind that religious identity is also part (indeed, the most important part) of his personality. For this reason, all social life has to be democratised, first of all starting with cultural democracy, the respect for every personality, which is the basis for democratic action in all other fields. The basis of this culture is Christianity, as a religion speaking out on behalf of human dignity, the highest order of justice and common good. The Christianisation of personal life is thus the starting point for the Christianisation and, at the same time, democratisation of all social life.

But this focus on the personal is in a way radical, as it leads to a critique of political democracy and even Christian Democracy, not only classically understood liberal democracy. Maceina saw liberalism as radically individualistic – ignoring other members of society, sacrificing morality in the name of freedom and an ideology that protects a partial, but not universally shared, common good. While Maceina was keen to follow a personalistic understanding of human nature and stressed that (a) humans are social beings and (b) as God's creation made in His image they should be developing their nature in accordance with God's will, that is, collectively expanding humanity's horizons as a group of creative cultural agents.[86] This self-understanding aggregates to a worldview common to all human beings; thus, liberal universalism as a rationalisation of societies is less developed than Christian universalism, which recognises differences and tries to preserve unity without eliminating pluralism. Integral democracy would integrate every human being. According to Maceina, "Integral democracy covers the full extent of life in the state. Not one sphere can remain where the principles of democracy would not be implemented. Integral democracy is not only political, but also regional, professional, cultural".[87]

A similar critique is expressed toward political democracy as tending to put the formal institutions of democracy before personhood, and thereby paradoxically diminishing democratic respect for the human person in the name of democracy. The real accomplishment of democracy is that it saved the human person from slavery to abstract principles; any refer-

86 Maceina, "Pilnutinės demokratijos pagrindai," 306-309.
87 Ibid, 319.

Justinas Dementavičius

ences to principles higher than personhood have a tendency to deny human dignity and real justice for all human beings. In Maceina's view, only principles expressed in the life of Christ were concrete and worthy of following. That is why liberalism, socialism and nationalism all got something right, but as they did not recognise Christ their claims were only partially true. In contrast, the Christian worldview was full (or integral), as its tendencies integrated all spheres of social and personal life, including religion, speaking about every social strata and human person and thereby constituting a perfect unity.[88]

At the same time, Maceina recognised a practical problem for the democratic ideal in the modern state, because every state acts as a set of law-giving institutions that cannot foresee all possible future changes. Even the best state represents only a vague possibility of a real divine Kingdom, which cannot be accomplished in this life, but should be seen as a perfect ideal, a full future realisation of democracy. According to Maceina, in theological terms this ideal can be understood as a communion of saints. The first step toward integral democracy should be seen as a person's attempts to be an integral human, a saint, as Maceina poetically presented in his book dedicated to the life of St. Francis in 1954.[89]

From this account of Maceina's thought, the possibilities for the critique of the Lithuanian philosophical understandings of Christian Democracy should already be clear. First, democracy cannot act only as Christian (or socialist, or national), because in its name it presupposes justice for every member of society. A Christian Democratic party is only a party, a part of society, which cannot be perfect as the world is not perfect. Since 1946, debating the relations of the FLF and the LCDP, Maceina had been convinced that party politics tend to become ideocratic, closed or even repressive, while Christianity does not need political violence.[90] Second, using Christianity as a motive in state politics, which always entails a use of force in one way or another, denies the possibility for a person to take decisions independently. Every human person is free, and even God "cannot compel free human beings", having given them free will to make choices on their own.[91]

---

88 Antanas Maceina, "Bažnyčia ir pasaulis," in *Raštai*, vol. 5 (Vilnius: Margi raštai, 1993), 18-21.
89 Maceina, *Saulės giesmė*; also, this idea can be found in his early, pre-World War II writings: Antanas Maceina, "Krikščioniškosios visuomenės klausimas," in *Raštai*, vol. 10 (Vilnius: Margi raštai, 2005), 314-318.
90 Antanas Maceina, "Politinis katalikų susiroganizavimas," NLL, F181-7.
91 Maceina, *Didysis inkvizitorius*, 103.

Maceina himself has no doubt that the Christian way is the right one, but a path that should be chosen freely, not taken out of fear or introduced by means of propaganda and seduction. To accomplish that – and here Maceina relies on Charles Journet and on Maritain's *Les droits de l'homme et la loi naturelle* – Christians had to recognise the so-called non-worldview (*nepasaulėžiūrinė*) politics. The guiding principle of this kind of politics was to avoid political decisions that would compromise the personal worldview and the cultural freedoms of communities.[92]

As it happened, the LCDP criticised these claims because in practical politics it is impossible to ignore beliefs that are part of one's convictions. The LCDP in its meetings and publications maintained that such an approach is dangerous because it leads to political and social ambiguity. For Christians, abandonment of worldview is impossible.[93] But for Maceina, the main argument was that it was not about "liberal neutrality", but rather that there exist certain spheres wherein the spirit of the person (or culture, in the case of the group) should be treated with respect.[94] Only respect for this principle can build real democratic institutions of free conscience, speech, publications, meetings, organisations and free personal or collective actions.[95] Such an integral democracy has the capacity to express personhood in its fullness, keeping in mind that the person is always culturally determined by family, nation and religion. But all of these social institutions are important only because they serve to develop a person as an image of God. It is true that Maceina avoided linking this theologically expressed goal of life to the political term of (Christian) democracy, but there is no doubt that, for him, the Christian worldview was inseparable from true democracy in the political, social and, above all, the cultural fields.

Conclusions

Summing up the history of the political organisations of Lithuanian Christians in exile, I have identified two competing ideas of democracy that can be called Christian democracy from below, and Christian democracy from

---

92 Antanas Maceina, "Politika ir pasaulėžiūra," *Aidai*, no. 19 (1948), 389-398.
93 Bagdanavičius, "Nepasaulėžiūrinės politikos klausimu," *Naujasis gyvenimas*, no. 10 (1948): 146-148; Bagdanavičius, "Nepasaulėžiūrinės politikos klausimu," *Naujasis gyvenimas*, no. 11 (1948): 164-168.
94 FLF, "Valstybinio gyvenimo pagrindai," NLL, F54-1324, 3.
95 FLF, "Į pilnutinę demokratiją," 592.

above. The first was expressed in the political writings of the FLF and Maceina. They defended Christianity as the most suitable cultural force for expressing every person's spiritual, material and social needs, a stance that the LCDP treated as liberal and demeaning of the priority of Catholic faith. The second interpretation of democracy was defended by the LCDP and Krupavičius. They gave priority to party interests and claimed that politics should be used in the Christianisation of public life, a position that Maceina and his fellows considered to be an undemocratic tendency.

Still, they can be treated as different sides of the same coin. Both of these interpretations of democracy were based on a common belief in political Catholicism – that other forms of democracy, be they socialist or liberal, do not represent real democracy, because democracy first of all means equal opportunities for personal freedom. A person had to be treated as the image of God. All ideologies that did not recognise this fact were therefore deserving of condemnation for enslaving and suppressing the human person in the name of collective (class or nation) economic needs or ideas; whereas the Christian worldview is best because (a) it refers to a transcendent ideal, which should be pursued everywhere, and also in politics; and (b) it is integral – combining one good thing with other good things to make them better.

These political debates changed over time, and their focus shifted from theoretical disagreement toward fighting for Lithuanian independence and preserving cultural identity. Christianity became a personal matter, overshadowed in public life by these national goals. But these Christian political interpretations and institutions did not pass into oblivion in the context of the Soviet occupations. The task of Lithuanian Christian Democrats as they understood it was to maintain the interwar traditions and present themselves as the real alternative (even in exile) to Soviet cultural politics. In the 1990s, after the collapse of the Soviet Union, this commitment to the idea of a free and Catholic Lithuania manifested itself in attempts to transfer Catholic institutions back to independent Lithuania. Even if this process cannot be called a success story, the intellectuals in the independent Lithuanian Republic treated Christian Democrats and Christian intellectuals in exile as an opportunity to continue what had been lost during the Soviet period.

9

HUNGARIAN CHRISTIAN DEMOCRACY IN EXILE
An Influential but Never Dominant Political Force

Katalin Kádár Lynn

The Christian Democratic movement emerged in Hungary in the 1930s, one of the most difficult periods in Hungarian history. Ten years after the end of World War I, Hungary's economy was in ruins, the world-wide economic depression having severely impacted a country dismembered by the Treaty of Trianon, reduced to one third of its former territory, and its means of production and markets in chaos. Overwhelmed by hundreds of thousands of Hungarian refugees fleeing the newly established successor states of Czechoslovakia, Yugoslavia and Romania, Hungary was near collapse. Regardless of the economic and social circumstances, the major issue and one which dominated all political action and policy was that of irredentism, revision of the Treaty that Hungarians regardless of social status, education, and economic means uniformly thought to be the greatest tragedy manifested on the nation in its history. While a great portion of its citizenry was absorbed with thc tragedy of Trianon, Hungary remained a semi-feudal nation, with a great portion of its assets still controlled by the former nobility, landowners and industrialists, a weak middle and professional class and a large, landless peasantry. It was evident to most that societal change was necessary in Hungary, but social and economic reform was largely set aside because of the upheaval resulting from Hungary's World War I losses.

A few forward-thinking Hungarian leaders emerged during this period who represented the rural citizenry and the working poor. The Smallholders Party, representing small farmers and rural constituencies, was re-constituted by Gaszton Gaál in 1930; the Social Democrats, although a small minority of elected officials, also developed a political following, led by Anna Kéthly. This was also the period when Hungarian Christian Democratic elements began to develop, although the country continued to be controlled by factions surrounding Regent Miklós Horthy.[1] During this period, pre-World War II Hungary, rejected by the West because of its irredentist stance, drifted into alliance with Nazi Germany, from which it later could not successfully extract itself. At the end of World War II Hungary, with no hope of regaining its historic lands of St. Stephen (some of which it had been awarded briefly in the First and Second Vienna Awards during World War II), found itself occupied by Soviet troops and its economy shattered without having made any progress toward solving the societal issues that haunted it during the inter-war period.

The brief period from the election of 1945, which the Smallholders Party won by a large majority, and 1947, after which its freely elected officials fled Hungary following the Soviet Union-engineered takeover by Hungarian communists, served to usher in the further development of the Christian Democratic movement in Hungary.

This chapter on Hungarian Christian Democratic movements in exile introduces the three major factions that can be regarded as Christian Democratic in Hungary that were active during the immediate post-World War II era. First are the Catholic social and professional movements that had already developed in Hungary in the 1930s. Second is a group of young intellectuals and journalists who were considered reformers or progressive Catholics, whose ideology incorporated Christian social teaching with a more pluralistic Catholic worldview. They are often referred to as the "Barankovics faction" (after their leader, István Barankovics). Third are the members of the Christian Democratic People's Party (Keresztény-demokrata Néppárt, KDNP), in existence since the turn of the nineteenth century as the official Catholic Party and the standard bearer for Christian social tradition. By 1949, four short years after the war's end and due to the Soviet occupation of Hungary, only the Barankovics faction remained in the country. All of the other Christian Democratic leaders had fled into exile or were under arrest, in line with the fate of Cardinal Mindszenty, the Primate of Hungary, and other key ecclesiastical leaders. When István Ba-

---

1 For a thorough and well-researched history of the Hungarian Christian Democratic movement during the inter-war period, see Peter Krisztián Zachar, "The Concept of Vocational Orders in Hungary Between the Two World Wars," *Estudos Históricos* (Rio de Janeiro) 31, no. 64 (May-August 2018): 259-276. A recently published compendium commemorating the 75th anniversary of the founding of the Hungarian Christian Democratic Party also provides valuable source material on this topic: Tibor Klesteniz, Éva Petrás, Viktor Attila Soós, eds, *Útkeresés Két Korszak Határán* (Agyakosszergény: Közi Horváth József Népfőiskola, 2018).

Katalin Kádár Lynn

rankovics and eleven other Democratic People's Party MPs fled Hungary in February 1949, they were the last of the Christian Democrats to leave. Twenty-two other leaders who remained in their homeland were jailed by the communist authorities.

This chapter examines how, ultimately, all of the Hungarian Christian Democratic elements moved into exile between 1945 and 1949. In exile, political changes were dictated by the constraints of statelessness and economic hardship but were also due to programmatic ideological shifts, as well as the pragmatic necessity for coalition-building on the part of the respective leaderships.

It is not possible to write the history of Hungarian Christian Democratic movements in exile without explaining their role within the respective worlds of the exile leadership, of the US-funded Hungarian National Council and, on a larger scale, within the parent organisation to all of the émigré groups, the (also US-funded) National Committee for a Free Europe/Free Europe Committee. It must be noted that leaders of the Christian Democrats in exile were always highly regarded and productive members of the diaspora but never held the highest and most influential positions. This, then, is a history of a political family that played a supporting – albeit productive and important – role, both in exile and in its reactivation in its homeland after 1989.

The Hungarian Christian Democratic movements also had strong elements of Christian nationalism within their ideology. They were not simply adhering to modern democratic ideas and Christian values, but in fact were – and remain – throughout their existence affiliated with ideologies related to religious nationalism, including during the period since the return of democracy in the Soviet satellites in 1989. Religious nationalism manifests itself, among others, in the Hungarian support for population growth by encouraging larger families, support of Blue laws and an emphasis on preserving Hungary's identity as a Christian nation.

This chapter shows the influence of the Christian Democrats in exile, both within their refugee communities, and on the governments in their various countries of exile. It addresses briefly the post-1989 restoration of the Christian Democratic People's Party in Hungary and the state of the party today. Sources include works by Hungarian authors specialising in religious history, authoritative histories of the emigration and the author's own two decades of research into the history of Hungarian immigration in the Hungarian National Committee archival materials housed at the Széchényi National Library in Budapest, the Hoover Institution Archives, the ACEN papers at the Immigration History Center at the University of Minnesota, the ABTL archives in Budapest, the Barankovics Foundation Archives in Budapest and the KDNP official website.

Post-war Christian Democratic movements in Hungary

Before reviewing the social and political composition of Hungarian Christian Democracy in exile, one needs to briefly examine the circumstances in which the Christian Democrats in Hungary found themselves in the spring of 1949. By then the country was occupied by the victorious Allies in the form of Soviet leadership and occupation troops, and all democratic elements had been eliminated or repressed.

According to Hungarian religious historian Jenő Gergely, post-war Hungarian Christian Democracy evolved from three sources. The first and most important group consisted of the Catholic social and professional movements that emerged in the 1930s.[2] In August 1943 these elements reorganised. They secretly met under the leadership of diocesan Bishop of Györ, Baron Vilmos Apor, and agreed to create a new Catholic party out of the remnants of the Egyesült Keresztény Párt (United Christian Party). The second group was made up primarily of young intellectuals and journalists who adhered to French neo-Thomism; they were referred to as the "progressive" Catholics and advocated a reform program. Leadership of this group included the historian Gyula Szekfű and political journalist István Barankovics, publisher of *Az Ország Útja* (The nation's road). Gergely notes that this "group formulated the programme of a modern Christian democracy with a European orientation".[3] But its most distinguishing aspect was the stand taken against Regent Horthy and his followers. The third of these groups, in existence since the beginning of the twentieth century, was social Catholicism – the official Catholic Party and guardian of Christian social tradition. It was this third group that in 1944-45 initiated contact among the three disparate groups and promoted the idea

---

2   These included the Association of Catholic Agrarian Youth Associations (Katolikus Agrárifjúsági Legényegyesületek, KALOT), the Parochial Departments of Workers (Egyházköségi Munkásszakosztályok, EMSZO) and the National Vocational Organisation of Hungarian Workers (Magyar Dolgozók Hivatásszervezetet). The three groups had a membership totalling almost a half-million members. The basis for Christian Democratic politics emerged as a response to the papal encyclical *Quadragesimo anno* and the social corporatist movements, principally led by members of the Society of Jesus. Of them, Father László Varga SJ was the most influential.

3   Jenő Gergely, "Christian Democracy in Hungary," in Michael Gehler and Wolfram Kaiser, eds, *Christian Democracy in Europe Since 1945* (London: Routledge, 2004), 115-172, at 156.

of consolidating their efforts under one party umbrella. This attempt at rapprochement was firmly rejected by Barankovics and his followers, who were unwilling to associate with the other two factions, both of which were seen as supporters of the Miklós Horthy regime that governed Hungary from 1920 until 1944 and had taken it into World War II on Germany's side.

Of the three factions, Barankovics's group emerged from the war years with the most favourable popular image, as its leadership had been active in anti-fascist resistance, and its pre-war public position regarding land reform and land re-distribution in semi-feudal Hungary continued to be a key policy, defined as "the sole way to ensure social peace and the nation's sustained existence".[4] As in the case of its sister parties in Europe, the Christian Democratic Party's "political innocence" was what differentiated it from the traditional Christian parties as they distanced themselves from the other two factions, which were tainted by their association with the pro-fascist Hungarian government.[5]

Regardless of the reluctance to cooperate among the three major Christian Democratic factions in Hungary, the Christian Democratic People's Party, Keresztény Demokrata Néppárt (KDNP), was illegally founded by József Pálffy on 13 October 1944 in the apartment of attorney László Varga while István Barankovics, leader of the Christian Democratic progressive faction, was still in hiding from the Arrow Cross and the Gestapo. The KDNP subsequently participated in the provisional national government formed in Debrecen in December 1944, and the party formalised its platform at a meeting in Szeged on 21 January 1945. After the Soviet takeover in Hungary in May 1947, leaders of this group of Christian Democrats – Pálffy, Béla Kovrig, Barankovics, Msgr. József Közi-Horváth, László Varga – were all driven into exile and were to become important figures in the Hungarian diaspora.

In 1945 the electoral commission in Hungary refused to recognise the KDNP, due to mistrust of its Church-related leadership, and did not allow its candidates to stand for election. Pálffy was removed from his position

---

4   István Barankovics, "Új földbirtok-reform felé" (Towards a new land reform), *Korunk Szava* 8 (1932): 1-15, at 13; *Korunk Szava / Keresztyéndemokrata Tudásbázis*, at www.barankovics.hu (1 November 2019).

5   As early as 1932 Barankovics is quoted as saying, "As the Catholic Church lost a major part of its power as a result of its temporary and harmful alliance with the ruling classes..." Éva Petrás, "The History of Christian Democracy in Hungary – From the Beginning to 1949," in Maria Rita Kiss, ed, *The Voyage of Hungarian Christian Democracy to the Heart of Europe* (Budapest: Barnakovics István Foundation, 2017), 10-25, at 22.

as head of the KDNP, and Barankovics, who had good relations with the Left, replaced him. After the war ended, at the party's inaugural meeting on 25 September 1945, Barankovics decided to remove "Christian" from the party's name and outlined its program. The name of the party changed, but its objectives did not. Since the national parliamentary elections were due to be held in November 1945, rather than mount its own candidates the now-DNP (Democratic People's Party, Demokratikus Neppárt) decided to support the slate of the Independent Smallholders Party (Független Kisgazda, Földmunkas és Polgári Part – FKgP).[6]

With the November elections imminent, the Catholic Church realised that Christian political forces needed to be unified and also threw its support behind the Smallholders Party and its candidates, rejecting the Barankovics faction because of its refusal to collaborate with the Church and Primate Mindszenty, who was known to be a staunch anti-communist and unwilling to appease or collaborate in any fashion with the occupying powers and their Hungarian minions.[7]

In 1945 the support of the Church added impetus to the Smallholders, resulting in their receiving 57 percent of the vote and 245 seats in Parliament. Monsignor Béla Varga, a Roman Catholic priest active in the Smallholders Party, was elected speaker of the Hungarian Parliament, and after the Hungarian leadership went into exile, he was the most important leader of the émigrés for three decades.[8]

Hungarian political leaders' exodus into exile

All factions of the Catholics then continued to play an important role within the Smallholders Party until Communist Party leader Mátyás Rákosi imposed his so-called "salami tactics" of fragmenting the existing parties, which continued to sub-divide, weakening themselves until rendered powerless. An illustration of the salami tactics occurred in March 1946 when twenty Smallholders MPs who had been labelled "reactionary and fascist" by the communists were expelled from the party. Sixteen of them went on to form the Hungarian Freedom Party – Magyar Szabadság Párt (MSZP) –

---

6 Gergely, "Christian Democracy in Hungary," 158.
7 Petrás, "History of Christian Democracy in Hungary," 22.
8 Katalin Kádár Lynn, "The Hungarian National Council," in Katalin Kádár Lynn, ed, *The Inauguration of Organized Political Warfare: Cold War Organizations Sponsored by the National Committee for a Free Europe/Free Europe Committee* (St. Helena, CA: Helena History Press, 2013), 237-308, at 259.

headed by Dezső Sulyok, known as the "most bourgeois of the bourgeois" politicians.[9] Further splits within the party leadership occurred, splintering the party, which the Smallholders were not successful in halting.

The Church managed to compound the problem, resulting in the further erosion of the democratic parties when, "despite the danger of a split of the political right, the Church readily supported the Hungarian Freedom Party led by Sulyok. Its policy statements show that of all the bourgeois parties it was closest to Christian democracy".[10] Of all the Hungarian parties invoking Christian principles, only the Hungarian Freedom Party included cooperation with Christian democratic parties from other countries in its mission. However, the Rákosi government soon passed a new electoral law that excluded voters on the grounds of membership in "prewar fascist parties", thus disenfranchising almost a tenth of the electorate. The Freedom Party as a result was not able to participate in the 1947 parliamentary elections. Protesting against the new election law, the Freedom Party dissolved itself in July 1947.

False accusations and a threat against his family rendered Smallholders prime minister Ferenc Nagy ineffective, and after a final meeting with Rákosi at which he was given no other choice but to resign, he fled into exile in May 1947. The communists consolidated their power, eventually controlling the entire country, and the Smallholders Party disintegrated. The communist takeover prompted a mass exodus of Hungarian politicians of various political persuasions. Seventy-four of them were spirited out of the country by James McCargar, a Budapest-based US intelligence officer.[11]

Those who remained, representing all the parties including the Smallholders, gravitated to the Democratic People's Party, the composition of which, in 1947, reflected Hungary's rural population. There were sixty DNP deputies elected that year – however there were seventy-one in total as there were eleven additional deputies who replaced others and entered parliament from the party list. Of the seventy-one, sixty were farmers and four were estate managers; all but two were Catholic. This illustrates the confessional divide at the time: the DNP was heavily Roman Catholic, while the Smallholders leadership had a strong representation of Protestants, including Prime Minister Ferenc Nagy. A second group of DNP deputies

---

9   Gergely, "Christian Democracy in Hungary," 162.
10   Ibid.
11   Christopher Felix [James McCargar], *A Short Course in the Secret War*, 4th ed. (Lanham, New York and Oxford: Madison Books, 2001), 261.

could be classed as intellectuals. They were thirty-three in number and included public servants, educators, soldiers, fourteen self-employed lawyers and solicitors (second in number only to the farmers), a large number of teachers and two priests.[12] The composition of the DNP mirrored that of its voting bloc, as 75.8 percent of its votes came from farmers.[13]

Although the DNP strove to continue constructive opposition politics in 1947 and 1948, it became increasingly clear that its hands were tied: the communist takeover was a done deal. Cardinal Mindszenty's arrest (26 December 1948) came at the same time as the dissolving of the DNP, "a party Mindszenty had never respected or openly supported".[14] Barankovics remained in Hungary at the helm of the DNP and attempted to work with the newly communist political apparatus; that lasted less than a month.[15] Historian Éva Petrás's assessment of political statements he made in 1945 and 1947 provides insight into the ideological nature of Hungary's Christian Democratic movement:

> Barankovics was aware of European trends and perceived their presence in Hungary, too, and argued for the existing need for the DNP on that basis … he took a firm stand supporting parliamentary democracy and fundamental human rights. He consistently assessed the social, political and economic events after 1945 with the measure of natural law: he supported the establishment of a new type of economic and social order, he agreed with land reform, with the nationalisation of strategic industries and agricultural estates, with transforming public administration and with need for a special relationship with the Soviet Union.[16]

In Barankovics's party programme speech delivered on 25 September 1945, he said the following about the political basis for a Christian party:

> Those, however, who do take into account the fact that the ideals, unique culture and faithful masses of Hungarian Christianity convey a political need that demands a place for itself in the contest of political parties and in shaping public life, those, who do not close their eyes to the immense religious needs that revive in the wake of great sufferings; those who rec-

12 Gergely, "Christian Democracy in Hungary," 164.
13 Ibid.
14 Ibid., 166.
15 At Barankovics's last meeting with Rakósi on 25 January 1949 he was told by Rakósi that his (party) activities against the government were exactly the same as those of Mindszenty, only that the DNP acted in a "much more devious" manner. Péter Miklós, "Mindszenty és Rakósi között," in Klesteniz, Petrás, Soós, *Útkeresés Két Korszak Határán*, 53-62, at 60.
16 Petrás, "History of Christian Democracy in Hungary," 23-24.

ognise the thousand year old roots of Hungarian Christianity, the roots
that could not be ripped out from the soul of the people in one take ... will
regard it as one of the key interests of the young Hungarian democracy
to have Christian organisations of faithful masses that are genuinely interested in establishing and sustaining democracy and protect it fervently
against any attack.

The cornerstone of this speech, however, was Barankovics outlining his
core belief that an ideal Christian state could exist. In his interpretation,
the state does not exist for its own purpose but is instead an institution
with a humane attitude, and it serves the public good. The "Christian ideal
state ... is implemented where the state sees its ultimate mission serving the human personality that possesses the divine privilege of freedom;
where public good is the state's guiding star and where all life-related actions of the state are governed and regulated by the law of justice".[17]

In the 1947 elections the DNP came in second to the Communist Party
with 820,000 clean, verifiable votes – its best result until present times.
It would have done even better had the communist apparatus not been
aligned against it – rampant fraud at the polls being the least of the communists' crimes. Basically, the DNP won the battle but lost the war: after
the elections it was allowed into parliament only temporarily, as window
dressing. Barankovics fought on through 1948 in hopes of retaining some
influence, and the party took a particularly strong stand against the nationalisation of Church schools, to no avail. Soon the full reality of Soviet
control of Hungary not only shattered his ideals but also endangered the
lives of the DNP politicians remaining in Hungary.

Announcing the dissolution of the DNP, Barankovics fled to Vienna on
2 February 1949. He was soon followed by eleven of the party's representatives. In 1950, he left Salzburg, where he had headed the refugee office
of the Hungarian National Council, and re-settled in New York City, where
the great majority of the Hungarian émigré leadership was based. There,
he chaired the Religious Affairs and Public Education Committee at the
Hungarian National Council from 1951 onward.[18] With the departure from
Hungary of Barankovics and the dissolution of the DNP, the role of Christian Democrats ended the brief era in which Barankovics could attempt

17 Ibid.
18 Kádár Lynn, "The Hungarian National Council," 264; Róbert Szabó, "A Christian Democratic
    Endeavour in East-Central Europe: The Democratic People's Party (1944-1949)," in Kiss, *The
    Voyage of Hungarian Christian Democracy to the Heart of Europe*, 26-42, at 42.

to put into practice within Hungarian society the ideals of the progressive brand of Christian Democracy that he espoused. He would never have that opportunity again.

Hungarian migration to the West: timing and composition

By September 1945, 235,000 Hungarian refugees were in the care of or had been repatriated by SHAEF (Supreme Headquarters, Allied Expeditionary Forces) in the West, and another 50,000 had been in the care of or were repatriated by Soviet forces. More than 100,000 additional refugees were not part of the official statistics because they received no aid from the military or little or none from civilian authorities.[19] Ultimately, approximately half a million Hungarians found their way to Western Europe from 1944 to 1946. Regardless of aggressive repatriation efforts on the part of the Allies, over 120,000 Hungarian refugees who had objections to repatriation or resettlement remained in the West. They came to be known as the *Nyugatosok*, the Westerners, and historians later referred to them as the 1945-ers – regardless of whether they left Hungary in 1944, 1945 or 1946.

The first wave of Hungarian refugees included a large number of officials, military personnel and others with ties to the pre-war government. They included the upper- and mid-level social and political elite, the professional officer corps of the Royal Hungarian Army or Hungarian police, and also the leaders of the various rightist political parties.

Those among this group of 45-ers who remained in the West reflected the conservative values, social structure, and political ideology of pre-war Hungary. They were potentially a good demographic fit and base of support for the Christian Democratic organisations that formed in the West after the war; however, according to historian Gyula Borbándi, a large percentage were not interested in politics. Those who were interested were split between supporters of Regent Horthy or of Arrow Cross leader Ferenc Szalási and were not concerned with anti-fascist political ideology.

---

19 Katalin Kádár Lynn, *Tibor Eckhardt: His American Years* (Boulder, CO: East European Monographs, 2007), 133; Malcolm J. Proudfoot, *European Refugees: 1939-1952. A Study in Forced Population Movement* (Evanston, IL: Northwestern University Press, 1956), 21, 158-159, 285-287. Proudfoot himself acknowledged that his statistics were understated. His statistics are, however, defensible, whereas the numbers quoted by historians of the emigration such as Gyula Borbándi are substantially higher than Proudfoot's and cannot be verified.

He quotes one survey in which 60 percent of Hungarian émigrés responded that they did not feel that political parties were necessary.[20]

The collapse of the Ferenc Nagy government and Nagy's subsequent flight into exile in May 1947 triggered a second wave of migration as Hungarians who had thought coexistence with their Soviet occupiers was possible began to recognise that the Sovietisation of Central and Eastern Europe was permanent. Another 40,000 Hungarians fled to the West, most of whom reflected various shades of liberalism and socialism and were known for their opposition to the right-wing views of the earlier refugees.

The Allies accorded the second wave of refugees more support and political credibility than the earlier, larger émigré group, as they were looked upon more favourably, as democrats, having generally not been associated with what was regarded as the fascist Horthy government. It was at this point that the US sponsored the formation of the Hungarian National Council (HNC), which assumed the role of a virtual Hungarian government in exile. This was first done secretly, under the auspices of the Department of State (1947), and later publicly through the Free Europe Committee. (That being said, funds came covertly, from the recently formed CIA.) In addition to its support for the HNC, the Department of State simultaneously provided funding to establish the Bulgarian National Committee, Council of Free Czechoslovakia and the Rumanian (*sic*) National Committee.[21]

Eager to either repatriate or resettle refugees housed in European camps, the Allied Control Commission, the International Refugee Organisation and various refugee agencies urged those who refused to return to their homelands to emigrate. The first of the Hungarian émigrés left Europe for Latin America (Argentina, Brazil and Venezuela) in 1947-48. By the late 1940s Australia and Canada also were accepting Hungarian refugees.[22] The passage of the Displaced Persons Act of 1948 cleared the way for the United States to finally open its doors to refugees from Central and Eastern Europe – although, in fact, the US had been admitting émigré politicians since long before the act was passed. In 1950 the first of some 16,000 Hungarians arrived in the US, uniting the 45-ers and 47-ers in migration if not in their politics.[23]

20 Gyula Borbándi, *A Magyar Emigráció Eletrajza - 1945-1985* (Bern: Európai Protestáns Magyar Szabadegyetem, 1985), 26, 62. "60 szazalek nem tartottta suksegesnek a politaki partokat." (This chapter references both the first – 1985 – and second Hungarian-language editions of this work).
21 Katalin Kádár Lynn, "At War While at Peace," in Kádár Lynn, ed, *Inauguration of Organized Political Warfare*, 7-70, at 33.
22 Nandor Dreiziger, *Church and Society in Hungary and in the Hungarian Diaspora* (Toronto: University of Toronto Press, 2016), 194.
23 Kádár Lynn, *Tibor Eckhardt*, 135-136.

Hungarian organisations in the West: the early years, 1945-1948

In Europe and in all the other nations of the emigration, various factions of the Hungarian military, which were substantial in number and had organised along professional lines, dominated many of the émigré groups, but representatives of Rome and the Catholic ecclesiastical hierarchy, as well as some Protestant leaders, also jockeyed for power.[24] The Apostolic Delegate to the Vatican for Germany, Zoltán Kótai, was a supporter of the Magyar Szabadság Mozgalom (Hungarian Freedom Movement) organised by General Ferenc Kisbarnaki Farkas in June 1946. Kótai invited ninety-four delegates of the Hungarian Parliament then in exile to a meeting in Altötting, Germany (in the American zone of occupation) for the purpose of voting the sitting parliament in Budapest out of existence and setting up a government in exile. The meeting's claim to legitimacy was that these were the last legally and freely elected members of the Hungarian Parliament, and according to Hungarian parliamentary law, only a quorum was required in order for them to assemble.[25]

The assembled MPs elected Farkas as regent to replace the abdicated Admiral Horthy. To convene the meeting, Kótai had chosen St. Stephen's Day, a major Hungarian holiday that included a pilgrimage by Hungarian refugees to the Shrine of Our Lady of Altötting, Bavaria's national shrine dedicated to the Virgin Mary. Twelve thousand Hungarian refugees from all over Germany participated.

Kótai was also instrumental in establishing one of the earliest refugee aid organisations in the fall of 1945, the Vatikani Tudakozó Iroda (Vatican Information Service) in Landshut, which provided families separated during the war with assistance in finding family members and also provided aid and social services.[26]

---

24 Of the military organisations, the Fraternal Association of Hungarian Veterans (Magyar Harcsosok Bajtarsi Köszössége – MHBK) and the Royal Hungarian Gendarmerie Benevolent Association (Magyar Királyi Csendőr Bajtársi Köszösség – MKCSBK) were by far the largest and most influential.

25 Borbándi, *Magyar Emigráció Életrajza*, 35-41.

26 Gábor Nyári, "Az altöttingi országgyűles és zarándoklat eseményi és hatása a magyar emigrációra" (The Altötting parliamentary meeting and pilgrimage events and their influence on Hungarian refugees), unpublished research paper, 17. After writing this paper, Nyári authored a monograph on the Hungarian emigration: *Menekültek az Új Hazában: A Német és Osztrák Területekben Élő Magyar Emigráció Története 1945-1956* (Budapest: Unikus Műhely, 2018).

The Free Europe years

As the various exile organisations were being formed, their funding principally originated from what was first called the Committee for Free Europe, later renamed the National Committee for a Free Europe and finally the Free Europe Committee. Incorporated in the State of New York on 11 May 1949 and ostensibly established as a private organisation of "freedom loving Americans," its formation was announced in the press by its board chairman, Ambassador Joseph C. Grew, on 1 June 1949 as part of the US initiative to counter the threat of the spread of communism worldwide.[27]

It is not an exaggeration to say that the entire structure of Central and East European émigré activities and organisations – not just in the US but throughout the world, during the Cold War – would not have existed were it not for the financial and organisational assistance provided by the NCFE/FEC. The national councils in all instances directed émigré activities within their various nationalities and formed the key structure by which the NCFE/FEC implemented US policy goals. This was accomplished either with the knowledge of the émigré leadership understanding the NCFE/FEC goals and providing support for them, or covertly by NCFE/FEC directing national council activities in such a manner that the national council leaders did not realise that they were being used as instruments of US intelligence. The national councils and their leaders were among the main tools used by the US in their Cold War propaganda efforts.

The national councils of Albania, Latvia, Lithuania, Estonia and Poland were established with the financial sponsorship of the NCFE, which also took over the four councils – Hungary, Bulgaria, Czechoslovakia and Romania – already quietly sponsored through the US Department of State.[28] These councils, courtesy of the NCFE, helped to direct funding to what they believed to be worthy organisations serving their constituencies. The majority of organisations founded within the émigré community that survived for even a few years were those that were funded through the NCFE/FEC. All of the members of the Hungarian National Council board received a monthly stipend from the FEC, as did other émigrés who were defined as "meritorious exiles" and had no officially defined functions. The two-fold goal on the part of the US was to provide financial support and to ensure

---

27 Peter Grose, *Gentleman Spy: The Life of Allen Dulles* (Boston and New York: Houghton Mifflin Company, 1994), 299-300.
28 It was agreed that while covert support was provided to the delegations from Russia, Belorussia, Ukraine and Yugoslavia, they would not be included in the ACEN and "not invited to join" the union of captive nations. See Kádár Lynn, "At War While at Peace," 49.

the loyalty of the exile leadership. During the lifetime of the NCFE/FEC (1949-71), the US government spent 76.1 million dollars on "Non-Radio Activities", which included the Committee for National Councils, exile relations programmes, Free Europe organisations and publications and their West European Operations Division.[29]

The NCFE/FEC also provided the exiled political leadership with a pipeline to its board members – all were distinguished diplomats, political figures, intelligence officials or leaders of industry – and through them to other influential contacts. While it is clear in the archival materials that a certain political hierarchy was to be respected, through the NCFE/FEC a few émigré political leaders had opportunities to meet heads of state or key government officials in the USA and abroad and gain real access to power. Msgr Béla Varga, for example, was invited to President Dwight D. Eisenhower's inauguration in 1953 and was seated in a place of honour. On the other hand, however often former Prime Minister Ferenc Nagy asked to meet with the US president, he was rebuffed.

The presidents of the NCFE/FEC made the decisions as to which leaders were given access to high officials. Among the Hungarians, Béla Varga, Tibor Eckhardt and János Pelényi (former ambassador to the US and president of the Free European University in Exile) enjoyed the greatest access, but one Christian Democrat also stood out. László Varga certainly had more access and visibility than any other Christian Democratic politician, due largely to his highly visible activities in human rights issues and the controversy over the seating of the Hungarian delegation at the United Nations, discussed below.

The Hungarian National Council/Hungarian National Committee

The Hungarian National Council held its first organisational meeting in Chicago in November 1947. On 18 November the principals – Tibor Eckhardt, Ferenc Nagy, Zoltán Pfeiffer, Desző Sulyok and Béla Varga – issued an "Appeal to the Hungarian People" stating, in part: "The problems and direction of the resistance [to communism in Hungary] will be accepted

---

29 Kádár Lynn, "At War While at Peace," 26-29; Comptroller General of the United States, US Government Monies provided to Radio Free Europe, Radio Liberty, NARA RG 263-CIA Archives 01. 25 May 1972, 102-4. The sum of 76 million dollars would be the equivalent of approximately 586 million dollars as of 1 January 2019.

as the responsibility of the Hungarian leadership living abroad".[30] Once formally established, in 1948, the new organisation added Msgr József Közi-Horváth, one of the most prominent Christian Democrats in exile, to its executive committee as chairman of culture and education and head of refugee affairs and aid. The executive committee also invited Christian Democrat József Pálffy to join the council.[31] At that point, the Christian Democratic leadership was still in Hungary, but after it made its way to the United States, István Barankovics, László Varga and Zoltán K. Kovács all accepted positions with the HNC and Radio Free Europe (established in 1950).

Hungarian Christian Democrats organise in Western Europe

As the first Hungarian refugees streamed into the West in the 1940s, it soon became clear that organisations, whether political or apolitical, needed to be formed by Hungarians to provide aid for their countrymen. Equally clear was the fact that these organisations had little chance of success without funding. Originally, the refugees' stay in the West was thought to be temporary, for surely the Soviet occupation would not last long. And so, for the first decade in exile, the organisations' activities, including retaining political ties, were oriented toward "return," which made the notion of maintaining political parties in exile seem a worthwhile effort. This was to bear fruit, as evidenced by the fact that according to historian Éva Petrás, during the 1956 Hungarian Revolution the Christian Democratic Party was "revitalised in seconds".[32] Reorganised by Sándor Keresztes and the sociologist Vid Mihelics – both former Democratic People's Party representatives – it functioned from 30 October until 4 November, when Soviet troops returned to put down the revolt. Following the suppression of the revolt, the party was banned and its leaders imprisoned.[33] Although

---

30 Kádár Lynn, "The Hungarian National Council," 241.
31 Minutes of the Preparatory Commission of the Hungarian National Council (Magyar Nemzeti Bizottmany), 14 July 1948, Emigració, Box 36 (temporary numbering), Országos Széchényi Könyvtár, Kézirattar, Hungarian National Library Archival Collections, Fond 470. Hereafter, OSZK Emigració.
32 Petrás, "History of Christian Democracy in Hungary," 83; Lajos Izsák, "Keresztény partok a forradalomban," in László Csorba, ed, *Az élő hagyomány: Barankovics István és a magyaroszági kereszténydemokracia öröksége* (Budapest: Barankovics István Alapitvány – Gondolat Kiadó, 2007), 177-191.
33 Gergely, "Christian Democracy in Hungary," 166.

the party in Hungary had been hounded out of public life, the values of Christian Democracy were preserved by individuals. Even after the revolution was brutally put down, Christian Democrats kept in touch with each other in Hungary and "later with those who fled the country. This contact keeping was as intense as the circumstances of living in a communist state allowed".[34]

One of the earliest organisations, the Hungarian Parliament in Exile organised by Zoltán Kótai, not only never received support but was also quickly scuttled by US authorities in Germany. The US Department of State refused to provide support, and shortly after the Altötting meeting, the military government demanded that all attempts to form a government in exile cease.[35] The Vatican envoy's attempt to influence the decision about governments in exile by staging the symbolic St. Stephen's Day event attended by thousands of émigrés went unheeded.

At this juncture, the segment of the Christian Democrats represented by traditionalists in the Roman Catholic Church did not find a political niche with which it could successfully associate itself. Yet in the case of the refugees' most immediate need – aid – the Roman Catholic hierarchy immediately stepped into the void. After Vatican envoy Kótai founded the Vatican Information Service in 1945 it continued to be successful under the leadership of Father Rozsály, establishing a branch of the Catholic aid organisation Caritas (Karitás) on 21 March 1947. The Hungarian Caritas was supported and funded partially through the auspices of Cardinal Michael Faulhaber of Bavaria. It was set up as a Catholic religious institution separate from the existing organisations but was later allowed to become a member of the German Caritas Association, thus bypassing the US authorities' rule forbidding Hungarian clergy from organising charitable activities.[36]

The first political organisation of Hungarian Christian Democrats was the Hungarian Christian People's Movement (Magyar Keresztény Népmozgalom). Founded in Paris in September 1948, its initial purpose was to provide refugee aid for Hungarians. It was established after the founding of the United States-sanctioned Hungarian National Council, and its founder and president, Msgr Közi-Horváth, was a member of the HNC's ex-

---

34 Petrás, "History of Christian Democracy in Hungary," 83.
35 Kádár Lynn, *Tibor Eckhardt*, 142-143.
36 Valerie Miké and John Miké, Jr, *Seeking Freedom and Justice for Hungary: John Madi-Miké (1905-1981), the Kolping Movement and the Years in Exile*, vol. 1: *Hungary and Germany* (Lanham, MD: Hamilton Books, 2015), 226-227.

ecutive committee. Funding through the HNC was immediate.[37] Közi-Horváth was highly regarded in émigré circles, being the only member of the Hungarian Parliament who, on the "third day of the German occupation – in the presence of German Wehrmacht officers and the Gestapo – spoke up against the violation of Hungary's sovereignty and demanded the immediate release of the arrested interior minister and several representatives".[38]

News of the Hungarian Christian People's Movement's founding was "met with a resounding echo throughout the Hungarian exile community here in Europe and also across the Ocean. Those masses of our émigré community who are unconditional followers of Cardinal Mindszenty are for the most part prepared to line up behind Közi-Horváth, because they see in this movement the representation of their worldview and of the principles assuring Hungary's survival and democratic development".[39] So wrote János Miké, a Munich-based Hungarian journalist who participated in the organisation's first meeting in Rome.

Many of the founding members had been key figures in the various parties involved in the Christian Democratic movement in Hungary and were now in exile, including László Varga (the jurist, not the priest) and Zoltán K. Kovács. At the organisation's founding, Baron Vilmos Apor, the former Hungarian delegate to the Vatican, also took part. Its initial efforts were directed toward providing aid to the Hungarian refugees living in refugee camps throughout the West. However, although the 1947 émigrés were fewer in number than their predecessors, they were politically more active, and their goals included preserving the Christian Democratic Party in exile with a view to its possible return to Hungary.

Several years after the founding of the Hungarian Christian People's Movement, it was joined by Democratic People's Party delegates newly arrived from Hungary. István Barankovics left Hungary in 1949 and in 1951 merged the DNP into the Hungarian Christian People's Movement. Közi-Horváth directed refugee aid efforts himself until 1952, after which he concentrated on the organisation's internal workings. In 1951 Barankovics took over the religion and education committee, and in 1958 he assumed the presidency of the Christian Democratic Union of Central Europe (CDUCE), discussed below, a post he held until his death in 1974.

---

37 "M/ Magyar Keresztény Népmozgalom," in *Magyar Katolikus Lexikon*, http://lexicon.katolikus. hu/M/Magyar Keresztény Népmozgalom.html (26 August 2019).

38 Miké and Miké, Jr, *Seeking Freedom and Justice for Hungary*, 272.

39 Ibid; Extract from an article written by János Miké, Munich, 4 December 1948.

Political organisations in exile: 1950 and beyond

By the early 1950s, both the Hungarian émigré community and its sponsors had realised that their exile was not temporary, and their stay in the West seemed increasingly permanent. The Cold War had escalated and the divide between the Soviet-occupied nations of Central and Eastern Europe and the West increased. With the creation of many kilometres of heavily guarded no-man's-land on the borders of its satellites, the Soviet Union tightened its grip on the region, and civil society in Central and Eastern Europe lost the few freedoms they had regained after World War II.

It was also true that, by 1953, the USA had come to see the national councils as something of a failed experiment. Continuing to fund the councils and political parties in exile was seen as an increasingly poor investment, given the diminishing likelihood of the émigrés' return to their native lands. However, the Cold War was, paradoxically, very hot, and organisations such as the national councils, the Congress for Cultural Freedom and the Free Europe University in Exile were important tools in the US propaganda arsenal to convince the world of the superiority of democracy over communism. So were the Crusade for Freedom, actively operating in the United States, and the media beaming propaganda to the Soviet satellites and Soviet Union – Radio Free Europe and Radio Liberty. US propaganda justifying the Cold War and promoting the superiority of democracy was aimed at nations in the West as well. This was the period when Greece, Italy, France and Spain had large active communist parties, and the US was paranoid about the possibility of communist governments seizing power in Western Europe.

Consequently, there was no way the USA could cut off support entirely, but there was nonetheless room for shifts in the budget allocations within the Free Europe Committee that reflected the changing values of the US administrations. With the singular exception of the year 1957, the year that followed the Hungarian Revolution, from 1953 onward a larger percentage of the budgets went to the radio broadcasts and ever less to the national councils.

Hungarians' collaboration with fellow Central and East European émigré leadership

When evaluating its position in the migration, the Hungarian leadership, like its Central and East European counterparts, always felt it should be aligned with the Western nations that would be the most sympathetic to Hungarian issues and beneficial allies.

On 25 July 1950, László Varga, in agreement with the influential leaders of the emigration and with the support of the NCFE/FEC, formed the Christian Democratic Union of Central Europe (Közep-európai keresztény-demokrat Unió). The CDUCE assembled the Christian Democratic Party politicians who had fled the Iron Curtain countries. In addition to Varga, who had emigrated to New York, the founding members included Polish, Hungarian, Czechoslovak, Lithuanian and Slovenian Christian Democratic parties and their leaders. The intention to "fight against Bolshevik tyranny" and the demand for "human rights for Oppressed Peoples" were included in the CDUCE's mission statement.[40] However, "its aim was not only to facilitate mutual understanding of the various situations of the six countries, but also to create a stronger force in their fight for their liberation. The peoples of the free world needed to understand these dangers coming from the east. It was jointly decided that the forces of the exiled groups holding Christian Democratic convictions would be more effective working together than each of them on their own".[41]

The newly established organisation chose as its president József Közi-Horváth, the president of the Hungarian Christian People's Movement. Konrad Sieniewicz, the secretary-general of the Polish Christian Labour Party (Stronnictwo Pracy), was elected CDUCE secretary.[42] Representing the countries of communist-dominated Central and Eastern Europe, the members formed a unified lobbying front against communism. President Közi-Horváth stated after their initial congress, "Our first and most important purpose is to bring the attention of the free world and particularly that of the people of the United States of America to the atrocities that are happening behind the Iron Curtain to millions of our brothers

---

40 Borbándi, *A Magyar Emigráció Életrajza*, 167-169.
41 Stanisław Gebhardt, "The Christian Democratic Union of Central Europe," in Piotr H. Kosicki and Sławomir Łukasiewicz, eds, *Christian Democracy Across the Iron Curtain: Europe Redefined* (London: Palgrave Macmillan, 2018), 411-424, at 412.
42 "M/ Magyar Keresztény Népmozgalom."

who are subjected to the tyranny of Moscow and are heroically enduring their suffering".[43]

One of the organisation's first priorities was a proposal to the United Nations General Assembly that it appoint a High Commissioner for Human Rights. First proposed in 1952, it was not passed until the late 1970s, long after the CDUCE's role in its origins had been forgotten.[44] The CDUCE also spent a great deal of time and effort working to publicise the physical threat posed to Western Europe by further Soviet expansion and by the ongoing military expansion within the Warsaw Pact nations.[45]

The CDUCE was one of the three "internationals" supported financially by the NCFE/FEC. The others were the International Peasant Union, representing the interests of agrarian and peasant citizens behind the Iron Curtain, and the International Center of Free Trade Unionists in Exile, which represented the exiled pre-war trade unionists of Poland, Hungary, Romania, Yugoslavia, Bulgaria, Lithuania, Latvia, Estonia and Ukraine.[46] Funding for the CDUCE was also provided by European governments, including those of West Germany and Italy, which had Christian Democratic governments, (as well as France, which had Christian Democratic leaders but provided less funding) with a commitment to European unity. Soon, CDUCE activities also included support for the emerging Christian Democratic parties of Latin America.[47]

Both the Hungarian Christian People's Movement and the CDUCE were members of the Nouvelles Équipes Internationales (NEI), a Christian Democratic international established in 1947 near Liège and counting among its founders eminent European statesmen such as Robert Schuman, Konrad Adenauer and Robert Bichet. It was founded originally to prevent countries from going communist as a response to the Soviets' founding of the Comintern. Rather quickly, the NEI realised that the best way to block the spread of communism was European integration, creating a united ideo-

---

43 Borbándi, *A Magyar Emigráció Életrajza*, 169.
44 Gebhardt, "Christian Democratic Union of Central Europe," 414.
45 Ibid.
46 Papers of Stanisław Mikołajczyk, Hoover Institution Archives, Stanford, CA, Box 133 International Peasant Union, Folder 15: Cooperating Organizations: Christian Democratic Union. Report of the Secretary General of the Christian Democratic Union of Central Europe presented by Konrad Sieniewicz at the First International Congress of the Christian Democratic Union of Central Europe, New York, 13 March 1953, 4. For the broader context, see Piotr H. Kosicki, "Christian Democracy's Global Cold War," in Kosicki and Łukasiewicz, *Christian Democracy across the Iron Curtain*, 221-256.
47 Kosicki, "Christian Democracy's Global Cold War"; Peter Van Kemseke, *Towards an Era of Development: The Globalization of Socialism and Christian Democracy, 1945-1965* (Leuven: Leuven University Press, 2017).

logical front in Western Europe. They focused on the social rather than economic aspects of defending Christian values and welcomed non-Catholics into the organisation. In 1965 it renamed itself the European Union of Christian Democrats, EUCD.

Émigré political activism

By the early 1950s the Hungarian émigré leadership, now concentrated principally in the United States, included Christian Democratic leaders such as Közi-Horváth as a member of the executive committee of the Hungarian National Committee and president of CDUCE; László Varga, on the board of HNC and high-ranking member of the CDUCE, as well as on the staff of Radio Free Europe; and Zoltán K. Kovács, also active in RFE and on the board of the Hungarian Christian People's Movement. They frequently turned to Western political leaders regarding issues in their homeland that they felt were critical and needed addressing. Political activism became an important component of their work, and shining a light on the atrocities resulting from communist rule of their homeland became a priority. Through their various organisations they were able to present the situation in Hungary to the world. Prompted by the émigré leadership, the foreign ministers of the USA, UK and France were contacted by Admiral Horthy in 1950 regarding the Hungarian soldiers still being held in Soviet internment camps. The Voice of America reported the story as "Hungarians Appeal for Prisoner Return".[48]

In 1951 the Rákosi government in Hungary, in an effort to rid Hungarian society of the influence of the former elite, termed them "enemies of the state" and began a campaign to remove them from the mainstream of the population. They initiated a programme of internal deportation of former political leaders, members of the nobility and the military and even members of the middle-class, wealthy landowning peasants or "kulaks". They displaced thousands, stripping them of their assets and sending them into exile in the countryside within their own homeland, where they were relegated to work as manual labourers at best, and slave labourers under armed guard at worst.[49] The HNC and related organisations such as the Magyar Harcosok Bajtársi Közössége (the Association of Hungarian

48 Radio Free Europe/Radio Liberty Corporate Files, Hungarian Refugee Committee. Hoover Institution Archives, Stanford, CA, Box 210/Folder 1.
49 Kinga Széchenyi, *Stigmatized: A History of Communist Hungary's Internal Deportations 1951-1958* (Reno, NV: Helena History Press, 2016).

Veterans) worked closely with the press to publicise the atrocities of the Hungarian Stalinist regime, and HNC correspondence files are full of appeals to the West to help Hungarian victims of internal exile.

In 1951 the Hungarian émigré leadership also staged protests at the United Nations against the forced labour practiced in the Soviet satellites and the domestic forced labour camps in Hungary, Romania and Bulgaria. In 1953 the HNC published (in English and Hungarian) a report on forced labour by László Varga that specifically addressed the document issued by the United Nations Ad Hoc Committee on Forced Labour which had been submitted to the UN Secretary General.[50]

While Barankovics continued in his role as the intellectual leader of the Christian Democrats in exile, László Varga served as its principal activist. In 1955 he founded the Federation of Free Hungarian Jurists and the Committee for Self Determination. Their primary functions were to keep pressure on the United Nations regarding (communist) Hungarian human rights violations and to work with the press and US authorities to bring them to the attention of the world. Both groups advocated on behalf of individuals whose human rights had been violated in Hungary.

The HNC also worked alongside a UN committee to stall Hungary's UN membership. Hungary was accepted as a member in 1955, at the same time as Bulgaria and Romania, and the Hungarian delegation was seated. After the Hungarian Revolution broke out, however, the United States proposed that its membership be suspended unless UN observers were promptly admitted to Hungary. The UN appointed Security Council Chair Sir Leslie Munro to head a Special Committee on the Question of Hungary, which, alongside the HNC, kept the Hungarian delegation from being formally (re-)seated until 1962. Among the Christian Democrats, László Varga led the protests organised by the Hungarian National Committee and was part of the delegation that preceded Nikita Khrushchev at every stop on his US tour. The delegation's mission was to alert the local media to Soviet crimes against humanity; the *San Francisco Call-Bulletin*, for example, ran the headline "Hungarians Arrive to offset Nikita Tour".[51]

---

50 László Varga, *A magyarországi kényszermunka rendszer jogi vonatkozásai* (New York: Magyar Nemzeti Bizottmány, 1954), deposited in OSZK, Emigracio, Box 10 (temporary numbering).
51 Quoted in Kádár Lynn, "Hungarian National Council," 291.

Collaboration among the émigré groups

It needs to be noted that the various national committees worked together and supported each other in exile as they had seldom done back in their homelands. Initiated by Gregoire (Grigore) Gafencu, the former foreign minister of Romania, their cooperative meetings began informally as the "Tuesday Panel" in the late 1940s and were later to become more formalised. This group organised an important demonstration of exile solidarity in Philadelphia, with its first gathering at Independence Hall on 11 February 1951. The meeting resulted in the "Declaration of the Aims and Principles of the Liberation of the Central and East European Peoples", which was signed by all the participants –195 Central and East European exile leaders as well as Alexander Kerensky, head of the Russian Provisional Government of 1917. An equally successful second conference was held in Williamsburg, Virginia, in 1952. It produced the Williamsburg Declaration, signed by, among others, former leaders from Albania, Bulgaria, Czechoslovakia, Estonia, Hungary, Latvia, Lithuania, Poland and Romania. The declaration endorsed the principles set forth in the 1776 Virginia Declaration of Rights (penned by Thomas Jefferson) and demanded that those rights be restored to citizens of the captive nations on their liberation.[52]

After the successes of the Philadelphia and Williamsburg conferences, the exile groups would next attempt to create a permanent umbrella organisation to work on their behalf on an ongoing basis. The Assembly of Captive European Nations (ACEN) was established in 1954 under the auspices of the Free Europe Committee and included representatives of Albania, the Baltic States, Bulgaria, Czechoslovakia, Hungary, Poland and Romania, as well as non-voting representatives from the Christian Democratic Union of Central Europe and the International Peasant Union. It met in its own General Assembly sessions at the same time as the United Nations. The ACEN's accomplishment was to provide a forum in which the Captive Nations' leaders could have an ongoing dialogue with each other and cooperate as a block to counter actions in the UN by the Soviet Union and its satellites. As I conclude in my essay "At War While at Peace", "This was remarkable in and of itself, as the nations that comprised the ACEN had not only historical animosities between their nations to overcome but also conflicts in the recent past, including Hungary's seizure of a third of

---

52   A.A. Berle Papers, FDR Presidential Library, Williamsburg Declaration Box 224/Folder NCFE.

Romania, Poland re-taking a portion of the Teschen area of Czechoslovakia and the Bulgarian participation in the dismemberment of Yugoslavia".[53]

The Hungarian Christian Democrats László Varga and John (János) Miké were members of the first ACEN Hungarian delegation, chaired by Tibor Eckhardt. The CDUCE also participated in all of the plenary sessions and ACEN conferences and had an opportunity to network with fellow Christian Democratic politicians from the other Central and East European nations. As a result of the relationships the CDUCE established and the CDUCE's acceptance into the family of European Christian Democratic parties, the CDUCE leadership built a working relationship with all the European parties in addition to those from Central and Eastern Europe.

These conferences reflected the commonly shared values and goals of those opposing the communist yoke in their native lands. A look at the correspondence between the Hungarian National Council and the other national councils after the failed Hungarian Revolution of 1956 also testifies to the immediate support all the captive nations' leadership gave the Hungarians.[54] As an example, a telegram sent on 31 October 1956 to Béla Varga by Constatin Visoianu, president of the Romanian National Committee, said:

> The Rumanian [sic] National Committee wishes to convey the most heartfelt admiration for the heroic struggle now being waged by the people of Hungary for freedom and independence…. We are deeply aware of the sacrifices brought by Magyar patriots to the common cause of our countries, now enslaved by Soviet Russia. We bow our heads in grateful homage to the many who have fallen in this glorious fight … From the depths of our hearts we wish the people of Hungary victory in their endeavour in behalf of liberty and we pray that Almighty God may be with them.[55]

Other letters of support expressing the same sentiment came from the Byelorussian-American Association, the Supreme Ukrainian Liberation Council, the Baltic Women's Council, the Council of Free Czechoslovakia, the Czechoslovak Party of Middle Class Exiles, the Estonian Consul Gen-

---

53 Kádár Lynn, "At War While at Peace," 49. Cut loose by the FEC in 1972 when the FEC was defunded, the ACEN continued operations as a transnational entity until 1989. Dr László Varga took over its presidency in 1985 and served until the organisation was disbanded. ACEN was one of the very few émigré organisations that had any life after the termination of FEC underwriting. More generally on the ACEN (prior to its defunding), see Anna Mazurkiewicz, *Voice of the Silenced Peoples in the Global Cold War: The Assembly of Captive European Nations, 1954-1972* (Berlin: de Gruyter, 2021).

54 Béla Varga Correspondence 1956-1957, OSZK, Emigració, Box 14 (temporary numbering).

55 Ibid.

eral, the Polish Minister of Foreign Affairs (London), the Free Slovaks and the All Russian Liberation Committee, among others.[56]

During the period from 1948 until 1971, the year that the national councils were defunded by the US, Hungarian Christian Democratic leaders played a major part in the ACEN, the Hungarian National Council, the CDUCE and social and cultural organisations in their communities, such as the New York Hungarian Theater, Hungarian House, the American Hungarian Library and Literary Society and particularly the Hungarian Scouts in Exteris.

In the spring of 1955, Barankovics, along with several members of his leadership group, split with the Paris-based, Közi-Horváth-founded Hungarian Christian People's Movement and re-established the Christian Democratic People's Party. He continued his participation in the CDUCE and in 1958 took over its presidency, which he held until his passing in 1974. He also continued as a member of the HNC and undertook a number of special assignments on its behalf, including spending half a year in Rome working with Hungarian dissident priests.

Worldwide activities of the Hungarian National Council

At the peak of its influence, the Hungarian National Council had offices in eighteen countries in addition to those in New York City and Washington, DC. The organisation's 1957 budget shows that stipends were received by each of the administrative offices in France, Italy, Belgium, Switzerland, England, Argentina, Germany, Turkey, Canada, Australia, Spain, Portugal, Brazil, Chile, Mexico, Uruguay and Morocco. Of these offices, two were administered by Christian Democrats – Rome (Apor) and Australia (Barcza) – however, the diaspora included many members who were or had been Hungarian Christian Democrats.[57]

The range of refugee assistance, cultural, educational and professional organisations funded through the HNC is extensive and beyond the scope of this chapter, but it suffices to say that almost every member of the postwar Hungarian diaspora was touched or aided in some way by the activities of the HNC during its lifetime. It is made very clear in researching

---

56 Kádár Lynn, "Hungarian National Council," 285-286.
57 Hungarian National Council, Statement of Expenditures, 30 June 1957, OSZK, Emigráció, Box 73 (temporary numbering).

the history of the Hungarian diaspora that it was not political parties or dogma that mattered to the average émigré; rather, the social, educational and cultural services the various organisations rendered were by far the most important and of lasting value, providing jobs, housing and educational opportunities and including assistance in re-settlement in a new homeland.

Regime change 1989: return of the party system in Hungary

Hungary's return to parliamentary democracy in 1989 after a forty-one-year hiatus also saw the return of the Christian Democratic People's Party (Kereszténydemokrata Néppárt, KDNP), led by Sándor Keresztes, a post-war member of the Hungarian Parliament (1946-48) who had remained in Hungary in the intervening years. The Christian Democrats were late in organising, and therefore joined the coalition organised by the dominant Magyar Democratic Forum (MDF), under the leadership and vision of József Antall. Antall's goal was to unite the centre-right parties that shared intellectual roots with the MDF, the Christian Democrats, the National Liberals and writers with conservative views as well as the regional intellectuals.

Although his credentials as a Christian Democrat appeared solid, Keresztes was soon sidelined by the Antall administration to a diplomatic posting. Leadership of the reconstituted Christian Democratic Party then fell to László Surjan.

Was there continuity between the Christian Democrats who had migrated West and retained their beliefs and the party that was formed in 1989? There was, although by the time the leadership of the post-war Hungarian Christian Democrats (such as László Varga and Zoltán K. Kovács, who had fled into exile after the war) returned to Hungary, the Christian Democratic Party had been relegated to a role as a minority-party player, and it remained so throughout its affiliation with the MDF and with its majority-party successors. The CD held its first party congress in 1992 and has continued to play a role as a subservient but loyal partner to the FIDESZ party of the current prime minister, Viktor Orbán. It is generally understood that today's Christian Democratic Party, led by Zsolt Semjén, cannot successfully mount its own election lists and therefore remains in coalition with FIDESZ.[58] Nevertheless, Semjén has served as deputy prime minister in the second, third and fourth Orbán governments, and the KDNP is the most important partner in the FIDESZ coalition in terms of influence. It is also worth noting that parties that were far more dominant in pre- and post-war politics in Hungary, such as the Smallholders Party, while revived could not successfully re-establish themselves in the post-communist era. Meanwhile, the KDNP, while remaining a minor player, is the only pre-communist party to survive in contemporary politics. The KDNP has a loyal but small constituency and continues to wield influence with the leadership of FIDESZ.

While the KDNP is the only post-war party that survived the transition from communism to democracy in Hungary, one would be remiss in not mentioning the powerful influence of two other political figures, both members of the Smallholders Party who returned to Hungary and again became active in politics,[59] Msgr Béla Varga and János Horváth. Varga returned to the position of Speaker of the Hungarian parliament that he vacated when he fled the country in 1947. Upon his return, his role as a senior moral authority was recognised by the state, and he was active in the leadership. An economist and professor at Butler University in the US, János Horváth returned to Hungary in 1997 at the invitation of Viktor Orbán and was elected to parliament in 1998. Having been the youngest member of parliament in 1945-47, he returned as its oldest member in 1998; Horváth represented many of the values of the defunct Peasant and Smallholders Parties within FIDESZ, which were also in concert with those of the Christian Democrats. While Varga was spirited west in 1947, Horváth remained in Hungary, was in prison at the breakout of the Hungarian Revolution and fled to the west in November of 1956. It can be said that both of these individuals played an important supporting role in the re-establishment of democracy in Hungary.

It is also true that there is very little ideological difference between the Smallholders leaders who returned as members of FIDESZ to Hungary and those who returned as Christian Democrats. They were all centre-right politicians with essentially the same core belief system.

58 Interview with former Hungarian Foreign Minister (1990-94) and diplomat, HE Géza Jeszenszky, 10 October 2019, Budapest; Kiss, *The Voyage of Hungarian Christian Democracy to the Heart of Europe*, 9. Kiss notes in the introduction to this compendium that the great part of the early DNP documents have been lost, and most party documents from after the re-launch of the KDNP's organised operations disappeared in 1997 when the party split.

59 The Smallholders party was re-established in September of 1988 and took part in the Hungarian parliament through the governments of József Antall, Péter Boross and Viktor Orbán. In the 2002 Hungarian parliamentary election it lost all its seats in parliament.

The returnee phenomenon in Hungary manifested itself as the politicians who returned to Hungary were those who left Hungary at a very young age. Thus, although four decades had passed under communism, they were able to return to make a contribution to its transition back to democracy. In 1947 when the communists consolidated their rule in Hungary, Zoltán K. Kovács was just twenty-three, János Horváth twenty-six, Béla Varga forty-four and László Varga thirty-seven. All lived to an advanced age and were thus able to return and contribute to the re-establishment of democracy in their homeland.

Returning to the role of the Christian Democrats, there is no question that the diminishing interest in the Christian Democratic philosophy on the part of the general population also mirrors the seismic social changes Hungarian society has experienced since World War II. The Roman Catholic Church, once all-powerful and representing 67.8 percent of all Hungarians as of 1949, represented only 37.1 percent in 2011. Protestants (Calvinist, Lutheran) accounted for another 13.8 percent in 2011, down from 27.1 percent in 1949. In 2011 16.7 percent of the Hungarian population declared "no religion", and another 27.1 percent chose not to answer regarding religious affiliation. By comparison, in 1949 only 0.2 percent of the population chose not to declare a religion.[60]

Despite the decline of the various religious denominations in Hungary, it would be wrong to state that there are no elements of continuity in the post-1989 Hungarian Christian Democratic movement and in the party. As already noted, two of the most dedicated Christian Democratic politicians, László Varga and Zoltán K. Kovács, returned to their homeland. Varga returned permanently in 1992 and was immediately named a minister in the Antall government. He went on to serve as vice-chair of the KDNP and was then elected to parliament in 1994. In 1997, when the KDNP went through its schism, he founded the Hungarian Christian Democratic Association and ran for election as a member of FIDESZ. In 2002 the courts returned the KDNP to its pre-1997 structure and the leadership of the KDNP again fell to Varga, who directed its activities until his death the following year. Zoltán K. Kovács is credited as the force behind the establishment of the István Barankovics Foundation in Budapest and for assuring the continuation of the Christian Democratic tradition in Hungary. As Barankovics's former secretary and then for decades a journalist at Radio Free Europe,

---

60   Központi Statisztikai Hivatal (KSH, [Hungarian] Central Statistical Office), Központi Statisztikai Hivatal/vallás (19 October 2019). Note: the 2011 Survey was the most recent available through the Hungarian Central Statistical Office.

Katalin Kádár Lynn

upon his return to Hungary Kovács dedicated himself to rebuilding the KDNP and writing and publishing its history. The KDNP celebrated its 75th anniversary in 2019, having achieved that longevity thanks in great part to the leadership of Varga and Kovács and the resources they contributed to their reconstituted party.

Thirty years after the fall of communism, the post-1989 Hungarian Christian Democrats have never been able to replicate the success that István Barankovics's (Christian) Democratic Party had in the 1947 elections. Yet they have carved out and played a role in government since the regime changes of 1989, no small feat in the constant evolution of politics and political parties after the fall of communism.

Ideologically, the present KDNP harkens back to the conservative values of the pre-Barankovics Christian Democrats supported by Cardinal Mindszenty. Its platform espouses marriage as between a man and woman, is anti-abortion and solidly supports the Orbán government's anti-immigration policies. It was able to pass legislation in 2016 (rescinded later that year) that closed retail establishments in Hungary on Sundays. Nevertheless, there are threads that bind the 1949 and 1989 parties together, as historian Éva Petrás rightly notes: "Thanks to the activities of politicians who were forced to emigrate from Hungary, an international network of contacts and organizational relations evolved in this era that served as a natural starting point for the re-founded KDNP in establishing its own international relations after 1989".[61]

As of 2020, the KDNP does not appear to be on a growth trajectory, but neither does it appear to be losing support within the electorate. Its support hovers under the 5% electoral base required for a party to be represented in the Hungarian parliament; thus, it survives as a result of its coalition with FIDESZ. Many of the key tenets of the FIDESZ political ideology – Euro-scepticism, anti-immigration, pro-Christian, pro-family – are core values within the KDNP and make their collaboration natural. Within the coalition, the KDNP took the lead in promoting the right to Hungarian citizenship of the Hungarian minority living outside its borders and was instrumental in over 1,100,000 ethnic Hungarians receiving Hungarian citizenship. It was also the KDNP that championed and saw passed a law lowering taxation for families in Hungary. The KDNP also led the charge within the Hungarian government for support for persecuted Christians abroad. Tristan Azbej (Vice President of KDNP) is the Deputy Secretary of State responsible for Hungary's outreach programme to Middle Eastern

---

61 Petrás, "History of Christian Democracy in Hungary," 82.

Christians, which the Hungarian government calls Hungary Helps.[62] The official KDNP website states the party mission as follows: "The KDNP has always conducted its activities within the Christian nationalist framework. We are currently working in close alliance with FIDESZ, representing our specific Christian Democratic goals within the alliance".[63]

In a film made to commemorate the 75th anniversary of the party, Hungarian Prime Minister Viktor Orbán refers to the KDNP as the party of "moral courage", and in describing the relationship of FIDESZ with the KDNP, he defines the role of FIDESZ as providing the large voting constituency and KDNP as providing the ideological high ground and says that both are necessary in order to govern.[64] The film also includes a recording in which Barankovics himself speaks of the party's goals:

> We are a party with a Christian worldview, but we are neither denominational nor a Church party; we're sworn enemies of every form of oppression and injustice; we preach the socialism of the gospels; we don't associate ourselves with either of the extremes; we don't veer to the left of our Christianity, and we do not veer to the right of our social and democratic convictions. In a nutshell our program is this: independent country, Christian Democracy and the socialism of the Gospels.[65]

And while perhaps some of the more progressive elements advocated by Barankovics in the late 1940s are no longer a part of the party platform, it seems as if the KDNP of 2020 in Hungary preserves clear continuity with many of the fundamental principles articulated by István Barankovics more than forty-six years ago.

62 Michael Igoe, "To direct more funding to Christians, USAID looks to Hungary," *Devex*, 25 November 2019, at https://www.devex.com/news/to-direct-more-funding-to-christians-usaid-looks-to-hungary-96055.

63 "A KDNP politikai tevékenységét mindig a keresztény–nemzeti–polgári oldal keretében végezte: Jelenleg a Fidesszel szoros szövetségben tevékenykedünk, a szövetségen belül képviseljük sajátos kereszténydemokrata célkitűzéseinket," *Kereszténydemokrata Néppárt (KDNP)*, at https://kdnp.hu (15 January 2020).

64 "KDNP 75 – Dokumentumfilm – Documentary in 5 languages on the history of the 75-year-old Hungarian Christian Democratic People's Party - Semjén Zsolt honlapja," at www.semjenzsolt.hu (16 January 2020).

65 Ibid.

Katalin Kádár Lynn

SECTION IV

CHILEAN EXILE IN WESTERN EUROPE AND THE AMERICAS 1973-1988

10
MULTIPLE CHRISTIAN DEMOCRATIC EXILES
Debating the Road Back to Democracy in Chile

Joaquín Fermandois

When the military ousted President Salvador Allende in 1973 and created a junta, the Christian Democrats in Chile faced a stark choice. Those who went into exile opposed the junta and, with two exceptions, Jaime Castillo and Andrés Zaldívar, were on the left of the party as opposed to the more conservative wing led by Eduardo Frei Montalva and Patricio Aylwin. Following two splits (1969 and 1971) among the Christian Democrats, the differences between the left and right wings within the Partido Demócrata Cristiano (PDC) had deepened. The left of the PDC – a loose group rather than an organised faction – was more amenable to negotiating with Allende, all while retaining its place among opposition parties. Its members stressed the objective of socialism, albeit in the Christian vein, more strongly at a time when all Christian Democrats spoke admiringly about some form of democratic socialism. The idea of "revolution" had been popular in Christian Democratic culture, although conceived mostly as accelerated social and economic change, with different shades. Members of the left of the PDC continued to pursue a more conciliatory approach to the Marxist coalition until 1973, even though after 1971 all groups inside the party supported liberal democracy, at least narrowly conceived, as political pluralism. They condemned the coup and in exile, too, remained open-minded about cooperation with the non-Christian Democratic Left. In contrast, the Frei wing at first showed sympathy, or at least tacit acceptance, of the coup.

Drawing on original sources, especially the correspondence among key members of the party located mainly in the private papers of Eduardo Frei, Patricio Aylwin and Gabriel Valdés, as well as memoirs and published sources, this chapter addresses the debates between PDC members in exile and those who stayed in Chile after the 1973 coup d'état. The chapter will focus on Christian Democrats' debates and exchanges prior to the overthrow of Allende, their initial reactions to the coup and Pinochet's Chile and the subsequent courses of action for reclaiming democracy.

The chapter's first section will describe the roots of the PDC in Chilean politics and its evolution in the 1960s and early 1970s, while briefly introducing the key protagonists. The second section revolves around the difficult questions of the reaction to the coup and the dichotomy between collaboration with and opposition to the dictatorship after 1973. The third section will deal with political disagreements over an alliance with the PDC left and over what sort of socialism – if any – would be desirable, with the exiled party members rapidly joining the ranks of the in-country PDC left in this debate. The fourth section explores the debate about the character of democracy and discussions about world affairs that influenced views about the party programme and its future. The political and intellectual evolution of both the Left and Christian Democracy in Western Europe mattered a great deal and opened the way for a new vision for the future in Chile, ultimately resulting in a convergence between the centrist forces and a renewed Left. The exiled Christian Democrats were not themselves significant agents of the transition to democracy in Chile. However, in a more general sense they were part of a broad transformation that led first to a re-evaluation of the social democratic tradition – rejected by the left wing of the PDC in the 1960s – and later helped close the gap between the revived Left and the PDC. This evolution included a clear break with Marxism, which had been so influential before the coup. This break was the seminal act of the future Concertación, the coalition that governed Chile from 1990 to 2010.

Roots: reform and polarisation until 1973

The PDC was a relatively new organisation in Chilean political history. Founded in 1957, it originated in the Falange Nacional, a splinter movement of one of the traditional and long-established parties of the nineteenth century, the Conservative Party, many of whose younger members were not content with the apparent lack of social sensitivity of the party leadership in the 1930s. To be born, the party had to murder the father. The 1930s generation of young Catholics – not just the *falangistas* – were committed to a sort of spiritual revolution alien to the majority of the establishment.[1]

At the same time, first within the framework of the Conservative Party and then after breaking away from it in 1938, these youths developed political acumen and capabilities that turned the small Falange into a significant political force. Like many political parties in Chile, even in some cases on the Left, the PDC comprised many traces of the old regime, for example through family traditions or marriage, especially in the cases of Frei, Radomiro Tomic and Bernardo Leighton. The main impulse had something of the *rebellion des notables* – people who, by virtue of belonging to an elite, continue under new social conditions to provide leadership and articulate social demands. The party's starting point was a critique of the Right and the offer of an alternative to communism. Part and parcel of this approach was the aim of acting as a vanguard of social reform: peaceful, or – if necessary – revolutionary changes, with the latter being of a moral nature only, at least until the late 1960s.

Once founded in 1957, the PDC became a mass party that was more ideologically motivated and oriented than other centrist or centre-right parties. In 1964 the party's candidate, Eduardo Frei Montalva, won the presidential race against Salvador Allende, the leader of the powerful Left. With 43.6% of the vote, the PDC obtained a majority of seats in the parliamentary elections of March 1965, by the largest margin ever in the twentieth century; the party reached an absolute majority of seats in the Chamber but, because only half of the Senate was replaced, gained only one-third of seats in the upper house.

The subsequent six-year period of Frei's presidency, from 1964 to 1970, has become a reference point in Chilean history. Frei was up against the main challenge of Chilean politics and society of those days, the combination of a developed and highly respected political system and electoral procedures, facing a pervasive sense of socio-economic underdevelopment. He had to deal with multiple demands for socio-economic reform, but the financial means to implement such reforms were limited. In this period, the PDC sought the support of the Left, but to no avail. The Marxist Left played a powerful role in Chilean politics and society, based on their increasing electoral strength. There was a race to offer more and more of

---

1   On the intellectual roots and politics of the PDC, see Andrea Botto, *Catolicismo chileno: controversias y divisiones (1930-1962)* (Santiago: Ediciones Universidad Finis Terrae, 2018); María Teresa Covarrubias, *1938: la rebelión de los jóvenes* (Santiago: Aconcagua, 1987); Diego González Cañete, *Una revolución del espíritu: política y esperanza en Frei, Eyzaguirre y Góngora en los años de entreguerras* (Santiago: Centro de Estudios Bicentenario, 2017).

what was widely referred to at the time as "real" democracy, which caused tensions at the heart of the PDC.[2]

Simultaneously, the forces of counterrevolution were beginning to gather strength. In the presidential election of September 1970, with the electorate divided roughly into thirds, Salvador Allende and the Marxist Left received nearly 36% of the vote. Having become president with PDC support and following legal procedures, the new Allende government's goal of paving the "Chilean road to socialism" accentuated the growing polarisation that had begun to take shape in the years of the Frei administration and ended with the coup of 11 September 1973.

Amidst the cultural changes of the 1960s, the PDC's young intelligentsia became fascinated by the Marxist and revolutionary ethos of the time. A first consequential split occurred in 1969, when many young and some middle-aged members, including one senator, Rafael Agustín Gumucio, scion of a founding father of the party, abandoned the PDC and created a new movement called Movimiento de Acción Popular Unitaria (MAPU). Here "unitarian" stood for alliance with the "true" Left, that is, the Marxist Left. Quickly, the MAPU came to speak a Marxist political language.

During the first year of the Allende government, a part of the PDC's remaining left-leaning intelligentsia again upset the party and joined a group of MAPU militants who were not so enthusiastic about the Marxist course. In response, they founded Izquierda Cristiana, espousing a type of Christian but not Marxist socialism. After a while, however, its political language became almost indistinguishable from that of the Marxist Left. The MAPU split again in 1973, with one faction more inclined to ally with the more gradual strategy of the Communists, and the other joining an informal alliance with the Castroite MIR, which supported an insurrection. Following Castro's guidance, however, they refrained from armed struggle so as not to disturb Allende's "Chilean road to socialism".

These multiple defections notwithstanding, the PDC continued to a certain extent to identify with Catholicism, or at least with certain self-styled Christian values, and not only in the social sense. Many of the leaders of this intelligentsia later became the core of the so-called renewal of the Left during the later 1970s and 1980s, leaving behind the Castroite or orthodox Marxism that they had espoused, instead embracing liberal democracy and social democracy. They were to form one pillar of the political class

---

2   For a general overview, see Arturo Olavarría, *Chile bajo la democracia cristiana* (Santiago: Nascimento, 1966).

of Concertación in the 1990s and 2000s and have only recently allowed younger generations to take over.

The vast majority of members and voters of the PDC opposed the Allende government, however. Allende and his coalition strove for their support, but they did not want the PDC as another member of Unidad Popular (UP) that would limit its revolutionary goals, even if pursued by constitutional means. After a second split in the party in 1971, the PDC had two wings. One of these was more amenable to coexistence with the Marxist government. It was led by the PDC's president until April 1973, Renán Fuentealba. Fuentealba, while supporting Allende's confirmation as president in 1970, joined an electoral alliance with the Right. Most members of this wing opposed the Pinochet Junta, and many of them went into exile. The other wing was headed by Aylwin, who succeeded Fuentealba as leader in April 1973, the latter supporting a more radical opposition to Allende. The two wings were under the spell of the old lion of the party, Frei, although he was closer to Aylwin.[3]

Protagonists: who were the exiles?

Who were the PDC leaders and active members who went into exile – whether voluntary or imposed – in the years of the dictatorship?[4] Some of them, like Bernardo Leighton and the 1970 presidential candidate Radomiro Tomic, left for self-imposed exile for a few years and were then prohibited from returning. In 1975, Leighton and his wife, Ana María Fresno, barely escaped an assassination attempt by the Pinochet secret police, which caused them severe injuries. Both were eventually allowed to return in 1979, but their activities and influence in Chile were severely restricted. Tomic returned after Frei's death in 1982. Fuentealba was the first important PDC leader whom the Pinochet dictatorship actively expelled in November 1974. Jaime Castillo followed in July 1975 but returned a few years later. Claudio Huepe was first arrested at the end of 1973 and later freed after he agreed to go into exile. He returned in the mid-1980s. Valdés had a post in the United Nations at the time of the coup and returned only around the time of Frei's death in early 1982. Zaldívar went to Europe

---

3   For the PDC in the Allende years, Wilhelm Hofmeister, *La opción por la democracia: democracia cristiana y desarrollo político en Chile, 1964-1994* (Santiago: Konrad-Adenauer-Stiftung, 1995), 159-189.
4   For concrete information about the composition of PDC exile groups, see Élodie Giraudier's chapter in this volume.

after the 1980 plebiscite on the Pinochet Constitution, and once abroad was prohibited from returning to Chile until 1983. Alongside these party leaders, many younger members also went into exile. However, the bulk of the party stayed behind and followed Aylwin and his policy until the late 1980s, when he became the undisputed leader of the PDC.

Generally, the Pinochet dictatorship treated Christian Democrats better than the supporters of the Allende coalition, with the notable exception of Leighton and his wife. This differentiation between victim groups signifies the dictatorship's more hesitant and delicate relationship with the PDC. Up to a point, Pinochet feared the international solidarity that awaited exiled members of the PDC. Thus, in a special case, Belisario Velasco, one of the members who remained in Chile and stayed critical of the Aylwin line following the coup, was twice exiled to a remote outpost within Chile, but neither sent abroad nor physically harmed.[5]

With the partial exception of Tomic, all of those mentioned above had been leading – and in many cases strident – opponents of Allende. Earlier on, Leighton had been a centrist Christian Democrat, but he increasingly became identified with the party's left wing, as were others such as Valdés, Tomic, Huepe and Fuentealba. Castillo had been a leading anti-Marxist inside the PDC. In exile, without changing his ideas, he interacted more with the exiles from other parties. Only Zaldívar followed the Aylwin line, but as one of his internal rivals within the party.

The coup and the aftermath: difficulties of a democratic coalition

Two days after the coup, Aylwin, as PDC president, delivered a radio declaration in which he effectively supported the coup, placing all blame on the extra-constitutional means and totalitarian goals of the Marxist coalition. It was a lukewarm blessing of the military takeover, however, trusting in the junta's promise to return power to the people by restoring "institutional normalcy".[6] Frei did not make a formal statement, but in one in-

5   His memoirs are useful for his differences with Aylwin and a posture that we may call "inner exile". Belisario Velasco, *Esta historia es mi historia* (Santiago: Catalonia, 2018). However, he was not strictly speaking an exile.

6   Patricio Aylwin, *El reencuentro de los demócratas Del golpe al triunfo del No* (Santiago de Chile: Zeta, 1998; Barcelona: Grupo Z, 1998), 31-34. For a general view of the PDC in the Pinochet years, Hofmeister, *La opción por la democracia*, 141-248; for international reactions to PDC behaviour, Raffaele Nocera, *Acuerdos y desacuerdos: la DC italiana y el PDC chileno, 1962-1973* (Santiago: Fondo de Cultura Económica, 2015), 83-208.

terview with the Spanish newspaper *ABC*, and in a long letter to Italian politician Mariano Rumor he justified the military takeover as a legitimate "right to rebellion", affirming that the vast majority of the PDC was behind his views.[7]

On the same day as Aylwin issued his statement, a group of party leaders formulated a very different interpretation, which they were not allowed to publish: the "Declaration of the 13," as it later became known. Among its most prominent authors were Leighton, a former minister in the Frei government, and former party leader Fuentealba. Most of the 13 later left the country voluntarily, were exiled by the regime or were forced to live in remote outposts within Chile.

The Group of 13 began their declaration by paying homage to the sacrifice of Allende – who killed himself during the coup, as an exhumation confirmed in 2011 – in defence of his "constitutional authority". They then asserted their peaceful opposition to Allende, designed to rectify the "mistakes" of his government: that the causes of the coup originated in the "sectarian dogmatism of Unidad Popular", which was unable "to build an authentic road to a democratic socialism", and that the far Left had behaved irresponsibly. The declaration concluded by demanding that "the Junta" (as it was initially called in Chile) return the power to the people as promised. The signatories' goal was a democratic and humanist transformation of Chile.[8]

This declaration contained significant clues that linked the reaction of the future exiles with the recent past and the positions to be adopted by them during the 1970s. They upheld Allende's constitutional position but rejected the concrete path that the UP coalition had followed. This somewhat ambivalent attitude reflected the political and moral views of the PDC signatories, with their roots in the quasi-Left, who had remained in the party after the 1971 Izquierda Cristiana split. At the same time, they did not explicitly oppose the declaration of the Chamber of Deputies of 22 August 1973, supported by the PDC and the Right, which in thinly veiled language asked the armed forces to intervene; this, in turn, had foreshadowed Aylwin's and Frei's reaction to the coup. Privately, however, Tomic wrote to Aylwin strongly criticising Frei's assessment and demanding that

---

7   Eduardo Frei, interviewed by Luis Calvo, "Los militares han salvado a Chile," *ABC*, 10 October 1973. In the letter to Mariano Rumor, Frei blamed the Unidad Popular for the breakdown of democracy because it had "totalitarian goals", quoted in Cristián Gazmuri, Patricia Arancibia, Álvaro Góngora, *Eduardo Frei Montalva y su época* (Santiago: Aguilar, 2000).

8   Jorge Donoso Pacheco and Grace Dunlop Echavarría, *Los 13 del 13: Los DC contra el golpe* (Santiago: RIL, 2013).

the party, "in this phase", keep its distance from the junta, which followed a capitalist and anti-democratic policy.[9]

Frei himself first publicly criticised the junta for the expulsion of Fuentealba in November 1974, followed by that of Castillo, the intellectual head of the dominant *freísta* wing of the party.[10] In an article published in 1977, Fuentealba stated that neither the PDC nor the UP as separated forces could lead on the task of recovering democracy. Instead, all democratic forces should be included in a new government. However, it was difficult to ask for "unity" in the opposition and better to speak of *concertación* – coordinated action. To begin with, this would require talking to the armed forces, taking into consideration existing "realities" and not demanding the realisation of "ultra-socialist" goals. Perhaps few of the remaining forces of the Left could take part in such a government, but it was nonetheless to be open to all of them.[11]

The discussion over responsibility for the coup played a central role in the first years after 1973. Leighton expressed harsh criticism of Frei's positions before and after the coup, albeit only in private correspondence with the former president. In his view, Frei had been passive before the coup, seeing it as inevitable. Leighton even insinuated that Frei saw the coup as the only solution to the crisis, although he conceded that the former head of state could not have anticipated how bloody such a coup would be.

Leighton maintained that, in the past, he had been accused of favouring the strategy of an "anti-fascist" front for the PDC, which in the Chile of the 1970s smacked of the communist strategy of manipulating the opposition to achieve non-democratic goals. Instead, Leighton proposed a coordination (*coordinación*), which would maintain separate organisations and tactics even if all parties to this cooperation agreed on defeating the dicta-

---

9   Radomiro Tomic to Patricio Aylwin, 15 October 1973, APA, 0907, Correspondence. In an interview to *In Messagero*, he testified that Aylwin did the utmost to find a constitutional solution to the crisis, but that "other" people in the PDC wanted Allende to be deposed. Attached to a letter from Radomiro Tomic to Patricio Aylwin, 27 September 1973, Repositorio Digital Archivo Patricio Aylwin (APA, http://www.archivopatricioaylwin.cl), 1771. Correspondence.

10 Summerscale to Foreign Office, 29 November 1974, N.A. (Manchester), Latin America, UK National Archives (Kew), 1/3.

11 "'Un entendimiento entre todos los que desean el retorno a la democracia es indispensable' Sostiene Renán Fuentealba," *Chile América*, nos. 28-29-30 (1977): 173-177. An episode of the exile was the meeting of Colonia Tovar, Venezuela, in 1975, referenced in Giraudier's chapter in this volume, between people of the Left coalition and PDC dissidents; the question was that the latter did not ask for permission from the PDC leadership in Chile, which was mandatory. Nevertheless, it was a step leading to later coordination with the moderate Left. Interview with Edgardo Riveros, 9 May 2019. Riveros, together with Mariano Fernández. Fernández was one of the young members of the PDC, closer to Aylwin but sharing an early aversion to the coup.

torship. Whatever the realities might have been, he at least claimed that in Europe – especially in Italy – all people saw such a coalition as something normal, as the means to defeat fascism. In any case, nobody would understand the PDC if it did not join a wide coalition against Pinochet. Leighton alluded to the "historic compromise" in 1970s Italy, the cooperation between Christian Democrats and Eurocommunists there, without however mentioning the man who coined the term, the leader of the Italian Communist Party, Enrico Berlinguer.[12]

In contrast to Leighton, Aylwin, having the bulk of the PDC in Chile behind him, wrote to Valdés that any frontal fight against the regime would be rejected by the majority of the people, who were opposed to anything smacking of communism or Marxism after the UP experience. Furthermore, Aylwin contended, the people would not live a freer and more just life if the alternative to the dictatorship was to be a Marxist-Leninist solution.[13] At the same time, the growing opposition of the PDC under Aylwin's leadership to the Pinochet regime contributed to closing the gap inside the country between those in a kind of inner exile and the Frei-Aylwin line.[14]

Probable coalitions and democracy

Behind this nascent debate about a possible pro-democracy coalition, there was still a wide rift between the notion of democracy held by the PDC and the parties of the UP. In the end, the fight against Pinochet, at first half-heartedly undertaken by the PDC inside Chile, united the opposition after a large part of the old Left abandoned the radical path of Marxism and changed their orientation in the direction of West European socialism. This shift occurred in the first half of the 1980s and has been one of the mainstays of democratic Chile since 1990. This path was by no means clear in 1973, however.

After the coup, Frei claimed that Leighton lent his name to a smear campaign against him, when the journal *Expresso* stated that the German

---

12 Bernardo Leighton to Eduardo Frei, Rome, 22 April 1975. Archivo Eduardo Frei Montalva (AF, Casa Museo Eduardo Frei Montalva, Santiago), Box 474.
13 Patricio Aylwin to Gabriel Valdés, 6 May 1976, APA, 0073, Correspondence. The day before he had just written to Leighton in the same vein, asking him where is that transformed communist system, in the Soviet Union, in East Germany, in Poland, etc. Patricio Aylwin to Bernardo Leighton, 5 May 1975, APA, 0072, Correspondence.
14 Patricio Aylwin to Claudio Huepe, 24 January 1974, APA, 0072. Huepe was in those days prisoner in Chacabuco, a concentration camp in the north. Aylwin did his best to intervene and later obtained his release, albeit into exile. Huepe would be a prominent exile close to Leighton.

Konrad Adenauer Foundation (KAS), which was close to the Christian Democratic Union there, paid Frei a lot of money annually.[15] In his letter to Frei of December 1974, Leighton in turn claimed that it was as necessary to oppose the dictatorship as to oppose Allende.[16] Leighton and others were convinced that real democrats could reach a consensus with the junta about its surrender of power. They largely retained this stance until just before the plebiscite in 1988. Early in 1975, Leighton stated that the Chilean Marxist parties would not fade away and that they would have to learn from the terrible lessons of the recent past. While still criticising Frei for his strict opposition to Allende and his support for the coup, Leighton nevertheless stated that he did not support an "anti-fascist" coalition with the UP parties.[17]

This long exchange of letters helps us to understand the Allende years, but it also contains clues for the development of the PDC after the coup and the position of exiles such as Leighton. Leighton went to Europe early in 1974. In his Italian exile, he began to interact with other politicians from the left of the PDC, and of the Marxist and far Left. Frei criticised these contacts, because of the harsh attacks on him by these groups before and after the coup. These letters – all written before the attempt on Leighton's life in September 1975 – reveal a slowly closing gap in the spectrum of attitudes towards the Left, with the PDC still considering itself as part of a democratic Left, in a painful effort to close the wounds inside the party. Thus, many exiles initially contributed to developing an anti-capitalist programme for a new Chilean democracy.

The anti-capitalist line for a new democracy

Valdés was the scion of an old family, foreign minister in the Frei government and an official of international organisations in which he reached high positions. He was also a member of the left wing of the party, and in the last phase of the Frei government the president did not always agree with him. During the Allende years, when he travelled from New York to Santiago, he frequently contacted UP politicians in the hope of arriving at an agreement. In one of his first pronouncements after the coup, a letter to PDC president Aylwin, he referred to the junta as "fascist", and he pro-

15 Memorandum from Frei to Tomás Reyes, 3 December 1974, AF, 472.
16 Leighton to Frei, 30 December 1974, AF, Box 474.
17 Leighton to Frei, 22 April 1975, AF, Box 474.

Joaquín Fermandois

tested against the PDC's support for the coup. He forgave Aylwin, however, because in Valdés's view, Aylwin had done all in his power to avoid it. However, the party had sold its soul to save its body, as he put it. The party, in his view, should stop criticising the UP and Allende. Valdés was harsh on Frei. He saw the letter from the PDC leaders to Pinochet as "submission" to the dictatorship. In his view, the PDC was at an end and had to be completely "cleaned" and equipped with new strategic goals.[18]

Aylwin's response to Valdés's sharp criticism was quite aggressive. He denied Valdés's authority to attack him, since Valdés had not lived in Chile during the UP years nor seen first-hand the persecution of the party by the Left, including the deaths of six of its members. Valdés, Aylwin continued, was not in Chile and could travel across the world as a moralist. "We recognize the fact of the dictatorship", stated Aylwin, adding that the great majority of the Chilean people asked for it, and there was still more support for it than opposition to it. He then justified the dictatorship as a reflection of the dilemma that many PDC members and other Chileans felt:

> We cannot consciously hide the fact that in present circumstances it would not be possible to have a democratic government. The power void, institutional crisis, economic disaster and social disintegration made necessary a period of "dictatorship" in the sense of an emergency government invested with full powers, as the Romans understood it.[19]

Nonetheless, to PDC members outside Chile, Aylwin's justification must have been incomprehensible. He clearly accepted the idea of a postponed democracy. Among them, Tomic protested to Aylwin that the PDC had not defended him publicly against attacks by the new authorities. In his letter to Aylwin, he argued:

> In our region, as in Asia and Africa and in large parts of Europe, it is capitalism which approaches its twilight. [It is] what must die because "that is the nature of things". And what is [now] born, under different forms and contents has a generic name: it is socialism. It is the substitution of the power of money by the power of work, from the few to the many.[20]

---

18 Letter from Patricio Aylwin and Osvaldo Olguín to Augusto Pinochet, 18 January 1974; and the reply of Gabriel Valdés, 27 February 1974, Archivo Histórico Gabriel Valdés (AGV, http://www.ahgv.cl).
19 Patricio Aylwin to Gabriel Valdés, 8 May 1974, AF.
20 Radomiro Tomic to Patricio Aylwin, 9 May 1974, AGV.

Even when taking into account Tomic's usually strong rhetoric, his words reveal the eschatological view underpinning his ideas, and the notion that any real coalition could only be formed with the traditional Left, for the purpose of creating a socialist socio-economic regime. Tomic was also ambiguous regarding democracy – or at least, liberal democracy. At times his thinking seemed to be quite closely aligned with that of the Tito regime in Yugoslavia. Not all PDC members in exile or on the party's left in Chile shared all of Tomic's views, but they largely agreed on the broad socialist direction.

In 1975, a group of exiled PDC members sent a collective letter to Aylwin critical of the party's position. They alluded to the Carnation Revolution with the possible threat of a Marxist usurpation of power in Portugal, which the party's majority around Frei and Aylwin saw as confirmation of the position that they had taken towards Allende and the coup. The exiles, however, asserted that the PDC's anti-Marxist position was "exhausted" and needed to be abandoned. In any case, Marxist parties in Europe were being transformed in a democratic spirit. In these circumstances, they asked, what could a future democracy look like?[21]

(We are convinced) that the moral and institutional crisis of the country [Chile] leaves no other way out than the construction of a new democracy, fruit of a gigantic effort of integration and participation of the people, in a context of high patriotic motivation and stern social discipline [...]. The PDC for the last four years has already defined itself as a communitarian and socialist force, democratic and pluralist. Especially in the present circumstances it is necessary to project this definition in a practical way, which demands political will, creative thinking and the necessary strategy and links.[22]

This collective letter, although it does not talk directly about the remains of the UP, reflected a broader trend to build closer relations and perhaps even a strategic alliance. The signatories were attached to the idea of socialism, which fascinated those in the *falangista* tradition. They conceded

21 In spite of odious criticism, links between the leaders were never broken. When Patricio Aylwin sent a letter to the president of the French Senate, he employed an exiled and former prisoner, Claudio Huepe, as messenger. Patricio Aylwin to Alain Poher, 15 June 1974, APA, 1842, Documents, Correspondence.
22 Letter from Bernardo Leighton, Renán Fuentealba, Claudio Huepe, Ricardo Hormazábal and Radomiro Tomic, to Patricio Aylwin, 7 April 1975, AGV. Previously, Aylwin wrote to Leighton reiterating that any frontal offensive against the Junta will not be supported by the population, which is in difficult economic straits, but uninterested in politics. Patricio Aylwin to Bernardo Leighton, 28 March 1975, APA, 0059, Correspondence.

Joaquín Fermandois

in relation to Aylwin's position that there should not be an "organic" union with the Left, but a "convergence", and that there should not be any public conflict over this inside the party. They were already speaking of a "new democracy".

Aylwin and the main current of the party inside Chile saw the process from a different perspective, as becomes clear in their view of the changes in Portugal. In an earlier letter to Leighton, Aylwin had stated that Portugal was an example of how prolonged rightist tyranny leads not to democracy, but to a communist dictatorship.[23] From this perspective, Aylwin accepted the return to democracy as a common goal shared with some democratic elements of the Left. At the same time, he insisted that the unity of the PDC, his main goal, aimed at the recovery of democracy: he did not want to support the dictatorship but was trying to give the armed forces a place in the future of the country. What those in exile did not understand, in his view, was that not more than 20% of the Chilean people were even interested in the re-establishment of democracy at that point in time.[24]

A *freísta* line to look for change and a promising future

Frei had more faith in men like Castillo, expelled from Chile a few months after Fuentealba. Castillo was from the PDC's *freísta* wing and extremely active in human rights matters following the coup. Writing to Frei on the day after the 1976 assassination of Orlando Letelier in his Washington exile by Pinochet's security forces, Castillo said that he suspected that the former Chilean diplomat had been one of the driving forces of the campaign against Frei. In his view, however, this did not matter in the face of the heinous crime committed by the Pinochet regime.[25] Shortly before this letter, Castillo's brother, Fernando Castillo Velasco, from the left wing of the PDC, had written to Frei from London, where he was staying in a sort of self-imposed exile, endorsing the former president's more recent statement advocating a "critical" position toward the regime. He added that

23 Patricio Aylwin to Bernardo Leighton, 28 March 1975, APA, 0059, Documents, Correspondence.
24 Patricio Aylwin to Bernardo Leighton, 5 May 1975, APA, 0072, Documents, Correspondence.
     Aylwin writes against "factionalism", so we can speculate that Leighton wanted himself and other exiles to be treated as a "group", as a part of the party distinct from the party inside the country. Aylwin considered that this position would cast a shadow over the legitimacy of his own steering of the party and (precarious) machine inside Chile and would be a service to the dictatorship. Patricio Aylwin to Renán Fuentealba, 24 March 1975, APA, 0058, Correspondence.
25 Frei to Jaime Castillo-Velasco, 22 September 1976, AF, Box 472.

two things seemed to worry the PDC: the character of the future democracy on the one hand, and any possible alliances with other forces, meaning the Marxist Left, on the other. Fernando Castillo proposed to forget about the future, and that the party should instead concentrate on fighting the dictatorship. In his view, this was the most urgent task of the time. He warned that the cases of Czechoslovakia and Portugal were not relevant to the case of Chile, because of the huge differences between them.[26]

Frei worried increasingly about the exiles, especially the people who had been close to him, like Zaldívar. After the plebiscite of 1980, this former minister from Frei's cabinet and former senator was not allowed by the dictatorship to return from travelling in Europe, and he had to stay abroad for about three years. In a public declaration, both men apparently agreed that if Zaldívar was permitted to return, it must be with dignity, and not as a mere concession by the regime. It should also not appear as if Frei was asking favours for special friends, but that he was in fact pleading for all Christian Democrats in exile.[27]

Later in 1981, in a letter to Tomás Reyes, then acting president of the PDC after Zaldívar was prevented from returning to Chile, Castillo apparently alluded to a future agreement with the Communists, or at least a common platform for reorganising trade unions. Without saying so, he appeared to accept the labour reforms introduced by the military regime in order to abolish the monopoly of one organisation. It seems that at this point he accepted some sort of negotiation with the Communists. However, they would dominate a joint organisation as they had done in the past.[28]

Frei's response is revealing. He agreed with Castillo Velasco that this was an urgent matter, but one that required caution. Certainly, the most important objective was the return to democracy: respect for human rights, freedom of information, workers' rights, university autonomy, security guaranties like in a normal civilised country and a timeline for free elections. Two premises were implicit in his statement. One is that there was a possibility that such a recovery of democracy could or should be negotiated with the armed forces. The second is that such a democracy would be akin to a liberal democracy, even if he recognised that the form of the future democracy could not be the same as in older times because the world had changed a lot. He said that he was not opposed to a broader alliance of political forces, despite the fact that UP had attacked him in the

26 Fernando Castillo to Frei, 5 June 1975, AF, Box 466.
27 A letter apparently written by Frei to Zaldívar, in the first days of January 1981, AF, Box 472.
28 Frei to Tomás Reyes, 17 September 1981, AF, Box 472.

Joaquín Fermandois

past and now he had to withstand attacks from "creole fascists".[29] At this point in time, Frei still retained some degree of optimism about a positive role of the state bureaucracy in a transition towards democracy.[30]

By 1980, the view of exiled PDC members about tactical questions continued to shift slightly. Valdés offers a key example. Writing to Eduardo Frei in 1979, already without the strong critical overtures of his earlier letters to Aylwin, Valdés congratulated the former president for an article in the press. He was not so optimistic as to the likelihood of avoiding violence in a transition to democracy, however. His main criticism was directed at Chile's economic policy under the dictatorship: "The international insertion of the Chilean economy corresponds to a perfect, sought-after asymmetry between the centre's interests and those of our countries". He added that he was very pessimistic about international development.[31]

Before 1980, Valdés had criticised Zaldívar for some of his statements, but after he was forced into exile, he showed respect for one of the leading representatives of the Frei orientation in the PDC. There appeared to be some rivalry in the search for funds dispersed by the Instituto Nuevo Chile in Rotterdam, which followed a more Socialist line from the late 1970s.[32] However, the Chileans in Rotterdam were overall more moderate and preferred a social democratic paradigm. Valdés insisted that he wanted to organise a study group in Santiago, where he would return in due course. He did not want to deprive the PDC of any resources, but he protested against Zaldívar for apparently forbidding him to maintain independent contacts in the Netherlands, adding:

> The party should be the voice of a new idea that illuminates the minds and hearts of its militants. We need answers for the 1980s in a Chile that is not the one of the 1950s, nor of 1964, 1970 nor 1973. [We] need to foster new mobilising ideas to ask, unite and allow creative liberty to emerge from all sides, because it is liberty inside the great current of democratic thought which will be able to give life to exhausted older forms.[33]

His words reflect more positive attitudes towards traditional democracy in the Western model. When Zaldívar was exiled, Aylwin, as de facto leader

---

29 Frei to Fernando Castillo Velasco, 8 July 1975, AF, Box 466.
30 Address of Eduardo Frei, in a seminar of former presidents of Latin American countries, Caracas, March 1979, Instituto de Altos Estudios de América Latina, Universidad Simón Bolívar.
31 Letter from Gabriel Valdés to Eduardo Frei, 24 June 1979, AGV.
32 See Élodie Giraudier's chapter in this volume.
33 Gabriel Valdés to Andrés Zaldívar, 10 March 1980, AGV.

of the PDC after Frei's death (through slow poisoning in two surgeries, as a Chilean court determined in 2019 after the exhumation of Frei's body), was intent on promoting a man close to him, Claudio Orrego, but he was unsuccessful.[34] Instead, the exiled Valdés became the successor of Zaldívar in 1982. Zaldívar reiterated the mainstream position in his interpretation of the Spanish transition as paradigmatic for Chile, where Adolfo Suárez had been his model, and a personal friend, as he succeeded in creating "a national consensus from Left to Right, which in Spain permitted to build up a democracy" in the period from 1977 to 1981-82.[35] Zaldívar did not believe that the world would be socialist in the sense of, or similar to, Brezhnev-style "real, existing socialism". Despite his rejection of the 1980 Pinochet Constitution, he also took the integration of the Right into account, as in his reference to Suárez, who after all had played a prominent role in the Spanish Falange and was state secretary in the government until Franco's death in November 1975.

Valdés returned to Chile in 1980, unmolested but with restrictions imposed on him, and became President of the PDC in 1982, to fill the vacuum left by an exiled leader, Zaldívar, and an acting leader without much power, Tomás Reyes. Valdés tried to maintain a centrist position inside the party. "In the PDC there are neither Marxists nor Rightists [derechistas] [...]. We reject that fashionable reductionism that one should be socialist or capitalist". Concerning the UP, he affirmed that he respected President Allende but that this did not "vindicate the UP because I believe that its ideas and actions were deeply mistaken".[36] His main intellectual references were somewhat traditional, reaching back to the pre-coup and pre Allende years, peppered with some reform ideas. In a letter to the recently created Democratic Alliance, a centre-left force including some former hard-line Marxists, Valdés enumerated the principles required for adhering to that persuasion: respect for human rights according to the prevailing Western definition; pluralism and alternation of power; the rejection of blocs in in-

---

34 Patricio Aylwin to Claudio Orrego, 10 March 1982, APA, 2826, Correspondence. The presumed assassination of Eduardo Frei has been intensely debated in Chile. The thesis is plausible, but, in my view and that of many others, there is no smoking gun in the alleged proof. The jury is still out, then - though, to complicate matters, the Appeals Court ruled on 25 January 2021 that Frei died of natural causes, declaring the accused to be innocent; as of this writing, part of the family has an appeal pending before the Supreme Court. Two basically sensationalistic oriented books explore the case in some detail: Lilian Olivares, *La verdad sin hora: quién mató al Presidente Frei?* (Santiago: Catalonia Ltd., 2020); Benedicto Castillo, *Magnicidio: la verdad del asesinato del Presidente de la República Eduardo Frei Montalva* (Santiago: Editorial Mare Nostrum, 2011).
35 Interview in *Hoy*, 29 July 1981.
36 Gabriel Valdés, *Por la libertad: Discursos y entrevistas 1982-1986* (Santiago: CESOC, 1986), 26.

ternational politics, and of "all means of struggle", which the communists advocated.[37]

This was a very different Valdés from the much more left-wing politician of 1973. By 1982 the clear anti-dictatorship line taken by the PDC leadership from 1975 on combined with the transformation of the Left in Western Europe, greatly facilitated a rapprochement undergone by both wings and views in the PDC. Moreover, the PDC was made illegal in 1977, which further contributed to the internal reconciliation. Even if rivalries among different groups persisted to some extent, they were under a common roof as enemies of the dictatorship, together with sectors of the former Left who themselves were now closer to an understanding with the self-avowed centrist PDC.

Zaldívar, in particular, wanted the PDC to be a centrist party. He assumed that radical Right regimes and dictatorships were usually succeeded by radical Left regimes, something that he was keen to avoid for Chile. Consequently, he advocated a peaceful and orderly transition back to democracy. Zaldívar demanded,

> That a real democracy be installed in the country. There is no way forward in following a democracy attached to some names, that only cover up that there is no democracy "like 'popular' democracy". There is only one democracy, and it is founded on one thing: that sovereignty comes from the people, and the people are the ones called upon to choose their authorities and to define by the [people's] mandate the rules that would govern their living together. Thus, these authorities are conditioned and limited by respect for fundamental human rights, and men are obliged to respect each other. These are the only limits [of democracy].[38]

Zaldívar's words mark the triumphant discourse of liberal democracy in Chile, that no longer needed to be translated into communitarian socialism to seem a legitimate alternative to the Pinochet dictatorship.

37 Gabriel Valdés to leaders of the Democratic Alliance, 10 November 1983, APA, 3141, Correspondence.
38 Andrés Zaldívar, interview by Antonio Martínez, in *Hoy*, 29 July 1981, reproduced in Andrés Zaldívar, *Por la democracia ahora y siempre* (Santiago: Aconcagua, Andante, 1984), 85-86.

Conclusion

The few but influential PDC exiles were not the main agents of the transition to democracy in Chile. However, to different degrees they participated in a major effort that led to the transition, and several of them were among the key actors in the first decade of the new democracy and beyond. The exiles had to align themselves with the leadership in Chile where the PDC continued to exist with its own structure and membership. They interacted with the huge mass of Latin American exiles of the 1960s up to the early 1980s.[39] Exile had the virtue of bringing the Christian Democrats into closer relations with the parties of the Left, at a time when many of its leaders and adherents were abandoning hard-line Marxist tenets. For the Left, the PDC was also a link – even if a weak one – with Chilean social elites and the economic establishment, important for developments in the late 1980s. Mainstream Christian Democrats could travel freely throughout this period, even if under surveillance and threats, and were links in a long chain. Exiled PDC leaders were not in the least a quiet group, but remained very active participants in Chilean and Latin American politics in exile.

When Valdés assumed the PDC's presidency in 1982, he led a policy of reconciliation of the two wings or strands. This process was facilitated by the weakening of the dictatorship following the 1982 economic crisis and the mass protests that followed, forcing the regime into a limited *apertura*, or opening. It was also made easier by parallel political processes in Europe, including the Spanish transition to democracy, where the socialists shed their Marxist traditions. This was something that increasingly also happened on the Left in Chile, which became more critical of "real, existing socialism". These processes facilitated the convergence between the political centre and the Left in Chilean politics.

---

39 For a recent study of the exiles from the Chilean Left in Western Europe, those who would in the end support a centre-left coalition for the return to democracy, containing many interviews with former exiles (including Christian Democrats) as important sources: Mariana Perry, *Exilio y renovación: Transferencia política del socialismo en Europa Occidental* (Santiago: Ariadna, 2020); in a wider context, see Mario Sznajder and Luis Roniger, eds, *The Politics of Exile in Latin America* (Cambridge: Cambridge University Press, 2009), on Chile, 229-243; on DC exile, 234. I differ with respect to the numbers. The people prohibited from returning amounted to ca. 30,000. Including families, these could reach some 200,000 or more; in addition, many people felt constrained or threatened and went into self-imposed exile. Including families, it would be wise to offer the number of ca. 300,000 exiles in those days. Economic migrants should be considered in a different category, not as exiles. Tellingly, the aforementioned book barely refers to the huge Cuban exile after the Revolution of 1959.

Joaquín Fermandois

The first wave of exiles were people who, with few exceptions, had opposed Allende's policies, but nevertheless held left-leaning political views. In part reacting to the coup and against the ensuing violence, they initially returned to left-wing notions of a Christian socialism. Most of them later on moved towards the model of a liberal democracy with a social face, as it was often called at the time. From this perspective, Zaldívar, who was more to the right, was relatively isolated, but his views were likely more in line with those of the bulk of the PDC members and voters. He and others helped to bring them along to create a centre-left majority that, together with international pressure, forced the Pinochet dictatorship to make concessions in the negotiations after the 1988 plebiscite.

Perhaps exile was not the actual cause of the reconciliation of the two wings or strands of the PDC. It was also no barrier to becoming more united again in one party and in opposition to the dictatorship. More importantly, the exiles from 1975 onward constituted a line of communication at first, and later an important link with the reform-oriented forces of the former Left coalition. They all formed part of a major realignment of the Chilean political party system in the run-up to the re-establishment of democracy.

11

CHILEAN CHRISTIAN DEMOCRATS IN EXILE IN THE AMERICAS AND IN EUROPE
Impact on Networks and Ideas

Élodie Giraudier

In 1964, Eduardo Frei Montalva became the first Christian Democrat elected President of Chile with his "Revolution in Liberty" programme and 56% of the votes. His victory caught the United States and European Christian Democrats' attention, especially as they had supported his presidential campaign.[1] This event is also important for understanding the Christian Democrats' reaction in the Americas and in Europe to the overthrow of Salvador Allende and his Popular Unity (UP), which included left-wing former Christian Democrats like Jacques Chonchol, who advocated overcoming capitalism.

In its declaration of 12 September 1973, the Partido Demócrata Cristiano (PDC) leadership "regretted" what had happened to Allende but blamed the socialist government and called for "the patriotic collaboration of all the sectors" to re-establish "constitutional normality".[2] These arguments were repeated in a letter that Frei Montalva sent to the president of the World Union of Christian Democrats (WUCD), Mariano Rumor, on 8 November 1973. In it he railed against "the continuous propaganda in the Marxist media welcomed by insignificant Christian Democrat groups".[3] At the same time, a dissident PDC group of 13 members led by the former MP and minister Bernardo Leighton signed a declaration on 13 Septem-

---

1 Piotr H. Kosicki, "Christian Democracy's Global Cold War," in Piotr H. Kosicki and Sławomir Łukasiewicz, eds, *Christian Democracy across the Iron Curtain: Europe Redefined* (London: Palgrave Macmillan, 2018), 221-255. See also Joaquín Fermandois's chapter in this volume.
2 Quoted in Patricio Aylwin, *El Reencuentro de los Demócratas: Del Golpe al Triunfo del No* (Santiago de Chile: Zeta, 1998; Barcelona: Grupo Z, 1998), 31-32.
3 Quoted in Cristián Gazmuri et al., *Eduardo Frei Montalva (1911-1982)* (Santiago: Fondo de cultura económica, 1996), 477.

ber 1973 that firmly condemned the military coup. They distributed their declaration to international news agencies and embassies, as the Chilean media refused to report or broadcast it.[4] In the context of the Cold War, the PDC division on the point of the military coup was also reproduced in Europe. In Germany, for example, the Christian Democratic Union (CDU) comprised left-Catholic, liberal and conservative wings, which explains their varied receptions of the Chilean coup.[5] Just like the West German party, the centrist Christian Democrats in Western Europe also saw the military coup differently depending on their domestic political positions.

Drawing on fresh archival sources from the Jean Jaurès, Frei and Konrad Adenauer Foundations, as well as interviews and press reporting, this chapter will analyse the dynamics of the exile of the Chilean Christian Democrats in the Americas and in Europe following the coup d'état. The key question is how the Chilean Christian Democratic exile experience bridged the national and global levels in the years of the military dictatorship. The chapter argues that the Chilean Christian Democrats who went into exile between 1973 and the early 1980s essentially chose host countries where they had pre-existing Christian Democratic contacts. The chapter also argues that, despite the heated controversies within the PDC and among Christian Democrats in exile, the exile experience nevertheless helped to bring Chilean Christian Democrats and socialists together to work for the democratic transition in Chile.

The chapter's first section will map the Chilean Christian Democratic exile in the Americas and in Europe: the individuals, the formats that they used for organising themselves and their interactions with other political refugees from Chile. The second section will then explore their connections within and across the host countries and their work with domestic Christian Democratic parties and foundations there. The third section will analyse the impact of exile on the Chilean Christian Democrats' political ideas and preferences, their relations with other political refugee groups, and their ideas about the future of Chile and Latin America.

---

4 Belisario Velasco, "Declaración de los 13," *La Tercera*, 24 August 2013.
5 Jean Julg, *La Démocratie chrétienne en République fédérale allemande* (Paris: Économica, 1985), 85.

Élodie Giraudier

Mapping the Chilean Christian Democratic exile in the Americas and in Europe

At least 400,000 people left Chile for political or economic reasons in the period after the coup.[6] The Chilean Christian Democratic exile has been studied less than the leftist one because it was less important and at the beginning of the dictatorship, only some leaders of the more progressive faction in the party were forced out of the country.[7] It is also difficult to quantify how many Christian Democrats actually were exiled. For example, some of them decided to study abroad as a way for them to protect themselves from repression. Other Christian Democrats were working in international organisations in the United States, without being formally exiled. Thus, who left Chile and when?

In the first year following the military coup, the Chilean Christian Democrats were part of the *chascones*, those who signed the Declaration of the 13. One of these signatories, Belisario Velasco, asserted during an interview that the military Junta wanted to shoot them at the beginning of the dictatorship because they firmly rejected the coup.[8] Renán Fuentealba and Claudio Huepe were also forced out of the country in 1974 and 1975. A former PDC president and senator, Fuentealba first went to Peru and then decided to stay in Costa Rica. After that, he lived in Venezuela from 1975 to 1983. A former deputy, Huepe, was arrested in mid-September 1973 for a few days, arrested again and detained for several months at Tres Alamos and Ritoque detention centres, without formal charges. He was released on 12 February 1975 and immediately departed Chile to seek refuge in England.[9] The well-known former minister Bernardo Leighton decided to accept the Italian DC's invitation and travelled to Europe in February 1974. He gave presentations about Chilean Christian Democracy and the military coup, and in September 1974, when he wanted to return to Chile, a military decree prohibited him from entering the country.

In the late 1970s and early 1980s, the forced eviction concerned instead the *guatones*: the dominant, more conservative PDC faction, which

---

6   Monica Quirico and Valentine Lomellini, "Italy: The 'Chilean Lesson' between the Legacy of the Struggle against Fascism and the Threat of New Authoritarian Shifts," in Kim Christiaens, Idesbald Goddeeris, and Magaly Rodríguez García, eds, *European Solidarity with Chile, 1970s-1980s* (Frankfurt am Main: Peter Lang, 2014), 239.

7   On the PDC, see Élodie Giraudier, *Le Parti démocrate-chrétien au Chili, 1957-2010: De la troisième voie au néolibéralisme* (PhD thesis, Université Sorbonne Nouvelle-Paris 3, 2018).

8   Interview with Belisario Velasco, Providencia, Chile, 26 August 2013.

9   United States Embassy, "Huepe Released," Cable, 13 February 1975, 1. DNSA collection: Chile and the United States.

had supported the military coup in the beginning but began fighting the dictatorship mainly from 1975 onward. For example, the Junta forced Andrés Zaldívar out of the country in 1980. Zaldívar, who had been a minister in the Frei government and who was the PDC president from 1976 onwards, took part in the opposition to the 1980 plebiscite on the military constitution. He was also in the Caupolicán Theatre when Frei gave his first public speech against the dictatorship on 27 August 1980.

The Chilean Christian Democrats essentially chose their host countries for links with local political parties and individual Christian Democrats. This depended largely on the international context and the domestic situation of Christian Democratic parties, as well as language skills. In the Americas, some of the Chilean Christian Democrats had been working in international or regional organisations such as the Organisation of American States or the United Nations. Others studied in the United States and lived on university campuses. They were involved in the Chilean community and participated in political meetings with other Chilean political leaders. For instance, the progressive Christian Democrat Raúl Allard obtained a grant from the Ford Foundation in April 1974 to study Political Science at Princeton University. After that, he worked for the Organisation of American States and lectured on and off at Harvard from 1979 to 1983.[10] In Princeton, Allard gathered other Chilean exiles such as the PhD student in Political Science, Juan Gabriel Valdés, son of a former Christian Democratic minister, and the physicist Claudio Bunster, the astronomer María Teresa Ruiz, the scientists Fernando Lund and Sergio Hojman, the public policy scholar Eugenio Lahera, the writer José Donoso and the economist Andrés Bianchi. In fact, the Chilean exiles played football every Saturday against other national teams as well as US students. The former Christian Democratic candidate in the 1970 election, Radomiro Tomic, visited them, and these Chilean exiles saw Eduardo Frei several times in New York in 1974-75.[11]

In Latin America, the Chilean Christian Democrats found refuge in Costa Rica, Mexico or Venezuela: like the other exiles, they went to neighbouring countries because they thought that the dictatorship might not last long given the strong democratic tradition in Chile.[12] They especially chose those countries in which links existed with local Christian Demo-

10 Interview with Raúl Allard, Providencia, Chile, 22 July 2013.
11 Raúl Allard, *Ambientes múltiples: Testimonio de cinco décadas en el desarrollo de Valparaíso, Chile y América* (Santiago: RIL Editores, 2013), 130-131.
12 Thomas C. Wright, "Chilean Political Exile in Western Europe," in Christiaens, Goddeeris, and Rodríguez García, *European Solidarity with Chile*, 50.

crats. In that regard, Venezuela was one of the key places where Chilean exiles lived. One example is the Christian Democratic thinker Jaime Castillo Velasco, who was forced out of the country twice – in 1976 and again in 1981. Venezuela granted him political asylum, and he met with President Caldera and with other Chilean exiles in the Caracas Group.

Between one-third and one-half of Chilean exiles settled in Western Europe. Countries such as Sweden, Belgium, the Netherlands and West Germany aided them financially, provided resettlement services, helped with language training and job placement. Exile in Europe was attractive because of the cultural, religious, social and political affinities. For the Chilean Christian Democrats, however, the most important host countries were Italy, the Netherlands and West Germany. A lot of Christian Democratic students or young leaders went to West Germany because the Konrad Adenauer Foundation (KAS), which was close to the CDU, offered them funding. This was the case, for example, for Otto Boye and Ricardo Hormazábal. Thanks to a KAS grant, Boye went to study Political Science in Heidelberg on 18 August 1973 and stayed on until October 1982 because of the dictatorship.[13] Ricardo Hormazábal studied for a postgraduate degree in Political Science and International Relations in Bonn from 1975 to 1977.[14] After the coup, 2,487 Chileans of all political persuasions lived in West Germany, and their number rose to 5,124 by 1979.[15]

Although France was not at first regarded as a site of the Chilean Christian Democrat "diaspora", the archives of the Jean Jaurès Foundation show that several of the PDC's mid-level politicians found refuge there and participated in the fight against the dictatorship alongside the former UP parties.[16] Thanks to the democratic transition, Spain became a host country for the Christian Democratic *guatones*: the most famous example was Andrés Zaldívar, who lived in Madrid in the early 1980s and led the Christian Democrat International (CDI) at that time.[17]

In comparison to the leftist exile, the duration of the Christian Democratic exile was shorter. Indeed, Bernardo Leighton, who together with his wife had been attacked on 6 October 1975 by the Condor Operation

---

13 Interview with Otto Boye, Santiago, Chile, 22 September 2006.
14 Interview with Ricardo Hormazábal, Santiago, Chile, 23 July 2013.
15 Georg Dufner, "West Germany: Professions of Political Faith, the Solidarity Movement and New Left Imaginaries," in Christiaens, Goddeeris, and Rodríguez García, *European Solidarity with Chile*, 167.
16 Coordinación de la Oposición Chilena, "Comunicado pública," 11 September 1986, Centre d'archives socialistes de la Fondation Jean Jaurès, 616 RI 45-47 Chili-Partis et mouvements politiques chiliens: actions et communiqués communs 1983-1986.
17 Interview with Andrés Zaldívar, Santiago, Chile, 28 December 2006.

in Rome, was able to return to Chile in June 1978. Because Leighton was severely hurt in the attack, he no longer represented a threat for the Junta. Most of the exiled Christian Democrats returned to Chile in 1983 thanks to a relative political liberalisation of the regime. Like the other exiles, they received help from Western European countries and repatriation committees.

For these different reasons the Chilean Christian Democrat exile was less numerous and shorter than the leftist one. First, members of the *chascona* faction and, from the late 1970s onward, the *guatona* faction, had been forced to live abroad. Their connections in and across the host countries and their work with domestic Christian Democratic parties and foundations while in exile helped them to create networks and collaborate with Chilean Socialists as well.

Chilean Christian Democrats' connections in and across the host countries

The Chilean Christian Democratic exile began as mobilisation against the Pinochet dictatorship was reported to be the most widespread international protest movement since the end of the Second World War.[18] The news of the Chilean coup had a strong impact on the Italian Communist Party (PCI), the largest in Western Europe, electorally dominant in many Italian regions and led by Enrico and Giovanni Berlinguer. On 12 September, the PCI's Central Committee met to analyse the Chilean situation as "a warning" for Italy and especially the Christian Democrats.[19] Within a few days, the PCI initiated a great media operation to place the Chilean case at the centre of national debate. The communist newspaper, *L'Unità*, dedicated its front pages to the Chilean situation until 25 September, and from 28 September, three articles by Enrico Berlinguer under the shared title "Reflections about Italy after the Chilean events" were published in the party's theoretical review, *Rinascita*.[20] On the initiative of the Italian Left, the debate in the Chamber of Deputies on 26 September focused on Chile.

18 Jan Eckel, "Allende's Shadow, Leftist Furor and Human Rights: The Pinochet Dictatorship in International Politics," in Christiaens, Goddeeris, and Rodríguez García, *European Solidarity with Chile*, 67-68.

19 Alessandro Santoni, *El comunismo y la vía chilena: Los orígenes de un mito político* (Santiago: RIL Editores/USACH, 2011), 198.

20 Berlinguer, "Imperialismo e coesistenza alla luce dei fatti cileni," *Rinascita*, no. 38, 28 September 1973: 3-4; "Via democratica e violenza reazionaria," *Rinascita*, no. 39, 5 October 1973: 3-4; "Alleanza sociali e schieramenti politici," *Rinascita*, no. 40, 12 October 1973: 3-5.

The debate among the Italian parties had started in the weeks before the coup. However, on 25 August *L'Unità* replied to the Christian Democrats' *Il Popolo* that "any opponent to Allende" should be called a fascist, asking the Italian Christian Democrats to condemn Frei openly "for minimising and justifying the fascist violence".[21] After 11 September, when Frei condoned the military action, the Italian DC distanced itself from him. As Amintore Fanfani stated, "Chile's drama does not tolerate neutrality; indeed, we are either with the oppressed, or with the oppressors".[22] The Italian Christian Democrats feared that the Chilean events could damage their image, as they and the German CDU had continued to support the PDC during the UP years.[23]

Subsequently, the Italian DC's relations with the PDC deteriorated, as is clear from the correspondence between Frei and Angelo Bernassola, who headed the DC's international department. In a letter written on 5 March 1974, Frei expressed his concern about what he alleged was happening in Italy: "The Communist Party uses the Chilean chaos to attack and black-mail the Italian DC".[24] According to Esteban Tomic, however, "the big obstacle to the success of the historic compromise" between the Eurocommunists and the DC, which was under discussion in Italy at the time, was the opposition of the United States; Secretary of State Henry Kissinger had announced that the US would not be "willing to have a plate of spaghettis with Chilean sauce".[25]

Italy, where the Chilean exile was politically more diverse than in France, witnessed the emergence of a strong solidarity between the Italian Christian Democrats and their South American partners. According to Olga Ulianova,[26] parliamentary groups organised solidarity campaigns with the exiles. The Italian DC felt a responsibility towards their fellow Catholics: Christian Democrats from the parties founded during and after the PDC's breakdown, such as the Movimiento de Acción Popular Unitaria (MAPU) and the Izquierda Cristiana (IC). The Istituto per le relazioni tra l'Italia, i paesi dell'Africa, dell'America Latina, Medio ed Estremo Oriente

---

21 Anonymous, "Perché *Il 'Popolo'* non condanna Frei?," *L'Unità*, 25 August 1973: 1. See also the interview with Giuliano Pajetta (Giancarlo Pajetta's brother) in Anonym, "La posta in gioco in Cile," *L'Unità*, 8 September 1973: 13.
22 Camera dei Deputati, VI legislatura, discussioni, 9168-9173.
23 CDU, Pressemitteilung, Bonn, 23 September 1974, Außenpolitik AZ Chile, von 01/01/1974 bis 30/04/1975, 0/073 Chile, Archiv für Christlich-Demokratische Politik (ACDP), KAS.
24 Letter from Angelo Bernassola to Eduardo Frei, 10 January 1974; Letter from Eduardo Frei to Angelo Bernassola, 5 March 1974, Fundación Frei, Correspondencia, CC/2.2 IT, MFN 1944.
25 Interview with Esteban Tomic, Santiago, Chile, 8 July 2013.
26 Interview with the historian Olga Ulianova, Providencia, Chile, 30 July 2013.

(IPALMO) in Rome organised seminars and workshops and made it possible for Chilean exiles to meet other Latin Americans. The DC deputy Gilberto Bonalumi travelled to Chile several times and worked on behalf of IPALMO to help the exiles. For example, the former PDC and IC leader Julio Silva Solar found a job there.[27] In addition, the deputy and co-founder of the Movement of Christian Workers, Giovanni Bersani, went to Chile and founded the Comitato europeo per la formazione e l'agricoltura (CEFA), a Bologna-based non-governmental organisation (NGO) of international volunteers to encourage economic development in Latin America as well as sub-Saharan Africa and the Balkans. Sometimes, he hosted his Latin American counterparts in this NGO: "We used small, but concrete non-financial ways to help the repressed and persecuted Christian Democrats".[28]

In West Germany in contrast, solidarity with the Chilean exiles at times appeared to depend on their affiliation to a particular PDC faction and their relations with a given group within the CDU or CSU. In addition, West Germany's political situation was different from Italy's because of Germany's division and proximity to the Eastern Bloc. Christian Democrats officially repudiated "the violation of human rights by the military dictatorship" and expressed regret for the violent overthrow of the democratically elected and constitutional government in Chile.[29] At the same time, many leading CDU/CSU members thought that the previous socialist government had been undemocratic. The CDU presidency requested that the Junta re-establish the Chilean constitution in its democratic tradition and organise the election of a democratic president.[30] Carl Carstens, the chairman of the CDU/CSU parliamentary group in the German Bundestag, stated that the "fall of President Allende's government clearly shows that the experiment to combine Marxism and liberal democratic foundations utterly failed". Allende's death was a "tragic symbol that the antagonisms between Marxism and democracy cannot be overcome".[31] Carstens, from the conservative wing of the CDU, was convinced that the Allende government had been aiming for a totalitarian dictatorship. Likewise, the Bavarian CSU leader Franz Josef Strauß and the CDU leader from Hesse, Alfred

27 Interview with the former Christian Democrat and IC Julio Silva Solar, Las Condes, Chile, 28 August 2013.
28 Interview with the Uruguayan Christian Democrat Bryan Palmer, Brussels, Belgium, 2 August 2014.
29 CDU Presse Mitteilungen, 1 October 1973. ACDP.
30 Chile/CDU, "CDU: Neue Machthaber sollen Verfassung wieder voll in kratz setzen," DPA, Bonn, 1 October, ACDP.
31 "Prof. Carstens zu den Ereignissen in Chile," Deutscher Union Dienst, 13 September 1973.

Dregger, both staunch conservatives, also supported the dictatorship publicly.[32]

The CDU dispatched the similarly conservative Bruno Heck and Kurt Vawrzik as official party envoys to Chile in mid-October to obtain first hand-information. Heck had been leading the KAS since 1968 and was on good terms with the former president Frei and with Cardinal Raúl Silva Henríquez. His statements after the visit provoked heated debate inside the CDU and in West Germany, as he joked during a press conference about the 3,000 prisoners in Santiago's National Stadium: "life in a stadium is quite pleasant in sunny weather" though it was surely "nasty in rainy weather". Heck stated that he had meant the opposite of what he said, though.[33] Having strongly supported the PDC under Frei's leadership, the CDU and CSU overall initially sided with Frei rather than the Group of 13 and other opponents of the military coup.

After the coup, the West German Left criticised the CDU's and CSU's hesitation in welcoming Chilean exiles. For the first time, they argued, the country had to help refugees from the other side of the Cold War divide. After initially opposing the social-liberal government's asylum programme for Latin American exiles, according to Felix A. Jiménez, "German Christian Democrats discovered the use of human rights talk and embraced it to attack the Chilean regime in the mid-1970s, something that they had only done before against 'totalitarian' states in the Communist Bloc. [...] It is clear that Christian Democrat criticism of the Chilean military regime sought to help their political allies in Chile while maintaining their ability to criticise the Social Democratic Party's policy of détente with East Germany and other 'real[ly] existing socialist countries'".[34]

Many PDC exiles opposed the conservative CDU and CSU leaders. As Ricardo Hormazábal recalls, "Many German Christian Democrats did not understand our criticism of Pinochet. I was living in West Germany because that regime had forced me to go for political reasons [...], but the KAS suddenly withdrew my grant [...]. Why? Because Heck, who was leading the KAS, was supporting an agreement with Pinochet. And as I was representing a position against Pinochet in the PDC, they withdrew my grant. But [CDU party leader] Kohl supported me [together with] the [West] German Young Christian Democrats [...]. Kohl understood perfectly that Christian

---

32 Dufner, "West Germany", 170-177.
33 BPA, MdB/CDU "Dr Bruno Heck, zu seinen Äußerungen über Chile," 4 November 1973, ACDP.
34 Felix A. Jiménez Botta, *Embracing Human Rights: Grassroots Solidarity Activism and Foreign Policy in Seventies West Germany* (PhD thesis, Boston College, 2018), 141.

Democracy could not support a dictatorship".[35] In this way, the conflict within the CDU and CSU over attitudes to Pinochet had a generational as well as ideological dimension.

After his turn against Pinochet, Frei's first contacts in Europe were in fact with European socialists, especially the West German Social Democratic Party and its leader Willy Brandt, possibly due to Frei's participation in the North-South Commission (1977-80). As Olga Ulianova recalls, networking was a "little Cold War game": if the KAS did not support the PDC sufficiently, it could go off and seek out the CDU's opponents.[36] CDU politicians thus came to realise that they could neither become nor remain a credible advocate for human rights in the Soviet Bloc if they failed to criticise abuses in right-wing regimes such as Chile's. Consequently, the CDU began to take a more openly critical stance towards the Pinochet regime from the mid-1970s onward. In so doing, they provoked the ire of the more conservative Bavarian CSU. CSU leaders strongly sympathised with Pinochet's heavy-handed suppression of communism and his government's radical neoliberal restructuring of the economy.[37] They continued to reject criticism of the regime's human rights records because they understood such criticism to be a product of leftist resentment and Soviet influence in the West.

According to Georg Dufner, the emerging rift between the CDU and the CSU over Chile primarily needs to be understood as the product of the power struggle between Kohl and Strauß for control of the Christian Democrats' policies.[38] This is also reflected in attitudes to the transition in Spain at this time and support for centrist or right-wing groups. According to Wolfram Kaiser, "their competition reflected their different more centre-right versus more right-wing ideological orientation and their different preferences for priority for [European Communities]-level cooperation in the [European People's Party] versus closer cooperation with conservative parties".[39] As the European Union of Christian Democrats and the European People's Party were not able financially to support the Spanish

35 Interview with the former deputy and PDC president, Ricardo Hormazábal, Santiago, Chile, 13 September 2006.
36 Interview with Olga Ulianova, Providencia, Chile, 30 July 2013.
37 Jiménez Botta, *Embracing Human Rights*, 141-142.
38 Georg Dufner, *Partner im Kalten Krieg: Die Politischen Beziehungen zwischen der Bundesrepublik Deutschland und Chile* (Frankfurt: Campus Verlag, 2014), 312-313.
39 Wolfram Kaiser, "Europeanization of Christian Democracy? Negotiating Organization, Enlargement, Policy and Allegiance in the European People's Party," in Wolfram Kaiser and Jan-Henrik Meyer, eds, *Societal Actors in European Integration: Policy-Building and Policy-Making 1958-1992* (Basingstoke: Palgrave Macmillan, 2013), 24.

Élodie Giraudier

Christian Democrats, the CDU and CSU played a key role in strengthening the Spanish Christian Democrats during the democratic transition. The CDU and its chairman Kohl aimed to create a Spanish People's Party akin to the CDU, whereas Strauß and the CSU supported moderate Francoists, who were strongly anti-communist and gathered in the Popular Alliance created in 1976.[40]

By the mid-1970s, the CDU increasingly sought to portray itself as a modern party that took international human rights seriously and supported the anti-Pinochet Chilean Christian Democrats. Meanwhile, the CSU continued to support the military regime, believing that the region needed a combination of authoritarian politics with a liberal business regime. When the Junta outlawed the PDC in 1977, the CDU wanted to support its first partner in South America. The CDU's support of the PDC was thus rooted in transnational networks and solidarity.[41] In the 1980s, the KAS focused strongly on working with the PDC. The foundation at this point dedicated over 40% of its budget to operations abroad in Latin America. Chile received much of this support.[42]

Finally, the Chilean exiles also received financial and political support from international party organisations. The CDI focused on rebuilding the PDC and preparing an alternative to the dictatorship. When Andrés Zaldívar became the CDI president in November 1982, he decided that the organisation had to fight against all dictatorships, and especially against Pinochet. He collaborated with the Socialist International (SI) which counted the Chilean Radical Party among its members.[43] In the early 1980s, the common call of the three Internationals – Socialist, Christian Democrat and Liberal – was "to obtain a consensus that would allow Latin America to recover democracy and ensure that human rights were respected".[44] Together with the CDI, the SI supported the pacification process in Central America and the transition to democracy in Argentina, Brazil and Guatemala in the period from 1983 to 1985.

---

40 Wolfram Kaiser and Christian Salm, "Transition und Europäisierung in Spanien und Portugal: Sozial- und christdemokratische Netzwerke im Übergang von der Diktatur zur parlamentarischen Demokratie," *Archiv für Sozialgeschichte*, no. 49 (2009): 269-277.
41 Jiménez Botta, *Embracing Human Rights*, 142-144.
42 Wright, "Chilean Political Exile in Western Europe", 55.
43 Interview with Andrés Zaldívar, Santiago, Chile, 28 December 2006.
44 Andrés Zaldívar, quoted in Anonymous, "El pacto del PDP con AP cuestiona su entrada en la Internacional DC," *La Vanguardia*, 15 March 1983: 16.

Impact of exile on the Christian Democrats' political ideas and relationships

The Chilean exile differed from other Latin American exiles due to its intense political activity and agitation against the Pinochet regime.[45] Exile in democratic countries dominated politically by socialists and/or Christian Democrats, as well as the experience of being on the receiving end of international solidarity, made it easier for PDC exiles to overcome the trauma of the UP experience for some and of the military coup for all. The convergence and cooperation between Chilean socialists and Christian Democrats first began in Europe, then in Latin and North American countries, before finally reaching Chile. It took place thanks to the work of organisations like the *Chile América* review, the Institute for the New Chile (INC) and the CDI. Despite the initial antagonism between the Christian Democrats abroad and the PDC in Chile, the exiles fostered the vision of collaboration between Christian Democrats and socialists working for the re-democratisation of Chile.

In fact, one inter-party organisation, Chile Democrático, was founded in Rome as early as the first month after the coup, in an early sign of cooperation between the UP parties and the *chascón* group. Its more general humanitarian aim was to fight for the protection of human rights in Chile by putting diplomatic pressure on the dictatorship and lobbying the United Nations Human Rights Commission and other human rights organisations. It founded the *Chile América* review in Rome in 1974: the Christian Democrats Esteban Tomic and Bernardo Leighton – as well as Julio Silva Solar (IC), José Antonio Viera-Gallo (MAPU), Eugenio Llona (MAPU) and the journalist and former communist Fernando Murillo – decided to create this broad-based publication produced by Chilean exiles. They then founded a documentation centre to edit the review. As Solar recalled the founders' motivations, "We wanted to reverse [...] the serious belligerence that had occurred between Christian Democracy and the UP, which had facilitated the path to the military coup".[46]

This review's launching and the ensuing collaboration with former UP members caused a crisis between Leighton and Tomic and the PDC leadership in Chile. The PDC vice-president, Andrés Zaldívar, sent a resoundingly anti-communist letter to Esteban Tomic, who was almost ejected from his

---

45 Wright, "Chilean Political Exile in Western Europe," 47.
46 Julio Silva Solar, Act of donation of Chile-América collection to the Museo de la Memoria y de los Derechos Humanos, 2012.

Élodie Giraudier

party but was supported by his father, the 1970 PDC presidential candidate, and by Leighton. When the review was founded, Gilberto Bonalumi promised a subsidy of 500,000 Italian lire. Franco Giornelli, Bonalumi's secretary, helped the Chilean exiles with typesetting, and the review was printed by the Leberit Company. The first edition was "a leap into the unknown" for Tomic, because it was produced without any prior funding guarantees.[47] From then until December 1983 the review's publication was guaranteed thanks to subscriptions and help from universities and organisations from 66 countries. For a brief period, some articles were also published in French and Italian. From the very beginning, most of the articles dealt with the subject of human rights, discussing and denouncing specific abuses of human rights by the Pinochet regime, and compiling a detailed list of victims.

Chilean Christian Democrats in political exile later met with leftist leaders abroad to develop a credible alternative to the military dictatorship. Thus, in Venezuela, where the so-called Caracas Group resided, the Friedrich Ebert Foundation close to the West German Social Democratic Party organised the International Seminar about Models and Alternatives of Democratic Development in Latin America. Taking place at the Alta Baviera Hotel of Colonia Tovar, some 70 kilometres from Caracas, this event lasted from 8 July to 10 July 1975, gathering Chilean Radicals, Socialists and Christian Democrats of different political orientation including Bernardo Leighton, Renán Fuentealba, Esteban Tomic and Gabriel Valdés, who attended in a private capacity, without consulting their party's executive. They established a consensus on opposition forces to follow common aims, specifically "to fight for the overthrow of the dictatorship and the re-establishment of a free political regime"[48] and to plan a government in Chile that would aim to "build a new socialist, democratic and pluralist society, with full workers' participation in power".[49] As some members were still supporting collaboration with the dictatorship, the PDC officially opposed Fuentealba's initiative. Andrés Zaldívar reckoned that Fuentealba and other advocates of cooperation with the socialists and radicals "violated party discipline"[50] and openly opposed the position adopted by the party, which had categorically rejected the possibility of a front with

47 Interview with Esteban Tomic, Santiago, Chile, 8 July 2013.
48 Quoted in Ignacio González, *Renán Fuentealba: En la génesis de la Concertación* (Santiago: Catalonia, 2007), 242-243.
49 "Declaración de personalidades democráticas reunidas en Colonia Tovar – Declaración," *Chile-América*, nos. 10-11, September-October 1975: 145.
50 Quoted in González, *Renán Fuentealba*, 247, 251.

Marxist-Leninist parties.[51] However, to Radomiro Tomic, the former PDC presidential candidate, the meeting had the great advantage of contradicting the Junta's narrative. According to Tomic, participation in the meeting of the Chilean Communist Party (PC) was "essential", as communists such as Gladys Marín and Volodia Teitelboim supported constructive talks with Fuentealba.[52]

Subsequently, Christian Democrats from the Group of 13 – especially Tomic, Valdés and Leighton – met in Fiano Romano, near Rome. Their purpose was to discuss the PDC's evolution in Chile and how to unite the people of Chile in the fight against the dictatorship. Then, from 13 to 17 December 1978, the Christian Democrats Tomic, Tomás Reyes (then PDC president), Edgardo Riveros, Ricardo Hormazábal, Claudio Huepe and Otto Boye participated in another meeting with socialists at the Institute for Social Studies in The Hague in the Netherlands. The discussions dealt especially with the dictatorship's social and economic policy. As Boye has recalled, "the atmosphere of dialogue between the former UP leaders and the Christian Democrats who were present over there was friendly, frank and focused on the future".[53]

Cross-party cooperation with other exiles also played out on other platforms. Thus, founded in Rotterdam in 1977 by the former socialist minister Orlando Letelier, the Institute for the New Chile (INC) was led by the socialist Jorge Arrate, with the participation of Otto Boye, a Christian Democrat working with Leighton. Fuentealba was part of the INC's Chilean Committee. Dutch Prime Minister Joop den Uyl and his government had rejected the coup straightaway and implemented political and economic measures against the military dictatorship.[54] The Dutch socialist-led and subsequently, beginning in 1977, Christian Democrat-led governments supported the Institute. The Dutch parliament allocated funds for the Institute's creation. The Dutch managed its finances, and the Institute also received help from the socialist-led Rotterdam local government to rent small premises. The INC organised workshops and published a magazine, *Plural*, as well as research results in English and Spanish. Its research activities focused, among other areas, on legal, institutional and socio-eco-

---

51 Quoted in "Declaración de personalidades democráticas reunidas en Colonia Tovar – Consecuencias de la reunión de Colonia Tovar en Chile," 145. The section was highlighted by Otto Boye, who donated his *Chile-América* collection to the Instituto Chileno de Estudios Humanísticos (ICHEH).
52 In boldface in the original. Quoted in González, *Renán Fuentealba*, 253.
53 Otto Boye, "Raíces externas de la Concertación," in Carlos Bascuñán, ed, *Mas acá de los sueños, mas allá de lo posible: la Concertación en Chile* (Santiago: LOM Ediciones, 2009), vol. 1, 86-88.
54 Mariana Perry, "Transferencia política en el exilio chileno en los Países Bajos, 1973-1989: El caso del Instituto para el Nuevo Chile," *Historia* 1, no. 50, January-June 2017: 185-187.

nomic issues, national security, international relations and Christian social movements.

The institute's eight International Summer Schools were its most important activities from 1981: to Jorge Arrate, their aims were to "re-live the spirit of freedom which was characteristic of Chilean universities when they used to work under democratic conditions", and to allow the Chilean and Latin American exile to "systematise scientific knowledge, cultural approaches and work experiences and studies acquired in contact with European societies".[55] Three of these Summer Schools took place in Rotterdam, four in Mendoza in Argentina and the last one in Santiago, during Patricio Aylwin's presidential campaign in September 1989. This summer school was inaugurated by Monsignor Raúl Silva Henríquez and closed by Aylwin, the candidate of the opposition to Pinochet, the Coalition of Parties for Democracy.

These meetings demonstrated the connection between the international level, exile and the national level. They gathered approximately 400 people in Rotterdam and 700 in Mendoza, of whom 600 were from Chile and roughly 100 exiles. The activities lasted one week. The institute received funding for the summer schools, which lasted five days, from some thirty European, Latin American and American foundations, with each summer school costing between 150,000 and 200,000 US dollars. The events helped the exiles to break out of their usual loneliness and to connect and network with nationals living in Chile. Topics under discussion included inter alia the contribution of Christians to moderate politics or whether they could participate in socialist party politics while remaining loyal to the PDC.[56] In this way, the summer schools served as platforms for the political transfer of ideas and practices from a European context to Latin American and Chilean exiles, and into Chile during and after the transition, with a focus on democracy.[57] The INC thus constituted a centre of Chilean socialist reinvention in Europe in a broad sense of the word, and of the democratic opposition's organisation in their fight against Pinochet. In that sense, Otto Boye qualified the role of the institute as one of the "Concertation's outside roots".[58]

In the Southern Cone, the Chilean exile was one among many during the Cold War. The military dictatorships and their repression in Brazil (1964-

---

55 Jorge Arrate, quoted in Perry, "Transferencia política en el exilio chileno en los Países Bajos, 1973-1989," 199-200.
56 Interview with Otto Boye, Santiago, Chile, 2 November 2006.
57 Perry, "Transferencia política en el exilio chileno en los Países Bajos, 1973-1989," 200.
58 Boye, "Raíces externas de la Concertación," 83.

85), Uruguay (1973-85) and Argentina (1976-83) triggered waves of exile either to other Latin American countries or to European countries. Studies on South American exiles tend to adopt a national or a comparative approach in terms of how to think about countries of origin and how to understand host countries where the exiles spent their years abroad. The exile had several stages: those who emigrated to neighbouring countries left Chile, Argentina and Uruguay when those were under military rule, too. As they struggled to adapt to the society and the climate, Argentinians in Israel and Brazilians in Sweden moved to a second host country.[59] Exiles tended to reside in national or Latin American clusters, which perhaps amplified the discrimination they suffered. Studies with a sociological or anthropological focus often underscore how exile impacted families, couples, individuals and friendships.[60]

With respect to Brazil, the emphasis has typically been on individual Brazilian exiles than on the phenomenon of exile as a whole. Indeed, Denise Rollemberg has characterised two exile waves, the "1964 generation" and the "1968 generation", according to the different stages of repression and distension during this long dictatorship. First, Reformist activists who supported the former president, João Goulart, emigrated to Uruguay, Chile, Mexico, Bolivia, France and Algeria. They planned to return soon to their home country. Then, the second wave was revolutionary, mostly connected to the student movement.[61] Whereas Argentinian exiles chose host countries such as Italy in part because of the migration history, their Chilean counterparts moved to countries dictated by political considerations. Argentinians struggled with integration: Peronism did not have an equivalent in Europe. On the contrary, Chile and Uruguay had a well-established political system, and their reality was easy to understand in Europe.[62] In general, exiles had a lower social status in their host countries. However, some Argentinians arriving in Mexico managed to reach important positions in universities, journalism, public administration and liberal profes-

59 Mario Sznajder and Luis Roniger, "Un extraño sitio de exilio para la izquierda argentina: Israel," in Pablo Yankelevich and Silvina Jensen, eds, *Exilios, destinos y experiencias bajo la dictadura militar* (Buenos Aires: Editorial del Zorzal, 2007), 21-61.
60 Samantha Viz Quadrat, "Exiliados argentinos in Brasil: una situación delicada," in Yankelevich and Jensen, *Exilios, destinos y experiencias bajo la dictadura militar*, 63-102.
61 Denise Rollemberg, *Exilio: entre raíces e radares* (Rio de Janeiro: Editora Record, 1999), 49-52.
62 Mario Sznajder and Luis Roniger, *The Politics of Exile in Latin America* (Cambridge: Cambridge University Press, 2009), 210-211.

Élodie Giraudier

sions.[63] In Brazil, Argentinian exiles helped to modernise the psychoanalytic traditions in Rio de Janeiro.[64]

Conclusions

Depending on their initial reaction to the military coup and the evolution of their attitudes to the Pinochet regime, Christian Democrats from Chile went into exile between 1973 and the early 1980s. During this time, the Christian Democratic networks were strong and could frequently rely on contacts from before 1973. The Chilean Christian Democrats essentially chose their host countries for links with local political parties and individual Christian Democrats. They settled in Venezuela, Mexico and Costa Rica within Latin America; in Western Europe, especially in West Germany and Italy; and in the United States. Crucially, they also received support from European socialist parties and organisations. Despite the heated controversies within the PDC and among Christian Democrats in exile, this experience abroad helped to bring together Chilean Christian Democrats and socialists. Their exile created new networks, and it increased the trust between the Christian Democrats and members of the former UP parties.

While Chilean Christian Democrats in exile assimilated and experimented with ideas and ideological positions of Christian Democrats in their host countries and transnationally, their exile had less impact on the PDC back in Chile than the exile of Chilean socialists had on the ideological renewal of the Chilean Socialist Party (PS) and its conversion to a non-revolutionary programme of European social democracy. Moreover, for most leading Christian Democrats, exile ended their political careers, at least at the national level. Thus, Leighton upon his return to Chile did not re-engage in national politics, and Fuentealba chose to have a regional political career instead of re-entering national politics.

Although the impact of exile on the PDC in Chile was less marked than in the case of the PS, the Chilean Christian Democrats abroad pointed the way towards overcoming the political conflict that had led to the military coup in the first place. Moreover, their exile also led to new international connections, networks and forms of collaboration that shaped the post-Pinochet period, deserving of greater attention in future research.

---

63 Ibid., 211-212.
64 Viz Quadrat, "Exiliados argentinos in Brasil: una situación delicada," 95-97.

LIST OF ABBREVIATIONS

ACDP	Archiv für Christliche Demokratische Politik
ACEN	Assembly of Captive European Nations
AECE	Association for European Cooperation
AFSC	American Friends Service Committee
ALS	Archivio Luigi Sturzo
ASILS	Archivio Storico Istituto Luigi Sturzo
AVASC	Agrupación Vasca de Acción Social Cristiana
BSC	British Security Coordination
BU KUL	Biblioteka Uniwersytecka Katolickiego Uniwersytetu Lubelskiego
CDI	Christian Democrat International
CDTSS	Christian Democratic Team of the Spanish State
CDU	Catalan Democratic Union
CDU	Christlich Demokratische Union Deutschlands
CDU/CSU	Christian Democratic Union
CDUCE	Christian Democratic Union of Central Europe
CEDA	Confederación Española de Derechas Autónomas
CEDI	European Centre for Documentation and Information
CEFA	Comitato europeo per la formazione e l'agricoltura
CEJ	Campagne Européenne de la Jeunesse
CFE	College of Free Europe
CISC	International Confederation of Christian Syndicates
COPEI	Comité de Organización Política Electoral Independiente
CSOM	Zjednoczenie Chrześcijańsko-Społecznych Organizacji Młodzieżowych (Polish Christian Social Youth Federation)
CSRM	Christian Social Youth Movement
CSU	Christlich-Soziale Union in Bayern
DC	Democrazia Cristiana
DNP	Democratic People's Party
DP	Displaced persons
DSC	Democracia Social Cristiana
ECSC	European Coal and Steel Community
EEC	European Economic Community
EM	European Movement
EMSZO	Egyházköségi Munkásszakosztályok
EPP	European People's Party
ETA	Euskadi ta Askatasuna
EUCD	European Union of Christian Democrats
FEC	Free Europe Committee
FEER	Free Europe Exile Relations
FIDESZ	Hungarian Civic Alliance
FLF	Fellows of the Lithuanian Front
HNC	Hungarian National Council
IC	Chile Izquierda Cristiana
ICDU	International Christian Democratic Union
ICHEH	Instituto Chileno de Estudios Humanísticos
IDC	Izquierda Demócratica Cristiana

IFCTU	International Federation of Christian Trade Unions
IIS	Institute für Internationale Solidarität
INC	Instituto para el Nuevo Chile
IPALMO	Istituto per le relazioni tra l'Italia, i paesi dell'Africa, dell'America Latina, Medio ed Estremo Oriente
IUYCD	International Union of Young Christian Democrats
JEF	Jeunesse Européenne Fédéraliste
JEL	Jeunesse Européenne Libérale
KALOT	Katolikus Agrárifjúsági Legényegyesületek
KAS	Konrad-Adenauer-Stiftung
KDNP	Kereszténydemokrata Néppárt
LAF	Lithuanian Activist Front
LCAS	Lithuanian Catholic Academy of Science
LCDP	Lithuanian Christian Democratic Party
LCDU	Lithuanian Christian Democratic Union
LF	Lithuanian Front
LIAV	International League of Friends of the Basques
MAPU	Chile Movimiento de Acción Popular Unitaria
MDF	Magyar Democratic Forum
MHBK	Magyar Harcsosok Bajtarsi Köszössége
MKCSBK	Magyar Királyi Csendőr Bajtársi Köszösség
MRP	Mouvement Républicain Populaire
MSZP	Magyar Szabadság Párt
NCFE	National Committee for a Free Europe
NCRLC	National Catholic Rural Life Conference
NCWC	National Catholic Welfare Conference
NEI	Nouvelles Équipes Internationales
NGO	Non-governmental organisation
NLL	National Library of Lithuania
NWT	National Worker's Confederation
OSS	US Office of Strategic Services
P & F	People and Freedom group
PC	Chilean Communist Party
PCCh	Partido Comunista de Chile
PCI	Partito Comunista Italiano
PDC	Partido Demócrata Cristiano
PIASA	Polish Institute of Arts and Sciences of America
PNKD	Polski Narodowy Komitet Demokratyczny
PNV	Basque Nationalist Party
PP	Spanish Partido Popular
PPI	Partito Popolare Italiano
PS	Partido Socialista de Chile
PSOE	Partido Socialista Obrero Español
RCS	Ruch Chrześcijańsko Społeczny
RIEV	Revista internacional de estudios vascos
SCLL	Supreme Committee for the Liberation of Lithuania
SÉCAL	Société d'études et de coopération artisanale Lorraine
SFCEM	Spanish Federal Council of the European Movement
SHAEF	Supreme Headquarters, Allied Expeditionary Forces
SI	Socialist International
SIPDIC	Secrétariat International des Partis Démocrates d'Inspiration Chrétienne
SP	Stronnictwo Pracy
SPD	Sozialdemokratische Partei Deutschlands
UD	Democratic Union

UDC	Christian Democratic Union
UDC	Unió Democràtica de Catalunya
UDC	Union of the Democratic Centre
UDF	Union of Democratic Forces
UE	Spanish Union
UFI	Union Fédéraliste Interuniversitaire
UNRRA	United Nations Relief and Rehabilitation Administration
UN	United Nations
UP	Unidad Popular
US	United States
VLIK	Vyriausiasis Lietuvos Išlaisvinimo Komitetas
WCL	World Community of Lithuanians
WUCD	World Union of Christian Democrats
YEPP	Youth of the European People's Party

BIBLIOGRAPHY

Acanfora, Paolo. "La Democrazia cristiana dega-speriana e il mito della nazione: le interpre-tazioni del Risorgimento." *Ricerche di storia politica*, no. 2 (2009): 177-196.

Acanfora, Paolo. "L'esilio antifascista negli Usa e la ricostruzione nazionale: I rapporti tra Luigi Sturzo e Max Ascoli." In *Oltreoceano: politica e comunicazione tra Italia e Stati Uniti nel Novecento*, edited by Davide Grippa, 169-196. Florence: Olschki, 2017.

Acanfora, Paolo. "Myths and the Political Use of Religion in Christian Democratic Culture." *Journal of Modern Italian Studies* 12, no. 3 (2007): 307-338.

Acerbi, Antonio. *Chiesa e Democrazia: Da Leone XIII al Vaticano II*. Milan: Vita e Pensiero, 1991.

Aguirre, José Antonio. *Obras Completas*. Volume 2. San Sebastian: Sendoa, 1981.

Ahonen, Pertti et al., editors. *People on the Move: Forced Population Movements in Europe in the Second World War and its Aftermath*. Oxford: Berg, 2008.

Aleksandravičius, Egidijus. *Karklo diegas: lietu-vių pasaulio istorija*. Vilnius: Versus aureus, 2002.

Aleksandravičius, Egidijus et al. *The Cultural Ac-tivities of Lithuanian Émigrés*. Vilnius: Versus aureus, 2002.

Alentorn, Miquel Coll i. *Escrits polítics, cívics i re-ligiosos*. Barcelona: Curial Edicions Catalanes; Publicacions de l'Abadia de Montserrat, 1993.

Allard, Raúl. *Ambientes múltiples: Testimonio de cinco décadas en el desarrollo de Valparaíso, Chile y América Latina*. Santiago: RIL Editores, 2013.

Álvarez de Miranda, Fernando. *La España que soñé: Memorias de un hombre de consenso*. Madrid: Esfera de los Libros, 2012.

Amat, Jordi. *Com una pàtria: vida de Josep Benet*. Barcelona: Edicions 62, 2017.

Applebaum, Anne. *Iron Curtain: The Crushing of Eastern Europe, 1944-1956*. New York: Ran-dom House, 2012.

Ariztimuño, José, J. de Urkina. *La democracia en Euzkadi*. San Sebastián: Editorial Euskaltza-leak, 1935.

Arrieta, Leyre. "Dilemas del nacionalismo vasco en la guerra civil." In *Desde la capital de la República: nuevas perspectivas y estudios so-bre la guerra civil*, edited by Sergio Valero and García Marta Carrión. Valencia: Universitat de Válencia, 2018.

Arrieta, Leyre. *Edición y estudio introductorio de La Causa del Pueblo Vasco de Francisco Javier Landaburu*. Leioa: Servicio de Publicaciones de EHU/UPV, 2017.

Arrieta, Leyre. "El nacionalismo vasco y Jacques Maritain (1936-1945)." *Ayer*, no. 13 (2019): 189-215.

Arrieta, Leyre. *Estación Europa: La política europeísta del PNV en el exilio (1945-1977)*. Madrid: Tecnos, 2007.

Arrieta, Leyre. "Por los derechos del Pueblo Vasco: El PNV en la Transición, 1975-1980." *Historia del Presente*, no. 19 (2012): 39-52.

Arski, Stefan. *Targowica leży nad Atlantykiem*. Warsaw: Książka i Wiedza, 1952.

Aschmann, Birgit. *Treue Freunde: Deutschland und Spanien in der Nachkriegszeit*. Stuttgart: Steiner, 1999.

Aylwin, Patricio. *El reencuentro de los demócra-tas: Del golpe al triunfo del No*. Santiago de Chile: Zeta, 1998; Barcelona: Grupo Z, 1998.

Azurmendi, José. "Pensamiento personalista en Euskadi en torno a la guerra." *Revista interna-cional de estudios vascos RIEV* 4, no. 1 (1996): 77-98.

Bagieński, Witold. *Wywiad cywilny Polski Ludowej w latach 1945-1961*. Volume 2. War-saw: Instytut Pamięci Narodowej, 2017.

Baldini, Alessandra and Paolo Palma, editors. *Gli antifascisti italiani in America (1942-1944): La 'legione' nel carteggio di Pacciardi con Borgese, Salvemini, Sforza e Sturzo*. Florence: Le Monnier, 1990.

Balkelis, Tomas. *The making of modern Lithua-nia*. London: Routledge, 2009.

Ball, Stuart. "The Politics of Appeasement: The Fall of the Duchess of Atholl and the Kinross and West Perth By-election, December 1938." *The Scottish Historical Review* LXIX, no.1 (1990): 49-83.

Banionis, Juozas. *Lietuvos laisvinimas Vakaruose 1940-1975.* Vilnius: LGGRTC, 2010.

Banionis, Juozas. *Lietuvos laisvinimas Vakaruose po Helsinkio akto 1975-1994.* Vilnius: LGGRTC, 2017.

Barba Prieto, Donato. *La democracia cristiana en España.* Volume 2. Madrid: Ediciones Encuentro, 2004.

Barbara, Frédérique. *Les populations réfugiés dans le Tarn pendant la seconde guerre mondiale.* Master's thesis, Université de Toulouse Le Mirail, 1990.

Barberà, Òscar. *Unió Democràtica de Catalunya (1976-1978): CiU-El pacte amb Convergència Democràtica de Catalunya.* Barcelona: Mediterrània, 2000.

Barrio López, Astrid. "Les arrels de Convergència Democràtica de Catalunya." In *El pal de paller: Convergència Democràtica de Catalunya, 1974-2000*, edited by Joan B. Culla i Clarà, 13-39. Barcelona: Pòrtic, 2001.

Benet, Josep. *L'intent franquista de genocidi cultural contra Catalunya.* Barcelona: Publicacions de l'Abadia de Montserrat, 1995.

Bernardi, Emanuele. *Il mais "miracoloso": Storia di un'innovazione tra politica, economia e religione.* Rome: Carocci, 2014.

Blažytė, Jurgita. "Religinis lietuvių gyvenimas DP stovyklose 1945-1950." *Oikos: lietuvių migracijos ir diasporos studijos*, no. 1 (2008): 83-103.

Borbándi, Gyula. *A Magyar Emigráció Eletrajza: 1945-1985.* Bern: Európai Protestáns Magyar Szabadegyetem, 1985.

Bordetas, Ivan and Anna Sánchez. *L'antifranquisme oblidat: de la dissidència al comunisme revolucionari, 1953-1972.* Barcelona: Base, 2019.

Borruso, Paolo. "The Impossibility of a Christian Democracy in Africa? The Uganda Experience." In *Christian Democrat Internationalism: Its Action in Europe and Worldwide from post-World War II until the 1990s*, edited by Jean-Dominique Durand. Volume 3, 97-106. Brussels: P.I.E. Peter Lang, 2014.

Botti, Alfonso. "La Iglesia vasca dividida: Cuestión religiosa y nacionalismo a la luz de la nueva documentación vaticana." *Historia Contemporánea*, no. 35 (2007): 451-489.

Botti, Alfonso. *Luigi Sturzo e gli amici spagnoli: Carteggi (1924-1951).* Bologna: Rubbettino, 2012.

Botto, Andrea. *Catolicismo chileno: controversias y divisiones (1930-1962).* Santiago: Ediciones Universidad Finis Terrae, 2018.

Bowd, Gavin. *Fascist Scotland: Caledonia and the Far Right.* Edinburgh: Birlinn, 2013.

Bowd, Gavin. "Scotland for Franco: Charles Saroléa v. The Red Duchess." *Journal of Scottish Historical Studies* 31, no. 2 (2011): 195-209.

Boye, Otto. "Raíces externas de la Concertación." In *Mas acá de los sueños, mas allá de lo posible: la Concertación en Chile.* Volume 1, edited by Carlos Bascuñán, 77-94. Santiago: LOM Ediciones, 2009.

Brandes, Detlef. "Confederation Plans in Eastern Europe during World War II." In *Wartime Plans for Postwar Europe 1940-1947*, edited by Michel Dumoulin, 83-94. Brussels: Bruylant, 1995.

Braojos Garrido, Alfonso and Leandro Alvarez Rey. *Epistolario Politico: Manuel Gimenez Fernandez (1896-1968).* Seville: Ayuntamiento de Sevilla, 2003.

Brenan, Gerald. *The Spanish Labyrinth: An Account of the Social and Political Background of the Spanish Civil War.* New York: Cambridge University Press, 2014.

Buchanan, Tom. *Britain and the Spanish Civil War.* Cambridge: Cambridge University Press, 1997.

Buchanan, Tom. "Great Britain." In *Political Catholicism in Europe, 1918-1965*, edited by Tom Buchanan and Martin Conway, 248-274. Oxford: Oxford University Press, 1996.

Buchanan, Tom. *The Spanish Civil War and the British Labour Movement.* Cambridge: Cambridge University Press, 1991.

Buchanan, Tom and Martin Conway, editors. *Political Catholicism in Europe 1918-1965.* Oxford: Oxford University Press, 1996.

Bučinskytė, Ilona. *Idealų vedami: Ateitininkai išeivijoje XX a: 5-7 dešimtmečiais.* Vilnius: Versus aureus, 2008.

Burke, Peter. *Exiles and Expatriates in the History of Knowledge, 1500-2000.* Waltham, Mass.: Brandeis University Press, 2017.

Burrin, Philippe. *France under the Germans: collaboration and compromise.* London: Arnold, 2000.

Caballer, Gemma. *Aidez les réfugiés! Josep Maria Trias i Peitx: un home d'acció entre catòlics i quàquers.* Maçanet de la Selva: Gregal, 2020.

Caballer, Gemma. "Josep Maria Trias Peitx: un català entre els quàquers." *Revista de Catalunya*, no. 301 (January-March 2018): 41-52.

Caballer, Gemma. "Pour la renaissance des villages abandonnés: Quaker Humanitarian Aid in a France at War." *Quaker Studies* 24, no. 1 (June 2019): 109-139. At: https://doi.org/10.3828/quaker.2019.24.1.6 (23 July 2019).

Caballer, Gemma. "Secours catholique international, una iniciativa catalana a França?" In *Postguerres / Aftermaths of War*, edited by Teresa Abelló, Giovanni Cattini, Víctor Gavín, Jordi Ibarz, Carles Santacana, Queralt Solé and Antoni Vives, 335-349. Barcelona: Universitat de Barcelona/Ventall, 2020.

Caballer, Gemma and Queralt Solé. "El Comitè Nacional Catòlic de Socors als Refugiats d'Espanya, una aproximació." In *Catalans du Nord et languedociens et l'aide à la République Espagnole, 1936-1946: actes de la Journée d'études de l'Association Maitron Languedoc-Roussillon...*, 109-134. Perpignan: Presses universitaires de Perpignan, 2009.

Caballer, Gemma and Queralt Solé, editors. *Fons Josep Maria Trias Peitx: 1900-1979.* Catarroja: Afers; Barcelona: Centre d'Estudis Històrics Internacionals, 2013.

Caballer, Gemma, Imma Tubella, and Eduard Vinyamata, editors. *La Solitud de la llibertat: memòries de Josep M. Trias i Peitx, secretari general d'Unió Democràtica de Catalunya durant la Guerra Civil.* Sant Cugat del Vallès: Símbol, 2008.

Camurri, Renato. "Idee in movimento: l'esilio degli intellettuali italiani negli Stati Uniti (1930-1945)." *Memoria e ricerca*, no. 31 (2009): 44-62.

Camurri, Renato. Introduction to "L'Europa in esilio: La migrazione degli intellettuali verso le Americhe tra le due guerre." *Memoria e ricerca*, no. 31 (2009): 5.

Camurri, Renato, editor. *Max Ascoli: Antifascista, intellettuale, giornalista.* Milan: Franco Angeli, 2012.

Canosa, Francesc. *Entre el sabre i la bomba: memòries d'un país i d'un partit: Unió Democràtica de Catalunya, 1931-1980.* Barcelona: Acontravent, 2012.

Casanova, Julian. *La Iglesia de Franco.* Madrid: Temas de Hoy, 2001.

Castillo, Benedicto. *Magnicidio: la verdad del asesinato del Presidente de la República Eduardo Frei Montalva.* Santiago: Editorial Mare Nostrum, 2011.

Castro, José Luis de. *La emergente participación política de las regiones en el proceso de construcción europea.* Bilbao: HAEE/IVAP, 1994.

Ceci, Lucia. *The Vatican and Mussolini's Italy.* Amsterdam: Brill, 2017.

Cenckiewicz, Sławomir. *Oczami bezpieki: Szkice i materiały z dziejów aparatu bezpieczeństwa PRL.* Krakow: Arcana, 2004.

Cervera, Javier. "De Vichy a la liberación." In *"Ay de los vencidos": el exilio y los países de acogida*, edited by Abdón Mateos, 41-70. Madrid: Eneida, 2009.

Cesarini, David and Tony Kushner, editors. *The Internment of Aliens in Twentieth Century Britain.* London: Frank Cass, 1993.

Chamedes, Giuliana. *A Twentieth-Century Crusade: The Vatican's Battle to Remake Christian Europe.* Cambridge, Mass: Harvard University Press, 2019.

Chappel, James. *Catholic Modern: The Challenge of Totalitarianism and the Remaking of the Church.* Cambridge, Mass.: Harvard University Press, 2018.

Chenaux, Philippe. "Bijdrage tot de internationale christen-democratie." In *Tussen staat en maatschappij 1945-1995: Christen-democratie in België*, edited by Wilfried Dewachter et al. Tielt: Lanoo, 1995.

Chenaux, Philippe. *Entre Maurras et Maritain: une génération intellectuelle catholique (1920-1930).* Paris: Cerf, 1999.

Christiaens, Kim, Idesbald Goddeeris, and Magaly Rodríguez García, editors. *European Solidarity with Chile, 1970s-1980s.* Frankfurt am Main: Peter Lang, 2014.

Clark, Christopher and Wolfram Kaiser, editors. *Culture Wars: Catholic-Secular Conflicts in Nineteenth-Century Europe.* Cambridge: Cambridge University Press, 2003.

Cohen, Susan. *Rescue the Perishing: Eleanor Rathbone and the Refugees.* London: Vallentine Mitchell, 2010.

Committee on Non-Represented Nations. *Statement by Don Fernando Alvarez de Miranda, 5 September 1961.* Strasbourg: Council of Europe, 1961.

Compagnon, Olivier. *Jacques Maritain et l'Amérique du Sud: Le modèle malgré lui.* Villeneuve d'Ascq: Presses universitaires du Septentrion, 2003.

Conway, Martin. "Legacies of Exile: The Exile Governments in London during World War II and the Politics of Postwar Europe." In *Europe in Exile: European Refugee Communities in Britain 1939-1945*, edited by Martin Conway and José Gotovitch, 255-274. Oxford: Oxford University Press, 2000.

Conway, Martin. "The Rise and Fall of Western Europe's Democratic Age, 1945-1973." *Contemporary European History* 13, no.1 (2004): 67-88.

Conway, Martin and José Gotovitch, editors. *Europe in Exile: European Exile Communities in Britain 1940-45*. New York: Berghahn, 2001.

Council of Europe. Consultive Assembly. Political Commission. *Resolution adopted by the Congress of the European Movement, in Munich, 8 June 1962*. Strasbourg: Council of Europe, 1962.

Coutouvidis, John and Jaime Reynolds. *Poland 1939-1947*. Leicester: Leicester University Press, 1986.

Covarrubias, María Teresa. *1938: la rebelión de los jóvenes*. Santiago: Edit. Aconcagua, 1987.

Crawford, Virginia. *Catholic Social Doctrine 1891-1931*. Oxford: The Catholic Social Guild, 1933.

Creixell, Joan. *Els Fets del Palau i el consell de guerra a Jordi Pujol*. Barcelona: Edicions de La Magrana, 2000, 2nd edition.

Culla i Clara, Joan B. *Unió Democràtica de Catalunya: el llarg camí (1931-2001)*. Barcelona: Unió Democràtica de Catalunya, 2002.

D'Agostino, Peter R. *Rome in America: Transnational Catholic Ideology from the Risorgimento to Fascism*. Chapel Hill and London: University of North Carolina Press, 2004.

Damušis, Adolfas. *Žvilgsnis, nukreiptas į idealų aukštumas: Adolfo Damušio tekstai*. Vilnius: Versus aureus, 2009.

Dapkutė, Daiva. *Lietuvių išeivijos liberaliosios srovės genezė*. Vilnius: Vaga, 2002.

De Felice, Renzo. "Prefazione." In *Gli antifascisti italiani in America (1942-1944): La "legione" nel carteggio di Pacciardi con Borgese, Salvemini, Sforza e Sturzo*, edited by Alessandra Baldini and Paolo Palma. Florence: Le Monnier, 1990.

De Marco, Vittorio. *Tempore belli: Sturzo, l'Italia, la guerra (1940-1946)*. Caltanissetta-Rome: Salvatore Sciascia Editore, 1995.

De Onaindia, Antonio. *Capitulos de mi vida II: Experiencias del exilio*. Buenos Aires: Ed. Vasca Ekin, 1974.

De Rosa, Gabriele. *Luigi Sturzo*. Turin: Unione Tipografico-Editrice Torinese, 1977.

De Rosa, Gabriele. "Luigi Sturzo nei documenti dell'Office of Strategic Service." In *Chiesa Società e Stato a Venezia: Miscellanea di studi in onore di Silvio Tramontin*, edited by Bruno Bertoli, 313-335. Venice: Edizioni Studium Cattolico Veneziano, 1994.

Delzell, Charles F. *Mussolini's Enemies: The Italian Anti-Fascist Resistance*. Princeton, NJ: Princeton University Press, 1961.

Denon-Birot, Marie-Nelly. *De la Démocratie chrétienne à Force démocrate: Échos d'une mutation politique*. Paris: L'Harmattan, 2000.

Devant la Crise Mondiale. New York: Ed. de la Maison Française, 1942.

Devin, Guillaume. *L'Internationale socialiste: Histoire et sociologie du socialisme international (1945-1990)*. Paris: Presses de la Fondation nationale des Sciences politiques, 1993.

Di Lascia, Alfred. "Luigi Sturzo nella cultura degli Stati Uniti." In *Luigi Sturzo e la democrazia europea*, edited by Gabriele De Rosa, 119-145. Rome-Bari: Laterza, 1990.

Doering, Bernard. *Jacques Maritain and the French Catholic Intellectuals*. South Bend, IN: University of Notre Dame Press, 1983.

Donskis, Leonidas. *Identity and Freedom: Mapping Nationalism and Social Criticism in Twentieth Century Lithuania*. London: Routledge, 2002.

Donskis, Leonidas. *Loyalty, Dissent, and Betrayal: Modern Lithuania and the East Central European Moral Imagination*. Amsterdam: Rodopi, 2005.

Dreiziger, Nandor. *Church and Society in Hungary and in the Hungarian Diaspora*. Toronto: University of Toronto Press, 2016.

Dufner, Georg. *Partner im Kalten Krieg: Die Politischen Beziehungen zwischen der Bundesrepublik Deutschland und Chile*. Frankfurt am Main: Campus Verlag, 2014.

Dufner, Georg. "West Germany: Professions of Political Faith, the Solidarity Movement and New Left Imaginaries." In *European Solidarity with Chile, 1970s-1980s*, edited by Kim Christiaens, Idesbald Goddeeris and Magaly Rodríguez García, 163-186. Frankfurt am Main: Peter Lang, 2014.

Dumoulin, Michel and Idesbald Goddeeris. "Introduction." In *Intégration ou représentation? Les exilés polonais en Belgique et la construction européenne*, edited by Michel Dumoulin and Idesbald Goddeeris, 5-12. Louvain-la-Neuve: Bruylant, 2005.

Dumoulin, Michel and Idesbald Goddeeris, editors. *Integration or representation? Polish exiles in Belgium and the European construction*. Louvain-la-Neuve: Bruylant, 2005.

Durand, Jean-Dominique. *L'Europe de la Démocratie Chrétienne*. Brussels: Éditions Complexe, 1995.

Durand, Jean-Dominique. "Exile as a Matrix of Christian Democrat Internationalism." In *Christian Democrat Internationalism: Its Action in Europe and Worldwide from post-World War II until the 1990s. Volume 1: The origins*, edited by Jean-Dominique Durand, 145-157. Brussels: Peter Lang, 2013.

Duranti, Marco. *The Conservative Human Rights Revolution*: *European Identity, Transnational Politics and the Origins of the European Convention*. Oxford: Oxford University Press, 2017.

Duverger, Maurice. *Cours de vie politique, en France et à l'étranger: rédigé d'après les notes et avec l'autorisation de M. Maurice Duverger,... Diplôme d'études supérieures de science politique: 1956-1957*. Paris: Les Cours de droit, 1957.

Eckel, Jan. "Allende's Shadow, Leftist Furor and Human Rights: The Pinochet Dictatorship in International Politics." In *European Solidarity with Chile, 1970s-1980s*, edited by Kim Christiaens, Idesbald Goddeeris and Magaly Rodríguez García, 67-92. Frankfurt am Main: Peter Lang Edition, 2014.

Eichenberg, Julia. "Macht auf der Flucht: Europäische Regierungen in London (1940-1944)." *Zeithistorische Forschungen* 15, no. 3 (2018): 452-473.

Eidintas, Alfonsas. *Antanas Smetona and his Lithuania: from the national liberation movement to an authoritarian regime*. Boston: Brill, 2015.

Elorza, Antonio. *Ideologías del nacionalismo vasco, 1876-1937: (de los "euskaros" a Jagi Jagi)*. San Sebastián: Luis Haranburu Editor, 1978.

Evans, Joseph. "Jacques Maritain and the Problem of Pluralism in Political Life." *Review of Politics* 22, no. 3 (July 1960): 307-323.

Farrell-Vinay, Giovanna. "The London Exile of Don Luigi Sturzo (1924-1940)." *The Heythrop Journal* 45, no. 2 (2004): 158-177.

Farrell-Vinay, Giovanna. "Viaggio nell'Italia del 1946: Quattro lettere di Barbara Barclay Carter a Luigi Sturzo." *Contemporanea* 13, no. 1 (2010): 79-102.

Felix, Christopher [James McCargar]. *A Short Course in the Secret War*. Lanham, New York and Oxford: Madison Books, 2001, 4th edition.

Fernández Baeza, Mario. "Solidaridad para la libertad, la democracia y la justicia social: 50 años de cooperación de la Fundación Konrad Adenauer con Chile." In *La Fundación Konrad Adenauer y la promoción de la democracia: Experiencias de 50 años de cooperación con Chile*, 26-64. Santiago de Chile: Fundación Konrad Adenauer, 2012.

Figueres Artigues, Josep M. "Hilari Raguer, historiador." In Hilari Raguer. *Escrits dispersos d'història*. Barcelona: Publicacions de la Presidència, 2018.

Flint, James. "'Must God go Fascist?' English Catholic Opinion and the Spanish Civil War." *Church History* 56, no. 3 (1987): 364-374.

Forgacs, David. "Sturzo e la Cultura Politica Inglese." In *Luigi Sturzo e la Democrazia Europea*, edited by Gabriele De Rosa. Rome: Laterza, 1990.

Formigoni, Guido. "Luigi Sturzo e la posizione internazionale dell'Italia nel secondo dopoguerra." In *Universalità e cultura nel pensiero di Luigi Sturzo*. Soveria Mannelli: Rubbettino, 2001.

Freeden, Michael. *Ideologies and Political Theory*. Oxford: Oxford University Press, 1996.

Friedlander, Judith. *A Light in Dark Times: The New School for Social Research and its University in Exile*. New York: Columbia University Press, 2019.

Gajewski, Ryszard. *Karol Popiel 1887-1977*. Suwałki: Wyższa Szkoła Służby Społecznej im. Księdza Franciszka Blachnickiego, 2008.

Galeote, Geraldine. "La temática europea en el discurso del Partido Nacionalista Vasco (PNV)." *Revista de Estudios Políticos*, no. 103 (1999): 259-278.

Gallagher, Charles R. *Vatican Secret Diplomacy: Joseph P. Hurley and Pope Pius XII*. New Haven and London: Yale University Press, 2008.

Gazmuri, Cristián et al. *Eduardo Frei Montalva (1911-1982).* Santiago de Chile: Fondo de Cultura Económica, 1996.

Gazmuri, Cristián, Patricia Arancibia and Álvaro Góngora. *Eduardo Frei Montalva y su época.* Santiago: Aguilar, 2000, 2 volumes.

Gebhardt, Stanisław "Korzenie." *Unia&Polska,* no. 21 (September 1999), at http:/www.unia-polska.pl/archive/98-99/9909_1/17_f.html.

Gebhardt, Stanisław. "Międzynarodowe organizacje chrześcijańsko–demokratyczne." In *Materiały do dziejów polskiego uchodźstwa niepodległościowego 1945-*1990. Volume 4: *Akcja niepodległościowa na terenie między-narodowym,* edited by Tomasz Piesakowski, 115-139. London: Polskie Towarzystwo Naukowe na Obczyźnie, 1999.

Gebhardt, Stanisław. "The Christian Democratic Union of Central Europe." In *Christian Democracy Across the Iron Curtain,* edited by Piotr H. Kosicki and Sławomir Łukasiewicz, 411-424. London: Palgrave Macmillan, 2018.

Gebhardt, Stanisław. "Zjednoczenie Młodzieży Chrześcijańsko–Społecznej." *Tygodnik Warszawski,* 18 June 2006, 8-9.

Gehler, Michael and Wolfram Kaiser, editors. *Christian Democracy in Europe Since 1945.* Volume 2. New York: Routledge, 2004.

Gehler, Michael et al., editors. *Transnationale Parteienkooperation der europäischen Christdemokraten und Konservativen.* Boston: de Gruyter, 2018.

Gellman, Irwin F. *Good Neighbor Diplomacy: United States Policies in Latin America, 1933-1945.* Baltimore: John Hopkins University Press, 1979.

Gemie, Sharif, Fiona Reid and Laure Humbert, with Louise Ingram. *Outcast Europe: Refugees and Relief Workers in an Era of Total War, 1936-48.* London and New York: Continuum, 2012.

Gentile, Emilio. *Contro Cesare: Cristianesimo e totalitarismo nell'epoca dei fascismi.* Milan: Feltrinelli, 2010.

Gentile, Emilio. "New Idols: Catholicism in the face of Fascist Totalitarianism." *Journal of Modern Italian Studies* 11, no. 2 (2011): 143-170.

Gerbi, Sandro. "Nelson Rockefeller e Max Ascoli: l'Office of Inter-American Affairs, la propaganda americana in America Latina e il caso del Perù." In *Max Ascoli: Antifascista, intellettuale, giornalista,* edited by Renato Camurri, 197-207. Milan: Franco Angeli, 2012.

Gergely, Jenő. "Christian Democracy in Hungary." In *Christian Democracy in Europe Since 1945,* edited by Michael Gehler and Wolfram Kaiser, 115-172. London: Routledge, 2004.

Gil Robles, José María. *Cartas del Pueblo Espanol.* Madrid: Afrodisio Aguado, 1966.

Gil Robles, José Maria. *Marginalia política.* Barcelona: Ariel, 1975.

Gillman, Peter and Leni Gillman. *'Collar the lot!' How Britain interned and expelled its Wartime Refugees.* London: Quartet Books, 1980.

Giraudier, Élodie. *Le Parti démocrate-chrétien au Chili, 1957-2010: De la troisième voie au néo-libéralisme.* PhD thesis, Université Sorbonne Nouvelle-Paris 3, 2018.

Girnius, Kęstutis et al., editors. *Lietuva, kurios nebuvo: pilnutinės demokratijos svarstymai ir vertinimai.* Vilnius: VU leidykla, 2016.

Giunipero, Carlo A. *Luigi Sturzo e la pace: Tra universalismo cattolico e internazionalismo liberale.* Milan: Guerini Associati, 2009.

Glees, Anthony. *Exile Politics during the Second World War: The German Social Democrats in Britain.* Oxford: Clarendon Press, 1982.

Goddeeris, Idesbald. "Exiles' Strategies for Lobbying in International Organisations: Eastern European Participation in the Nouvelles Équipes Internationales." *European Review of History / Revue européenne d'histoire* 11, no. 3 (2004): 383-400.

Goichot, Émile. "I Maritain e gli Anni Americani." In *Luigi Sturzo e gli Intellettuali Cattolici Francesi: Carteggi (1925-1945).* Soveria Mannelli: Rubettino, 2003.

Goiogana, Iñaki. "Alberto Onaindía: Ideas y contenidos de un democristiano precursor de la Europa de la posguerra." In *Dos vascos humanistas en la UNESCO: Alberto Onaindia, José Miguel de Azaola,* 18-34. Bilbao: UNESCO Etxea, 2016.

Goldner, Franz. *Die österreichische Emigration 1938 bis 1945.* Vienna and Munich: Herold, 1972.

González Cañete, Diego. *Una revolución del espíritu: política y esperanza en Frei, Eyzaguirre y Góngora en los años de entreguerras.* Santiago: Ediciones Centro de Estudios Bicentenario, 2018.

González, Ignacio. *Renán Fuentealba: En la génesis de la Concertación.* Santiago: Catalonia, 2007.

Granja, José Luis de la. *Ángel o demonio: Sabino Arana.* Madrid: Tecnos, 2015.

Grasso, Giovanni, editor. *Luigi Sturzo e i Rosselli tra Londra, Parigi e New York: Carteggio (1929-1945)*. Soveria Mannelli: Rubbettino, 2003.

Gray, Lawrence. "L'America di Roosevelt negli anni dell'esilio di Luigi Sturzo fra Jacksonville e New York: quale America ha conosciuto?" In *Universalità e cultura nel pensiero di Luigi Sturzo*, 521-549. Soveria Mannelli: Rubbettino, 2001.

Grenville, Anthony and Andrea Reiter, editors. *Political Exile and Exile Politics in Britain after 1933*. Amsterdam: Radopi, 2011.

Grippa, Davide. *Un antifascista tra Italia e Stati Uniti*. Milan: Franco Angeli, 2009.

Grose, Peter. *Gentleman Spy: The Life of Allan Dulles*. Boston and New York: Houghton Mifflin Company, 1994.

Guixé Coromines, Jordi. *La República perseguida: exilio y represión en la Francia de Franco, 1937-1951*. València: Universitat de València, 2012.

Habielski, Rafał. *Życie społeczne i kulturalne emigracji*. Warsaw: Biblioteka Więzi, 1999.

Halloran Lumsdaine, David, editor. *Evangelical Christianity and Democracy in Asia*. Oxford: Oxford University Press, 2009.

Heidar, Knut. "Party membership and participation." In *Handbook of Party Politics*, edited by Richard S. Katz and William Crotty, 301-315. Los Angeles and London: Sage, 2014.

Herzog, Jonathan P. *The Spiritual-Industrial Complex: America's Religious Battle against Communism in the early Cold War*, 55-71. New York: Oxford University Press, 2011.

Hetherington, S.J. *Katherine Atholl 1874-1960: Against the Tide*. Aberdeen: Aberdeen University Press, 1989.

Heumos, Peter. *Die Emigration aus der Tschechoslowakei nach Westeuropa und dem Nahen Osten 1938-1945*. Munich: Oldenbourg, 1989.

Hofmeister, Wilhelm. *La opción por la democracia: Democracia Cristiana y desarrollo político en Chile 1964-1994*. Santiago: Konrad-Adenauer-Stiftung, 1995.

Holmes, Colin. *John Bull's Island: Immigration and British Society, 1871-1971*. Basingstoke: Macmillan, 1988.

Horn, Gerd-Rainer. *The Spirit of Vatican II: Western European Progressive Catholicism in the Long Sixties*. Oxford: Oxford University Press, 2015.

Hörster-Philipps, Ulrike. *Joseph Wirth 1879-1956: Eine politische Biographie*. Paderborn: Schöningh, 1998.

Ignesti, Guiseppe. "Momenti del Popolarismo in Esilio." In *I Cattolici tra Fascismo e Democrazia*, edited by Pietro Scoppola and Francesco Traniello, 75-183. Bologna: Mulino, 1975.

Igoe, Michael. "To direct more funding to Christians, USAID looks to Hungary." *Devex*, 25 November 2019. At https://www.devex.com/news/to-direct-more-funding-to-christians-usaid-looks-to-hungary-96055.

Invernizzi Accetti, Carlo. *What is Christian Democracy? Politics, Religion and Ideology*. Cambridge: Cambridge University Press, 2019.

Izsák, Lajos. "Keresztény partok a forradalomban." In *Az élő hagyomány: Barankovics István és a magyaroszági kereszténydemokracia öröksége*, 177-191. Budapest: Barankovics István Alapitvány - Gondolat Kiadó, 2007.

Jensen, Thomas and Steven Van Hecke. *At Europe's Service: The Origins and Evolution of the European People's Party*. Berlin: Springer, 2011.

Jesień, Leszek. "The Social Virtues of Christian Democracy, European and Polish: The Case of Jan Kułakowski." In *Christian Democracy across the Iron Curtain: Europe Redefined*, edited by Piotr H. Kosicki and Sławomir Łukasiewicz, 277-290. London: Palgrave Macmillan, 2018.

Jiménez Botta, Felix A. *Embracing Human Rights: Grassroots Solidarity Activism and Foreign Policy in Seventies West Germany*. PhD thesis, Boston College, 2018.

Jiménez de Aberásturi, Juan Carlos and Rafael Moreno Izquierdo. *Al servicio del extranjero: Historia del Servicio Vasco de Información (1936-43)*. Madrid: Antonio Machado Libros, 2008.

Julg, Jean. *La Démocratie chrétienne en République fédérale allemande*. Paris: Économica, 1985.

Kádár Lynn, Katalin. "At War While at Peace." In *The Inauguration of "Organized Political Warfare": The Cold War Organizations Sponsored by the National Committee for a Free Europe / Free Europe Committee*, edited by Katalin Kádár Lynn, 7-70. St. Helena, Calif.: Helena History Press, 2013.

Kádár Lynn, Katalin. "The Hungarian National Council." In *The Inauguration of "Organized Political Warfare": The Cold War Organizations Sponsored by the National Committee for a Free Europe / Free Europe Committee*, edited by Katalin Kádár Lynn, 237-308. St. Helena, Calif.: Helena History Press, 2013.

Kádár Lynn, Katalin. *Tibor Eckhardt: His American Years*. Boulder, Colo.: East European Monographs, 2007.

Kaiser, Wolfram. *Christian Democracy and the Origins of European Union*. Cambridge: Cambridge University Press, 2007.

Kaiser, Wolfram. "Co-Operation of European Catholic Politicians in Exile in Britain and the USA during the Second World War." *Journal of Contemporary History* 35, no. 3 (2000): 439-465.

Kaiser, Wolfram. "Europeanization of Christian Democracy? Negotiating Organization, Enlargement, Policy and Allegiance in the European People's Party." In *Societal Actors in European Integration: Policy-Building and Policy-Making 1958-1992*, edited by Wolfram Kaiser and Jan-Henrik Meyer, 15-37. Basingstoke: Palgrave Macmillan, 2013.

Kaiser, Wolfram. "No Second Versailles: Transnational Contacts in the People and Freedom Group and the International Christian Democratic Union, 1936-1945." In *Christian Democracy in 20th Century Europe*, edited by Michael Gehler, Wolfram Kaiser and Helmut Wohnout, 616-641. Vienna: Böhlau Verlag, 2001.

Kaiser, Wolfram. "Transnational Christian Democracy: From the Nouvelles Équipes Internationales to the European People's Party." In *Christian Democracy in Europe Since 1945*, edited by Michael Gehler and Wolfram Kaiser. Volume 2, 194-208. New York: Routledge, 2004.

Kaiser, Wolfram. "Trigger-Happy Protestant Materialists? The European Christian Democrats and the United States." In *Between Alliance and Empire: America and Europe During the Cold War*, edited by Marc Trachtenberg, 63-82. Lanham, MD: Rowman and Littlefield, 2003.

Kaiser, Wolfram and Christian Salm. "Transition und Europäisierung in Spanien und Portugal: Sozial- und christdemokratische Netzwerke im Übergang von der Diktatur zur parlamentarischen Demokratie." *Archiv für Sozialgeschichte*, no. 49 (2009): 259-282.

Kalyvas, Stathis and Kees van Kersbergen. "Christian Democracy." *Annual Review of Political Science* 13 (2010).

Katzenstein, Peter J., Theodore J. Lowy and Sidney Tarrow, editors. *Comparative theory and political experience: Mario Einaudi and the liberal tradition*. Ithaca, New York: Cornell University Press, 1990.

Keating, Joan. "Looking to Europe: Roman Catholicism and Christian Democracy in 1930s Britain." *European History Quarterly* 26, no. 1 (1996): 57-79.

Kemseke, Peter Van. *Towards an Era of Development: The Globalization of Socialism and Christian Democracy, 1945-1965*. Leuven: Leuven University Press, 2006.

Kershner, Howard E. *Quaker Service in Modern War: Spain and France, 1939-1940*. New York: Prentice-Hall, 1950.

Kertzer, David. *The Pope and Mussolini: The Secret History of Pius XI and the Rise of Fascism in Europe*. New York: Random House, 2014.

Killinger, Charles. "Fighting Fascism from the Valley: Italian Intellectuals in the United States." In *The Dispossessed: An Anatomy of Exile*, edited by Peter I. Rose, 135-145. Amherst: University of Massachusetts Press, 2005.

Kirby, Dianne. "The Cold War, the Hegemony of the United States and the Golden Age of Christian Democracy." In *The Cambridge History of Christianity, 1914-2000*, edited by Hugh McLeod, Volume 9, 285-303. Cambridge: Cambridge University Press, 2006.

Kiss, Maria Rita, editor. *Voyage of Hungarian Christian Democracy to the Heart of Europe*. Budapest: Istvan Barankovics Foundation, 2017.

Klesteniz, Tibor, Éva Petrás and Viktor Attila Soós, editors. *Útkeresés Két Korszak Határán*. Agyakosszergény: Közi Horváth József Népfőiskola, 2018.

Knox, William W.J. *Lives of Scottish Women: Women and Scottish Society, 1800-1980*. Edinburgh: Edinburgh University Press, 2006.

Kochanski, Halik. *The Eagle Unbowed: Poland and the Poles in the Second World War*. Cambridge, Mass.: Harvard University Press, 2012.

Kosicki, Piotr H. "Beyond 1989: The Disappointed Hopes of Christian Democracy in Post-Communist Central and Eastern Europe." In *Christian Democracy and the Fall of Communism*, edited by Michael Gehler, Piotr H. Kosicki and Helmut Wohnout, 305-326. Leuven: Leuven University Press, 2019.

Kosicki, Piotr H. *Catholics on the Barricades: Poland, France and "Revolution," 1891-1956.* New Haven, CT: Yale University Press, 2018.

Kosicki, Piotr H. "Christian Democracy's Global Cold War." In *Christian Democracy across the Iron Curtain: Europe Redefined*, edited by Piotr H. Kosicki and Sławomir Łukasiewicz, 221-256. London: Palgrave Macmillan, 2018.

Krupavičius, Mykolas. *Atsiminimai.* Chicago: Draugo spaustuvė, 1972.

Krupavičius, Mykolas. "Darbininkas ir darbas." In *Visuomeniniai klausimai*, 206-221. Chicago: Popiežiaus Leono XIII fondas, 1983.

Krupavičius, Mykolas. "Enciklika *Graves de communi.*" In *Visuomeniniai klausimai*, 143-166. Chicago: Popiežiaus Leono XIII fondas, 1983.

Krupavičius, Mykolas. "Enciklika *Mater et Magistra.*" In *Visuomeniniai klausimai*, 371-384. Chicago: Popiežiaus Leono XIII fondas, 1983.

Kułakowski, Jan. *Spotkania na Bagateli.* Warsaw: Wydawnictwo Rhetos, 2004.

La Bella, Gianni. "Latin America: Rafael Caldera, Eduardo Frei, Napoleone Duarte." In *Christian Democrat Internationalism: Its Action in Europe and Worldwide from post-World War II until the 1990s.* Volume 2: *The Development (1945-1979): The role of Parties, Movements, People*, edited by Jean-Dominique Durand. Brussels: Peter Lang, 2013.

La Bella, Gianni. *Luigi Sturzo e l'esilio negli Stati Uniti.* Brescia: Morcelliana, 1990.

Labanauskas, Ramūnas. *The Young Catholic Movement: Genesis, Ideological Principles and Putting them into Practice (1919-1940).* Kaunas: Lithuanian Academic Libraries Network, 2011.

Landaburu, Francisco Javier. *La causa del pueblo vasco.* Bilbao: Editorial Geu, 1977.

Landaburu, Francisco Javier. *Obras completas de Francisco Javier Landaburu.* Bilbao: Idatz Ekintza, 1982-1984, 5 volumes.

Łaptos, Józef. "L'apport des exilés d'au-delà du rideau de fer à la construction européenne." In *Intégration ou représentation? Les exilés polonais en Belgique et la construction européenne*, edited by Michel Dumoulin and Idesbald Goddeeris, 187-212. Louvain-la-Neuve: Bruylant, 2005.

Larronde, Jean Claude. *Exilio y Solidaridad: La Liga Internacional de Amigos de los Vascos.* Bilbao: Bidasoa, 1988.

Laurent, Pierre-Henri. "Reality not rhetoric: Belgian-Dutch diplomacy in wartime London, 1940-1944." In *Making the New Europe: European Unity and the Second World War*, edited by M.L. Smith and Peter M.R. Stirk, 133-141. London: Pinter, 1990.

Letamendia, Pierre. *Le Mouvement Républicain Populaire: Histoire d'un grand parti français.* Paris: Beauchesne, 1995.

Lida, Miranda. *Historia del Catolicismo en la Argentina entre el siglo XIX y el XX.* Buenos Aires: Siglo Veintiuno Editores, 2015.

Linz, Juan José. *The Breakdown of Democratic Regimes: Crisis, Breakdown and Equilibration.* Baltimore, MD: Johns Hopkins University Press, 1978.

Lipgens, Walter. *Europa-Föderationspläne der Widerstandsbewegungen 1940-1945.* Munich: Oldenbourg, 1968.

Lorés, Jaume. "Aproximació al pujolisme." *Taula de canvi*, no. 23-24 (September-December 1980): 5-37.

Lowe, Sid. *Catholicism, War, and the Foundation of Francoism: The Juventud de Accion Popular in Spain, 1931-1939.* Portland, Oregon: Sussex University Press, 2010.

Luconi, Stefano. "Italian Americans and the New Deal Coalition." *Transatlantica: American Studies Journal*, no. 1 (2006).

Łukasiewicz, Sławomir. "A Shadow Party System: The Party Politics of Cold War Polish Exiles." *Journal of Cold War Studies* [forthcoming, 2021].

Łukasiewicz, Sławomir. "Młodzi polscy chadecy na emigracji." *Zeszyty Historyczne (Paris)*, no. 163 (2005): 50-99.

Łukasiewicz, Sławomir. *Polacy w europejskim ruchu federalnym po II wojnie światowej.* Warsaw: Centrum Europejskie Natolin, 2006.

Łukasiewicz, Sławomir. *Third Europe: Polish Federalist Thought in the United States 1940-1970s*, trans. Witold Zbirohowski-Ko**ścia**. Budapest: Helena History Press, 2016.

Luykx, Theo. "De rol van August De Schryver in het politieke leven tot en met de Tweede Wereldoorlog." In *Veertig jaar Belgische politiek: Liber amicorum aangeboden aan Minister van Staat A.E. De Schryver ter gelegenheid van zijn 70ste verjaardag*, 121-211. Antwerp and Utrecht: Standaard Wetenschappelijke Uitg., 1968.

Maceina, Antanas. *Antano Maceinos laiškai pre: Pranciškui Jurui*. Vilnius: Katalikų akademija, 1997.

Maceina, Antanas. "Bažnyčia ir pasaulis." In Antanas Maceina. *Raštai*. Volume 5. Vilnius: Margi raštai, 1993.

Maceina, Antanas. *Didysis inkvizitorius*. Weilheim: Atžalynas, 1946.

Maceina, Antanas. "Krikščioniškosios visuomenės klausimas." In Antanas Maceina. *Raštai*. Volume 10. Vilnius: Margi raštai, 2005.

Maceina, Antanas. "Nuo ko mes bėgom?" In Antanas Maceina. *Raštai*. Volume 12, 308-332. Vilnius: Margi raštai, 2007.

Maceina, Antanas. "Pilnutinės demokratijos pagrindai." In *Lietuva, kurios nebuvo: pilnutinės demokratijos svarstymai ir vertinimai*, edited by Kęstutis K. Girnius et al. Vilnius: VU leidykla, 2016.

Maceina, Antanas et al. "Į reformuotą demokratiją." In *Lietuva, kurios nebuvo: pilnutinės demokratijos svarstymai ir vertinimai*, edited by Kęstutis K. Girnius et al. Vilnius: VU leidykla, 2016.

Machcewicz, Paweł. *Emigracja w polityce międzynarodowej*. Warsaw: Biblioteka "Więzi," 1999.

Maimann, Helene. *Politik im Wartesaal: Österreichische Exilpolitik in Grossbritannien 1938-1945*. Vienna, Cologne and Graz: Böhlau, 1975.

Mainwaring, Scott and Timothy R. Scully, editors. *Christian Democracy in Latin America: Electoral Competition and Regime Conflicts*. Stanford, Calif.: Stanford University Press, 2003.

Malandrino, Corrado. "I rapporti di Luigi Sturzo con Mario Einaudi negli anni dell'esilio americano." In *Universalità e cultura nel pensiero di Luigi Sturzo*, 551-596. Soveria Mannelli: Rubbettino, 2001.

Malandrino, Corrado. "L'iniziativa sturziana del People and Freedom Group of America nell'esilio di Jacksonville (1940-1944)." In *Luigi Sturzo e la democrazia nella prospettiva del terzo millennio: Atti del seminario internazionale, Erice 7-11 ottobre 2000*, edited by Eugenio Guccione, 193-213. Florence: L.S. Olschki, 2004.

Malgeri, Francesco. *Luigi Sturzo*. San Paolo: Cinisello Balsamo, 1993.

Malgeri, Francesco. "Luigi Sturzo nel "difficile" esilio americano (1940-46)." *Analisi storica*, no. 2 (1984): 5-38.

Malgeri, Francesco. "Sturzo e Maritain." In *Jacques Maritain e la Società Contemporanea*, edited by Roberto Papini. Milan: Massimo, 1978.

Mans, G.M.V. "Ideas of Netherlands Exiles on the Postwar International Order." In *Documents on the History of European Integration*. Volume 2: *Plans for European Union in Great Britain and in Exile, 1939-1945*, edited by Walter Lipgens, 451-475. Berlin: de Gruyter, 1986.

Maritain, Jacques. *Antimoderne*. Paris: Éditions de la Revue des Jeunes, 1922.

Maritain, Jacques. *Christianity and Democracy and the Rights of Man and Natural Law*. San Francisco: Ignatius Press, 1943.

Maritain, Jacques. *Humanisme Intégral*. Paris: Aubier, 1936.

Maritain, Jacques. *Integral Humanism: Temporal and Spiritual Problems of a New Christendom*. Translated by Joseph Evans. New York: Scribner and Sons, 1968.

Maritain, Jacques. *Man and the State*. Chicago: University of Chicago Press, 1951.

Maritain, Jacques. *Oeuvres Complètes*. Volume VIII. Paris: Saint Paul Éditions, 1984.

Maritain, Jacques. *Reflections on America*. New York: Scribner, 1958.

Mariuzzo, Andrea. *Una biografia intellettuale di Mario Einaudi: Cultura e politica da sponda a sponda*. Florence: Olschki, 2016.

Masłowska, Teresa. *Łącznik z Paryża*. Leszno: Instytut im. Gen. Stefana "Grota" Roweckiego, 2007.

Mauro, Diego. "Católicos antifascistas en Argentina (1936-1943): Luigi Sturzo y las tramas locales de People & Freedom Group." *Itinerantes: Revista de Historia y Religión*, no. 7 (2017): 10-11.

Mauro, Diego. "I popolari en la Argentina: Luigi Sturzo y el antifascismo católico de entreguerras." *Anuario IEHS*, nos. 29-30 (2014-2015): 267-287.

Mayeur, Jean-Marie. *Des partis catholiques à la démocratie chrétienne*. Paris: A. Colin, 1980.

Mazurkiewicz, Anna, editor. *East Central European Migrations during the Cold War: A Handbook*. Berlin: de Gruyter, 2019.

Mazurkiewicz, Anna, editor. *East Central Europe in Exile*. Cambridge: Cambridge Scholars, 2013.

Mazurkiewicz, Anna. *Uchodźcy polityczni z Europy Środkowo-Wschodniej w amerykańskiej polityce zimnowojennej 1948-1954*. Warsaw: Instytut Pamięci Narodowej/Uniwersytet Gdański, 2016.

Mazurkiewicz, Anna. *Voice of the Silenced Peoples in the Global Cold War: The Assembly of Captive European Nations, 1954-1972*. Berlin: de Gruyter, 2021.

McAvoy, Thomas. "Liberalism, Americanism, Modernism." *Records of the American Catholic Historical Society of Philadelphia* 63, no. 4 (1952): 225-231.

McAvoy, Thomas. *The Americanist Heresy in Roman Catholicism 1895-1900*. Notre Dame: University of Notre Dame Press, 1963.

McGreevy, John. *Catholicism and American Freedom: A History*. New York: Norton, 2003.

Meer, Fernando de. *El Partido Nacionalista Vasco ante la guerra de España (1936-1937)*. Pamplona: Ediciones de la Universidad de Navarra EUNSA, 1992.

Mees, Ludger et al. *La política como pasión: El lehendakari José Antonio Aguirre (1904-1960)*. Madrid: Tecnos, 2014.

Mendizábal Villalba, Alfredo. *Los orígenes de una tragedia*. Madrid: Centro de Estudios Políticos y Constitucionales, 2012.

Mendizábal Villalba, Alfredo. *Pretérito imperfecto: Memorias de un utopista*. Oviedo: Real Instituto de Estudios asturianos, 2009.

Miké, Valerie and John Miké Jr, editors. *Seeking Freedom and Justice for Hungary: John Madi-Miké (1905-1981), the Kolping Movement and the Years in Exile, Hungary and Germany*. Volume 1. Lanham, MD: Hamilton Books, 2015.

Misner, Paul. "Christian Democratic Social Policy: Precedents for Third Way Thinking." In *European Christian Democracy: Historical Legacies and Comparative Perspectives*, edited by Thomas Kselman and Joseph Buttigieg. Notre Dame: University of Notre Dame Press, 2003.

Mitchell, Maria. *The Origins of Christian Democracy: Politics and Confession in Modern Germany*. Ann Arbor: University of Michigan Press, 2012.

Molas, Isidre. *El sistema de partits polítics a Catalunya, 1931-1939*. Barcelona: Edicions 62, 1972.

Molt, Peter. *Die Anfänge der Entwicklungspolitik der Bundesrepublik in der Ära Adenauer*. Düsseldorf: Droste, 2017.

Montero García, Feliciano. "La démocratie chrétienne pendant le franquisme." In *Centre et centrisme en Europe aux XIXᵉ et XXᵉ siècles*, edited by Sylvie Guillaume and Jean Garrigues, 95-105. Brussels, Bern and Berlin: PIE-P. Lang, 2006.

Mosse, George L. *Intervista su Aldo Moro*, edited by Alfonso Alfonsi. Soveria Mannelli: Rubbettino, 2015.

Mota Zurdo, David. *Un sueño americano: El Gobierno Vasco en el exilio y Estados Unidos (1937-1979)*. Oñati: IVAP, 2016.

Moyn, Samuel. *Christian Human Rights*. Philadelphia: University of Pennsylvania Press, 2015.

Moyn, Samuel. *The Last Utopia: Human Rights in History*. Cambridge, Mass.: Belknap Press of Harvard University Press, 2010.

Müller, Guido. "Anticipated Exile of Catholic Democrats: The Secrétariat International des Partis Démocratique d'Inspiration Chrétienne." In *Political Catholicism in Europe 1918-45*, edited by Wolfram Kaiser and Helmut Wohnout, 252-264. London: Routledge, 2004.

Nadal, Jordi. *El fracaso de la Revolucion industrial en España, 1814-1913*. Barcelona: Ariel, 1975.

Naimark, Norman M. and Leonid Gibianskii, editors. *The Establishment of Communist Regimes in Eastern Europe, 1944-1949*. Boulder, Colo.: Westview Press, 1998.

Nocera, Raffaele. *Acuerdos y desacuerdos: La DC italiana y el PDC chileno: 1962-1973*. Santiago: Fondo de Cultura Económica, 2015.

Nyári, Gábor. *Menekültek az Új Hazában: A Német és Osztrák Területekben Élő Magyar Emigráció Törenete 1945-1956.* Budapest: Unikus Műhely, 2018.

Olavarría, Arturo. *Chile bajo la democracia Cristiana.* Santiago: Nascimento, 1966-1970.

Olivares, Lilian. *La verdad sin hora: quién mató al Presidente Frei?* Santiago: Catalonia Ltd., 2020.

Olivé, Oriol. "Unió Democràtica de Catalunya durant el franquisme." *Diàlegs,* no. 32-33 (April-September 2006): 53-66.

Orłowski, Marek. *Generał Józef Haller 1873-1960.* Krakow: Arcana, 2007.

Ortega y Gasset, Jose. *Discursos políticos.* Madrid: Alianza Editorial, 1990.

Pablo, Santiago de, et al. *El Péndulo Patriótico: Historia del Partido Nacionalista Vasco.* Barcelona: Crítica, 1999-2001.

Pablo, Santiago de, et al. *La diócesis de Vitoria: 150 años de historia (1862-2012).* Vitoria: Editorial ESET, Diócesis de Vitoria, 2013.

Pacheco, Jorge Donoso and Grace Dunlop Echavarría. *Los 13 del 13: Los DC contra el golpe.* Santiago: RIL, 2013.

Pagès Blanch, Pelai et al. *L'Exili republicà als Països Catalans: una diàspora històrica.* Barcelona: Base, 2014.

Papini, Roberto. *The Christian Democrat International.* Translated by Robert Royal. Lanham: Rowman & Littlefield Publisher, 1997.

Papini, Roberto, editor. *Jacques Maritain e la Società Contemporanea.* Milan: Massimo, 1978.

Pasture, Patrick. *Histoire du syndicalisme chrétien international: La difficile recherche d'une troisième voie.* Paris: L'Harmattan, 1999.

Pasture, Patrick. "Jan Kułakowski: From Exile to International Trade Union Leader and Diplomat." In *Intégration ou représentation? Les exilés polonais en Belgique et la construction européenne,* edited by Michel Dumoulin and Idesbald Goddeeris, 99-120. Louvain-la-Neuve: Academia-Bruylant, 2005.

Payne, Stanley. *A History of Fascism, 1914-1945.* London: UCL Press, 1995.

Payne, Stanley. *Spain's First Democracy: The Second Republic, 1931-1936.* Madison: University of Wisconsin Press, 1993.

People & Freedom Group, editors. *For Democracy.* London: People & Freedom Group, 1939.

Perry, Mariana. *Exilio y renovación: Transferencia política del socialismo en Europa Occidental.* Santiago: Ariadna, 2020.

Perry, Mariana. "Transferencia política en el exilio chileno en los Países Bajos, 1973-1989: El caso del Instituto para el Nuevo Chile." *Historia* (Santiago) 1, no. 50 (January-June 2017): 175-207.

Petrás, Éva. "The History of Christian Democracy in Hungary – From the Beginning to 1949." In *The Voyage of Hungarian Christian Democracy to the Heart of Europe,* edited by Maria Rita Kiss, 10-25. Budapest: Barankovics István Foundation, 2017.

Pigenet, Phryné. *Les catalans espagnols en France au XXème siècle: exil et identités à l'épreuve du temps.* PhD thesis, Université de Paris Ouest La Défense – Laboratoire IDHE, 2014.

Piñol, Josep M. *El nacionalcatolicisme a Catalunya i la resistència: 1926-1966.* Barcelona: Ajuntament de Barcelona; Edicions 62, 1993.

Piva, Francesco and Francesco Malgeri. *Vita di Luigi Sturzo.* Rome: Edizione Cinque Lune, 1972.

Poguntke, Thomas. "Political parties and other organizations." In *Handbook of Party Politics,* edited by Richard S. Katz and William Crotty, 396-405. Los Angeles and London: Sage, 2014.

Polska emigracja polityczna: Informator [a reprint from 1962], edited by Sławomir Cenckiewicz. Warsaw: Adiutor, 2004.

Popiel, Karol. *Od Brześcia do "Polonii".* London: Odnowa, 1967.

Possenti, Vittorio, editor. *Jacques Maritain: Oggi.* Milan: Vita e Pensiero, 1983.

Povilaitis, Pranas and Audronė Škiudaitė, editors. *Lietuviai krikščionys demokratai išeivijoje: 1946-2008 m.* Vilnius: Baltijos kopija, 2013.

Powell, Charles. "The Tacito Group and Democracy." In *Elites and Power in Twentieth Century Spain,* edited by Paul Preston and Frances Lannon, 249-268. Oxford: Oxford University Press, 1990.

Preston, Paul. *The Coming of the Spanish Civil War: Reform, Reaction and Revolution in the Second Republic.* London: Routledge, 1994.

Preston, Paul. *The Spanish Civil War: Reaction, Revolution and Revenge.* New York: WW Norton, 2007.

Prokop, Piotr. "Analiza działalności i rozwoju polskich młodzieżówek partii politycznych w latach 2001-2007." *Zeszyty Naukowe Uniwersytetu Szczecińskiego Acta Politica*, no. 28 (2014): 97-106.

Proudfoot, Malcolm J. *European Refugees: 1939-1952: A Study in Forced Population Movement*. Evanston, IL: Northwestern University Press, 1956.

Prządka, Ewa, editor. *Świadectwa: Testimonianze*. Volume 4: *Pro publico bono: Polityczna, społeczna i kulturalna działalność Polaków w Rzymie w XX wieku*. Rome: Fondazione Romana Marchesa J.S. Umiastowska, 2006.

Quirico, Monica and Valentine Lomellini. "Italy: The 'Chilean Lesson' between the Legacy of the Struggle against Fascism and the Threat of New Authoritarian Shifts." In *European Solidarity with Chile, 1970s-1980s*, edited by Kim Christiaens, Idesbald Goddeeris and Magaly Rodríguez García, 239-256. Frankfurt am Main: Peter Lang, 2014.

Rabiński, Jarosław. "The Elimination of Christian Democracy in Poland after World War II." In *Christian Democracy across the Iron Curtain: Europe Redefined*, edited by Piotr H. Kosicki and Sławomir Łukasiewicz, 153-176. London: Palgrave Macmillan, 2018.

Rabiński, Jarosław. *Stronnictwo Pracy we władzach naczelnych Rzeczypospolitej Polskiej na uchodźstwie w latach 1939-1945*. Lublin: Wydawnictwo KUL, 2012.

Radkau, Joachim. *Die deutsche Emigration in den USA: Ihr Einfluß auf die amerikanische Europapolitik 1933-1945*. Düsseldorf: Bertelsmann, 1971.

Raguer, Hilari. *Escrits dispersos d'història*. Barcelona: Publicacions de la Presidència, 2018.

Raguer, Hilari. *La pólvora y el incienso: La Iglesia y la guerra civil española (1936-1939)*. Barcelona: Península, 2001.

Raguer, Hilari. *La Unió Democràtica de Catalunya i el seu temps (1931-1939)*. Monserrat: Publicacions de l'Abadia de Monserrat, 1976.

Raguer, Hilari. "Maritain i la guerra d'Espanya." *Qüestions de vida cristiana*, no. 67 (1973): 111-125.

Rémond, René with Aline Coutrot. *Les catholiques, le communisme et les crises: 1929-1939*. Paris: A. Colin, 1961.

Resch, Alice. *Over the Highest Mountains: A Memoir of Unexpected Heroism in France during World War II*. Pasadena, Calif.: International Productions, 2005.

Ritchie, J.M. *German Exiles: British Perspectives*. New York: Peter Lang, 1997.

Rivas, Darlene. *Missionary Capitalist: Nelson Rockefeller in Venezuela*. Chapel Hill: University of North Carolina Press, 2003.

Robinson, Richard A.H. *The Origins of Franco's Spain: The Right, the Republic and Revolution, 1931-1936*. Pittsburgh: University of Pittsburgh Press, 1970.

Rollemberg, Denise. *Exilio: entre raíces e radares*. Rio de Janeiro: Editora Record, 1999.

Rosa, Gabriele De. *Luigi Sturzo*. Turin: Unione Tipografico-Editrice Torinese, 1977.

Rosenboim, Or. *The Emergence of Globalism: Visions of World Order in Britain and the United States, 1939-1950*. Princeton, NJ: Princeton University Press, 2017.

Saldukas, Linas. *Lithuanian diaspora*. Vilnius: Vaga, 2002.

Salvati, Mariuccia. *Da Berlino a New York: Crisi della classe media e futuro della democrazia nelle scienze sociali degli anni Trenta*. Bologna: Cappelli, 1989.

Santoni, Alessandro. *El comunismo y la vía chilena: Los orígenes de un mito político*. Santiago: RIL Editores/USACH, 2011.

Satrústegui, Joaquin and Fernando Álvarez de Miranda, editors. *Cuando la Transición se hizo posible*. Madrid: Tecnos, 1992.

Scoppola, Pietro. "L'esperienza dell'esilio: aspetti religiosi." In *Universalità e cultura nel pensiero di Luigi Sturzo*, 37-60. Soveria Mannelli: Rubbettino, 2001.

Seabrook, Jeremy. *The Refuge and the Fortress: Britain and the Persecuted 1933-2013*. Basingstoke: Palgrave Macmillan, 2013.

Serrahima, Maurici. *Del passat quan era present*. Barcelona: Edicions 62; Publicacions de l'Abadia de Montserrat, 2003-2006, 4 volumes.

Seyfert, Michael. "'His Majesty's Most Loyal Internees': Die Internierung und Deportation deutscher und österreichischer Flüchtlinge als 'enemy aliens': Historische, kulturelle und literarische Aspekte." In *Exil in Großbritannien: Zur Emigration aus dem nationalsozialistischen Deutschland*, edited by Gerhard Hirschfeld, 155-182. Stuttgart: Klett Cotta, 1983.

Shannon, Marie and Tony Shannon. *Jacques Maritain*. London: Catholic Truth Society, 1983.

Siegelberg, Mira L. *Statelessness: A Modern History*. Cambridge, Mass.: Harvard University Press, 2020.

Sieniewicz, Konrad. "Chrześcijańska Demokracja na świecie." In *Chrześcijańska myśl społeczna na emigracji*, edited by Zygmunt Tkocz, 242-250. London and Lublin: Odnowa, 1991.

Sigmund, Paul E. "Maritain on Politics." In *Understanding Maritain: Philosopher and Friend*, edited by Deal W. Hudson and Matthew J. Mancini, 153-170. Macon, GA: Mercer University Press, 1987.

Škiudaitė, Audronė, editor. *Krikščionys demokratai Lietuvoje 1989-2015.* Vilnius: Baltijos kopija, 2015.

Śleszyński, Janusz. "Stronnictwo Pracy i Łacińsko–Amerykańska Chrześcijańska Demokracja." In *Chrześcijańska myśl społeczna na emigracji*, edited by Zygmunt Tkocz, 251-254. London and Lublin: Odnowa, 1991.

Smetana, Vít and Kathleen Geaney, editors. *Exile in London: The Experience of Czechoslovakia and the other Occupied Nations, 1939-1945*. Prague: Charles University Karolinum Press, 2017.

Solé, Queralt and Gemma Caballer. "Aproximación biográfica a Josep Maria Trias Peitx (Barcelona, 1900 - Prada de Conflent, 1979): un hombre de Unió Democràtica de Catalunya (UDC) clave para el exilio republicano en los campos de internamiento franceses." *Pasado y memoria: revista de historia contemporánea*, no. 12 (2013): 163-178.

Spiecker, Carl. *Germany - from Defeat to Defeat*. London: Macdonald, 1943.

Stachura, Peter D. "The Poles in Scotland, 1940-50." In *The Poles in Britain 1940-2000: From Betrayal to Assimilation*, edited by Peter D. Stachura, 48-58. London: Frank Cass, 2004.

"Stanisław Mieczysław Gebhardt." In *Świadectwa: Testimonianze*. Volume 4: *Pro publico bono: Polityczna, społeczna i kulturalna działalność Polaków w Rzymie w XX wieku*, edited by Ewa Prządka, 321-322. Rome: Fondazione Romana Marchesa J.S. Umiastowska, 2006.

Stewart-Murray, Katherine Duchess of Atholl. *Searchlight on Spain*. London: Penguin, 1937.

Stewart-Murray, Katherine Duchess of Atholl. *The Tragedy of Warsaw and its documentation.* London: John Murray, 1945.

Stewart-Murray, Katherine Duchess of Atholl. *Working Partnership: Being the Lives of John George, 8th Duke of Atholl and of His Wife Katharine Marjory Ramsay*. London: Arthur Baker, 1958.

Studnicki, Konrad. "Parę uwag o ruchach politycznych na emigracji." *Zjednoczenie Chrześcijańsko–Społecznych Organizacji Młodzieżowych*, no. 2 (December 1949): 10.

Sturzo, Luigi. *La mia battaglia da New York*. Cernusco Sul Naviglio: Grazanti, 1949.

Sturzo, Luigi. *La mia battaglia da New York*. Rome: Edizioni di Storia e Letteratura, 2004.

Sturzo, Luigi. *Nationalism and Internationalism*. New York: Roy Publishers, 1946.

Sturzo, Luigi. *Opera Omnia, Prima Serie*. Volumes VI, VIII, IX, X. Bologna: Nicola Zanichelli Editore, 1939.

Sturzo, Luigi and Mario Einaudi. *Corrispondenza americana (1940-1944)*, edited by Corrado Malandrino. Florence: Olschki, 1998.

Suppan, Arnold. "Catholic People's Parties in East Central Europe: The Bohemian Lands and Slovakia." In *Political Catholicism in Europe 1918-45*, edited by Wolfram Kaiser and Helmuth Wohnout, 217-234. London: Routledge, 2004.

Svarauskas, Artūras. "The Restoration of Christian Democracy in Lithuania, 1989-1990: Continuities and Ruptures." In *Christian Democracy and the Fall of Communism*, edited by Michael Gehler, Piotr H. Kosicki and Helmut Wohnout, 275-286. Leuven: Leuven University Press, 2019.

Sword, Keith, Norman Davies and Jan Ciechanowski. *The Formation of the Polish Community in Great Britain, 1939-1950*. London: School of Slavonic and East European Studies, 1989.

Szabó, Róbert. "A Christian Democratic Endeavour in East-Central Europe: The Democratic People's Party (1944-1949)." In *The Voyage of Hungarian Christian Democracy to the Heart of Europe*, edited by Maria Rita Kiss, 26-42. Budapest: Barankovics István Foundation, 2017.

Széchenyi, Kinga. *Stigmatized: A History of Communist Hungary's Internal Deportations 1951-1958*. Reno, NV: Helena History Press, 2016.

Sznajder, Mario and Luis Roniger. "Un extraño sitio de exilio para la izquierda argentina: Israel." In *Exilios, destinos y experiencias bajo la dictadura militar*, edited by Pablo Yankelevich and Silvina Jensen, 21-61. Buenos Aires: Editorial del Zorzal, 2007.

310

Sznajder, Mario and Luis Roniger, editors. *The Politics of Exile in Latin America*. Cambridge: Cambridge University Press, 2009.

Tarka, Krzysztof. *Emigracyjna dyplomacja: Polityka zagraniczna Rządu RP na Uchodźstwie 1945-1990*. Warsaw: Rytm, 2003.

Tarka, Krzysztof. "Hugo Hanke premier-agent." *Zeszyty Historyczne*, no. 152 (2005): 26-44.

Tarka, Krzysztof. "Powrót premiera: Emigracja o sprawie Hugona Hankego." *Przegląd Polonijny*, no. 3 (2001): 19-33.

Trenscényi, Balázs et al. *A history of modern political thought in East Central Europe*. Volume 2, Part 1: *Negotiating Modernity in the "Short Twentieth Century" and Beyond*. Oxford: Oxford University Press, 2018.

Tusell, Javier. *Historia de la democracia cristiana en España*. Madrid: Cuadernos para El Dialogo, 1974, 2 volumes.

Ugalde, Alexander. *La Acción Exterior del Nacionalismo Vasco (1890-1939): Historia, Pensamiento y Relaciones internacionales*. Oñati: HAEE/IVAP, 1996.

Urigüen López de Sandaliano, Natalia. *A imagen y semejanza: la democracia cristiana alemana y su aportación a la Transición Española*. Madrid: Consejo Superior de Investigaciones Científicas, 2018.

Ūsaitė, Kristina. *Pasaulio lietuvių jaunimo sąjunga XX a. 6-9 dešimtmečiais*. Vilnius: Versus Aureus, 2013.

Valdés, Gabriel. *Por la libertad: Discursos y entrevistas 1982-1986*. Santiago: CESOC, 1986.

Valiušaitis, Vidmantas, editor. *Gairė - pilnutinė demokratija: "Į Laisvę" fondo dešimtmetis Lietuvoje*. Kaunas: Į Laisvę fondo Lietuvos filialas, 2001.

Vardys, V. Stanley. *Lithuania: The Rebel Nation*. Boulder, Colo.: Westview Press, 1997.

Vardys, V. Stanley. *The Catholic Church, dissent and nationality in Soviet Lithuania*. Boulder, Colo.: East European Quarterly, 1978.

Varsori, Antonio. *Gli alleati e l'emigrazione democratica antifascista (1940-1943)*. Florence: Sansoni, 1982.

Varsori, Antonio. "Gli Stati Uniti paese di rifugio e l'emigrazione politica italiana fra le due guerre." In *L'émigration politique en Europe aux XIXe et XXe siècles: Actes du colloque de Rome* (3-5 Mars 1988), 171-187. Rome: École française de Rome, 1991.

Velasco, Belisario. "Declaración de los 13." *La Tercera*, 24 August 2013.

Velasco, Belisario. *Esta historia es mi historia*. Santiago: Catalonia, 2018.

Vilanova, Francesc. "Entre la espada y la pared: el franquismo, la III República Francesa y los exiliados republicanos en 1939-1940." In *"Ay de los vencidos": el exilio y los países de acogida*, edited by Abdón Mateos, 13-40. Madrid: Eneida, 2009.

Vilanova, Francesc. *Exiliats, proscrits, deportats: el primer exili dels republicans espanyols: dels camps francesos al llindar de la deportació*. Barcelona: Empúries, cop. 2006.

Vilar, Sergio. *Historia del Anti-Franquismo 1949-1975*. Barcelona: Plaza & Janes, 1984.

Villis, Tom. *British Catholics & Fascism: Religious Identity and Political Extremism Between the Wars*. Basingstoke: Palgrave, 2013.

Vincent, Mary. *Catholicism in the Second Spanish Republic: Religion and Politics in Salamanca, 1930-1936*. Oxford: Clarendon Press, 1996.

Vincent, Mary. "Religion: The Idea of Catholic Spain." In *Metaphors of Spain: Representations of Spanish National Identity in the Twentieth Century*, edited by Javier Moreno Luzón and Xosé M. Núñez Seixas, 122-141. New York: Berghahn, 2018.

Vinyamata, Eduard. "Josep Maria Trias Peitx, primer secretari general d'Unió Democràtica de Catalunya." In *Miscel·lània d'homenatge a Josep Benet*, 373-391. Barcelona: Publicacions de l'Abadia de Montserrat, 1991.

Viotto, Piero. *De Gasperi e Maritain: Una Proposta Politica*. Rome: Armando, 2013.

Viotto, Piero. *Introduzione a Maritain*. Bari: Laterza, 2000.

Vitkuvienėm, Indrė and Kęstutis Žemaitis. "Lietuvių išeivių pastoracijos modelis Vakarų Europoje 1946-1949 metais." *Soter*, no. 94 (2018): 25-49.

Viz Quadrat, Samantha. "Exiliados argentinos in Brasil: una situación delicada." In *Exilios, destinos y experiencias bajo la dictadura militar*, edited by Pablo Yankelevich and Silvina Jensen, 63-102. Buenos Aires: Editorial del Zorzal, 2007.

Warren, Donald. *Radio Priest: Charles Coughlin, the Father of Hate Radio*. New York: Free Press, 1996.

Weidling, Paul. "'For the Love of Christ': Strategies of International Catholic Relief and the Allied Occupation of Germany, 1945-1948." *Journal of Contemporary History* 43, no. 3 (2008): 477-492.

Wright, Thomas C. "Chilean Political Exile in Western Europe." In *European Solidarity with Chile, 1970s-1980s*, edited by Kim Christiaens, Idesbald Goddeeris and Magaly Rodríguez García, 47-66. Frankfurt am Main: Peter Lang, 2014.

Wróbel, Janusz. *Na rozdrożu historii: Repatriacje obywateli polskich z Zachodu w latach 1945-1949*. Łódź: Instytut Pamięci Narodowej, 2009.

Yankelevich, Pablo and Silvina Jensen, editors. *Exilios, destinos y experiencias bajo la dictadura militar*. Buenos Aires: Editorial del Zorzal, 2007.

Zabłocki, Janusz. *Chrześcijańska Demokracja w kraju i na emigracji 1947-1970*. Lublin: Ośrodek PZKS w Lublinie, 1999.

Zachar, Peter Krisztián. "The Concept of Vocational Orders in Hungary Between the Two World Wars." *Estudos Históricos* (Rio de Janeiro) 31, no. 64 (May-August 2018): 257-276.

Zahra, Tara. *The Great Departure: Mass Migration from Eastern Europe and the Making of the Free World*. New York: WW Norton & Co., 2016.

Zaldívar, Andrés. *Por la democracia ahora y siempre*. Santiago: Aconcagua, Andante, 1984.

Ziętara, Paweł. "Seweryna Eustachiewicza przypadki." *Zeszyty Historyczne,* no. 158 (2006): 35-71.

LIST OF CONTRIBUTORS

Paolo Acanfora is Associate Professor of Contemporary History at the University of Rome La Sapienza. His main research interests concern the history of political Catholicism from national and international perspectives in the Cold War years and the relationship between politics and religion in mass society. His publications include *L'Inter Press Service e il nuovo ordine internazionale: Informazione e terzomondismo negli anni della Guerra fredda* (2019); *Adolfo Sarti e le crisi della Repubblica* (2018); *Miti e ideologia nella politica estera DC* (2013); and *Un nuovo umanesimo cristiano: Aldo Moro e Studium* (2011).

Leyre Arrieta is Professor of Modern History and History of Political Thought at the University of Deusto in Bilbao and San Sebastián, Spain. She has published widely on Basque nationalism, Basque exile and symbols as tools of communication and transmission of collective identity. Her most noteworthy publications are: *Estación Europa: La política europeísta del PNV en el exilio (1945–1977)* (2007); *Diccionario ilustrado de símbolos del nacionalismo vasco* (with others, 2012); and *Estudio introductorio: La Causa del Pueblo Vasco de F. J. Landaburu* (2017).

Gemma Caballer is a librarian and a historian. She works at the CRAI Library of the University of Barcelona, currently in the Rare Books and Manuscripts section, and she also teaches History at the Open University of Catalonia. In recent years, her research has focused on the Catalan Christian Democratic politician Josep Maria Trias Peitx. She has published, among others, *Aidez les réfugiés: Josep Maria Trias Peitx, un home d'acció entre catòlics i quàquers* (2020) and *La Solitud de la llibertat: memòries de Josep Maria Trias i Peitx, secretari general d'Unió Democràtica de Catalunya, durant la Guerra Civil* (2008).

Justinas Dementavičius is Associate Professor of Ideology Studies at Vilnius University, Institute of International Relations and Political Science. He has published studies on the transformation of modern Lithuanian political thought, analysing it as a part of transnational intellectual history. Among these studies are articles and a book dedicated to the ideological imaginaries of Lithuanian centre-right parties and Christian political movements.

Joaquín Fermandois is Professor of Contemporary History at the Catholic University of Chile and at the Universidad San Sebastián, both in Santiago. He received the Guggenheim Fellowship in 1989. His latest books include *La revolución inconclusa: La izquierda chilena y el gobierno de la Unidad Popular* (2013) and *La democracia en Chile: Trayectoria de Sísifo* (2020).

Élodie Giraudier is a Visiting Scholar in History at Harvard University. She has published articles on the twentieth-century Chilean history of Christian Democracy and Catholicism. Her PhD dissertation, *Le Parti démocrate-chrétien au Chili, 1957-2010: De la troisième voie au néolibéralisme*, will be published in 2021 (Éditions du Cerf).

Carlo Invernizzi Accetti is Associate Professor of Political Science at the City University of New York (City College) and Associate Researcher at the Institut d'Études Politiques de Paris (Sciences Po). He is the author of *What is Christian Democracy? Politics, Religion and Ideology* (2019) and *Relativism and Religion: Why Democratic Societies Do Not Need Moral Absolutes* (2015). He has also edited *Ideologies and the European Union* (2020, with Jonathan White).

Katalin Kádár Lynn, PhD, is a historian specialising in twentieth-century Hungarian history, with an emphasis on the Hungarian immigration in the West, its organisations and political movements. She is also the founder and editor in chief of Helena History Press LLC, a publishing house specialising in scholarly works in English about and from Central and Eastern Europe. Her publications include the edited volume *The Inauguration of Organized Political Warfare: Cold War Organizations sponsored by the National Committee for a Free Europe/Free Europe Committee* (2013).

Wolfram Kaiser is Professor of European Studies at the University of Portsmouth and Visiting Professor at the College of Europe in Bruges. He has published widely on nineteenth- and twentieth-century European and global history and the history of Christian Democracy, including *The European Ambition: The Group of the European People's Party and European Integration* (with others, 2020) and *Christian Democracy and the Origins of European Union* (2007).

Piotr H. Kosicki is Associate Professor of History at the University of Maryland and Adjunct Professor of History at McGill University. He has published widely on the history of the Catholic Church, on the intellectual entanglements of Poland and France and on the Cold War, including *Catholics on the Barricades: Poland, France and "Revolution", 1891-1956* (2018) and, as editor, *Christian Democracy and the Fall of Communism* (2019, with Michael Gehler and Helmut Wohnout), *Christian Democracy across the Iron Curtain* (2018, with Sławomir Łukasiewicz) and *Vatican II behind the Iron Curtain* (2016).

Sławomir Łukasiewicz is Professor at the John Paul II Catholic University of Lublin, Visiting Scholar at the Davis Center for Russian and Eurasian Studies at Harvard University and staff historian at the Institute of National Remembrance's Lublin Branch. A 2019-20 recipient of the Fulbright Senior Scholar Award, he has published widely on the history, politics and political concepts of Polish and Central European Cold War exile, including *Third Europe: Polish Federalist Thought in the United States, 1940-1970s* (2016) and *Christian Democracy across the Iron Curtain* (2018, with Piotr H. Kosicki).

Christopher Stroot is a PhD candidate in modern European history at the University of California San Diego. His dissertation focuses on the relationship between Catholic politics and democracy in interwar Europe, and particularly Spain, looking at the role of the large, confessionally oriented Confederation of the Autonomous Right (CEDA) in the rise and fall of the Second Republic (1931-1936).

INDEX OF PERSONS

Hull, Cordell 68
Hurdes, Felix 32

Irujo, Manuel de 43, 104, 106, 110, 122, 142, 149
Ivinskis, Zenonas 200-201

Jiménez, Felix A. 283
Johnson, Alvin 66
Journet, Charles 220
Juan (Don): see Borbón, Don Juan de

Kähler, Alfred 66
Kairys, Steponas 207
Kaiser, Wolfram 284
Kallen, Horace M. 66
Kavolis, Vytautas 193
Kerensky, Alexander 245
Keresztes, Sándor 237, 248
Kershner, Howard E. 147
Kéthly, Anna 224
Khrushchev, Nikita 173, 205, 244
Kissinger, Henry 281
Kohl, Helmut 283-285
Kosicki, Piotr H. 184
Kótai, Zoltán 234, 238
Kovács, Zoltán 237, 239, 243, 248, 250-251
Kovrig, Béla 227
Közi-Horváth, József 186, 227, 237-239, 241, 243, 247
Krek, Miha 186
Krupavičius, Mykolas 21, 194, 196, 198, 202, 206, 208-215, 221
Kułakowski, Jan 169, 172, 183, 187-190
Kulczycki, Jerzy 188
Kwiatkowski, Michał 42, 47

La Guardia, Fiorello 68-69
Lahera, Eugenio 278
Landaburu (Landáburu), Javier (Xabier) Francisco 41, 106, 132
La Pira, Giorgio 82
Lardone, Francesco 59
Lederer, Emile 66
Lehmann, Fritz 66
Leich, John Foster 178
Leighton, Bernardo 257, 259-264, 267, 275-277, 279-280, 286-288, 291
Lenin, Vladimir 12
Leo XIII 74, 140, 210, 214-215
Letelier, Orlando 267, 288
Ligutti, Luigi 61
Linz, Juan 93
Littauer, Rudolf 66
Llona, Eugenio 286

Llopis, Rodolfo 105-106, 113
Loeb, James 65
Lorés, Jaume 156
Lund, Fernando 278

Maceina, Antanas 20-21, 194-196, 199-201, 206-212, 215-221
Mačiulis-Maironis, Jonas 191
Madariaga, Salvador de 94, 101, 107
Majonica, Ernst 172
Malgeri, Francesco 63
Mann, Thomas 49
Manning, Henry 38
Maragall, Joan 151
Marc, Alexandre 127
Mardones, Francisco de 55, 57
Marín, Gladys 288
Maritain, Jacques 11, 17-18, 21-22, 25, 39, 41, 54-55, 70, 73-74, 81-89, 97, 102-104, 128-129, 131, 143-144, 150, 206, 210, 216, 218, 220
Maritain, Raïssa 82
Marshall, Cicely 9, 37-38
Marx, Karl 86
Mathieu, Clément Joseph 144
Matulaitis, Jurgis 211
Mauriac, François 128, 144, 151, 210
Maurras, Charles 81, 87, 102
Mayer, Carl 66
Mazzini, Giuseppe 63-65, 67-68
McAvoy, Thomas 74
McCargar, James 179, 229
McIntyre, James Francis 56
Mendizábal, Alfredo 41, 104, 128
Menthon, François de 32
Meyer, Karl 46
Mihelics, Vid 237
Miké, János 239, 246
Mille, Pierre 147
Mindszenty, József 22, 224, 228, 230, 239, 251
Monnet, Jean 105
Moore, Anthony 68
Morawski, Maciej 169, 178
Morawski, Stanisław August 189
Moreno Baez, Enrique 112-113
Morlion, Felix 62
Moulin, Jean 32
Mounier, Emmanuel 127-128, 150, 210, 216
Moyen, Samuel 97
Múgica, Mateo 123
Müller, Josef 32
Munro, Leslie 244
Murillo, Fernando 286

COLOPHON

Final editing
Godfried Kwanten, KADOC
Luc Vints, KADOC

Copy editing
Lieve Claes, KADOC

Lay-out
Alexis Vermeylen, KADOC

Printing and binding
Wilco B.V., Amersfoort

CIVITAS
Forum of Archives and Research on Christian Democracy
c/o KADOC
Vlamingenstraat 39
B - 3000 Leuven
https://civitas-farcd.eu

Leuven University Press
Minderbroedersstraat 4
B - 3000 Leuven
http://lup.be